Fodor's 2008

U.S. & BRITISH VIRGIN ISLANDS

Where to Stay and Eat
for All Budgets

Must-See Sights
and Local Secret

Ratings You Car

D1445800

.972
+wD

Fodor's Travel Publications   New York, Toronto, London, Sydney, Auckland
www.fodors.com

FODOR'S U.S. & BRITISH VIRGIN ISLANDS 2008
Editors: Mark Sullivan

Editorial Production: Astrid deRidder
Editorial Contributors: Carol M. Bareuther, Lynda Lohr
Maps: David Lindroth, *cartographer;* Bob Blake and Rebecca Baer, *map editors*
Design: Fabrizio La Rocca, *creative director;* Guido Caroti, *art director;* Melanie Marin, *senior picture editor*
Production/Manufacturing: Angela L. McLean
Cover Photo: Dave Bartruff

ISBN 978–1–4000–1817–8

ISSN 1070–6380

SPECIAL SALES
This book is available for special discounts for bulk purchases for sales promotions or premiums. Special editions, including personalized covers, excerpts of existing books, and corporate imprints, can be created in large quantities for special needs. For more information, write to Special Markets/ Premium Sales, 1745 Broadway, MD 6-2, New York, New York 10019, or e-mail specialmarkets@ randomhouse.com.

AN IMPORTANT TIP & AN INVITATION
Although all prices, opening times, and other details in this book are based on information supplied to us at press time, changes occur all the time in the travel world, and Fodor's cannot accept responsibility for facts that become outdated or for inadvertent errors or omissions. So **always confirm information when it matters,** especially if you're making a detour to visit a specific place. Your experiences—positive and negative—matter to us. If we have missed or misstated something, **please write to us.** We follow up on all suggestions. Contact the Virgin Islands editor at editors@ fodors.com or c/o Fodor's at 1745 Broadway, New York, New York 10019.

Be a Correspondent for Fodor's

Your opinion matters. It matters to us. It matters to your fellow Fodor's travelers, too. And we'd like to hear it. In fact, we *need* to hear it.

When you share your experiences and opinions, you become an active member of the Fodor's community. That means we'll not only use your feedback to make our books better, but we'll publish your names and comments whenever possible. Throughout our guides, look for "Word of Mouth," excerpts of your unvarnished feedback.

Here's how you can help improve Fodor's for all of us.

Tell us when we're right. We rely on local writers to give you an insider's perspective. But our writers and staff editors—who are the best in the business—depend on you. Your positive feedback is a vote to renew our recommendations for the next edition.

Tell us when we're wrong. We're proud that we update most of our guides every year. But we're not perfect. Things change. Hotels cut services. Museums change hours. Charming cafés lose charm. If our writer didn't quite capture the essence of a place, tell us how you'd do it differently. If any of our descriptions are inaccurate or inadequate, we'll incorporate your changes in the next edition and will correct factual errors at fodors.com *immediately.*

Tell us what to include. You probably have had fantastic travel experiences that aren't yet in Fodor's. Why not share them with a community of like-minded travelers? Maybe you chanced upon a beach or bistro or B&B that you don't want to keep to yourself. Tell us why we should include it. And share your discoveries and experiences with everyone directly at fodors.com. Your input may lead us to add a new listing or highlight a place we cover with a "Highly Recommended" star or with our highest rating, "Fodor's Choice."

Give us your opinion instantly at our feedback center at www.fodors.com/feedback. You may also e-mail editors@fodors.com with the subject line "Virgin Islands Editor." Or send your nominations, comments, and complaints by mail to Virgin Islands Editor, Fodor's, 1745 Broadway, New York, NY 10019.

You and travelers like you are the heart of the Fodor's community. Make our community richer by sharing your experiences. Be a Fodor's correspondent.

Happy traveling!

Tim Jarrell, Publisher

CONTENTS

HOW TO USE THIS BOOK

Our Ratings

Sometimes you find terrific travel experiences and sometimes they just find you. But usually the burden is on you to select the right combination of experiences. That's where our ratings come in.

As travelers we've all discovered a place so wonderful that its worthiness is obvious. And sometimes that place is so experiential that superlatives don't do it justice: you just have to be there to know. These sights, properties, and experiences get our highest rating, **Fodor's Choice**, indicated by orange stars throughout this book.

Black stars highlight sights and properties we deem **Highly Recommended**, places that our writers, editors, and readers praise again and again for consistency and excellence.

By default, there's another category: any place we include in this book is by definition worth your time, unless we say otherwise. And we will.

Disagree with any of our choices? Care to nominate a place or suggest that we rate one more highly? Visit our feedback center at www.fodors.com/feedback.

Budget Well

Hotel and restaurant price categories from ¢ to $$$$ are defined in the opening pages of each chapter. For attractions, we always give standard adult admission fees; reductions are usually available for children, students, and senior citizens. Want to pay with plastic? **AE, D, DC, MC, V** following restaurant and hotel listings indicate if American Express, Discover, Diners Club, MasterCard, and Visa are accepted.

Restaurants

Unless we state otherwise, restaurants are open for lunch and dinner daily. We mention dress only when there's a specific requirement and reservations only when they're essential or not accepted—it's always best to book ahead.

Hotels

Hotels have private bath, phone, TV, and air-conditioning and operate on the European Plan (a.k.a. EP, meaning without meals), unless we specify that they use the Continental Plan (CP, with a Continental breakfast), Breakfast Plan (BP, with a full breakfast), Modified American Plan (MAP, with breakfast and dinner), Full American Plan (FAP, with all meals), or are all-inclusive (AI, includ-

ing all meals and most activities). We always list facilities but not whether you'll be charged an extra fee to use them, so when pricing accommodations, find out what's included.

Many Listings
★	Fodor's Choice
★	Highly recommended
⊠	Physical address
⊹	Directions
⊕	Mailing address
☎	Telephone
🖷	Fax
⊕	On the Web
✐	E-mail
⊴	Admission fee
☉	Open/closed times
►	Start of walk/itinerary
Ⓜ	Metro stations
▭	Credit cards

Hotels & Restaurants
☶	Hotel
⇱	Number of rooms
⌂	Facilities
℩◯℩	Meal plans
✕	Restaurant
⌂	Reservations
▥	Dress code
⅃	Smoking
₿₽	BYOB
✕☶	Hotel with restaurant that warrants a visit

Outdoors
⅄	Golf
⚠	Camping

Other
⏣	Family-friendly
🛈	Contact information
⇨	See also
⊠	Branch address
☞	Take note

WHAT'S WHERE

ST. THOMAS 	The familiar and foreign mingle on this U.S.-owned island, where you'll recognize everything from major hotel chains to fast food restaurants and at the same time be able to relax in the exotic ambience of a tropical destination. Go for the shopping, sights, and water sports. Stores that sell gold, diamonds, and emeralds line Main Street in Charlotte Amalie. Seventeenth-century-built Fort Christian dates back to the island's colonization, while breathtaking vistas await from Mountain Top and Paradise Point. Opportunities for swimming, snorkeling, scuba diving, sailing, sports fishing, and even submarining abound in the surrounding seas. Don't go for uninhabited tranquility. St. Thomas is the most cosmopolitan of the three U.S. Virgins, and she has a buffet of choices to show visitors a good time.
ST. CROIX 	The largest of the U.S. Virgin Islands, St. Croix is 40 mi south of St. Thomas. Its northwest is relatively lush, but the drier East End—where you'll find most of the resorts—is spotted with cacti. The main towns are Frederiksted on the West End and Christiansted on the East End. Ironically, the island's best beaches are on the West End, far from the best resorts. Go to St. Croix if you like history. Ruins of old plantations stand crumbling in long-fallow fields and Christiansted National Historic Site beckons with its old fort and other Danish-era remnants. You'll want to linger at interesting restaurants, browse in the island's eclectic collection of stores, or enjoy an afternoon at your hotel's beach when you're finished exploring the island's past. Don't go if you prefer a more back-to-nature experience.
ST. JOHN 	Only 3 mi from St. Thomas but still a world apart, St. John is the least developed of the USVI. Although two-thirds of its tropical hills remain protected as a U.S. national park, a bit of hustle and bustle has come to Cruz Bay, the main town. Although many people visit on a day-trip from their cruise ship or from St. Thomas, the island is a great place to unwind for a week or more. If you want to get in touch with nature, go to St. John, where you can enjoy all that Virgin Islands National Park has to offer. This doesn't mean, of course, that you'll have to camp. The island has a couple of posh hotels, some condos, lots of vacation villas, and even some pretty cushy campgrounds.

TORTOLA 	A day might not be enough to tour this island—all 10-square-mi of it—not because there's so much to see and do but because you're meant to relax while you're here. Time stands still even in Road Town, the biggest community, where the hands of the central square's clock occasionally move, but never tell the right time. The harbor, however, is busy with sailboats—this is the charter-boat capital of the Caribbean. Tortola's roads dip and curve and lead to lovely, secluded accommodations. Go to Tortola if you want to do some shopping and enjoy a larger choice of good restaurants than you'll find on the other British Virgins.
VIRGIN GORDA 	Progressing from laid-back to more laid-back, mountainous and arid Virgin Gorda fits right in. Its main road sticks to the center of the island, connecting the odd-shaped north and south appendages; sailing is the preferred mode of transportation. Spanish Town, the most noteworthy settlement, is on the southern wing, as are The Baths. Here smooth, giant boulders are scattered about the beach and form delightful sea grottoes just offshore. Choose Virgin Gorda if you want better beaches, but the trade-off is fewer restaurants and many fewer shopping opportunities.
JOST VAN DYKE 	Jost Van Dyke, a sparsely populated island northwest of Tortola, has a disproportionate number of surprisingly lively bars and is a favorite haunt of yachties. There are also a few places to stay here, in case you really want to get away from it all. Go to Jost if you want to get a taste of what the Caribbean used to be like.
ANEGADA 	Flat Anegada lurks 20 mi northeast of Virgin Gorda. It rises just 28 feet above sea level, but its reef stretches out underwater, practically inviting wrecks. The scores of shipwrecks that encircle the island attract divers and a bounty of fish. Choose Anegada if you're a diver and want easier access to the best BVI dive sights. The beaches are also excellent, but don't expect luxury accommodations or dining.
OTHER VIRGIN ISLANDS 	There are actually about 50 islands in the British Virgin chain, many of them completely uninhabited, but others have a single hotel or at least a beach that is popular with sailors. Choose one of these resorts if you want to be pampered and pampered some more. A few are exclusive and popular with the jet-set, though more for their potential for relaxation than their lavish amenities.

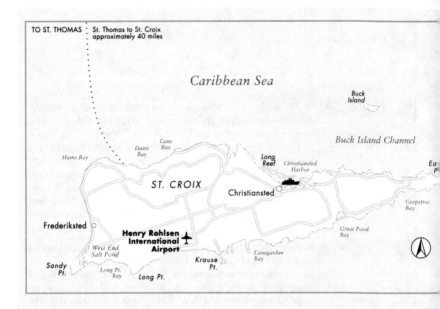

TO ST. THOMAS : St. Thomas to St. Croix
approximately 40 miles

Caribbean Sea

Buck
Island

Buck Island Channel

Hams Bay

Davis
Bay

Cane
Bay

Long
Reef

Christiansted
Harbour

Ea
P

ST. CROIX

Christiansted

Grapetree
Bay

Frederiksted

**Henry Rohlsen
International
Airport**

Great Pond
Bay

West End
Salt Pond

Canegarden
Bay

Sandy
Pt.

Long Pt.
Bay

Long Pt.

Krause
Pt.

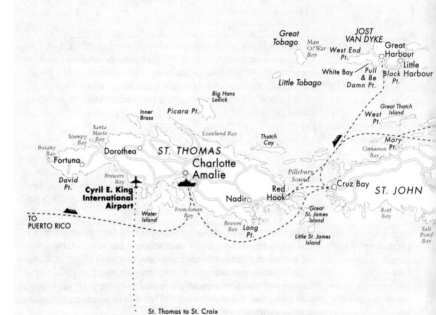

A T L A N T I C   O C E A N

Great
Tobago

Man
O?War
Bay

**JOST
VAN DYKE**

West End
Pt.

Great
Harbour

Little

White Bay

Pull
& Be
Damn Pt.

Black Harbour
Pt.

Little Tobago

Big Hans
Lollick

Inner
Brass

Picara Pt.

Great Thatch
Island

West
Pt.

Santa
Maria
Bay

Loveland Bay

Thatch
Cay

Mary
Pt.

Stumpy
Bay

Dorothea

ST. THOMAS

Cannamon
Bay

Botany
Bay

Fortuna

Charlotte
Amalie

Pillsbury
Sound

Cruz Bay

ST. JOHN

David
Pt.

Brewers
Bay

**Cyril E. King
International
Airport**

Nadir

Red
Hook

Great
St. James
Island

Reef
Bay

Water
Island

Frenchman
Bay

TO
PUERTO RICO

Bovoni
Bay

Long
Pt.

Little St. James
Island

Salt
Pond
Bay

TO ST. CROIX : St. Thomas to St. Croix
approximately 40 miles

The Virgin Islands

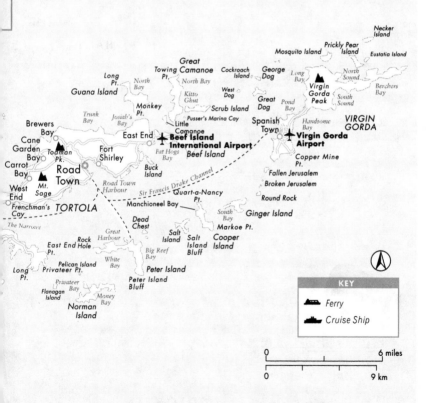

West End
Pt.

Bones
Bight

Loblolly
Bay   Table Bay

Flamingo   *Red*
Pond   *Pond*

The
Settlement

ANEGADA
(15 miles north of Necker Is.)

Lower
Bay

Budrock Horse
Pond   Shoe
Reef

White
Bay

Necker
Island

Prickly Pear
Mosquito Island   Island   Eustatia Island

Great
Towing Camanoe   Cockroach   George
Pt.   Island   Dog

Long   *North*   North Bay
Pt.   *Bay*
Guana Island

Kitto   West
Ghut   Dog

Long   *North*
Bay   *Sound*

Great   *Pond*
Dog   *Bay*

Virgin
Gorda   *South*
Peak   *Sound*

Berchers
Bay

Monkey
Pt.

Scrub Island

Spanish
Town

Handsome
Bay

VIRGIN
GORDA

Trunk   *Josiah's*
Bay   *Bay*

Pusser's Marina Cay

Little
Comanoe

Brewers
Bay

East End   Beef Island
International Airport

Virgin Gorda
Airport

Cane
Garden   *Todman*
Bay   *Pk.*

Fort
Shirley

Fat Hogs   Beef Island
Bay

Copper Mine
Pt.

Carrot
Bay

Road
Town

Buck
Island

Fallen Jerusalem

West   *Mt.*
End   *Sage*

Road Town
Harbour

Broken Jerusalem

Frenchman's   TORTOLA
Cay

Sir Francis Drake Channel

Quart-a-Nancy
Pt.

Round Rock

Manchioneel Bay

The Narrows

Great
Harbour

Dead
Chest

South
Bay   Ginger Island

East End Hole
Pt.

Rock   Salt   Salt   Markoe Pt.
Island   Island   Cooper
Bluff   Island

Long
Pt.

Pelican Island
Privateer Pt.

White
Bay

Big Reef
Bay

Peter Island

Privateer
Bay

Money
Bay

Peter Island
Bluff

Flanagan
Island

Norman
Island

KEY

🚢 Ferry

🚢 Cruise Ship

0 ——————— 6 miles

0 ——————— 9 km

U.S.A.

Miami

Key West

Nassau ✪

THE BAHAMAS

Havana ✪

Turks and
Caicos Islands

CUBA

Cuba

Little
Cayman

George
Town ✪

Cayman
Brac

Puerto Plata

HAITI

*Grand
Cayman*

Montego
Bay

Ocho
Rios

Hispaniola

Port-au-Prince ✪

Jamaica

G R E A T E R

C a r i b b e a n

0 _____ 200 mi

0 _____ 200 km

*Panama
Canal*

PANAMA

Cartagena

COLOMBIA

Maracaibo

Caribbean

ATLANTIC OCEAN

DOMINICAN REPUBLIC

LEEWARD ISLANDS

St. John   Tortola
St. Thomas   Virgin Gorda
San Juan   Anguilla
                                   St. Barthélemy
Santo   St. Maarten/
Domingo   St. Martin   Saba   Barbuda
        Puerto   St.   St. Eustatius
        Rico   Croix   St. Kitts   Antigua
                              Nevis
ANTILLES   Montserrat   Marie
                     Guadeloupe   Galante

S e a   Dominica

                          Martinique
                          Fort-de-France   WINDWARD ISLANDS

                                St. Lucia

                            St. Vincent   Barbados
                               Bequia   Bridgetown
                          The Grenadines
Aruba   Carriacou
Curaçao   Bonaire   Islas Los   St. George's
         Roques   LESSER ANTILLES
   Willemstad   Grenada
                                        Tobago

                                Port of Spain
La Guaira   Trinidad
Caracas

VENEZUELA

IF YOU LIKE

The Beach

With their warm, clear days, unspoiled sandy strands, and beautiful turquoise water, the Virgin Islands are a beach bum's paradise. Even if you're not a connoisseur, a day or two on the sand is central to a complete vacation here. Your hotel may border a beach or provide transportation to one nearby, but don't limit yourself. You could spend one day at a lively, touristy beach that has plenty of water-sports facilities and is backed by a bar, and another at an isolated cove that offers nothing but seclusion. Of course, these beaches are just jumping-off points to the underwater world. Here are our favorites:

- **The Baths, Virgin Gorda, BVI.** Swimming among the giant boulders here is a highlight of any trip despite the crowds.

- **Buck Island, St. Croix, USVI.** The softest sandy beach in St. Croix isn't exactly *on* St. Croix.

- **Cane Garden Bay, Tortola, BVI.** This silky beach is often Tortola's busiest.

- **Coki Beach, St. Thomas, USVI.** Come here for St. Thomas's best off-the-beach snorkeling.

- **Long Bay West, Tortola, BVI.** Although the water is not calm, this is one of Tortola's finest beaches and still quite swimmable.

- **Magens Bay, St. Thomas, USVI.** St. Thomas's busiest beach is one of the most beautiful in the Caribbean, if not the world.

- **Trunk Bay, St. John, USVI.** This natural park beach is picture-perfect and has an underwater snorkeling trail.

- **West End Beaches, St. Croix, USVI.** Find a spot near Sunset Grill and relax.

- **White Bay, Jost Van Dyke, BVI.** You won't have to travel far to find a bar on this long stretch of sand.

Diving & Snorkeling

Clear water and numerous reefs afford wonderful opportunities for both diving and snorkeling in the Virgin Islands. Serious divers usually head to the BVI, but don't neglect St. Croix, which is also a good dive destination.

- **Anegada, BVI.** The reefs surrounding this flat coral and limestone atoll are a sailor's nightmare but a scuba diver's dream.

- **The Baths, Virgin Gorda, BVI.** Snorkelers in the BVI need not worry that they will miss out because they can't reach the deeper reefs and wrecks. Virgin Gorda's most popular beach is dotted with giant boulders that create numerous tidepools, making it a great place to explore underwater. It's especially good for kids.

- **Buck Island, St. Croix, USVI.** Buck Island Reef National Monument is St. Croix's best-known snorkeling spot, where there's a marked trail among the coral formations. Take a catamaran for a more relaxing trip.

- **The Reefs of St. Croix, USVI.** Cane Bay Wall is the most popular dive site in St. Croix, and that's where you'll find the high concentration of dive operators.

- **Snorkeling Tours, St. John, USVI.** If you want to do a daysail and snorkeling trip, then St. John is a good place to leave from. You'll have easy access to a wide variety of islets and cays so the boat can drop anchor in several places during a full-day sailing trip.

- **The Wreck of the *Rhone*, off Tortola, BVI.** This exceptionally well-preserved royal mail steamer, which sank in 1867, is one of the most famous wreck dives in the Caribbean. But snorkelers won't feel left out in these clear waters.

History

Columbus, pirates, European colonizers, and plantation farmers and their slaves are among the people who have left their marks on these islands, all of which are benefiting the tourism industry, a relatively recent development. The U.S. National Park Service maintains several sites in the U.S. Virgin Islands, so keep your annual America the Beautiful Pass handy for free or discount admissions.

- **Annaberg Plantation, St. John, USVI.** You can sometimes see living history demonstrations at the most popular plantation ruins on St. John.

- **Christiansted, St. Croix, USVI.** With several historic buildings, including Fort Christiansvaern, the island's main town is a place to do more than just shop and dine.

- **Copper Mine Point, Virgin Gorda, BVI.** The remains of a 16th-century copper mine are a popular tourist site here.

- **Old Government House Museum, Tortola, BVI.** The former seat of the island's government is now a museum. It can be found right in the heart of Road Town.

- **Seven Arches Museum, St. Thomas, USVI.** A trip to this museum, in a restored 18th-century home, will give you a sense of how St. Thomas residents lived in the colonial heyday.

- **Whim Plantation Museum, St. Croix, USVI.** A lovingly restored plantation house and estate is St. Croix's best-preserved historical treasure. It's also an island cultural center.

Sleeping in Style

The Virgin Islands have some fine resorts, though not all the best places are necessarily the most luxurious. St. Croix in particular is known more for its small inns than for big, splashy resorts. In the British Virgin Islands (and even St. John), the best options are usually much more laid-back. You're paying for a sense of exclusivity and personal attention, not lavish luxury. You won't be disappointed by these choices.

- **Caneel Bay, St. John, USVI.** Caneel has been a standard-bearer since it opened in the 1950s, but the sense of luxury here is decidedly laid-back. Still, we can't resist those seven gorgeous beaches.

- **Carringtons, St. Croix, USVI.** We have loved Claudia and Roger Carrington's small, friendly B&B in the hills outside Christiansted from the beginning and see no reason to change our mind now.

- **Cooper Island Beach Club, BVI.** Our favorite private-island retreat in the BVI is not the most luxurious—not by a long shot. But we can think of no better place to get away from it all without having to raid the kids' college fund.

- **Ritz-Carlton, St. Thomas, USVI.** Built like a palatial Italian villa, there's elegance everywhere. This is the best Ritz-Carlton in the Caribbean.

- **Sugar Mill Hotel, Tortola, BVI.** We love this small hotel's romantic, tropical ambience, and the restaurant is one of our favorites on Tortola.

- **Villa Greenleaf, St. Croix, USVI.** This B&B comes with the frills, but it's hardly a resort-like experience. Think of a visit to a well-heeled aunt in the Caribbean. We like that thought.

WHEN TO GO

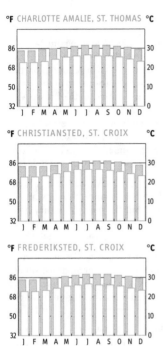

°F CHARLOTTE AMALIE, ST. THOMAS °C

°F CHRISTIANSTED, ST. CROIX °C

°F FREDERIKSTED, ST. CROIX °C

The high season in the USBVI is traditionally winter—from December 15 to the week after the St. Thomas Carnival, usually the last week in April—when northern weather is at its worst. During this season, you're guaranteed the most entertainment at resorts and the most people with whom to enjoy it. It's also the most fashionable, the most expensive, and the most popular time to visit—and most hotels are heavily booked. You must make reservations at least two or three months in advance for the very best places (sometimes a year in advance for the most exclusive spots). Hotel prices drop 20% to 50% after April 15; airfares and cruise prices also fall. Saving money isn't the only reason to visit the USBVI during the off-season. Summer is usually one of the prettiest times of the year; the sea is even calmer, and things move at a slower pace (except for the first two weeks of August on Tortola when the BVI celebrate Carnival). The water is clearer for snorkeling and smoother for sailing in the Virgin Islands in May, June, and July.

Climate

Weather in the USBVI is a year-round wonder. The average daily temperature is about 80°F, and there isn't much variation from the coolest to the warmest months. Rainfall averages 40 to 44 inches per year. But in the tropics, rainstorms tend to be sudden and brief, often erupting early in the morning and at dusk.

In May and June what's known as the Sahara Dust sometimes moves through, making for hazy spring days and spectacular sunsets.

Toward the end of summer, of course, hurricane season begins in earnest, with the first tropical wave passing by in June. Islanders pay close attention to the tropical waves as they form and travel across the Atlantic from Africa. In an odd paradox, tropical storms passing by leave behind the sunniest and clearest days you'll ever see. (And that's saying something in the land of zero air pollution.)

🄵 **Weather Channel Connection** (☎ 900/932-8437 95¢ per minute from a Touch-Tone phone ⊕ www.weather.com).

ON THE CALENDAR

	The USBVI's top seasonal events are listed below, and any one of them could provide the stuff of lasting memories. Contact local tourism authorities for exact dates and for further information.
ONGOING Oct.–Apr.	The Candlelight Concert Series at Whim Plantation is an ongoing classical music program—the only such program of its kind on St. Croix—that presents concerts on Friday and Saturday evenings throughout the year on the grounds of the historic plantation.
WINTER Dec.	For the best in local *fungi* bands (bands that make music using household items as instruments), stop by the Scratch–Fungi Band Fiesta during the last two weeks of December.
Dec. and Jan.	St. Croix celebrates Carnival with its Crucian Christmas Festival, which starts in late December. After weeks of beauty pageants, food fairs, and concerts, the festival wraps with a parade in early January.
SPRING Mar.	Locals and yachties gather at Foxy's bar on Jost Van Dyke in the British Virgin Islands for the annual St. Patrick's Day celebration.
	The annual St. John Blues Festival brings musicians from all over to play for five nights in Coral Bay and Cruz Bay.
Mar. and Apr.	During Easter weekend, St. Thomas Yacht Club hosts the Rolex Cup Regatta, which is part of the three-race Caribbean Ocean Racing Triangle (CORT) that pulls in yachties and their pals from all over.
	The internationally known BVI Spring Regatta & Sailing Festival, which includes the competition for the Nation's Challenge Cup, begins during the last week in March and continues into the first weekend in April, with parties and sailing competitions on Tortola and Virgin Gorda.
Apr.	Join the fun at the Virgin Gorda Festival, which culminates with a parade on Easter Sunday.
May	Every May, hordes of people head to Tortola for the three-day BVI Music Festival to listen to reggae, gospel, blues, and salsa music by musicians from around the Caribbean and the U.S. mainland.
	The St. Croix Half Ironman Triathlon attracts international-class athletes as well as amateurs every May for a 1-mi (2-km) swim, a 7-mi (12-km) run, and a 34-mi (55-km) bike ride; it includes a climb up the Beast on Route 69.

ON THE
CALENDAR

SUMMER	
June–July	Events of the St. John Festival celebrating the island's heritage and history continue throughout the month of June—including beauty pageants and a food fair—culminating with the annual parade on Independence Day.
July	The St. Thomas Gamefishing Club hosts its July Open Tournament over the Fourth of July weekend. There are categories for serious marlin anglers, just-for-fun fishermen, and even kids who want to try their luck from docks and rocks.
	All three islands celebrate Independence Day on July 4 with fireworks, though the biggest celebration is on St. John.
Aug.	Try your hand at sportfishing, as anglers compete to land the largest catch at the BVI Sportfishing Tournament.
	August sees two weeks of joyful revelry during Tortola's BVI Emancipation Festival celebrations.

United States Virgin Islands

Snorkelers, St. Thomas

WORD OF MOUTH

"Magens Bay St. Thomas would be my vote for best and most beautiful beach we've been to."   —Fran

"St. John is where you want to be. We took our whole family last summer and had a wonderful time. Very laid back."
                                                                                        —regansmom

"When on St. Croix, make sure you take a day trip over to Buck Island. . . ."   —Leigh

WELCOME TO THE UNITED STATES VIRGIN ISLANDS

ATLANTIC

Big Hans Lollick

Inner Brass

Picara Pt.

Santa Maria Bay

Botany Bay

Stumpy Bay

Dorothea

Magens Bay

Lovelund Bay

Thatch Cay

Fortuna

David Pt.

Brewers Bay

see detail map pages 26–27

Cyril E. King International Airport

Charlotte Amalie

ST. THOMAS

Hassel Island

Pillsbury Sound

Red Hook

Water Island

Nadir

Greg St. Jar Islan

Frenchman Bay

Bovoni Bay

Long Pt.

Little St. James Island

Charlotte Amalie is the busiest cruise-ship port in the Caribbean. On a busy port day in the high season, as many as 8 ships may anchor in the harbor.

Cane Bay

Davis Bay

Hams Bay

Frederiksted

Henry E. Rohlsen International Airport

West End Salt Pond

Krause Pt

Long Pt. Bay

Long Pt.

Sandy Pt.

AMERICA'S CARIBBEAN

About 1,000 mi (1,600 km) from the southern tip of Florida, the U.S. Virgin Islands were acquired from Denmark in 1917. St. Croix, at 84 square mi (216 square km) is the largest of the islands; St. John, at 20 square mi (52 square km) is the smallest. Together, they have a population of around 110,000, half of whom live on St. Thomas.

A perfect combination of the familiar and the exotic, the U.S. Virgin Islands are a little bit of home set in an azure sea. With hundreds of idyllic coves and splendid beaches, chances are that on one of the three islands you'll find your ideal Caribbean vacation spot.

UNITED STATES VIRGIN ISLANDS

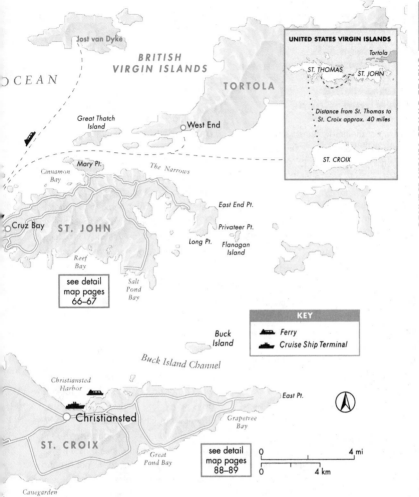

TOP 4 REASONS TO VISIT THE UNITED STATES VIRGIN ISLANDS

1 St. Thomas is one of the Caribbean's major sailing centers.

2 Two-thirds of St. John is a national park, which is criss-crossed by excellent hiking trails.

3 Though Magens Bay on St. Thomas and Trunk Bay on St. John are two of the most perfect beaches you'll ever find, St. Croix's west-end beaches are fetching in their own way.

4 Shopping on both St. Thomas and St. Croix is stellar.

U.S. VIRGIN ISLANDS PLANNER

Getting to the U.S. Virgin Islands

Most major airlines fly nonstop to St. Thomas (STT) from the U.S. There are also a few nonstops to St. Croix (STX). Otherwise, you may have to connect in San Juan. It's also possible to take a seaplane between St. Thomas and St. Croix. There are no flights to St. John because it has no airport; the only option is a ferry from either Red Hook or Charlotte Amalie in St. Thomas. Both Caneel Bay and the Westin have private ferries.

St. Thomas's Cyril E. King Airport sits at the western end of the island. St. Croix's Henry Rohlsen Airport sits outside Frederiksted; the east end is 45 minutes away. The ferry dock in St. John is right in the heart of Cruz Bay.

Hassle Factor: Low to Medium

Activities

St. Thomas is one of the Caribbean's most important centers for **sailing. Beaches** are excellent on both St. Thomas and St. John, good on St. Croix. Of the three, St. Croix is more known for **diving.** Other activities are too varied and numerous to list, particularly on St. Thomas, which is the most developed of the three islands, but you'll find every imaginable kind of water- and land-based activity, **historic sights, golf** (except on St. John), **biking, horseback riding,** and **hiking,** to mention but a few. Since most of St. John is a national park, the island is in pristine condition and well worth exploring on foot. St. Croix's Buck Island and its surrounding reefs are also a protected part of the national park system.

On the Ground

In St. Thomas, shared taxi vans are plentiful at the airport. Fees (set by the VI Taxi Commission) are per person. You'll usually be charged a small fee for each piece of luggage. East End resorts are typically a half-hour from the airport. In St. Croix, you'll pay $10 to $20 for a taxi to your hotel. In St. John, safari-style taxi vans meet all the ferries and will drop you at your hotel; as on St. Thomas, the rates are per person.

Renting a Car

If you are renting a villa on any of the three islands, you'll need a car. Otherwise, it's possible to get by with taxis on St. Thomas, but this can be expensive if you need one every day. You'll probably want a car on St. Croix, if only for a few days, to explore the island; if you are staying near Christiansted and your hotel has a shuttle into Christiansted, you might do without one entirely. In St. John, you will probably need a car to get around and to the beach unless you are staying at Caneel Bay or the Westin.

You need only a valid driver's license and credit card to rent a car; the minimum age for drivers is 18, although many agencies won't rent to anyone under the age of 25. Always make a reservation for a car during the high season.

Where to Stay

St. Thomas is the most developed of the Virgin Islands; choose it if you want extensive shopping opportunities and a multitude of activities and restaurants. The more luxurious resorts tend to be at the east end of the island. St. John is the least developed of the three and has a distinct following; it's the best choice if you want a small-island feel and easy access to great hiking. However, most villas there aren't directly on the beach. St. Croix is a sleeper. With a wide range of accommodations, from simple inns to luxury resorts, including some dive-oriented resorts on the north coast, it's remarkably diverse, but none of the beaches is as breathtaking as those on St. Thomas and St. John.

TYPES OF LODGINGS

Resorts: Whether you are looking for a luxury retreat or a moderately priced vacation spot, there's going to be something for you in the USVI. St. Thomas has the most options. St. John has only two large resorts, both upscale; others are small, but it has some unique eco-oriented camping options. St. Croix's resorts are more mid-sized. The island also has two gay-oriented resorts.

Small Inns: Particularly on St. Croix, you'll find a wide range of attractive and accommodating small inns; if you can live without being directly on the beach, these friendly, homey places are a good option. St. Thomas also has a few small inns.

Villas: Villas are plentiful on all three islands, but they are especially popular on St. John, where they represent more than half the available lodging. They're always a good bet for families who can do without a busy resort environment.

Hotel & Restaurant Costs

Assume that hotels operate on the European Plan (**EP**—with no meals) unless we specify that they use either the Continental Plan (**CP**—with a Continental breakfast), Breakfast Plan (**BP**—with full breakfast), or the Modified American Plan (**MAP**—with breakfast and dinner). Other hotels may offer the Full American Plan (**FAP**—including all meals but no drinks) or may be All-Inclusive (**AI**—with all meals, drinks, and most activities).

WHAT IT COSTS in Dollars

	$$$$	$$$	$$	$	¢
Restaurants	over $30	$20–$30	$12–$20	$8–$12	under $8
Hotels*	over $350	$250–$350	$150–$250	$80–$150	under $80
Hotels**	over $450	$350–$450	$250–$350	$125–$250	under $125

*EP, BP, CP   **AI, FAP, MAP
Restaurant prices are for a main course at dinner excluding tip. Hotel prices are for two people in a double room in high season excluding 8% tax, service, and energy charges (which can vary significantly), and meal plans (except for all-inclusives).

When to Go

High season coincides with that on most other Caribbean islands, from December through April or May; before and after that time, rates can drop by as much as 25% to 50%, depending on the resort.

St. Thomas's **International Rolex Regatta** in March is a big draw, as are the big **sport-fishing tournaments**, which usually begin in May and go through the summer. The St. Croix **Half Ironman Triathlon** attracts international-class athletes as well as amateurs every May. In February and March, the **St. Croix Landmarks Society House Tours** give you a chance to peek inside many historic homes that aren't usually open to the public. There aren't too many big events on St. John, but **Carnival** tends to bring many people to all three islands.

By Carol M.
Bareuther &
Lynda Lohr

WE PILED INTO THE TAXI VAN, BAGS IN THE BACK, and set off for our hotel on the opposite end of the island. Minutes later, cars slowed as we crept through the heart of town. But this traffic jam came with a view. Ballast-brick-walled 19th-century buildings touted contemporary buys on gold, diamonds, and emeralds, while turquoise seas glittered on the other side. Then our world turned topsy-turvy. Up we drove at a 45-degree angle or steeper, along former donkey trails to the mountain-ridge road that runs down the spine of the island. From this vantage point, the red-roof buildings and harbor below looked like miniatures on a postcard. Back on level ground, we pulled up to a green-painted van parked alongside stands brimming with tropical produce. "Sorry, I didn't have lunch," our driver apologized as he hopped back into his seat while holding a large paper bag. He pulled out a fried-bread oval, took a bite and passed the rest of the bag back to us. "Here, try a johnnycake," he offered. We were still happily munching as we finally pulled into our hotel. In 40 minutes, we had not merely reached where we were going but had a good idea of where we'd come. True, the U.S. flag blows here, but "America's Paradise" is in reality a delightful mix of the foreign and familiar that offers something for everyone to enjoy.

The U.S. Virgin Islands—St. Thomas, St. John, and St. Croix—float in the Greater Antilles between the Atlantic and Caribbean seas and some 1,000 mi (1,600 km) from the southern tip of Florida. History books give credit to Christopher Columbus for "discovering" the New World. In reality, the Virgin Islands, like the rest of the isles in the Caribbean chain, were populated as long ago as 2000 BC by nomadic waves of seagoing settlers as they migrated north from South America and eastward from Central America and the Yucatán Peninsula.

Columbus met the descendants of these original inhabitants during his second voyage to the New World, in 1493. He anchored in Salt River, a natural bay west of what is now Christiansted, St. Croix, and sent his men ashore in search of fresh water. Hostile arrows rather than welcoming embraces made for a quick retreat. In haste, Columbus named the island Santa Cruz (Holy Cross) and sailed north. He eventually claimed St. John, St. Thomas, and what are now the British Virgin Islands for Spain and at the same time named this shapely silhouette of 60-some islands Las Once Mil Virgenes, for the 11,000 legendary virgin followers of St. Ursula. Columbus believed the islands barren of priceless spices, so he sailed off leaving more than a century's gap in time before the next Europeans arrived.

Pioneers, planters, and pirates from throughout Europe ushered in the era of colonization. Great Britain and the Netherlands claimed St. Croix in 1625. This peaceful coexistence ended abruptly when the Dutch governor killed his English counterpart, thus launching years of battles for possession that would see seven flags fly over this southernmost Virgin isle. Meanwhile, St. Thomas's sheltered harbor proved a magnet for pirates like Blackbeard and Bluebeard. The Danes first colonized the island in 1666, naming their main settlement Taphus for its many beer halls. In 1691 the town received the more respectable name of Charlotte Amalie in honor of Danish king Christian V's wife. It wasn't until

1718 that a small group of Dutch planters raised their country's flag on St. John. As on its sibling Virgins, a plantation economy soon developed.

Plantations depended on slave labor, and the Virgin Islands played a key role in the triangular route that connected the Caribbean, Africa, and Europe in the trade of sugar, rum, and human cargo. By the 1800s a sharp decline in cane prices due to competing beet sugar and an increasing number of slave revolts motivated Governor General Peter von Scholten to abolish slavery in the Danish colonies on July 3, 1848. This holiday is now celebrated as Emancipation Day.

After emancipation, the island's economy slumped. Islanders owed their existence to subsistence farming and fishing. Meanwhile, during the American Civil War, the Union began negotiations with Denmark for the purchase of the Virgin Islands in order to establish a naval base. However, the sale didn't happen until World War I, when President Theodore Roosevelt paid the Danes $25 million for the three largest islands; an elaborate Transfer Day ceremony was held on the grounds of St. Thomas's Legislature Building on March 31, 1917. A decade later, Virgin Islanders were granted U.S. citizenship. Today the U.S. Virgin Islands is an unincorporated territory, meaning that citizens govern themselves, vote for their own governors, but cannot vote for president or congressional representation.

Nowadays, Virgin Islanders hail from more than 60 nations. Descendants of African slaves are the largest segment of the population, so it's not surprising that they also provide the largest percentage of workers and owners of restaurants, resorts, and shops. The Danish influence is still strong in architecture and street names. Americana is everywhere, too, most notably in recognizable fast-food chains, familiar shows on cable TV, and name-brand hotels. Between this diversity and the wealth that tourism brings, Virgin Islanders struggle to preserve their culture. Their rich, spicy West Indian–African heritage comes to full bloom at Carnival time, when celebrating and playing *mas* (with abandon) take precedence over everything else.

About 60,000 people live on 32-square-mi (83-square-km) St. Thomas (about the size of Manhattan); 51,000 on the 84 square mi (216 square km) of pastoral St. Croix; and about 5,000 on 20-square-mi (52-square-km) St. John, two-thirds of which is a national park. The backbone of the islands' economy is tourism, but at their heart is an independent, separate being: a rollicking hodgepodge of West Indian culture with a sense of humor that puts sex and politics in almost every conversation. Lacking a major-league sports team, Virgin Islanders follow the activities and antics of their 15 elected senators with the rabidity of Washingtonians following the Redskins. Loyalty to country and faith in God are the rules in the USVI, not the exceptions. Prayer is a way of life, and ROTC is one of the most popular high-school extracurricular activities.

Although the idyllic images of a tropical isle are definitely here, there's evidence, too, of growing pains. Traffic jams are common, a clandestine drug trade fuels crime, and—particularly on St. Thomas—there are few beaches left that aren't fronted by a high-rise hotel. Virgin Islanders are friendly folks, yet they can be prone to ungracious moments. Saying "Good morning" to the woman behind the jewelry counter, "Good afternoon" to the man who drives your cab, or "Good evening" as you arrive at a restaurant for dinner will definitely pave the way for more pleasantries. Despite fairly heavy development, wildlife has found refuge here. The brown pelican is on the endangered list worldwide but is a common sight in the USVI. The endangered native boa tree is protected, as is the hawksbill turtle, whose females lumber onto the beaches to lay eggs.

With three islands to choose from, you're likely to find your piece of paradise. Check into a beachfront condo on the East End of St. Thomas; then eat burgers and watch football at a beachfront bar and grill. Or stay at an 18th-century plantation greathouse on St. Croix, dine on everything from local food to Continental cuisine, and go horseback riding at sunrise. Rent a tent or a cottage in the pristine national park on St. John; then take a hike, kayak off the coast, read a book, or just listen to the sounds of the forest. Or dive deep into "island time" and learn the art of limin' (hanging out, Caribbean-style) on all three islands.

ST. THOMAS

By Carol M.
Bareuther

If you fly to the 32-square-mi (83-square-km) island of St. Thomas, you land at its western end; if you arrive by cruise ship, you come into one of the world's most beautiful harbors. Either way, one of your first sights is the town of Charlotte Amalie. From the harbor you see an idyllic-looking village that spreads into the lower hills. If you were expecting a quiet hamlet with its inhabitants hanging out under palm trees, you've missed that era by about 300 years. Although other islands in the USVI developed plantation economies, St. Thomas cultivated its harbor, and it became a thriving seaport soon after it was settled by the Danish in the 1600s.

The success of the naturally perfect harbor was enhanced by the fact that the Danes—who ruled St. Thomas with only a couple of short interruptions from 1666 to 1917—avoided involvement in some 100 years' worth of European wars. Denmark was the only European country with colonies in the Caribbean to stay neutral during the War of the Spanish Succession in the early 1700s. Thus, products of the Dutch, English, and French islands—sugar, cotton, and indigo—were traded through Charlotte Amalie, along with the regular shipments of slaves. When the Spanish wars ended, trade fell off, but by the end of the 1700s Europe was at war again, Denmark again remained neutral, and St. Thomas continued to prosper. Even into the 1800s, while the economies of St. Croix and St. John foundered with the market for sugarcane, St. Thomas's economy remained strong. This prosperity led to the development of shipyards, a well-organized banking system, and a large merchant class. In 1845 Charlotte Amalie had 101 large importing houses owned by the English, French, Germans, Haitians, Spaniards, Americans, Sephardim, and Danes.

Charlotte Amalie is still one of the world's most active cruise-ship ports. On almost any day at least one and sometimes as many as eight cruise ships are tied to the dock or anchored outside the harbor. Gently rocking in the shadows of these giant floating hotels are just about every other kind of vessel imaginable: sleek sailing mono- and multihulls that will take you on a sunset cruise complete with rum punch and a Jimmy Buffett soundtrack, private megayachts that spirit busy executives away, and barnacle-encrusted sloops—with laundry draped over the lifelines—that are home to world-cruising gypsies. Huge container ships pull up in Sub Base, west of the harbor, bringing in everything from breakfast cereals to tires. Anchored right along the waterfront are down-island barges that ply the waters between the Greater Antilles and the Leeward Islands, transporting goods like refrigerators, VCRs, and disposable diapers.

The waterfront road through Charlotte Amalie was once part of the harbor. Before it was filled to build the highway, the beach came right up to the back door of the warehouses that now line the thoroughfare. Two hundred years ago those warehouses were filled with indigo, tobacco, and cotton. Today the stone buildings house silk, crystal, linens, and leather. Exotic fragrances are still traded, but by island beauty queens in air-conditioned perfume palaces instead of through open market stalls. The pirates of old used St. Thomas as a base from which to raid merchant ships of every nation, though they were particularly fond of the gold- and silver-laden treasure ships heading to Spain. Pirates are still around, but today's versions use St. Thomas as a drop-off for their contraband: illegal immigrants and drugs.

Where to Stay

Of the USVI, St. Thomas has the most rooms and the greatest number and variety of resorts. You can let yourself be pampered at a luxurious resort—albeit at a price of $300 to more than $500 per night, not including meals. If your means are more modest, there are fine hotels (often with rooms that have a kitchen and a living area) in lovely settings throughout the island. There are also guesthouses and inns with great views (if not a beach at your door) and great service at about half the cost of what you'll pay at the beachfront pleasure palaces. Many of these are east and north of Charlotte Amalie or overlooking hills—ideal if you plan to get out and mingle with the locals. There are also inexpensive lodgings (most right in town) that are perfect if you just want a clean room to return to after a day of exploring or beach-bumming. You can learn more about the smaller properties on the island from the **St. Thomas–St. John Hotel & Tourism Association** (⇨ Visitor Information *in* U.S. Virgin Islands Essentials).

East-end condominium complexes are popular with families. Although condos are pricey (winter rates average $350 per night for a two-bedroom unit, which usually sleeps six), they have full kitchens, and you can definitely save money by cooking for yourself—especially if you bring some of your own nonperishable foodstuffs. (Virtually everything on St. Thomas is imported, and restaurants and shops pass shipping costs on to you.) Though you may spend some time laboring in the kitchen, many condos ease your burden with daily maid service and on-site restaurants; a few also have resort amenities, including pools and ten-

St. Thomas

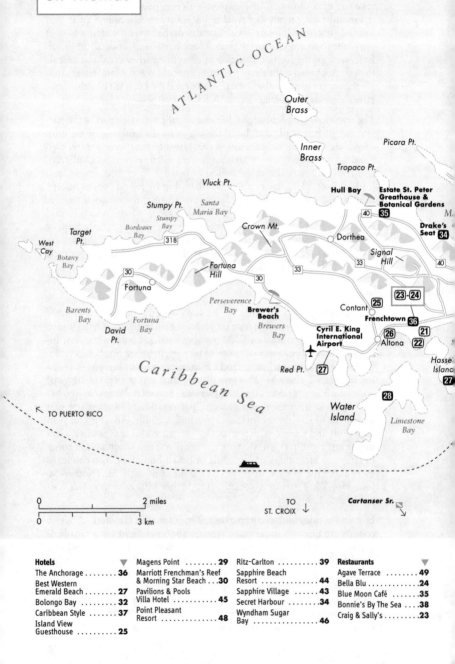

ATLANTIC OCEAN

Outer Brass

Inner Brass

Picara Pt.

Tropaco Pt.

Vluck Pt.

Hull Bay

Estate St. Peter Greathouse & Botanical Gardens

Stumpy Pt.

Santa Maria Bay

Stumpy Bay

Crown Mt.

Dorthea

Drake's Seat **34**

40 **35**

Bordeaux Bay

318

Target Pt.

West Cay

Botany Bay

Signal Hill

33

40

Fortuna Hill

33

30

Fortuna

30

Perseverance Bay

Brewer's Beach

Contant

25

23 - **24**

Barents Bay

Fortuna Bay

Brewers Bay

Frenchtown **36**

David Pt.

Cyril E. King International Airport

26 **21**

Altona **22**

Hassel Island

27

Caribbean Sea

Red Pt. **27**

Water Island

28

Limestone Bay

← TO PUERTO RICO

| 0 | | 2 miles |
| 0 | | 3 km |

TO ST. CROIX ↓

Cartanser Sr.

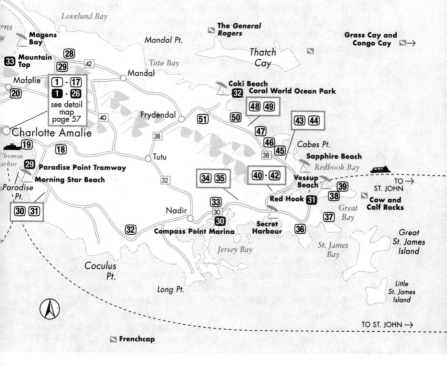

KEY

- ⚓ Beaches
- 🚢 Cruise Ship Terminal
- ◣ Dive Sites
- 1 Exploring Sights
- 🚤 Ferry
- ① Hotels & Restaurants

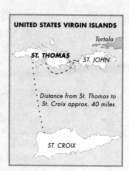

UNITED STATES VIRGIN ISLANDS

Tortola

ST. THOMAS   ST. JOHN

Distance from St. Thomas to St. Croix approx. 40 miles

ST. CROIX

Hans Lollick

Lovelund Bay

Magens Bay

33 **Mountain Top**

28
29   42

Mafolie

20

1 · 17
1 · 26
see detail map page 57

Mandal Pt.

Tutu Bay

Mandal

The General Rogers

Thatch Cay

Grass Cay and Congo Cay

Charlotte Amalie

19

40

Frydendal

Coki Beach
32 **Coral World Ocean Park**

48 49

51   50

47

46   45

38

Cabes Pt.

43 44

Sapphire Beach
Redhook Bay

TO ST. JOHN →

29
18

Paradise Point Tramway

Morning Star Beach

Tutu

32

34 35

40 · 42

Vessup Beach

39
38

Cow and Calf Rocks

Thomas Harbor

Paradise Pt.

30 31

Nadir

33
30
30

Compass Point Marina

32

Red Hook 31

Secret Harbour

37

Great Bay

36

St. James Bay

Great St. James Island

Coculus Pt.

Jersey Bay

Long Pt.

Little St. James Island

TO ST. JOHN →

◣ **Frenchcap**

nis courts. The east end is convenient to St. John, and it's a hub for the boating crowd, with some good restaurants. The prices below reflect rates in high season, which runs from December 15 to April 15. Rates are 25% to 50% lower the rest of the year.

Hotels

CHARLOTTE
AMALIE Accommodations in town and near town offer the benefits of being close to the airport, shopping, and a number of casual and fine-dining restaurants. The downside is that this is the most crowded and noisy area of the island. Crime can also be a problem. Don't go for a stroll at night in the heart of town. Use common sense and take the same precautions you would in any U.S. city. Those properties located up along the hillsides are less likely to have crime problems, plus they command a steady breeze from the cool trade winds. This is especially important if you're visiting in summer and early fall.

$$$ 🏨 **Best Western Emerald Beach Resort.** You get beachfront ambience at this reasonably priced miniresort tucked beneath the palm trees, but the tradeoff is that it's directly across from a noisy airport runway. You'll definitely want to spend time on the white-sand beach, which can be seen from nearly every room in the four three-story, peach-color buildings. Rooms are acceptable, but the tropical-print bedspreads and rattan furnishings look worn. Stay here if you need the beach on a budget or if you have an early-morning flight. ⊠ *8070 Lindberg Bay, 00802* ☎ *340/777–8800 or 800/780–7234* 🖷 *340/776–3426* ⊕ *www. emeraldbeach.com* ⤱ *90 rooms* ⚷ *In-room: refrigerator, dial-up. In-hotel: restaurant, bar, tennis courts, pool, gym, beachfront, no elevator* ▤ *AE, D, MC, V* ❙❂❙ *CP.*

$$–$$$ 🏨 **Holiday Inn St. Thomas.** Business travelers, those on the way to the British Virgin Islands, or laid-back vacationers who want the convenience of being able to walk to duty-free shopping, sights, and restaurants stay at this harborfront hotel. But if your ideal Caribbean beach vacation means having the beach at your doorstep, this isn't the place for you, despite the presence of a free beach shuttle. Contemporary rooms have such amenities as coffeemakers, hair dryers, ironing boards, and irons. An introductory dive lesson with Admiralty Dive Center is complimentary. In 2006, a lounge opened on the ground level that provides complimentary high-speed computer terminals to guests who are Ambassador or Platinum Priority Club members. ⊠ *Waterfront Hwy., Box 640, 00804* ☎ *340/774–5200 or 800/524–7389* 🖷 *340/774–1231* ⊕ *www.holidayinn.st-thomas.com* ⤱ *140 rooms, 11 suites* ⚷ *In-room: safe, refrigerator, dial-up. In-hotel: restaurant, room service, bar, pool, gym, diving, laundry service, public Internet* ▤ *AE, D, DC, MC, V* ❙❂❙ *EP.*

$–$$$ 🏨 **Hotel 1829.** Antique charm is readily apparent in this rambling 19th-century merchant's house, from the hand-painted Moroccan tiles to a Tiffany window. Rooms on several levels range from stylish and spacious suites with vaulted ceilings to small and cozy rooms. The bar is open nightly and attracts locals as well as hotel guests. The second-floor botanical gardens and open-air champagne bar make a romantic spot for sunset viewing. Main Street, with its duty-free shops, is down the hill one block away. ⊠ *Government Hill, Box 1567, 00804* ☎ *340/776–*

1829 or 800/524–2002 🖷 340/776–4313 ⊕ *www.hotel1829.com* ➼ *15 rooms* ♿ *In-room: no phone, refrigerator. In-hotel: bar, pool, no kids under 11, no elevator* ☰ *AE, D, MC, V* ﹗◎﹗ *CP.*

$–$$ 🏨 **The Green Iguana.** Atop Blackbeard's Hill, this B&B offers the perfect mix of gorgeous harbor views, proximity to town and shopping (five minutes away by foot), and secluded privacy provided by the surrounding flamboyant trees and bushy hibiscus. Accommodations range from a roomy, top-floor junior suite with two queen beds to a balcony room with queen bed and full kitchen. All rooms have air-conditioning, refrigerators, microwave ovens, and coffeemakers. Guests have use of washers and dryers. There's also a picnic area with a gas barbecue grill. The managing couple lives on the property and is very helpful in giving restaurant, sightseeing, or beach suggestions. ⊠ *37B Blackbeard's Hill, 00802* 🕿 *340/776–7654 or 800/484–8825* 🖷 *340/777–4312* ⊕ *www. thegreeniguana.com* ➼ *6 rooms* ♿ *In-room: kitchen (some), refrigerator. In-hotel: pool, laundry facilities, no-smoking rooms, no elevator* ☰ *AE, D, MC, V* ﹗◎﹗ *EP.*

$–$$
Fodor's Choice
★   🏨 **Villa Santana.** Built by exiled General Antonio López Santa Anna of Mexico, this 1857 landmark provides a panoramic view of the harbor and plenty of West Indian charm, which will make you feel as if you're living in a charming slice of Virgin Islands history. Each of the rooms is unique and lovely. Our two favorites are La Mansion, a former library that is now an elegant villa with a large living area crowned by cathedral ceilings, full kitchen, two baths, and four-poster bed; and El Establo, a three-bedroom house with a full kitchen and laundry facilities that is rented by the week. Modern amenities aren't lacking; you can even sit by the pool with your laptop and indulge in wireless Internet access. ⊠ *2D Denmark Hill, 00802* 🕿 *340/776–1311* 🖷 *340/776–1311* ⊕ *www.villasantana.com* ➼ *6 rooms* ♿ *In-room: no a/c (some), no phone, kitchen (some), no TV (some), Wi-Fi. In-hotel: pool, no elevator* ☰ *AE, MC, V* ﹗◎﹗ *EP.*

$ 🏨 **Island View Guesthouse.** Perched 545 feet up the face of Crown Mountain, this small inn has a homey feel; the hands-on owners can book tours or offer tips about the best sightseeing spots. Rooms range from a suite with a kitchenette that's perfect for families to two simply furnished verandah rooms that share a bath. The two verandah rooms and six poolside rooms have no air-conditioning, but at this altitude there's always a breeze. Six of the rooms have kitchenettes, so you wouldn't have to eat out for every meal. Laundry facilities are on-site. There's an honor bar for drinks and snacks and a communal verandah where guests congregate for Continental breakfasts and home-cooked dinners. You'll need a car to explore the island. ⊠ *Rte. 332, Box 1903, Estate Contant 00803* 🕿 *340/774–4270 or 800/524–2023* 🖷 *340/774–6167* ⊕ *www. islandviewstthomas.com* ➼ *16 rooms, 14 with private bath* ♿ *In-room: no a/c (some), kitchen (some). In-hotel: pool, laundry facilities, no elevator* ☰ *AE, MC, V* ﹗◎﹗ *CP.*

$ 🏨 **Mafolie Hotel.** The view and the value are the selling points of this 1970s-era hotel perched 700 feet above Charlotte Amalie harbor. The rooms at this family-run place are simply furnished rather than resort elegant, and a few of those at pool level don't have much of a view or a constant flow of trade winds, which makes air-conditioning a must. Rooms above the restaurant are really small and lack privacy in the evening due to the steady stream of diners. Rooms 8 and 9 have a connecting door, which is great for families or other groups. The restaurant is known for its well-prepared Continental cuisine, featuring fresh seafood, steaks, and chicken. A daily shuttle takes guests to and from Magens Bay Beach and to Charlotte Amalie, although you need to find your own way back once you are downtown. ✉ *Rte. 35, Box 7091, Estate Mafolie, 00802* ☎ *340/774–2790 or 800/225–7035* ☒ *340/774–4091* ⊕ *www. mafolie.com* ⇆ *22 rooms* ⚐ *In-room: refrigerator. In-hotel: restaurant, bar, pool, no elevator* ⊟ *AE, MC, V* ⊚∣ *CP.*

EAST END   You can find most of the large, luxurious beachfront resorts on St. Thomas's east end. The downside is that these properties are about a 30-minute drive from town and 45-minute drive from the airport (substantially longer during peak hours). On the upside, these properties tend to be self-contained, plus there are a number of good restaurants, shops, and water-sports operators in the area. Thus, once you've arrived, you don't need to travel far to have many activities and services at your fingertips.

🕒 **$$$$**
Fodor'sChoice
★

Ritz-Carlton, St. Thomas. Everything sparkles at the island's most luxurious resort, especially after a $40 million renovation and expansion in 2006 that upgraded everything from in-room furnishings to tiling for the walkways. Spacious guest rooms, with high-speed Internet access, private balconies, and marble bathrooms with deep soaking tubs, are in six buildings fanning out from the main building. Six tall, somewhat institutional-looking buildings, composing the Ritz-Carlton Club, are two- and three-bedroom condos on their own adjacent beach. There are also two new villas. The spa, salon, and fitness center serve adults, both body and soul; the Ritz Kids program packs in a full day of activities for kids, including collecting seashells and feeding iguanas. A 54-foot catamaran is a must-do for a day or sunset sail. ✉ *Rte. 317, Box 6900, Estate Great Bay 00802* ☎ *340/775–3333 or 800/241–3333* ☒ *340/ 775–4444* ⊕ *www.ritzcarlton.com* ⇆ *255 rooms, 20 suites, 2 villas, 81 condos* ⚐ *In-room: safe, refrigerator, Wi-Fi. In-hotel: 4 restaurants, room service, bars, tennis courts, pools, gym, spa, beachfront, water sports, concierge, children's programs (ages 4–12), laundry service, public Internet, airport shuttle, no-smoking rooms* ⊟ *AE, D, DC, MC, V* ⊚∣ *EP.*

🕒 **$$$$**
Fodor'sChoice
★

Wyndham Sugar Bay Resort & Spa. Though this terra-cotta high-rise is surrounded by palm trees and lush greenery, rooms and the walkways between them have a bit of a generic feel. However, the sixth and seventh levels of building D have spectacular ocean views. A $3 million renovation completed in 2006 added plantation-style guest-room furnishings, plush carpeting, and marble-tile bathrooms. The beach is small, although the nearby pool is replete with waterfalls and colorful cabanas housing hair braiders and henna tattoo artists that make a day of lounging here idyllic. It's a 99-step hike from guest rooms, however. Health buffs will enjoy the full-service spa and fitness center, as well as the outdoor fitness trail. If you're feeling lucky, head to the Wyndham Sugar Bay Gaming Center, where there are more than 50 video slot machines. ✉ *Rte. 38, Box 6500, Estate Smith Bay 00802* ☎ *340/777–7100 or*

800/927–7100 🖷 *340/777–7200* ⊕ *www.wyndham.com* ⬎ *300 rooms, 9 suites* ⚓ *In-room: safe, refrigerator, dial-up. In-hotel: 2 restaurants, room service, bar, tennis courts, pool, gym, spa, beachfront, water sports, concierge, children's programs (ages 4–12), laundry service* ▭ *AE, D, DC, MC, V* ⍥ *AI.*

$$$–$$$$ ⌂ **Point Pleasant Resort.** Hilltop suites give you an eagle's-eye view of the east end and the BVI beyond, while those in a building adjacent to the reception area offer incredible sea views. Sea-level junior suites, where the sounds of lapping waves will lull you to sleep, are smaller. There's a resort shuttle, but some walking is necessary and hills are steep. The beach is tiny, though some may call it wonderfully private, but three pools give you more swimming and sunning options. The property also has a labyrinth of well-marked nature trails to explore. If you like seafood, don't miss dinner at the Agave Terrace restaurant; Fungi's on the Beach is a casual alternative. ⊠ *6600 Rte. 38, Estate Smith Bay 00802* ☎ *340/775– 7200 or 800/524–2300* 🖷 *340/776–5694* ⊕ *www.pointpleasantresort. com* ⬎ *128 suites* ⚓ *In-room: safe, kitchen, dial-up. In-hotel: 2 restaurants, bar, tennis court, pools, gym, beachfront, concierge, laundry facilities, public Internet, no elevator* ▭ *AE, D, DC, MC, V* ⍥ *EP.*

$$$–$$$$ ⌂ **Secret Harbour Beach Resort & Villas.** There's not a bad view from these low-rise studio, one-, and two-bedroom condos, which are either beachfront or perched on a hill overlooking the inviting cove beyond. All units, which have white-tile floors and tropical-print wood and wicker furnishings, are spacious; even the studios are more than 600 square feet and certainly big enough for a family with two children. The pool is small, but the beach is the real focal point here. Calm seas make for excellent swimming, and snorkeling is especially good near the small dock to the east of the cove, where coral outcroppings attract a bevy of marine life. Watch spectacular sunsets from your balcony or the beachfront bar. Kids under 13 stay free, making this a good value for families. ⊠ *Rte. 317, Box 6280, Estate Nazareth 00802-1104* ☎ *340/775–6550 or 800/524–2250* 🖷 *340/ 775–1501* ⊕ *www.secretharbourvi.com* ⬎ *49 suites, 15 studios* ⚓ *In-room: kitchen. In-hotel: restaurant, bar, tennis courts, pool, gym, beachfront, diving, water sports, no elevator* ▭ *AE, MC, V* ⍥ *CP.*

$$–$$$ ⌂ **Magens Point Resort.** This small resort is tucked into the lush, green countryside 10 minutes from town and close to both Magens Bay Beach and the Mahogany Run golf course, to which there are free shuttles. Be forewarned that renovations are needed for the large, multilevel suites, which have full kitchens. Most units are available as time-shares. A plus is the Sunday-morning poolside talk about what to see and do on the island. The restaurant, Indigo, has upscale yet reasonably priced fare served up in a casual, laid-back setting. ⊠ *Rte. 35, Magens Bay Rd., Estate St. Joseph 00802* ☎ *340/777–6000 or 800/524–2031* 🖷 *340/777– 6055* ⊕ *www.magenspoint.com* ⬎ *52 suites* ⚓ *In-hotel: restaurant, bar, tennis courts, pool, gym, concierge* ▭ *AE, D, MC, V* ⍥ *EP.*

$$–$$$ ⌂ **Pavilions & Pools Villa Hotel.** Although the rates might lead you to believe you're buying resort ambience, the reality is that you get fairly basic accommodations but also a private swimming pool right outside your bedroom. Perfect for couples who crave privacy, the villas have full kitchens, lots of space, and sunken garden showers. The informal bar and open-air dining area, built around a pond filled with tilapia, is a great place to congregate over a Continental breakfast and chat with other guests. Karl's Cajun and Creole Kitchen offers casual dinners Wednesday through Saturday. Prices range from $10 for a plate of the famous tamales served with beans and rice, to over $20 for blackened catfish or crawfish etouffee. There's no beach, but Sapphire Bay is less than a 10-minute walk away. ✉ *6400 Rte. 38, Estate Smith Bay 00802* ☎ *340/775–6110 or 800/524–2001* 🌐 *www.pavilionsandpools.com* *25 1-bedroom villas* *In-room: safe, kitchen. In-hotel: restaurant, pools, no elevator* 💳 *AE, D, MC, V* 🍽 *CP.*

$$–$$$ **Sapphire Beach Resort & Marina.** A beautiful half-mile-long white-sand beach is the real ace here. After a long succession of owners, Antilles Resorts took control of the property in 2006 and began much-needed refurbishments to the rooms. Changes include new curtains and bedspreads. The property is nicely landscaped on the ocean side, but away from the beach is a long-awaited convention center, marina office, and shopping complex that is still just a big grassy spot occupied by the odd car and piece of construction equipment. The kid's club program no longer exists. Only the pool bar and restaurant are open, but the resort runs a nightly shuttle to the Wyndham Sugar Bay Beach Club & Resort to give guests two more dinner options. Snorkeling equipment, floating mats, one windsurfing lesson, and one sail on a Sunfish are complimentary, as is a two-day car rental. ✉ *6720 Estate Smith Bay 00802* ☎ *800/524–2090, 340/773–9150, or 800/874–7897* 📠 *340/778–4009* 🌐 *www.sapphirebeachresort.net* *171 suites* *In-room: kitchen (some). In-hotel: restaurant, bar, tennis courts, pool, gym, beachfront, water sports, concierge, laundry facilities, no elevator* 💳 *AE, MC, V* 🍽 *EP.*

SOUTH SHORE

The south shore of St. Thomas connects town to the east end of the island via a beautiful road that rambles along the hillside with frequent peeks between the hills for a view of the ocean and, on a clear day, of St. Croix some 40 mi (60 km) to the south. The resorts here are on their own beaches. They offer several opportunities for water sports, as well as land-based activities, fine dining, and evening entertainment.

$$$$ **Marriott Frenchman's Reef & Morning Star Beach Resorts.** Set majestically on a promontory overlooking the east side of Charlotte Amalie's harbor, Frenchman's Reef is the high-rise full-service superhotel, while Morning Star is the even more upscale boutique property nestled along the fine white-sand beach. Renovations completed in 2006 at Frenchman's Reef property include 8-foot-wide mahogany headboards, flat-screen televisions, and Wi-Fi in all the rooms. Meals here include lavish buffets for breakfast and dinner. The former Lobby Bar is now a rum bar featuring bottles from around the Caribbean and beyond. Live entertainment and dancing, scheduled activities for all ages, and an hourly boat that shuttles guests to town make having fun easy. ✉ *Rte. 315, Box 7100, Estate Bakkeroe 00801* ☎ *340/776–8500 or 800/233–6388* 📠 *340/715–6193* 🌐 *www.marriott.com/property/propertypage/sttfr* *479 rooms, 27 suites* *In-room: safe, refrigerator, dial-up, Wi-Fi. In-hotel: 4 restaurants, room service, bar, tennis courts, pools, gym, spa, beachfront, concierge, children's programs (ages 4–12)* 💳 *AE, D, DC, MC, V* 🍽 *EP.*

$$$ ▥ **Bolongo Bay Beach Club.** All the rooms at this small, family-run resort tucked along a 1,000-foot-long palm-lined beach have balconies with ocean views; down the beach are 12 studio and two-bedroom condos with full kitchens. This place is more homey than fancy, but the friendliness of the longtime staff keeps visitors, including many honeymooners and even some families, coming back. The beach is a bit rocky for swimming, but sails aboard the resort's 53-foot catamaran and excursions arranged by the on-site dive shop are popular. You can opt out of the all-inclusive plan and pay less, but then you'd have to rent a car because the resort is a bit removed from the main parts of the island. The creative Caribbean cuisine at the Beach House, especially the seven-course tasting menu, which is paired with wines, shouldn't be missed. ⊠ *Rte. 30, Box 7150, Estate Bolongo 00802* ☎ *340/775–1800 or 800/524–4746* 🖷 *340/775–3208* ⊕ *www.bolongobay.com* ⇨ *65 rooms, 12 studio and 2-bedroom condos* ♻ *In-room: safe, kitchen (some), refrigerator. In-hotel: 2 restaurants, bar, tennis courts, pool, beachfront, diving, water sports, no elevator* ⊟ *AE, D, DC, MC, V* ⋈ *EP.*

Villas & Condominiums

All the villa and condominium complexes listed here are on the East End of St. Thomas.

☾ $$$-$$$$ ▥ **The Anchorage.** A beachfront setting and homey conveniences that include full kitchens and washer-dryer units are what you can find in these two- and three-bedroom suites on Cowpet Bay next to the St. Thomas Yacht Club. The complex has two lighted tennis courts, a freshwater pool, and an informal restaurant. ⊠ *Rte. 317, Estate Nazareth* 🖅 *Antilles Resorts, Box 24786, Christiansted, St. Croix 00824-0786* ☎ *800/874–7897* 🖷 *340/778–4009* ⊕ *www.antillesresorts.com* ⇨ *11 suites* ♻ *In-room: kitchen. In-hotel: restaurant, bar, gym, tennis courts, pool, beachfront, laundry facilities, no elevator* ⊟ *AE, D, MC, V* ⋈ *EP.*

$$ ▥ **Sapphire Village.** These high-rise towers feel more like apartment buildings than luxury resorts, so if you're looking for a home away from home, this might be the place. There are full kitchens, so you can avoid pricey restaurant meals. The view from your balcony is the marina and the Atlantic Ocean. The beach, a spectacular half mile of white sand, is a five-minute walk down the hill. There's a restaurant on property and two more down the hill at the Sapphire Beach Resort & Marina. Additional restaurants, a shopping complex, and ferries to St. John are a mile away in Red Hook. ⊠ *Rte. 38, Sapphire Bay* 🖅 *Antilles Resorts, Box 24786, Christiansted, St. Croix 00824-0786* ☎ *340/779–1540 or 800/874–7897* 🖷 *340/778–4009* ⊕ *www.antillesresorts.com* ⇨ *15 condos* ♻ *In-room: kitchen. In-hotel: restaurant, bar, tennis courts, pools, beachfront, water sports, laundry facilities, no elevator* ⊟ *AE, D, MC, V* ⋈ *EP.*

★ $ ▥ **Caribbean Style.** Couples will enjoy the romantic feel of these private, individually decorated condos. Each has a king-size bed, a reading and video library, and a kitchen stocked with breakfast foods and special requests, such as your favorite ice cream or preferred brand of rum. You can literally toss an ice cube into the sea from the hammock or lounge chairs on the private porches of the two smaller condos, while the two larger condos are only about 20 feet away from the rocky waterfront.

Vessup Beach and water sports are a 10-minute walk away. Couples who would like to tie the knot will find that wedding arrangements, including professional photography, are the owner's specialty. ⊠ *Rte. 317, at Cabrita Point, Estate Vessup Bay* ⌖ *6501 Red Hook Plaza, Suite 201, 00802* ☏ *340/715–1117 or 800/593–1390* ⊕ *www.cstylevi.com/cstyle new/html* ⊳ *4 1-bedroom condos* ⌂ *In-room: kitchen. In-hotel: pool, water sports, no kids under 15, no-smoking rooms, no elevator* ⊟ *AE, MC, V* ⦿ *CP.*

PRIVATE VILLAS   You can arrange private villa rentals through various agents that represent luxury residences and usually have both Web sites and brochures that show photos of the properties they represent. Some are suitable for travelers with disabilities, but be sure to ask specific questions regarding your own needs. **Calypso Realty** (⌖ Box 12178, 00801 ☏ 340/774–1620 or 800/747–4858 ⊕ www.calypsorealty.com) specializes in rental properties around St. Thomas. **McLaughlin-Anderson Villas** (⊠ 100 Blackbeard's Hill, Suite 3, 00802 ☏ 340/776–0635 or 800/537–6246 ⊕ www. mclaughlinanderson.com) handles rental villas throughout the U.S. Virgin Islands, British Virgin Islands, and Grenada.

Where to Eat

The beauty of St. Thomas and its sister islands has attracted a cadre of professionally trained chefs who know their way around fresh fish and local fruits. You can dine on everything from terrific cheap local dishes such as goat water (a spicy stew) and fungi (a cornmeal polentalike side dish) to imports such as hot pastrami sandwiches and raspberries in crème fraîche.

Restaurants are spread all over the island, although fewer are found on the west and northwest parts of the island. Most restaurants out of town are easily accessible by taxi and have ample parking. If you dine in Charlotte Amalie, take a taxi. Parking close to restaurants can be difficult to find, and walking around after dark isn't advisable for safety reasons.

If your accommodations have a kitchen and you plan to cook, there's good variety in St. Thomas's mainland-style supermarkets. Just be prepared for grocery prices that are about 20% higher than those in the United States. As for drinking, outside the hotels a beer in a bar will cost between $2 and $3 and a piña colada $5 or more.

What to Wear
Dining on St. Thomas is informal. Few restaurants require a jacket and tie. Still, at dinner in the snazzier places shorts and T-shirts are inappropriate; men would do well to wear slacks and a shirt with buttons. Dress codes on St. Thomas rarely require women to wear skirts, but you can never go wrong with something flowing.

Charlotte Amalie
AMERICAN   ✕ **Greenhouse Bar & Restaurant.** The eight-page menu at this bustling wa-
☺ **$–$$$**   terfront restaurant offers burgers, salads, sandwiches, and pizza served all day long, along with more upscale entrées like peel-and-eat shrimp, Maine lobster, Alaskan king crab, and certified Black Angus prime rib

that are reasonably priced. This is generally a family-friendly place, though the Two-for-Tuesdays happy hour and Friday-night live reggae music that starts thumping at 10 PM draw a lively young-adult crowd. ✉ *Waterfront Hwy. at Storetvaer Gade* ☎ 340/774–7998 ➡ *AE, D, MC, V.*

ⓒ ¢–$
Fodor'sChoice
★
✕ **Jen's Gourmet Cafe & Deli.** This hole-in-the-wall eatery is the closest thing you'll find to a New York–style Jewish deli. Choose the smoked salmon platter for breakfast or hot pastrami on rye at lunch. Homemade desserts like chocolate layer cake, apple strudel, and peaches-and-cream-cheese strudel are yummy. ✉ *Grand Galleria, 43-46 Norre Gade* ☎ 340/777–4611 ➡ *AE, MC, V* ⊘ *No dinner. Closed Sun.*

BARBECUE
ⓒ ¢–$
✕ **Texas Pit BBQ.** The smell of smoky barbecue ribs, beef brisket, and chicken wafts enticingly from these mobile stands, which set up daily around 4 PM. Austin native and longtime Virgin Islands resident Bill Collins perfected his sauce recipe, which received a thumbs-up from the late culinary great James Beard. Choice of homemade seasoned rice, coleslaw, or potato salad completes the meal. Takeout only. Besides the two Charlotte Amalie branches, you can also find one in Red Hook at the northern end of Red Hook Shopping Center. ✉ *Waterfront, across from Holiday Inn St. Thomas* ☎ 340/776–9579 ✉ *Wheatley Center* ☎ 340/714–5775 ➡ *No credit cards* ⊘ *No lunch.*

CARIBBEAN
$$
✕ **Cuzzin's Caribbean Restaurant & Bar.** The top picks in this restaurant in a 19th-century livery stage are Virgin Islands staples. For lunch, order tender slivers of conch stewed in a rich onion butter sauce, savory braised oxtail, or curried chicken. At dinner, the island-style mutton, served in a thick gravy and seasoned with locally grown herbs, offers a tasty treat that's deliciously different. Side dishes include peas and rice, boiled green bananas, fried plantains, and potato stuffing. ✉ *7 Wimmelskafts Gade, also called Back St.* ☎ 340/777–4711 ➡ *AE, MC, V.*

$–$$
Fodor'sChoice
★
✕ **Gladys' Cafe.** Even if the local specialties—conch in butter sauce, salt fish and dumplings, hearty red bean soup—didn't make this a recommended café, it would be worth coming for Gladys's smile. While you're here, pick up a $5 or $10 bottle of her special hot sauce. There are mustard-, oil and vinegar-, and tomato-based versions; the last is the hottest. ✉ *Waterfront, at Royal Dane Mall* ℗ *28 Dronningens Gade, Charlotte Amalie St. Thomas 00802* ☎ 340/774–6604 ➡ *AE* ⊘ *No dinner.*

ECLECTIC
$$$–$$$$
Fodor'sChoice
★
✕ **Banana Tree Grille.** The eagle's-eye view of the Charlotte Amalie harbor from this open-air restaurant is as fantastic as the food. Arrive before 6 PM and watch the cruise ships depart from the harbor and the sun set over the sea while you enjoy a drink at the bar. Liz Buckalew, in the restaurant business since the early 1980s, always gives you a warm welcome. For starters, try the combination of lobster, shrimp, scallops, and squid marinated in a savory herb vinaigrette. The dark rum, honey, and brown sugar–glazed salmon is an excellent entrée. ✉ *Bluebeard's Castle, Bluebeard's Hill* ℗ *Box 302913, Charlotte Amalie St. Thomas 00803* ☎ 340/776–4050 ◬ *Reservations essential* ➡ *AE, D, MC, V* ⊘ *Closed Mon. No lunch.*

★ $$–$$$
✕ **Randy's Bar & Bistro.** There's no view here—even though you're at the top of a hill—but the somewhat hidden location has helped to keep this

one of the island's best dining secrets. This wineshop and deli caters to a local lunch crowd. At night, you forget you're tucked into a nearly windowless building. The table-side bread for starters is a thick, crusty focaccia flavored with nearly 10 different vegetables. Try the Brie-stuffed filet mignon or rack of lamb. After-dinner cigars and wine complete the experience. ⊠ *Al Cohen's Plaza, atop Raphune Hill, ½ mi (¾ km) east of Charlotte Amalie* ☎ *340/777–3199* ▤ *AE, D, MC, V.*

FRENCH
★ $$$–$$$$

✕ **Hervé Restaurant & Wine Bar.** In the glow of candlelight—at tables impeccably dressed with fine linens, silver settings, and sparkling crystal—you can start off with French-trained Hervé Chassin's crispy conch fritters served with a spicy-sweet mango chutney, then choose from such entrées as black-sesame-crusted tuna with a ginger-raspberry sauce or succulent roast duck with a ginger-tamarind sauce. The passion-fruit cheesecake is to die for. For lunch, lighter fare like quiche, salads, and grilled sandwiches is served in the open-air bistro on the first floor. ⊠ *Government Hill* ☎ *340/777–9703* ⚜ *Reservations essential* ▤ *AE, MC, V.*

ITALIAN
★ $$$–$$$$

✕ **Virgilio's.** For the island's best northern Italian cuisine, don't miss this intimate, elegant hideaway tucked on a quiet side street. Eclectic art covers the two-story brick walls, and the sound of opera sets the stage for a memorable meal. Come here for more than 40 homemade pastas topped with superb sauces—cappellini with fresh tomatoes and garlic or peasant-style spaghetti in a rich tomato sauce with mushrooms and prosciutto. House specialties include osso buco and tiramisu—expertly crafted by chef Ernesto Garrigos, who has prepared these two dishes on the Discovery Channel's "Great Chefs of the World" series. ⊠ *18 Main St.* ☎ *340/776–4920* ⚜ *Reservations essential* ▤ *AE, MC, V* ☉ *Closed Sun.*

$$

✕ **Café Amici.** Set within the historic stonework and cascading tropical blossoms of A. H. Riise Alley, this charming open-air eatery has an Italian name but boasts a menu with Caribbean flair. Choose anything from brick-oven pizzas to fresh salads, open-faced sandwiches, and unique pasta dishes that are cooked to order. House specialties include tamarind barbecued shrimp salad and pizza topped with housemade sausage and apples. ⊠ *37 Main St.* ☎ *340/776–0444* ▤ *AE, MC, V* ☉ *Closed Sun. No dinner.*

JAPANESE
$–$$

✕ **Beni Iguana's Sushi Bar & Restaurant.** Edible art is an apt description of the sushi and sashimi feast on display at this Japanese restaurant tucked into the historic Grand Galleria Hotel. There are nearly 30 vegetarian and seafood rolls to choose from, including avocado, spicy crab, and red snapper. The real favorite here is steamed mussels in a house-made creamy sesame dressing dubbed "iguana sauce," which is, happily, not made from the spiny reptile that roams the island's hillsides and roadways. ⊠ *Grand Galleria, Tolbod Gade at Norre Gade* ☎ *340/777–8744* ▤ *AE, MC, V.*

SPANISH
★ $$$–$$$$

✕ **Café Amalia.** Tucked into the alleyway of Palm Passage, this open-air café owned by Antiguan-born Randolph Maynard and his German wife, Helga, serves authentic Spanish cuisine. Try tapas such as mussels in brandy sauce, escargots with mushrooms and herb butter, or Galician-style octopus and baby eels served in a sizzling garlic sauce. Paella is a house specialty, as is the caramel flan. ✉ *Palm Passage, 24 Dronnigens Gade* ☎ *340/714–7373* 🖃 *AE, MC, V.*

East End

AMERICAN
☼ $$–$$$$
✕ **Blue Moon Café.** Watch the serene scene of sailboats floating at anchor while supping; sunsets are especially spectacular here. Enjoy French toast topped with toasted coconut for breakfast, a grilled mahimahi sandwich with black olive–caper mayonnaise at lunch, or red snapper with pecans, bananas, and a coconut rum sauce for dinner. ✉ *Secret Harbour Beach Resort, Rte. 32, Red Hook* ☎ *340/779–2080* 🖃 *AE, D, MC, V.*

CARIBBEAN
☼ $$–$$$
✕ **Fungi's on the Beach.** Watch the windsurfers, jet skiers, and swimmers out on the bay as you tuck into native-style foods at this open-air, gaily painted restaurant. Try creole-style fish with a side of fungi. Callaloo, roti bread with a curried chicken or conch filling, and a grilled lobster tail with garlic butter are also good choices. All-American burgers and hot dogs are available, too. ✉ *Point Pleasant Resort, Rte. 38, Estate Smith Bay* ☎ *340/775–4142* 🖃 *AE, MC, V.*

ECLECTIC
$$–$$$$
Fodor'sChoice
★
✕ **Old Stone Farmhouse.** Dine in the splendor of a beautifully restored plantation house. Start with appetizers such as the caramelized onion, ricotta cheese, and poppy-seed crepe with a duck confit salad, then move on to entrées like tilapia with a mushroom and baby-pea risotto. For a truly memorable meal, forget the menu entirely. Chef Steven Jankowski will note your table's likes and dislikes, then surprise you with a customized six-course meal. That kind of personalized attention makes dining here a delight. ✉ *Rte. 42, 1 mi (1½ km) west of entrance to Mahogany Run Golf Course, Estate Lovenlund* ☎ *340/777–6277* ⚑ *Reservations essential* 🖃 *AE, MC, V* ⊘ *Closed Mon.*

☼ $$–$$$
✕ **Bonnie's by the Sea.** Wriggle your toes in the sand while you tuck into burgers, sandwiches, and pizza for lunch. For dinner, there's fancier fare like crab cakes, grilled New York strip steak, or fresh grilled snapper in a butter, banana liqueur, and mango chutney sauce. The island-style pig roast on Sunday afternoons isn't to be missed. ✉ *Elysian Beach Resort, 6800, Estate Nazareth* ☎ *340/774–8868* 🖃 *AE, D, MC, V.*

$
✕ **Duffy's Love Shack.** If the floating bubbles don't attract you to this zany eatery, the lime-green shutters, loud rock music, and fun-loving waitstaff just might. It's billed as the "ultimate tropical drink shack," and the bartenders shake up such exotic concoctions as the Love Shack Volcano—a 50-ounce flaming extravaganza. The menu has a selection of burgers, tacos, burritos, and salads. Try the grilled mahimahi taco salad or jerk Caesar wrap. Wednesday night is usually a theme party complete with giveaways. ✉ *Rte. 32, Red Hook* ☎ *340/779–2080* 🖃 *No credit cards.*

ENGLISH
$$–$$$
✕ **Toad & Tart English Pub.** You may not notice this unassuming restaurant on first drive-by, but inside, owner Anna Clarke has created a homey, lively pub atmosphere in which to serve favorites like fish-and-chips on Friday and prime rib with Yorkshire pudding on Saturday. There are always three draft beers on tap. The strawberry rhubarb pie is a win-

ner for dessert. ⊠ *Rte. 38, across from Kilnwork's Pottery & Caribbean Art Gallery, Estate Smith Bay* ☎ *340/775–1153* ▭ *AE, MC, V.*

GERMAN
$$–$$$

✕ **Petra's Schnitzel Haus.** If you have a hankering for German food, this is the one and only place on St. Thomas to find it. Owner Petra Dedekind, a native of Hamburg, has crafted a menu that features favorites like Wiener schnitzel and jäger schnitzel, along with pot roast, bratwurst, chicken, and apple strudel to top off the meal. You can also get four brands of imported German beer, or Dedekind makes her own apple schnapps, which is light and delightful. ⊠ *Rte. 32, next to Fish Hawk Marina, Estate Frydenhoj* ☎ *340/776–7198* ⚐ *Reservations essential* ▭ *AE, MC, V* ☾ *Closed Sun.*

IRISH
☾ $$–$$$

✕ **Molly Molone's.** This open-air eatery has a devout following among locals who live and work on boats docked nearby. Traditional Irish dishes include bangers and mash (sausage and mashed potatoes), as well as fresh fish, oversize deli sandwiches, and rich soups and stews. Beware: the iguanas will beg for table scraps—bring your camera. Upstairs, the same owners run A Whale of a Tale, a pricier seafood eatery that also serves freshly made pasta dishes and fine wines. ⊠ *Rte. 32, at American Yacht Harbor, Bldg. D, Red Hook* ☎ *340/775–1270* ▭ *MC, V.*

ITALIAN
★ $$$–$$$$

✕ **Romanos.** Inside this huge old stucco house is a delightful surprise: a spare yet elegant restaurant serving superb northern Italian cuisine. Try the pastas, either with a classic sauce or a more unique creation such as cream sauce with mushrooms, prosciutto, pine nuts, and Parmesan. ⊠ *Rte. 388, at Coki Point, Estate Frydendal* ☎ *340/775–0045* ⚐ *Reservations essential* ▭ *MC, V* ☾ *Closed Sun. No lunch.*

SEAFOOD
$$–$$$$

✕ **Agave Terrace.** At this open-air restaurant in the Point Pleasant Resort, fresh fish is the specialty, served as steaks or fillets, and the catch of the day is listed on the blackboard. More than a dozen sauces, including teriyaki-mango and lime-ginger, liven up your entrée. If you get lucky on a sportfishing day charter, the chef will cook your catch if you bring the fish in by 3 PM. Come early and have a drink at the Lookout Lounge, which has breathtaking views of the British Virgins. ⊠ *Point Pleasant Resort, Rte. 38, Estate Smith Bay* ☎ *340/775–4142* ▭ *AE, MC, V* ☾ *No lunch.*

$$–$$$

✕ **Off the Hook.** The fish is so fresh here that you may see it coming in from one of the boats tied up at the dock just steps away. For starters, try the crispy conch fritters with sweet-hot banana-chili chutney. Entrées include a rib-sticking fish stew with scallops, shrimp, mahimahi, mussels, conch, and calamari swimming in a coconut curry broth. Steak, poultry, and pasta lovers will also find something to please at this open-air eatery. There's also a children's menu. ⊠ *Rte. 32, Red Hook* ☎ *340/775–6350* ▭ *AE, MC, V* ☾ *No lunch.*

South Shore

ECLECTIC
$$–$$$$
Fodor$Choice
★

✕ **Havana Blue.** The cuisine here is described as Cuban/Asian, but the dining experience is out of this world. You're met by a glowing wall of water as you enter, then sit at a table laid with linen and silver that is illuminated in a soft blue light radiating from above. Be sure to sample the mango mojito, made with fresh mango, crushed mint, and limes.

1

Entrées include coconut-chipotle ceviche, sugarcane-glazed pork tenderloin medallions, and the signature dish, miso sea bass. Hand-rolled cigars and aged rums finish the night off in true Cuban style. For something really special, request an exclusive table for two set on Morning Star Beach—you get a 7-course tasting menu, champagne, and your own personal waiter, all for $375 for two. ⊠ *Morningstar Beach Resort, Rte. 315, Box 7100* ⓓ *5 Estate Bakkeroe, St. Thomas 00802* ☎ *340/715–2583* ⚖ *Reservations essential* ⊘ *No lunch.*

Frenchtown

AMERICAN
ⓒ **$$–$$$**

✕ **Sib's Mountain Bar & Restaurant.** Here you can find live music, football on the TV, burgers, barbecue ribs and chicken, and beer. It's the perfect place for a casual dinner after a day at the beach. ⊠ *Rte. 35, Estate Mafolie* ☎ *340/774–8967* ⊟ *AE, MC, V.*

ⓒ **$–$$**

✕ **Tickle's Dockside Pub.** Nautical types as well as the local working crowd come here for casual fare with homey appeal: chicken-fried steak, meat loaf and mashed potatoes, and baby back ribs. Hearty breakfasts feature eggs and pancakes, while lunch is a full array of burgers, salads, sandwiches, and soups. From November through April, the adjacent marina is full of megayachts that make for some great eye candy while you dine. ⊠ *Crown Bay Marina, Rte. 304, Estate Contant* ☎ *340/776–1595* ⊟ *AE, D, MC, V.*

ECLECTIC
$$$–$$$$

✕ **Oceana Restaurant & Wine Bar.** In the old Russian consulate greathouse at the tip of the Frenchtown peninsula, this restaurant offers superb views along with fresh seafood dishes expertly prepared by longtime Virgin Islands chef Patricia LaCourte and her staff. Specialties include a pan-seared sea bass served on a saffron risotto cake with white truffle butter as well as bouillabaisse chockfull of mussels, manila clams, shrimp, and Caribbean lobster simmered in a tomato-saffron broth. ⊠ *Villa Olga* ☎ *340/774–4262* ⊟ *AE, D, MC, V* ⊘ *No dinner Sun.*

$$–$$$$
Fodor'sChoice
★

✕ **Craig & Sally's.** In the heart of Frenchtown, culinary wizard Sally Darash creates menus with a passionate international flavor using fresh ingredients and a novel approach that makes for a delightful dining experience at this friendly, casual eatery. Sally's constantly changing menu is never the same, which means your favorite dish may not appear again. But there's always something new to tantalize your taste buds, such as yellowtail tuna swimming in a mango, key lime, and habanero sauce. Husband Craig maintains a 300-bottle wine list that's received accolades. ⓓ *22 Honduras St., St. Thomas 00802* ☎ *340/777–9949* ⊟ *AE, MC, V* ⊘ *Closed Mon. and Tues. No lunch weekends.*

MEDITERRANEAN
ⓒ **$$–$$$$**

✕ **Bella Blu.** Tucked into a quaint building in Frenchtown, this place has thrown out its Austrian menu—though the menu still has a couple of schnitzels—and lightened up the decor. Alexander Treml's Mediterranean-style menu now includes souvlaki or skewered lamb, snapper Provençal, and chicken breast stuffed with spinach, feta, and pine nuts. ⊠ *Frenchtown Mall, 24-A Honduras* ☎ *340/774–4349* ⊟ *AE, MC, V* ⊘ *Closed Sun.*

SEAFOOD
ⓒ **$$**

✕ **Hook, Line & Sinker.** Anchored right on the breezy Frenchtown waterfront, adjacent to the pastel-painted boats of the local fishing fleet, this harbor-view eatery serves quality fish dishes. The almond-crust yellowtail snapper is a house specialty. Spicy jerk-seasoned swordfish and grilled tuna topped with a yummy mango-rum sauce are also good bets. This is one of the few independent restaurants serving Sunday brunch. ⊠ *2 Honduras, in Frenchtown Mall* ☎ *340/776–9708* ▤ *AE, MC, V.*

Beaches

All 44 St. Thomas beaches are open to the public, although you can reach some of them only by walking through a resort. Hotel guests frequently have access to lounge chairs and floats that are off-limits to nonguests; for this reason you may feel more comfortable at one of the beaches not associated with a resort, such as Magens Bay (which charges an entrance fee to cover beach maintenance) or Coki. Whichever one you choose, remember to remove your valuables from the car and keep them out of sight when you go swimming.

Brewer's Beach. Watch jets land at the Cyril E. King Airport as you dip into the usually calm seas. Rocks at either end of the shoreline, patches of grass poking randomly through the sand, and shady tamarind trees 30 feet from the water give this beach a wild, natural feel. Civilization is here, though (one or two mobile food vans park on the nearby road). Buy a fried-chicken leg and johnnycake or burgers, chips, and beverages to munch on at the picnic tables. ⊠ *Rte. 30, west of University of the Virgin Islands.*

☾ **Coki Beach.** Funky beach huts selling local foods like meat pates (fried
FodorsChoice   turnovers with a spicy ground-beef filling), picnic tables topped with
★   umbrellas sporting beverage logos, and a brigade of hair braiders and taxi men give this beach overlooking picturesque Thatch Cay a Coney Island feel. But this is the best place on the island from which to snorkel and scuba dive. Fish, including grunts, snappers, and wrasses, team in schools like an effervescent cloud you can wave your hand through. Ashore, find conveniences like restrooms, changing facilities, rentals for masks, fins, air tanks, and even fish food. ⊠ *Rte. 388, next to Coral World Marine Park.*

Hull Bay. Watch surfers ride the waves here from December to March, when huge swells roll in from north Atlantic storms. The rest of the year, tranquility prevails. Homer's Snorkel & Scuba Tours, led by Hugo "Homer" Calloway, is based here, and Homer will happily lead you on a day or night snorkel trip to the nearby reefs and out to the uninhabited island of Hans Lollick. Enjoy hot pizza, barbecue ribs, and a game of darts or pool at the Hull Bay Hideaway bar and restaurant. ⊠ *Rte. 37, at end of road on north side.*

☾ **Magens Bay.** Deeded to the island as a public park, this ½-mi (¾-km)
FodorsChoice   heart-shape stretch of white sand is considered one of the most beauti-
★   ful in the world. The bottom of the bay here is flat and sandy, so this is a place for sunning and swimming rather than snorkeling. On weekends and holidays the sounds of music from groups partying under the sheds fill the air. There's a bar, snack bar, and beachwear boutique; bathhouses with restrooms, changing rooms, and saltwater showers are also here. Sunfish and paddleboats are the most popular rentals at the water-

sports-equipment kiosk. East of the beach is Udder Delight, a one-room shop at St. Thomas Dairies that serves a Virgin Islands tradition—a milk shake with a splash of Cruzan rum. Kids can enjoy virgin versions, which have a touch of soursop, mango, or banana flavoring. If you arrive between 8 AM and 5 PM, you have to pay an entrance fee of $3 per person, $1 per vehicle, and 25¢ per child under age 12. ⊠ *Rte. 35, at end of road on north side of island.*

★ **Morningstar Beach.** Nature and nurture combine at this ¼-mi-long (½-km-long) beach between Marriott Frenchman's Reef and Morning Star Beach Resorts, where amenities range from water-sports rentals to beachside bar service. A concession rents floating mats, snorkeling equipment, sailboards, and Jet Skis. Swimming is excellent; there are good-size rolling waves year-round, but do watch the undertow. If you're feeling lazy, rent a lounge chair with umbrella and order a libation from one of two full-service beach bars. At 7 AM and again at 5 PM, watch the megacruise ships glide majestically out to sea from the Charlotte Amalie harbor. ⊠ *Rte. 315, 2 mi (3 km) southeast of Charlotte Amalie, past Havensight Mall and cruise-ship dock.*

★ **Sapphire Beach.** A steady breeze makes this beach a boardsailor's paradise. The swimming is great, as is the snorkeling, especially at the reef near Pettyklip Point. Beach volleyball is big on the weekends. There's also a restaurant, bar, and water-sports rentals at Sapphire Beach Resort & Marina. ⊠ *Rte. 38, Sapphire Bay.*

Secret Harbour. Placid waters make it an easy job to stroke your way out to a swim platform offshore from the Secret Harbour Beach Resort & Villas. Nearby reefs give snorkelers a natural show. There's a bar and restaurant, as well as a dive shop. ⊠ *Rte. 32, Red Hook.*

Vessup Beach. This wild, undeveloped beach is lined with sea-grape trees and century plants, and it's close to Red Hook harbor, so you can watch the ferries depart. Calm waters are excellent for swimming. West Indies Windsurfing is located here, so you can rent Windsurfers, kayaks, and other water toys. There are no restroom or changing facilities. It's popular with locals on weekends. ⊠ *Off Rte. 322, Vessup Bay.*

Sports & the Outdoors

Air Tours

On the Charlotte Amalie waterfront next to Tortola Wharf, **Air Center Helicopters** (⊠ Waterfront, Charlotte Amalie ☎ 340/775–7335 or 800/619–0013 ⊕ www.aircenterhelicopters.com) offers two tours, both pretty pricey: a 17-minute tour of St. Thomas and St. John priced at $256, and a 25-minute tour that includes St. Thomas, St. John, and Jost Van Dyke priced at $348. Both are for up to four passengers. If you can afford the splurge, it's a nice ride, but in truth, you can see most of the aerial sights from Mountain Top or Paradise Point, and there's no place you can't reach easily by car or boat.

Boating & Sailing

Calm seas, crystal waters, and nearby islands (perfect for picnicking, snorkeling, and exploring) make St. Thomas a favorite jumping-off spot for day- or weeklong sails or powerboat adventures. With more than 100 vessels from which to choose, St. Thomas is the charter-boat center of the U.S. Virgin Islands. You can go through a broker to book a sailing vessel with a crew or contact a charter company directly. Crewed charters start at $1,500 per person per week, while bareboat charters can start at $1,200 per person for a 50- to 55-foot sailboat (not including provisioning), which can comfortably accommodate up to six people. If you want to rent your own boat, hire a captain. Most local captains are excellent tour guides.

Single-day charters are also a possibility. You can hire smaller power boats for the day, including the services of a captain if you wish to have someone take you on a guided snorkel trip around the islands.

Island Yachts (✉ 6100 Red Hook Quarter, 18B, Red Hook ☎ 340/775–6666 or 800/524–2019 ⊕ www.iyc.vi) offers sail- or powerboats with or without crews. Luxury is the word at **Magic Moments** (✉ American Yacht Harbor, Red Hook ☎ 340/775–5066 ⊕ www.yachtmagicmoments. com), where the crew of a 45-foot Sea Ray offers a pampered island-hopping snorkeling cruise. Nice touches include icy-cold eucalyptus-infused washcloths to freshen up and a gourmet wine and lobster lunch. **Stewart Yacht Charters** (✉ 6501 Red Hook Plaza, Suite 20, Red Hook ☎ 340/775–1358 or 800/432–6118 ⊕ www.stewartyachtcharters.com) is run by longtime sailor Ellen Stewart, who is an expert at matching clients with yachts for weeklong crewed charter holidays. Bareboat sail and powerboats, including a selection of stable trawlers, are available at **VIP Yacht Charters** (✉ South off Rte. 32, Estate Frydenhoj ☎ 340/774–9224 or 866/847–9224 ⊕ www.vipyachts.com), at Compass Point Marina.

Awesome Powerboat Rentals (✉ 6100 Red Hook Quarter, Red Hook ☎ 340/775–0860 ⊕ www.powerboatrentalsvi.com), at "P" dock next to the Off the Hook restaurant, offers 22- to 26-foot twin-engine catamarans for day charters. Rates range from $345 to $385 for a half or full day. A captain can be hired for $115 for a day. If you want to explore the east end of St. Thomas, **Mangrove Adventures** (✉ Rte. 32, Estate Nadir ☎ 340/779–2155 ⊕ www.viecotours.com) offers inflatable boat rentals for $100 per day. **Nauti Nymph** (✉ 6501 Red Hook Plaza, Suite 201, Red Hook ☎☎ 340/775–5066 ☎ 800/734–7345 ⊕ www. st-thomas.com/nautinymph) has a large selection of 25- to 29-foot powerboats. Rates vary from $345 to $540 a day, including snorkel gear, water skis, and outriggers, but not including fuel. You can hire a captain for $115 more.

Cycling

Water Island Adventures (✉ Water Island ☎ 340/714–2186 or 340/775–5770 ⊕ www.waterislandadventures.com) offers a cycling adventure to the USVI's "newest" Virgin. You take a ferry ride from the West Indian Company dock near Havensight Mall to Water Island before jumping on a Cannondale mountain bike for a 90-minute tour over rolling hills on dirt and paved roads. Explore the remains of the Sea Cliff Hotel, the inspiration for Herman Wouk's book *Don't Stop the Carnival,* then take a cooling swim at beautiful Honeymoon Beach. Helmets, water, a guide, juices, and ferry fare are included in the $65 cost.

Diving & Snorkeling

Popular dive sites include such wrecks as the *Cartanser Sr.,* a beautifully encrusted World War II cargo ship sitting in 35 feet of water, and the *General Rogers,* a Coast Guard cutter resting at 65 feet. Here you'll find a gigantic resident barracuda. Reef dives offer hidden caves and archways at **Cow and Calf Rocks,** coral-covered pinnacles at **Frenchcap,** and tunnels where you can explore undersea from the Caribbean to the Atlantic at **Thatch Cay, Grass Cay,** and **Congo Cay.** Many resorts and charter yachts offer dive packages. A one-tank dive starts at $75; two-tank dives are $90 and up. Call the USVI Department of Tourism to obtain a free eight-page guide to Virgin Islands dive sites. There are plenty of snorkeling possibilities too.

Admiralty Dive Center (⌧ Holiday Inn St. Thomas, Waterfront Hwy., Charlotte Amalie ☎ 340/777–9802 or 888/900–3483 ⊕ www.admiraltydive. com) provides boat dives, rental equipment, and a retail store. Four-tank to 12-tank packages are available if you want to dive over several days. **BOB Underwater Adventure** (⌧ Crown Bay Marina, Rte. 304, Charlotte Amalie ☎ 340/715–0348 ⊕ www.bobusvi.com) offers an alternative to traditional diving in the form of an underwater motor scooter called BOB, or Breathing Observation Bubble. A half-day tour, including snorkel equipment, rum punch, and towels, is $99 per person. **Blue Island Divers** (⌧ Crown Bay Marina, Rte. 304, Estate Contant ☎ 340/774–2001 ⊕ www.blueislanddivers.com) is a full-service dive shop that offers both day and night dives to wrecks and reefs. **Chris Sawyer Diving Center** (☎ 340/775–7320 or 877/929–3483 ⊕ www.sawyerdive.vi) is a PADI five-star outfit that specializes in dives to the 310-foot-long *Rhone,* in the British Virgin Islands. Hotel–dive packages are offered through the Wyndham Sugar Bay Beach Club & Resort. **Coki Beach Dive Club** (⌧ Rte. 388, at Coki Point, Estate Frydendal ☎ 340/775–4220 ⊕ www. cokidive.com) is a PADI Gold Palm outfit run by avid diver Peter Jackson. Snorkel and dive tours in the fish-filled reefs off Coki Beach are available, as are classes from beginner to underwater photography. **Snuba of St. Thomas** (⌧ Rte. 388, at Coki Point, Estate Smith Bay ☎ 340/ 693–8063 ⊕ www.visnuba.com) offers something for nondivers, a cross between snorkeling and scuba diving: a 20-foot air hose connects you to the surface. The cost is $68. Children must be eight or older to participate. **Underwater Safaris** (⌧ Havensight Mall, Bldg. VI, Rte. 30, Charlotte Amalie ☎ 340/774–1350 ⊕ www.scubadivevi.com) is another PADI five-star center that offers boat dives to the reefs around Buck Island and nearby offshore wrecks.

Fishing

★ Fishing here is synonymous with blue marlin angling—especially from June through October. Four 1,000-pound-plus blues, including three world records, have been caught on the famous North Drop, about 20 mi (32 km) north of St. Thomas. A day charter for marlin with up to six anglers costs $1,500 for the day. If you're not into marlin fishing, try hooking sailfish in the winter, dolphin (the fish, not the mammal) in the spring, and wahoo in the fall. Inshore trips for two to four hours range in cost from $200 to $550, respectively. To find the trip that will best suit you, walk down the docks at either American Yacht Harbor or Sapphire Beach Marina in the late afternoon and chat with the captains and crews.

🜨 For marlin, Captain Red Bailey's *Abigail III* (⊠ Rte. 38, Sapphire Bay ☎ 340/775–6024 ⊕ www.sportfishvi.com) operates out of the Sapphire Beach Resort & Marina. The **Charter Boat Center** (⊠ 6300 Red Hook Plaza, Red Hook ☎ 340/775–7990 ⊕ www.charterboat.vi) is a major source for sportfishing charters, both marlin and inshore. Capt.

🜨 Eddie Morrison, aboard the 45-foot Viking *Marlin Prince* (⊠ American Yacht Harbor, Red Hook ☎ 340/693–5929 ⊕ www.marlinprince. com), is one of the most experienced charter operators in St. Thomas

🜨 and specializes in fly-fishing for blue marlin. For inshore trips, **Peanut Gallery Charters** (⊠ Crown Bay Marina, Rte. 304, Estate Contant ☎ 340/775–5274 ⊕ www.fishingstthomas.com) offers trips on its 18-foot *Dauntless* or 28-foot custom sportfishing catamaran.

Golf

★ The **Mahogany Run Golf Course** (⊠ Rte. 42, Estate Lovenlund ☎ 340/ 777–6006 or 800/253–7103 ⊕ www.mahoganyrungolf.com) attracts golfers for its spectacular view of the British Virgin Islands and the challenging 3-hole Devil's Triangle. At this Tom and George Fazio–designed par-70, 18-hole course, there's a fully stocked pro shop, snack bar, and open-air club house. Greens and half-cart fees for 18 holes are $150. The course is open daily, and there are frequently informal weekend tournaments. It's the only course on St. Thomas.

HORSE RACING   The **Clinton Phipps Racetrack** (⊠ Rte. 30, Estate Nadir ☎ 340/775– 4555) schedules races—especially on local holidays—with sanctioned betting. Be prepared for large crowds.

Parasailing

The waters are so clear around St. Thomas that the outlines of coral reefs are visible from the air. Parasailers sit in a harness attached to a parachute that lifts them off a boat deck until they're sailing through the sky. Parasailing trips average a 10-minute ride in the sky that costs $75 per person. Friends who want to ride along pay $20 for the boat trip. **Caribbean Watersports & Tours** (⊠ 6501 Red Hook Plaza, Red Hook ☎ 340/775– 9360 ⊕ www.viwatersports.com) makes parasailing pickups from 10 locations around the island, including many major beachfront resorts. It also rents Jet Skis, kayaks, and floating battery-powered chairs.

Sea Excursions

Landlubbers and seafarers alike will enjoy the wind in their hair and salt spray in the air while exploring the waters surrounding St. Thomas. Several businesses can book you on a snorkel-and-sail to a deserted cay for the day that costs on average $85 to $125 per person; a luxury daylong motor-yacht cruise complete with gourmet lunch for $325 or more per person; or an excursion over to the British Virgin Islands starting at $115 per person.

For a soup-to-nuts choice of sea tours, contact the **Adventure Center** (⊠ Marriott's Frenchman's Reef Hotel, Rte. 315, Estate Bakkeroe ☎ 340/774–2992 or 866/868–7784 ⊕ www.adventurecenters.net). The

Charter Boat Center (✉ 6300 Red Hook Plaza, Red Hook ☎ 340/775–7990 ⊕ www.charterboat.vi) specializes in day trips to the British Virgin Islands and day- or weeklong sailing charters. **Limnos Charters** (✉ Compass Point Marina, Rte. 32, Estate Frydenhoj ☎ 340/775–3203 ⊕ www.limnoscharters.com) offers one of the most popular British Virgin Islands day trips, complete with lunch, open bar, and snorkel gear. Destinations include The Baths in Virgin Gorda and the sparsely inhabited island of Jost Van Dyke. Jimmy Loveland at **Treasure Isle Cruises** (✉ Rte. 32, Box 6616, Estate Nadir ☎ 340/775–9500 ⊕ www.treasureislecruises.com) can set you up with everything from a half-day sail to a seven-day U.S. and British Virgin Islands trip that combines sailing with accommodations and sightseeing trips onshore.

Sea Kayaking

Fish dart, birds sing, and iguanas lounge on the limbs of dense mangrove trees deep within a marine sanctuary on St. Thomas's southeast shore. Learn about the natural history here in a guided kayak–snorkel tour to Patricia Cay or via an inflatable boat tour to Cas Cay for snorkeling and hiking. Both are 2½ hours long. The cost is $65 per person. ☾ **Mangrove Adventures** (✉ Rte. 32, Estate Nadir ☎ 340/779–2155 ⊕ www.viecotours.com) rents its two-person sit-atop ocean kayaks and inflatable boats for self-guided exploring. In addition, many resorts on St. Thomas's eastern end also rent kayaks.

Sightseeing Tours

Accessible Adventures (☎ 340/775–2346 ⊕ www.accessvi.com) provides a 2- to 2½-hour island tour aboard a special trolley that's especially suitable for those in wheelchairs. Tours include major sights like Magens Bay and Mountain Top and provide a stop for shopping and refreshments. The cost is $34 per person. **Tropic Tours** (☎ 340/775–1855 or 800/524–4334 ⊕ www.tropictours-virginislands.com) offers half-day shopping and sightseeing bus tours of St. Thomas six days a week. The cost is $4 per person. The company also has a full-day ferry tour to St. John that includes snorkeling and lunch. The cost is $90 per person. **V. I. Taxi Association St. Thomas City-Island Tour** (☎ 340/774–4550 ⊕ www.vitaxi.com) gives a two-hour tour for two people in an open-air safari bus or enclosed van; aimed at cruise-ship passengers, this $29 tour includes stops at Drake's Seat and Mountain Top. Other tours include a three-hour trip to Coki Beach with a shopping stop in downtown Charlotte Amalie for $35 per person, a three-hour tour that includes a trip up the St. Thomas Skyride for $38 per person, a three-hour trip to the Coral World Ocean Park for $45 per person, and a five-hour beach tour to St. John for $75 per person. For $35 to $40 for two, you can hire a taxi for a customized three-hour drive around the island. Make sure to see Mountain Top, as the view is wonderful.

STARGAZING Without the light pollution so prevalent in more densely populated areas, the heavens appear supernaturally bright. On a **Star Charters Astronomy Adventure** (☎ 340/774–9211) you can peer into the Caribbean's largest telescope—an 18-inch Newtonian reflector—and learn the science and lore of the stars from a well-informed celestial guide.

Submarining

Dive 90 feet under the sea to one of St. Thomas's most beautiful reefs without getting wet. **Atlantis Adventures** (⊠ Havensight Mall, Bldg. VI, Charlotte Amalie ☎ 340/776–5650 ⊕ www.atlantisadventures.com) has a 46-passenger submarine that takes you to a watery world teeming with brightly colored fish, vibrant sea fans, and the occasional shark. A guide narrates the one-hour underwater journey, while a diver makes a mid-tour appearance for a fish-feeding show. The cost is $89. No children shorter than 36 inches are allowed.

TENNIS The Caribbean sun is hot, so be sure to hit the courts before 10 AM or after 5 PM (many courts are lighted). You can indulge in a set or two even if you're staying in a guesthouse without courts; most hotels rent time to nonguests. **Marriott Frenchman's Reef and Morning Star Beach Resorts** (⊠ Rte. 315, Estate Bakkeroe ☎ 340/776–8500 Ext. 6818) has two courts, with nonguests charged $15 per hour per court. Two courts are available at the **Ritz-Carlton, St. Thomas** (⊠ Rte. 317, Box 6900, Estate Great Bay ☎ 340/775–3333), where nonguests can reserve lessons for $80 per hour and $40 per half hour. **Sapphire Beach Resort & Marina** (⊠ Sapphire Bay ☎ 340/775–6100 Ext. 8135) has four courts that fill up fast in the cool early morning hours. The cost for nonguests is $15 per hour. At **Wyndham Sugar Bay Beach Club & Resort** (⊠ Rte. 38, Box 6500, Estate Smith Bay ☎ 340/777–7100) nonguests can rent any of the four courts for $15 per hour. Lessons are by appointment, and rates start at $45 for a half hour.

Lindberg Bay Park (⊠ Rte. 302, Estate Lindberg Bay) has two courts that are open to the public; it's opposite the Cyril E. King Airport. There are two public tennis courts at **Sub Base** (⊠ Rte. 306, next to Water and Power Authority, Estate Contant), open on a first-come, first-served basis at no cost. Lights are on until 10 PM.

Walking Tours

The *St. Thomas–St. John Vacation Handbook,* available free at hotels and tourist centers, has an excellent self-guided walking tour of Charlotte Amalie.

Blackbeard's Castle (☎ 340/776–1234 or 340/776–1829 ⊕ www.blackbeardscastle.com) conducts a 45-minute to one-hour historic walking tour that starts at Blackbeard's Castle, then heads downhill to Villa Notman, Haagensen House, and the 99 steps. The cost is $35 per person and includes a tour of Haagensen House and a rum punch.

Cindy Born (☎ 340/714–1672 ⊕ www.st-thomas.com/walktour) conducts a two-hour historical walking tour of Charlotte Amalie at 9:30 each weekday that starts at Emancipation Garden. The tour covers all the in-town sights and can be narrated in Spanish, Danish, German, and Japanese as well as in English. The cost is $20 per person; wear a hat and comfortable walking shoes. The tour is offered again at 12:30, but you must make a reservation.

The **St. Thomas Historical Trust** (☎ 340/774–5541 ⊕ www.stthomashistoricaltrust.org) has published a self-guided tour of the historic district; it's available in book and souvenir shops for $1.95. Trust members also conduct a two-hour guided historic walking tour by reservation only. Call for more information and to make a reservation.

Windsurfing

Expect some spills, anticipate the thrills, and try your luck clipping through the seas. Most beachfront resorts rent Windsurfers and offer one-hour lessons for about $75. One of the island's best-known independent windsurfing companies is **West Indies Windsurfing** (⊠ Vessup Beach, No. 9, Estate Nazareth ☎ 340/775–6530). Owner John Phillips is the board buff who introduced the sport of kite boarding to the USVI; it entails using a kite to lift a boardsailor off the water for an airborne ride. A private kite-boarding lesson costs $125 per hour, while a semi-private lesson starts at $85 per hour. Allow 2 to 4 hours to get the hang of this demanding, yet thrilling, sport. Speedy WindRider 17 trimarans are popular water toys here. They rent for $125 an hour or $350 a day.

Shopping

FodorsChoice
★

St. Thomas lives up to its billing as a duty-free shopping destination. Even if shopping isn't your idea of how to spend a vacation, you still may want to slip in on a quiet day (check the cruise-ship listings—Monday and Sunday are usually the least crowded) to browse. Among the best buys are liquor, linens, china, crystal (most stores will ship), and jewelry. The amount of jewelry available makes this one of the few items for which comparison shopping is worth the effort. Local crafts include shell jewelry, carved calabash bowls, straw brooms, woven baskets, and dolls. Creations by local doll maker Gwendolyn Harley—like her costumed West Indian market woman—have been little goodwill ambassadors, bought by visitors from as far away as Asia. Spice mixes, hot sauces, and tropical jams and jellies are other native products.

On St. Thomas, stores on Main Street in Charlotte Amalie are open weekdays and Saturday 9 to 5. The hours of the shops in the Havensight Mall (next to the cruise-ship dock) and the Crown Bay Commercial Center (next to the Crown Bay cruise-ship dock) are the same, though occasionally some stay open until 9 on Friday, depending on how many cruise ships are anchored nearby. You may also find some shops open on Sunday if cruise ships are in port. Hotel shops are usually open evenings, as well.

There's no sales tax in the USVI, and you can take advantage of the $1,200 duty-free allowance per family member (remember to save your receipts). Although you can find the occasional salesclerk who will make a deal, bartering isn't the norm.

Areas & Malls

The prime shopping area in **Charlotte Amalie** is between Post Office and Market squares; it consists of two parallel streets that run east–west (Waterfront Highway and Main Street) and the alleyways that connect them. Particularly attractive are the historic **A. H. Riise Alley, Royal Dane Mall, Palm Passage,** and pastel-painted **International Plaza.**

Made in St. Thomas

Date palm brooms, frangipani-scented perfume, historically clad dolls, sun-scorched hot sauces, aromatic mango candles: these are just a few of the handicrafts made in St. Thomas.

Justin Todman, aka the Broom Man, keeps the dying art of broom-making alive. It's a skill he learned at the age of six from his father. From the fronds of the date palm, Todman delicately cuts, strips, and dries the leaves, a process that can take up to a week. Then he creatively weaves the leaves into distinctively shaped brooms with birch-berry wood for handles. His styles? There are feather brooms, cane brooms, multicolor yarn brooms, tiny brooms to fit into a child's hand, and tall long-handled brooms to reach cobwebs on the ceiling. Some customers buy Todman's brooms—sold at the Native Arts & Crafts Cooperative—not for cleaning but rather for celebrating their nuptials. It's an old African custom for the bride and groom to jump over a horizontally laid broom to start their new life.

Gail Garrison puts the essence of local flowers, fruits, and leaves into perfumes, powders, and body splashes. Her Island Fragrances line includes frangipani-, white ginger-, and jasmine-scented perfumes; aromatic mango, lime, and coconut body splashes; and bay rum aftershave for men. Garrison compounds, mixes, and bottles the products herself in second-floor offices on Charlotte Amalie's Main Street. You can buy the products in the Tropicana Perfume Shop.

Gwendolyn Harley preserves Virgin Islands culture in the personalities of her hand-sewn, softly sculptured historic dolls for sale at the Native Arts & Crafts Cooperative. There are quadrille dancers clad in long, colorful skirts; French women with their neat peaked bonnets; and farmers sporting handwoven straw hats. Each one-of-a-kind design is named using the last three letters of Harley's first name; the dolls have names like Joycelyn, Vitalyn, and Iselyn. From her adoption log, she knows her dolls have traveled as far as Asia.

Cheryl Miller cooks up ingredients like sun-sweetened papayas, fiery Scotch bonnet peppers, and aromatic basil leaves into the jams, jellies, and hot sauces she sells under her Cheryl's Taste of Paradise line. Five of Miller's products—Caribbean Mustango Sauce, Caribbean Sunburn, Mango Momma Jam, Mango Chutney, and Hot Green Pepper Jelly—have won awards at the National Fiery Foods Show in Albuquerque, New Mexico. Miller makes her products in a professional kitchen in the Compass Point Marina and sells them from a storefront there as well as from Cost-U-Less and the Native Arts & Crafts Cooperative.

Jason Budsan traps the tropically enticing aromas of the islands into sumptuously scented candles he sells at his Tillett Gardens workshop and at stores throughout the island such as the Native Arts & Crafts Cooperative. Among the rich scents are Ripe Mango, Night Jasmine, Lime in de Coconut, Frenchie Connection (with vanilla and lavender), and Ripe Pineapple. Some candles, such as the Ripe Mango, are uniquely set in beautiful tonna shells or wrapped in aromatic sea-grape leaves.

Vendors Plaza, on the waterfront side of Emancipation Gardens in Charlotte Amalie, is a central location for vendors selling handmade earrings, necklaces, and bracelets; straw baskets and handbags; T-shirts; fabrics; African artifacts; and local fruits. Look for the many brightly colored umbrellas.

West of Charlotte Amalie, the pink-stucco **Nisky Center,** on Harwood Highway about ½ mi (¾ km) east of the airport, is more of a hometown shopping center than a tourist area, but there's a bank, clothing store, record shop, and Radio Shack.

At the Crown Bay cruise-ship pier, the **Crown Bay Center,** off the Harwood Highway in Sub Base about ½ mi (¾ km) has quite a few shops.

Havensight Mall, next to the cruise-ship dock, may not be as charming as downtown Charlotte Amalie, but it does have more than 60 shops. It also has an excellent bookstore, a bank, a pharmacy, a gourmet grocery, and smaller branches of many downtown stores. The shops at **Port of $ale,** adjoining Havensight Mall (its buildings are pink instead of brown), sell discount goods. Next door to Port of $ale is the **Yacht Haven Grande** complex, with many upscale shops.

East of Charlotte Amalie on Route 38, **Tillett Gardens** is an oasis of artistic endeavor across from the Tutu Park Shopping Mall. The late Jim and Rhoda Tillett converted this old Danish farm into an artists' retreat in 1959. Today you can watch artisans produce silk-screen fabrics, candles, watercolors, jewelry, and other handicrafts. Something special is often happening in the gardens as well: the Classics in the Gardens program is a classical music series presented under the stars, Arts Alive is an annual arts-and-crafts fair held in November, and the Pistarckle Theater holds its performances here. **Tutu Park Shopping Mall,** across from Tillett Gardens, is the island's one and only enclosed mall. More than 50 stores and a food court are anchored by Kmart and Plaza Extra grocery store. Archaeologists have discovered evidence that Arawak Indians once lived near the grounds.

Red Hook has **American Yacht Harbor,** a waterfront shopping area with a dive shop, a tackle store, clothing and jewelry boutiques, a bar, and a few restaurants.

Don't forget **St. John.** A ferry ride (an hour from Charlotte Amalie or 20 minutes from Red Hook) will take you to the charming shops of **Mongoose Junction** and **Wharfside Village,** which specialize in unusual, often island-made articles.

Specialty Items

ART **Camille Pissarro Art Gallery.** This second-floor gallery, in the birthplace of St. Thomas's famous artist, offers a fine collection of original paintings and prints by local and regional artists. ✉ *14 Main St., Charlotte Amalie* ☎ *340/774–4621.*

The Color of Joy. Find locally made arts and crafts here, including pottery, batik, hand-painted linen and cotton clothing, glass plates and ornaments, and watercolors by owner Corinne Van Rensselaer. There are also original prints by many local artists. ⊠ *Rte. 317, about 100 yards west of Ritz-Carlton, Red Hook* ☏ *340/775–4020.*

Gallery St. Thomas. Fine art and collectibles are found in this charming gallery, including paintings, wood sculpture, glass, and jewelry that are from or inspired by the Virgin Islands. ⊠ *1 Main St., 2nd fl., Charlotte Amalie* ☏ *340/777–6363.*

Kilnworks Pottery & Caribbean Art Gallery. A 12-foot statue of a green iguana marks the entrance to this pottery paradise. Owner Peggy Seiwert is best known for her lizard-themed ceramic cups, bowls, and platters. There are also pottery pieces by other local artists, as well as paintings and gift items. ⊠ *Rte. 38, across from the Toad & Tart English Pub, Estate Smith Bay* ☏ *340/775–3979.*

Mango Tango. Works by popular local artists—originals, prints, and note cards—are displayed (there's a one-person show at least one weekend a month) and sold here. There's also the island's largest humidor and a brand-name cigar gallery. ⊠ *Al Cohen's Plaza, ½ mi (¾ km) east of Charlotte Amalie* ☏ *340/777–3060.*

BOOKS **Dockside Bookshop.** This place is packed with books for children, travelers, cooks, and historians, as well as a good selection of paperback mysteries, best sellers, art books, calendars, and prints. It also carries a selection of books written in and about the Caribbean and the Virgin Islands. ⊠ *Havensight Mall, Bldg. VI, Rte. 30, Charlotte Amalie* ☏ *340/ 774–4937.*

CAMERAS & **Boolchand's.** Brand-name cameras, audio and video equipment, and ELECTRONICS binoculars are sold here. ⊠ *31 Main St., Charlotte Amalie* ☏ *340/ 776–0794* ⊠ *Havensight Mall, Bldg. II, Rte. 30, Charlotte Amalie* ☏ *340/776–0302.*

Royal Caribbean. Shop here for cameras, camcorders, stereos, watches, and clocks. ⊠ *23 Main St., Charlotte Amalie* ☏ *340/776–5449* ⊠ *33 Main St., Charlotte Amalie* ☏ *340/776–4110* ⊠ *Havensight Mall, Bldg. I, Rte. 30, Charlotte Amalie* ☏ *340/776–8890.*

CHINA & CRYSTAL **The Crystal Shoppe at A. H. Riise.** All that glitters is here, from the Swarovski and Waterford crystal to the figurines by Hummel, Daum, and Royal Copenhagen, and china by Belleek, Kosta Boda, and several Limoges factories. There's also a large selection of Lladró figurines. ⊠ *37 Main St., at Riise's Alley, Charlotte Amalie* ☏ *340/776–2303.*

Little Switzerland. All of this establishment's shops carry crystal from Baccarat, Waterford, and Orrefors; and china from Kosta Boda, Rosenthal, and Wedgwood, among others. There's also an assortment of Swarovski cut-crystal animals, gemstone globes, and many other affordable collectibles. It also does a booming mail-order business; ask for a catalog. ⊠ *5 Dronningens Gade, across from Emancipation Garden, Charlotte Amalie* ☏ *340/776–2010* ⊠ *3B Main St., Charlotte Amalie* ☏ *340/776– 2010* ⊠ *Havensight Mall, Bldg. II, Rte. 30, Charlotte Amalie* ☏ *340/ 776–2198.*

Scandinavian Center. The best of Scandinavia is here, including Royal Copenhagen, Georg Jensen, Kosta Boda, and Orrefors. Owners Soøren and Grace Blak make regular buying trips to northern Europe and are a great source of information on crystal. Online ordering is available if you want to add to your collection once home. ⊠ *Havensight Mall, Bldg. III, Rte. 30, Charlotte Amalie* ☎ *340/776–5030 or 800/524–2063.*

CLOTHING **Fresh Produce.** You won't find lime-green mangoes, peachy-pink guavas, or sunny-yellow bananas in this store. But you will find these fun, casual colors in the Fresh Produce clothing line. This is one of only 16 stores to stock 100% of this California-created, tropical-feel line of apparel for women. Find dresses, shirts, slacks, and skirts in small to plus sizes as well as accessories such as bags and hats. ⊠ *Riise's Alley, Charlotte Amalie* ☎ *340/774–0807.*

Keep Left. This friendly shop features something for everyone in the family, including Patagonia dresses, Quiksilver swim wear, Jams World shirts, Watership Trading hats, and NAOT sandals. ⊠ *American Yacht Harbor, Bldg. C, Rte. 32, Red Hook* ☎ *340/775–9964.*

Local Color. Men, women, and children will find something to choose from among brand-name wear like Jams World, Fresh Produce, and Urban Safari. There's also St. John artist Sloop Jones's colorful, hand-painted island designs on cool dresses, T-shirts, and sweaters. Find tropically oriented accessories like big-brim straw hats, bold-color bags, and casual jewelry. ⊠ *Royal Dane Mall, at Waterfront, Charlotte Amalie* ☎ *340/774–2280.*

Nicole Miller. The New York designer has created an exclusive motif for the USVI: a map of the islands, a cruise ship, and a tropical sunset. Find this print, and Miller's full line of other designs, on ties, scarves, boxer shorts, sarongs, and dresses. ⊠ *24 Main St., at Palm Passage, Charlotte Amalie* ☎ *340/774–8286.*

Tommy Hilfiger Boutique. Stop by this shop for classic American jeans and sportswear, as well as trendy bags, belts, ties, socks, caps, and wallets. ⊠ *Waterfront Hwy. at Trompeter Gade, Charlotte Amalie* ☎ *340/777–1189.*

FOODSTUFFS **The Belgian Chocolate Company.** Everything at this confectionery tastes as good as it smells. Watch chocolates made daily before your eyes. Specialties include triple-chocolate rum truffles. Gift boxes are available. You can find imported chocolates here as well. Both the homemade and imported come in decorative boxes, so they make great gifts. ⊠ *Royal Dane Alley., Charlotte Amalie* ☎ *340/774–6675.*

Cost-U-Less. The Caribbean equivalent of Costco and Sam's Club sells everything from soup to nuts, but in giant sizes and case lots. The meat-and-seafood department, however, has family-size portions. A well-stocked fresh produce section and a case filled with rotisserie chicken were added in 2006. ⊠ *Rte. 38, ¼ mi (½ km) west of Rte. 39 intersection, Estate Donoe* ☎ *340/777–3588.*

Food Center. Fresh produce, meats, and seafood, plus an on-site bakery and deli with hot-and-cold prepared foods, are the draw here, especially for those renting villas, condos, or charter boats in the East End area. ⊠ *Rte. 32, Estate Frydenhoj* ☎ *340/777–8806.*

Fruit Bowl. For fresh fruits and vegetables, this is the best place on the island to go. ⊠ *Wheatley Center, Rtes. 38 and 313 intersection, Charlotte Amalie* ☎ *340/774–8565.*

Gourmet Gallery. Visiting millionaires buy their caviar here. There's also an excellent and reasonably priced wine selection, as well as specialty ingredients for everything from tacos to curries to chow mein. A full-service deli offers imported meats, cheeses, and in-store prepared foods that are perfect for a gourmet picnic. ⊠ *Crown Bay Marina, Rte. 304, Estate Contant* ☎ *340/776–8555* ⊠ *Havensight Mall, Bldg. VI, Rte. 30, Charlotte Amalie* ☎ *340/774–4948.*

Marina Market. You won't find better fresh meat or seafood anywhere on the island. ⊠ *Rte. 32, across from Red Hook ferry, Red Hook* ☎ *340/779–2411.*

Plaza Extra. This large U.S.-style supermarket has everything you need from produce to meat, including fresh seafood, an excellent deli, and a bakery. There's a liquor department, too. ⊠ *Tutu Park Shopping Mall, Rte. 38, Estate Tutu* ☎ *340/775–5646.*

PriceSmart. Everything from electronics to housewares is found in this warehouse-size store. The meat, poultry, and seafood departments are especially popular. A small café in front sells pizzas, hot dogs, and the cheapest bottled water on the island—just 75¢ a pop. ⊠ *Rte. 38, west of Fort Mylner, Estate Tutu* ☎ *340/777–3430.*

Pueblo Supermarket. This Caribbean chain carries stateside brands of most products—but at higher prices because of shipping costs to the islands. ⊠ *Sub Base, ½ mi (¾ km) east of Crown Bay Marina, Estate Contant* ☎ *340/774–4200* ⊠ *Rte. 30, 1 mi (1½ km) north of Havensight Mall, Estate Thomas* ☎ *340/774–2695.*

HANDICRAFTS **Caribbean Marketplace.** This is a great place to buy handicrafts from the Caribbean and elsewhere. Also look for Sunny Caribee spices, teas from Tortola, and coffee from Trinidad. ⊠ *Havensight Mall, Rte. 30, Charlotte Amalie* ☎ *340/776–5400.*

Dolphin Dreams. Look for gaily painted Caribbean-theme Christmas ornaments, art glass from the Mitchell-Larsen studio, and jewelry made from recycled coral. Signature clothing lines include Bimini Bay and Rum Reggae. This boutique is the exclusive Red Hook source for the famous Caribbean Hook Bracelet, originated by the Caribbean Bracelet Company on St. Croix. ⊠ *American Yacht Harbor, Bldg. C, Rte. 32, Red Hook* ☎ *340/775–0549.*

Down Island Traders. These traders deal in hand-painted calabash bowls; finely printed Caribbean note cards; jams, jellies, spices, hot sauces, and herbs; teas made of lemongrass, passion fruit, and mango; coffee from Jamaica; and handicrafts from throughout the Caribbean. ⊠ *Waterfront Hwy. at Post Office Alley, Charlotte Amalie* ☎ *340/776–4641.*

Into the Sea. Find a wide variety of arts and crafts made by Virgin Islands artists. There are ceramics, glass art, paintings and prints, tropical perfumed soaps, and Caribbean Christmas ornaments. ⊠ *2-A Royal Dane Mall, Charlotte Amalie* ☎ *340/779–1280.*

Native Arts & Crafts Cooperative. More than 40 local artists—including schoolchildren, senior citizens, and people with disabilities—create the handcrafted items for sale here: African-style jewelry, quilts, calabash bowls, dolls, carved-wood figures, woven baskets, straw brooms, note cards, and cookbooks. ⊠ *Tolbod Gade, across from Emancipation Garden, Charlotte Amalie* ☎ *340/777–1153.*

JEWELRY **Amsterdam Sauer.** Many fine one-of-a-kind designs are displayed at this jeweler's three locations. The Imperial Topaz Collection at the Main Street store is a stunner. ⊠ *1 Main St., Charlotte Amalie* ☎ *340/774–2222* ⊠ *Havensight Mall, Rte. 30, Charlotte Amalie* ☎ *340/776–3828* ⊠ *Ritz-Carlton, Rte. 317, Estate Great Bay* ☎ *340/779–2308.*

Cardow Jewelry. A chain bar—with gold in several lengths, widths, sizes, and styles—awaits you here, along with diamonds, emeralds, and other precious gems. You're guaranteed 40% to 60% savings off U.S. retail prices or your money will be refunded within 30 days of purchase. ⊠ *33 Main St., Charlotte Amalie* ☎ *340/776–1140* ⊠ *Havensight Mall, Bldg. I, Rte. 30, Charlotte Amalie* ☎ *340/774–0530 or 340/774–5905* ⊠ *Marriott Frenchman's Reef Resort, Rte. 315, Estate Bakkeroe* ☎ *340/774–0434.*

Colombian Emeralds. Well known in the Caribbean, this store offers set and unset emeralds as well as gems of every description. The watch boutique carries upscale brands like Ebel, Tissot, and Jaeger LeCoultre. ⊠ *30 Main St., Charlotte Amalie* ☎ *340/777–5400* ⊠ *Waterfront at A. H. Riise Mall, Charlotte Amalie* ☎ *340/774–1033* ⊠ *Havensight Mall, Bldg. V, Rte. 30, Charlotte Amalie* ☎ *340/774–2442.*

Diamonds International. Choose a diamond, emerald, or tanzanite gem and a mounting, and you can have your dream ring set in an hour. Famous for having the largest inventory of diamonds on the island, this shop welcomes trade-ins, has a U.S. service center, and offers free diamond earrings with every purchase. ⊠ *31 Main St., Charlotte Amalie* ☎ *340/774–3707* ⊠ *3 Drakes Passage, Charlotte Amalie* ☎ *340/775–2010* ⊠ *7AB Drakes Passage, Charlotte Amalie* ☎ *340/774–1516* ⊠ *Havensight Mall, Bldg. II, Rte. 30, Charlotte Amalie* ☎ *340/776–0040* ⊠ *Wyndham Sugar Bay Beach Club & Resort, Rte. 38, Estate Smith Bay* ☎ *340/714–3248.*

H. Stern Jewelers. The World Collection of jewels set in modern, fashionable designs and an exclusive sapphire watch have earned this Brazilian jeweler a stellar name. ⊠ *8 Main St., Charlotte Amalie* ☎ *340/776–1939* ⊠ *Havensight Mall, Bldg. II, Rte. 30, Charlotte Amalie* ☎ *340/776–1223* ⊠ *Marriott Frenchman's Reef Resort, Rte. 315, Estate Bakkeroe* ☎ *340/776–3550.*

Jewels. Name-brand jewelry and watches are in abundance here. Designer jewelry lines include David Yurman, Bulgari, Chopard, and Penny Preville. The selection of watches is extensive, with brand names including Jaeger le Coultre, Tag Heuer, Breitling, Movado, and Gucci. ⊠ *Main St., at Riise's Alley, Charlotte Amalie* ☎ *340/777–4222* ⊠ *Waterfront at Hibiscus Alley, Charlotte Amalie* ☎ *340/777–4222* ⊠ *Havensight Mall, Bldg. II, Rte. 30, Charlotte Amalie* ☎ *340/776–8590.*

Rolex Watches at A. H. Riise. As the Virgin Islands' official Rolex retailer, this shop offers one of the largest selections of these fine timepieces in the Caribbean. An After Sales Service Center assures that your Rolex keeps on ticking for a lifetime. ⊠ *37 Main St., at Riise's Alley, Charlotte Amalie* ☎ *340/776–2303* ⊠ *Havensight Mall, Bldg. II, Rte. 30, Charlotte Amalie* ☎ *340/776–4002.*

LEATHER GOODS **Coach Boutique at Little Switzerland.** Find a full line of fine leather handbags, belts, gloves, and more for women, plus briefcases and wallets for men. Accessories for both sexes include organizers, travel bags, and cell-phone cases. ⊠ *5 Main St., Charlotte Amalie* ☎ *340/776–2010.*

Longchamp Boutique. Classic Longchamp brings you authentic French handcrafted leather goods like handbags, briefcases, wallets, key chains, belts, and luggage. The exclusive line of canvas and leather travel bags is as beautiful as it is practical. ⊠ *25 Main St., Charlotte Amalie* ☎ *340/777–5240.*

Ⓒ **Zora's.** Fine made-to-order leather sandals are the specialty here. There's also a selection of locally made backpacks, purses, and briefcases in durable, brightly colored canvas. ⊠ *Norre Gade, across from Roosevelt Park, Charlotte Amalie* ☎ *340/774–2559.*

LINENS **Fabric in Motion.** Fine Italian linens share space with Liberty's of London silky cottons, colorful batiks, cotton prints, ribbons, and accessories at this small shop. ⊠ *Storetvaer Gade, Charlotte Amalie* ☎ *340/774–2006.*

Mr. Tablecloth. The friendly staff here will help you choose from the floor-to-ceiling selection of linens, from Tuscany lace tablecloths to Irish linen pillowcases. The prices will please. ⊠ *6–7 Main St., Charlotte Amalie* ☎ *340/774–4343.*

LIQUOR & **A. H. Riise Liquors & Tobacco.** This Riise venture offers a large selection
TOBACCO of tobacco (including imported cigars), as well as cordials, wines, and rare vintage Armagnacs, cognacs, ports, and Madeiras. It also stocks fruits in brandy and barware from England. Enjoy rum samples at the tasting bar. ⊠ *37 Main St., at Riise's Alley, Charlotte Amalie* ☎ *340/776–2303* ⊠ *Havensight Mall, Bldg. I, Rte. 30, Charlotte Amalie* ☎ *340/776–7713.*

Al Cohen's Discount Liquor. The wine selection at this warehouse-style store is extremely large. ⊠ *Rte. 30 across from Havensight Mall, Charlotte Amalie* ☎ *340/774–3690.*

Tobacco Discounters. Find here a full line of discounted brand-name cigarettes, cigars, and tobacco accessories. ⊠ *Port of $ale Mall, Rte. 30, next to Havensight Mall, Charlotte Amalie* ☎ *340/774–2256.*

MUSIC **Modern Music.** Shop for the latest stateside and Caribbean CD releases,
Ⓒ plus oldies, classical, and New Age music. ⊠ *Rte. 30, across from Havensight Mall, Charlotte Amalie* ☎ *340/774–3100* ⊠ *Nisky Center, Rte. 30, Charlotte Amalie* ☎ *340/777–8787.*

Ⓒ **Parrot Fish Music.** A stock of standard stateside CDs, plus a good selection of Caribbean artists, including local groups, can be found here. You can browse through the collection of calypso, soca, steel band, and reggae music online. ⊠ *Back St., Charlotte Amalie* ☎ *340/776–4514* ⊕ *www.parrotfishmusic.com.*

PERFUME **Tropicana Perfume Shoppe.** Displayed in an 18th-century Danish building is a large selection of fragrances for men and women, including those locally made by Gail Garrison from the essential oils of tropical fruits and flowers like mango and jasmine. ⊠ *2 Main St., Charlotte Amalie* ☎ *340/774–0010.*

SUNGLASSES **Davante.** This designer eyewear store carries brands like Cartier, Dunhill, Giorgio Armani, and Christian Dior. ⊠ *Riise's Alley, Charlotte Amalie* ☎ *340/714–1220.*

Fashion Eyewear. Take your pick from name-brand eyewear. A real plus here is prescription sunglasses, copied from your present eyewear, ready in a half hour for $99. ⊠ *International Plaza, Charlotte Amalie* ☎ *340/776–9075.*

TOYS **Quick Pics.** Birds sing, dogs bark, and fish swim in this animated toy land, which is part of a larger electronics and souvenir store. Adults have as much fun trying out the wares as do kids. ⊠ *Havensight Mall, Bldg. IV, Rte. 30, Charlotte Amalie* ☎ *340/774–3500.*

Nightlife & the Arts

On any given night, especially in season, you can find steel-pan orchestras, rock and roll, piano music, jazz, broken-bottle dancing (actual dancing atop broken glass), disco, and karaoke. Pick up a copy of the free, bright yellow *St. Thomas–St. John This Week* magazine when you arrive (it can be found at the airport, in stores, and in hotel lobbies). The back pages list who's playing where. The Friday edition of the *Daily News* carries complete listings for the upcoming weekend.

Nightlife

BARS **Agave Terrace.** Island-style steel-pan bands are a treat that should not be missed. Steel pan music resonates after dinner here on Tuesday and Thursday. ⊠ *Point Pleasant Resort, Rte. 38, Estate Smith Bay* ☎ *340/775–4142.*

Duffy's Love Shack. A live band and dancing under the stars are the big draws for locals and visitors alike. ⊠ *Red Hook Plaza, Red Hook* ☎ *340/779–2080.*

Epernay Bistro. This intimate nightspot has small tables for easy chatting, wine and champagne by the glass, and a spacious dance floor. Mix and mingle with island celebrities. The action runs from 4 PM until the wee hours Monday through Saturday. ⊠ *Frenchtown Mall, 24-A Honduras, Frenchtown* ☎ *340/774–5348.*

Greenhouse Bar & Restaurant. Once this favorite eatery puts away the salt-and-pepper shakers at 10 PM, it becomes a rock-and-roll club with a DJ or live reggae bands raising the weary to their feet six nights a week. ⊠ *Waterfront Hwy. at Storetvaer Gade, Charlotte Amalie* ☎ *340/774–7998.*

Iggies Beach Bar. Sing along karaoke-style to the sounds of the surf or the latest hits at this beachside lounge. There are live bands on the weekends, and you can dance inside or kick up your heels under the stars. At the adjacent Beach House restaurant, there's Carnival Night, complete with steel-pan music on Wednesday. ⊠ *Bolongo Bay Beach Club & Villas, Rte. 30, Estate Bolongo* ☎ *340/775–1800.*

Ritz-Carlton, St. Thomas. On Monday nights, catch steel pan music at this resort's bar. ⊠ *Rte. 317, Estate Great Bay* ☎ *340/775–3333.*

The Arts

THEATER **Pistarkle Theater.** In the Tillett Gardens complex, this air-conditioned theater with more than 100 seats is host to a dozen or more productions annually, plus a children's summer drama camp. ⊠ *Tillett Gardens, Rte. 38, across from Tutu Park Shopping Mall, Estate Tutu* ☎ *340/775–7877.*

Reichhold Center for the Arts. This amphitheater has its more expensive seats covered by a roof. Schedules vary, so check the paper to see what's on when you're in town. Throughout the year there's an entertaining mix of local plays, dance exhibitions, and music of all types. ⊠ *Rte. 30, across from Brewers Beach, Estate Lindberg Bay* ☎ *340/693–1559.*

Exploring St. Thomas

St. Thomas is only 13 mi (21 km) long and less than 4 mi (6½ km) wide, but it's extremely hilly, and even an 8- or 10-mi (13- or 16-km) trip could take well over an hour. Don't let that discourage you, though; the mountain ridge that runs east to west through the middle and separates the island's Caribbean and Atlantic sides has spectacular vistas.

Charlotte Amalie

Look beyond the pricey shops, T-shirt vendors, and bustling crowds for a glimpse of the island's history. The city served as the capital of Denmark's outpost in the Caribbean until 1917, an aspect of the island often lost in the glitz of the shopping district.

Emancipation Gardens, right next to the fort, is a good place to start a walking tour. Tackle the hilly part of town first: head north up Government Hill to the historic buildings that house government offices and have incredible views. Several regal churches line the route that runs west back to the town proper and the old-time market. Virtually all the alleyways that intersect Main Street lead to eateries that serve frosty drinks, sandwiches, burgers, and West Indian fare. There are public restrooms in this area, too. Allow an hour for a quick view of the sights.

A note about the street names: In deference to the island's heritage, the streets downtown are labeled by their Danish names. Locals will use both the Danish name and the English name (such as Dronningens Gade and Norre Gade for Main Street), but most people refer to things by their location ("a block toward the Waterfront off Main Street" or "next to the Little Switzerland Shop"). You may find it more useful if you ask for directions by shop names or landmarks.

Numbers in the margin correspond to points of interest on the Charlotte Amalie map.

㉒ All Saints Anglican Church. Built in 1848 from stone quarried on the island, the church has thick, arched window frames lined with the yellow brick that came to the islands as ballast aboard ships. Merchants left the brick on the waterfront when they filled their boats with molasses, sugar, mahogany, and rum for the return voyage. The church was built in celebration of the end of slavery in the USVI. ⊠ *Domini Gade* ☎ *340/774–0217* ۞ *Mon.–Sat. 9–3.*

㉕ Cathedral of St. Peter & St. Paul. This building was consecrated as a parish church in 1848 and serves as the seat of the territory's Roman Catholic diocese. The ceiling and walls are covered with murals painted in 1899 by two Belgian artists, Father Leo Servais and Brother Ildephonsus. The San Juan–marble altar and side walls were added in the 1960s. ⊠ *Lower Main St.* ☎ *340/774–0201* ۞ *Mon.–Sat. 8–5.*

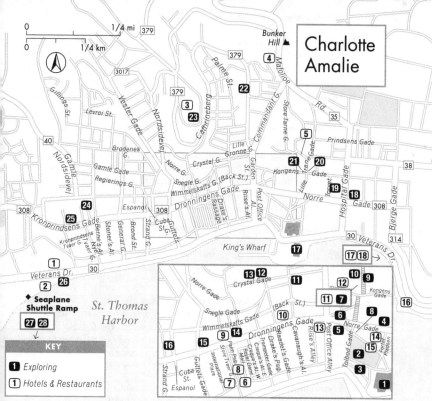

Charlotte Amalie

Bunker Hill

St. Thomas Harbor

Seaplane Shuttle Ramp

King's Wharf

KEY

1 *Exploring*

1 *Hotels & Restaurants*

㉓ Danish Consulate Building. Built in 1830, this structure once housed the Danish Consulate. Although the Danish Consul General, Soøren Blak, has an office in Charlotte Amalie, the Danish Consulate is now in the Scandinavian Center in Havensight Mall. This building is not open to the public. ⊠ *Take stairs north at corner of Bjerge Gade and Crystal Gade to Denmark Hill.*

⓫ Dutch Reformed Church. This church has an austere loveliness that's amazing considering all it's been through. Founded in 1744, it's been rebuilt twice following fires and hurricanes. The unembellished cream-color hall gives you a sense of peace—albeit monochromatically. The only other color is the forest green of the shutters and the carpet. Call ahead if you need to visit at a particular time; the doors are sometimes locked. ⊠ *Nye Gade and Crystal Gade* ☎ *340/776–8255* ☉ *Weekdays 9–5.*

❻ Educators Park. A peaceful place amid the town's hustle and bustle, the park has memorials to three famous Virgin Islanders: educator Edith Williams, J. Antonio Jarvis (a founder of the *Daily News*), and educator and author Rothschild Francis. The last gave many speeches here. ⊠ *Main St., across from post office.*

㉖ Edward Wilmoth Blyden Marine Terminal. Locally called Tortola Wharf, it's where you can catch the *Native Son* and other ferries to the BVI. The restaurant upstairs is a good place to watch the Charlotte Amalie harbor traffic and sip an iced tea. Next door is the ramp for the *Seaborne Airlines* seaplane, which offers commuter service to St. Croix, the BVI, and Puerto Rico. ⊠ *Waterfront Hwy.*

☚ ❷ Emancipation Garden. Built to honor the freeing of slaves in 1848, the garden was the site of a 150th anniversary celebration of emancipation. A bronze bust of a freed slave blowing a symbolic conch shell commemorates this anniversary. The gazebo here is used for official ceremonies. Two other monuments show the island's Danish-American connection—a bust of Denmark's King Christian and a scaled-down model of the U.S. Liberty Bell. ⊠ *Between Tolbod Gade and Fort Christian.*

☚ ⓯ Enid M. Baa Public Library. Like so many other structures on the north side of Main Street, this large pink building is a typical 18th-century town house. Merchants built their houses (stores downstairs, living quarters above) across from the brick warehouses on the south side of the street. The library was once the home of merchant and landowner Baron von Bretton. It's the island's first recorded fireproof building, meaning it was built of ballast brick instead of wood. Its interior of high ceilings and cool stone floors is the perfect refuge from the afternoon sun. You can browse through historic papers or just sit in the breeze by an open window reading the paper. ⊠ *Main St.* ☎ *340/774–0630* ☉ *Weekdays 9–5, Sat. 10–3.*

☚ ❶ Fort Christian. St. Thomas's oldest standing structure, this monument was built between 1672 and 1680 and now has U.S. National Landmark status. The clock tower was added in the 19th century. This remarkable building has, over time, been used as a jail, governor's residence, town hall, courthouse, and church. Closed for major structural renovations since 2005, the building was scheduled to reopen in 2007. It houses the **Virgin Islands Museum,** where you can see exhibits on USVI history, natural history, and turn-of-the-20th-century furnishings. Local artists display their works in the gallery. A gift shop sells local crafts, books, and other souvenirs. This is also the site of the Chamber of Commerce's Hospitality Lounge, where there are brochures, public restrooms, and a place where you can stash your luggage for some last-minute shopping before heading to the airport. ⊠ *Waterfront Hwy., east of shopping district* ☎ *340/776–4566.*

④ Frederick Lutheran Church. This historic church has a massive mahogany altar, and its pews—each with their own door—were once rented to families of the congregation. Lutheranism is the state religion of Denmark, and when the territory was without a minister, the governor—who had his own elevated pew—filled in. ⊠ *Norre Gade* ☎ *340/776–1315* ☺ *Mon.–Sat. 9–4.*

㉑ Government House. Built in 1867, this neoclassical white brick-and-wood structure houses the offices of the governor of the Virgin Islands. Inside, the staircases are of native mahogany, as are the plaques hand-lettered in gold with the names of the governors appointed and, since 1970, elected. Brochures detailing the history of the building are available, but you may have to ask for them. ⊠ *Government Hill* ☎ *340/ 774–0294* ☜ *Free* ☺ *Weekdays 8–5.*

⑧ Grand Hotel. This imposing building stands at the head of Main Street. Once the island's premier hotel, it has been converted into offices and shops. ⊠ *Tolbod Gade at Norre Gade* ☎ *340/774–7282* ☺ *Weekdays 8–5, Sat. 9–noon.*

⑩ Haagensen House. Behind Hotel 1829, this lovingly restored home was built in the early 1800s by Danish entrepreneur Hans Haagensen and is surrounded by an equally impressive cookhouse, outbuildings, and terraced gardens. A lower-level banquet hall now showcases antique prints and photographs. Guided walking tours begin at the lookout tower at Blackbeard's Castle and continue to the circa-1860s Villa Notman, Haagensen House, and Hotel 1829. The first tour starts at 9:30 AM. ⊠ *Government Hill* ☎ *340/776–1234 or 340/776–1829* ☜ *Tours $29* ☺ *Oct.–May, daily 9–4; June–Sept., by appointment only.*

㉗ Hassel Island. East of Water Island in Charlotte Amalie harbor, Hassel Island is part of the Virgin Islands National Park, as it has the ruins of a British military garrison (built during a brief British occupation of the USVI during the 1800s) and the remains of a marine railway (where ships were hoisted into dry dock for repairs). You can opt for a three-hour guided tour, which departs from the dock at Marriott's Frenchman's Reef Resort. For $49 per person you can see the Garrison House ruins, Fort Willoughby, and the island's flora and fauna.

⑦ Hotel 1829. As its name implies, the hotel was built in 1829, albeit as the private residence of a prominent merchant named Lavalette. The building's coral-color façade is accented with fancy black wrought iron, and the interior is paneled in dark wood, which makes it feel delightfully cool. From the terrace there's an exquisite view of the harbor framed by brilliant orange bougainvillea. You can combine a visit to this hotel with a walking tour of Haagensen House, Villa Notman, and the lookout tower at Blackbeard's Castle just behind the hotel. ☒ *Government Hill* ☎ *340/776–1829 or 340/776–1234* ⊕ *www.hotel1829.com* ☎ *Tour $20* ⊙ *Oct.–May, daily 9–4; June–Sept., by appointment only.*

⓱ Legislature Building. Its pastoral-looking lime-green exterior conceals the vociferous political wrangling of the Virgin Islands Senate inside. Constructed originally by the Danish as a police barracks, the building was later used to billet U.S. Marines, and much later it housed a public school. You're welcome to sit in on sessions in the upstairs chambers. ☒ *Waterfront Hwy., across from Fort Christian* ☎ *340/774–0880* ⊙ *Daily 8–5.*

⓰ Market Square. A truck accident in 2004 knocked the roof off the market, yet a cadre of old-timers continues to sell local fruit such as mangoes and papayas, strange-looking root vegetables, and herbs, while sidewalk vendors offer African fabrics and artifacts and tie-dyed cotton clothes at good prices. A new roof, along with a new sidewalk, benches, and landscaping, were set for 2007. ☒ *North side of Main St., at Strand Gade.*

⓲ Memorial Moravian Church. Built in 1884, this church was named to commemorate the 150th anniversary of the Moravian Church in the Virgin Islands. ☒ *17 Norre Gade* ☎ *340/776–0066* ⊙ *Weekdays 8–5.*

☝ ⓽ 99 Steps. This staircase "street," built by the Danes in the 1700s, leads to the residential area above Charlotte Amalie and Blackbeard's Castle. The castle's tower, built in 1679, was once used by the notorious pirate Edward Teach. If you count the stairs as you go up, you will discover, as have thousands before you, that there are more than 99. ☒ *Look for steps heading north from Government Hill.*

⓮ Pissarro Building. Housing several shops and an art gallery, this was the birthplace and childhood home of Camille Pissarro, who later moved to France and became an acclaimed impressionist painter. The art gallery contains three original pages from Pissarro's sketchbook and two pastels by Pissarro's grandson, Claude. ☒ *Main St., between Raadets Gade and Trompeter Gade.*

☝ ⓳ Roosevelt Park. You can see members of the local legal community head to the nearby court buildings while you rest on a bench in this park— a good spot to people-watch. The small monument on the park's south side is dedicated to USVI war veterans. Kids enjoy the playground made of wood and tires. ☒ *Norre Gade.*

㉔ Savan. A neighborhood of small streets and houses, Savan was first laid out in the 1700s as the residential area for a growing community of middle-class black artisans, clerks, and shopkeepers. There's a row of Rastafarian shops along the first block and restaurants that sell spicy vegetarian fare. It's best not to walk here at night and to exercise caution even in daylight. ☒ *Turn north off lower Main St. onto General Gade.*

★ ⑳ **Seven Arches Museum.** This restored 18th-century home is a striking example of classic Danish–West Indian architecture. There seem to be arches everywhere—seven to be exact—all supporting a "welcoming arms" staircase that leads to the second floor and the flower-framed front doorway. The Danish kitchen is a highlight: it's housed in a separate building off the main house, as were all cooking facilities in the early days (for fire prevention). Inside the house you can see mahogany furnishings and gas lamps. ⊠ *Government Hill, 3 bldgs. east of Government House* ☎ *340/774–9295* ☒ *$5 donation* ☉ *Oct.–July, daily 10–4; Aug. and Sept., by appointment only.*

⑫ **Synagogue of Beracha Veshalom Vegmiluth Hasidim.** The synagogue's Hebrew name translates as the Congregation of Blessing, Peace, and Loving Deeds. The small building's white pillars contrast with the rough stone walls, as does the rich mahogany of the pews and altar. The sand on the floor symbolizes the exodus from Egypt. Since the synagogue first opened its doors in 1833 it has held a weekly Sabbath service, making it the oldest synagogue building in continuous use under the American flag and the second-oldest (after the one on Curaçao) in the western hemisphere. Guided tours are available. Brochures detailing the key structures and history are also available. Next door, the Weibel Museum showcases Jewish history on St. Thomas. ⊠ *15 Crystal Gade* ☎ *340/774–4312* ⊕ *new.onepaper.com/synagogue* ☉ *Weekdays 9–4.*

⑤ **U.S. Post Office.** While you buy your postcard stamps, contemplate the murals of waterfront scenes by *Saturday Evening Post* artist Stephen Dohanos. His art was commissioned as part of the Works Project Administration (WPA) in the 1930s. ⊠ *Tolbod Gade and Main St.*

☽ ③ **Vendors Plaza.** Here merchants sell everything from T-shirts to African attire to leather goods. Look for local art among the ever-changing selections at this busy market. ⊠ *Waterfront, west of Fort Christian* ☉ *Weekdays 8–6, weekends 9–1.*

㉘ **Water Island.** This island, once owned by the U.S. Department of the Interior and about ¼ mi (½ km) out in Charlotte Amalie Harbor, was once a peninsula. A channel was cut through so that U.S. submarines could get to their base in a bay just to the west, known as Sub Base. Today, this is the fourth-largest U.S. Virgin Island. A ferry goes between Crown Bay Marina and the island several times daily, at a cost of $5 or $10 round-trip.

⑬ **Weibel Museum.** In this museum next to the synagogue, 300 years of Jewish history on St. Thomas are showcased. The small gift shop sells a commemorative silver coin celebrating the anniversary of the Hebrew congregation's establishment on the island in 1796. There are also tropically inspired items, like a shell seder plate and menorahs painted to resemble palm trees. ⊠ *15 Crystal Gade* ☎ *340/774–4312* ☒ *Free* ☉ *Weekdays 9–4.*

Around the Island

To explore outside Charlotte Amalie, rent a car or hire a taxi. Your rental car should come with a good map; if not, pick up the pocket-size "St.

Thomas–St. John Road Map" at a tourist information center. Roads are marked with route numbers, but they're confusing and seem to switch numbers suddenly. Roads are also identified by signs bearing the St. Thomas–St. John Hotel and Tourism Association's mascot, Tommy the Starfish. More than 100 of these color-coded signs line the island's main routes. Orange signs trace the route from the airport to Red Hook, green signs identify the road from town to Magens Bay, Tommy's face on a yellow background points from Mafolie to Crown Bay through the north side, red signs lead from Smith Bay to Four Corners via Skyline Drive, and blue signs mark the route from the cruise-ship dock at Havensight to Red Hook. These color-coded routes are not marked on most visitor maps, however. Allow yourself a day to explore, especially if you want to stop to take pictures or to enjoy a light bite or refreshing swim. Most gas stations are on the island's more populated eastern end, so fill up before heading to the north side. And remember to drive on the left!

Although the eastern end has many major resorts and spectacular beaches, don't be surprised if a cow or a herd of goats crosses your path as you drive through the relatively flat, dry terrain. The north side of the island is more lush and hush—fewer houses and less traffic. Here there are roller-coaster routes (made all the more scary because the roads have no shoulders) and incredible vistas. Leave time in the afternoon for a swim. Pick up some sandwiches from delis in the Red Hook area for a picnic lunch, or enjoy a slice of pizza at Magens Bay. A day in the country will reveal the tropical pleasures that have enticed more than one visitor to become a resident.

Numbers in the margin correspond to points of interest on the St. Thomas map.

30 **Compass Point Marina.** It's fun to park your car and walk around this marina. The boaters—many of whom have sailed here from points around the globe—are easy to engage in conversation. Turn south off Route 32 at the well-marked entrance road just east of Independent Boat Yard. ☒ *Estate Frydenhoj.*

32 **Coral World Ocean Park.** This interactive aquarium and water-sports center lets you experience a variety of sea life and other animals. The park has several outdoor pools where you can pet baby sharks, feed stingrays, touch starfish, and view endangered sea turtles. There is also a walk-through aviary where colorful rainbow lorikeets might drink nectar right from your hands. Other activities include the Sea Trek Helmet Dive that lets you walk along an underwater trail with a high-tech helmet that provides a continuous supply of air. A Shark Encounter program lets you observe juvenile sharks as they swim around you. A sea-lion pool, scheduled to open in 2007, is where you can get a big, wet sea-lion kiss. Coral World also has an offshore underwater observatory, an 80,000 gallon living coral-reef exhibit (one of the largest in the world), and a nature trail full of lush tropical flowers, ducks, and tortoises. Daily feedings take place at most every exhibit. ☒ *Coki Point, north of Rte. 38, Estate Frydendal* ☎ *6450 Estate Smith Bay, St. Thomas 00802* ☎ *340/775–1555* ⊕ *www.coralworldvi.com* ☒ *$18, Sea Trek $68, Shark Encounter $43* ☉ *Daily 9–5.*

FodorśChoice
★

☾ ③④ Drake's Seat. Sir Francis Drake was supposed to have kept watch over his fleet and looked for enemy ships from this vantage point. The panorama is especially breathtaking (and romantic) at dusk, and if you arrive late in the day you can miss the hordes of day-trippers on taxi tours who stop here to take a picture and buy a T-shirt from one of the many vendors. ⊠ *Rte. 40, Estate Zufriedenheit.*

③⑤ Estate St. Peter Greathouse & Botanical Gardens. This unusual spot is perched on a mountainside 1,000 feet above sea level, with views of more than 20 islands and islets. You can wander through a gallery displaying local art, sip a complimentary rum punch while looking out at the view, or follow a nature trail that leads you past nearly 70 varieties of tropical plants, including 17 varieties of orchids. ⊠ *Rte. 40, Estate St. Peter* ☎ *340/774–4999* ⊕ *www.greathouse-mountaintop.com* ⊠ *$12* ☉ *Mon.–Sat. 9–4:30.*

③⑥ Frenchtown. Popular for its bars and restaurants, Frenchtown is also the home of descendants of immigrants from St. Barthélemy (St. Barths). You can watch them pull up their brightly painted boats and display their equally colorful catch of the day along the waterfront. If you chat with them, you can hear speech patterns slightly different from those of other St. Thomians. Get a feel for the residential district of Frenchtown by walking west to some of the town's winding streets, where tiny wooden houses have been passed down from generation to generation. Next to Joseph Aubain Ballpark, the **French Heritage Museum** (⊠ Intersection of rue de St. Anne and rue de St. Barthélemy ☎ 340/774–2320) houses century-old artifacts such as fishing nets, accordions, tambourines, mahogany furniture, and historic photographs that illustrate the lives of the French descendants during the 18th through 20th centuries. The museum is open Monday through Saturday from 9 AM to 6 PM; admission is free. ⊠ *Turn south off Waterfront Hwy. at post office.*

★ ☾ ③③ Mountain Top. Stop here for a banana daiquiri and spectacular views from the observation deck more than 1,500 feet above sea level. There are also shops that sell everything from Caribbean art to nautical antiques, ship models, and T-shirts. Kids will like talking to the parrots—and hearing them answer back. ⊠ *Head north off Rte. 33, look for signs* ⊕ *www.greathouse-mountaintop.com.*

★ ☾ ②⑨ Paradise Point Tramway. Fly skyward in a gondola to Paradise Point, an overlook with breathtaking views of Charlotte Amalie and the harbor. There are several shops, a bar, restaurant, and a wedding gazebo; kids enjoy the tropical-bird show held daily at 10:30 AM, 1:30 PM, and 3:30 PM. A ¼-mi (½-km) hiking trail leads to spectacular views of St. Croix to the south. Wear sturdy shoes; the trail is steep and rocky. ⊠ *Rte. 30, across from Havensight Mall, Charlotte Amalie* ☎ *340/774–9809* ⊕ *www.paradisepointtramway.com* ⊠ *$16* ☉ *Thurs.–Tues. 9–5, Wed. 9–9.*

③① Red Hook. In this nautical center there are fishing and sailing charter boats, dive shops, and powerboat-rental agencies at the American Yacht Harbor marina. There are also several bars and restaurants, including Molly Molone's, Duffy's Love Shack, and Off the Hook. One grocery store and two delis offer picnic fixings—from sliced meats and cheeses to rotisserie-roasted chickens, prepared salads, and freshly baked breads.

ST. JOHN

By Lynda Lohr

The sun slipped up over the horizon like a great orange ball, streaking the sky with wisps of gold. Watching from my porch overlooking Coral Bay, I thanked Mother Nature, as I do almost every day, for providing glorious sunrises, colorful rainbows and green hillsides, and the opportunity to enjoy them all. It was a magnificent start to another gorgeous St. John day, an island where nature is the engine that fuels the economy and brings more than 800,000 visitors a year.

St. John's heart is Virgin Islands National Park, a treasure that takes up a full two-thirds of St. John's 20 square mi (53 square km). The park helps keep the island's interior in its pristine and undisturbed state, but if you go at midday, you'll probably have to share your stretch of beach with others, particularly at Trunk Bay.

The island is booming, and it can get a tad crowded at the ever-popular Trunk Bay Beach during the busy winter season; parking woes plague the island's main town of Cruz Bay, but you won't find traffic jams or pollution. It's easy to escape from the fray, however: just head off on a hike or go early or late to the beach. The sun won't be as strong, and you may have that perfect crescent of white sand all to yourself.

St. John doesn't have a grand agrarian past like her sister island, St. Croix, but if you're hiking in the dry season, you can probably stumble upon the stone ruins of old plantations. The less adventuresome can visit the repaired ruins at the park's Annaberg Plantation and Caneel Bay resort.

In 1675 Jorgen Iverson claimed the unsettled island for Denmark. By 1733 there were more than 1,000 slaves working more than 100 plantations. In that year the island was hit by a drought, hurricanes, and a plague of insects that destroyed the summer crops. With famine a real threat and the planters keeping them under tight rein, the slaves revolted on November 23, 1733. They captured the fort at Coral Bay, took control of the island, and held on to it for six months. During this period, about 20% of the island's total population was killed, the tragedy affecting both black and white residents in equal percentages. The rebellion was eventually put down with the help of French troops from Martinique. Slavery continued until 1848, when slaves in St. Croix marched on Frederiksted to demand their freedom from the Danish government. This time it was granted. After emancipation, St. John fell into decline, with its inhabitants eking out a living on small farms. Life continued in much the same way until the national park opened in 1956 and tourism became an industry.

Of the three U.S. Virgin Islands, St. John, which has 5,000 residents, has the strongest sense of community, which is primarily rooted in a desire to protect the island's natural beauty. Despite the growth, there are still many pockets of tranquility. Here you can truly escape the pressures of modern life for a day, a week—perhaps, forever.

St. John Archaeology

Archaeologists continue to unravel St. John's past through excavations at Trunk Bay and Cinnamon Bay, both prime tourist destinations within Virgin Islands National Park.

Work began back in the early 1990s, when the park wanted to build new bathhouses at the popular Trunk Bay. In preparation for that project, the archaeologists began to dig, turning up artifacts and the remains of structures that date to AD 900. The site was once a village occupied by the Taino, a peaceful group that lived in the area for many centuries. A similar but not quite as ancient village was discovered at Cinnamon Bay.

By the time the Tainos got to Cinnamon Bay—they lived in the area from about AD 1000 to 1500—their society had developed to include chiefs, commoners, workers, and slaves. The location of the national park's busy Cinnamon Bay campground was once a Taino temple that belonged to a king or chief. When archaeologists began digging in 1998, they uncovered several dozen *zemis*, which are small clay gods used in ceremonial activities, as well as beads, pots, and many other artifacts.

Near the end of the Cinnamon Bay dig, archaeologists turned up another less ancient but still surprising discovery. A burned layer indicated that a plantation slave village had also stood near Cinnamon Bay campground; it was torched during the 1733 revolt because its slave inhabitants had been loyal to the planters. Since the 1970s, bones from slaves buried in the area have been uncovered at the water's edge by beach erosion.

Where to Stay

St. John doesn't have many beachfront hotels, but that's a small price to pay for all the pristine sand. However, the island's two excellent resorts—Caneel Bay Resort and the Westin St. John Resort & Villas—*are* on the beach. Sandy, white beaches string out along the north coast, which is popular with sunbathers and snorkelers and is where you can find the Caneel Bay Resort and Cinnamon and Maho Bay campgrounds. Most villas are in the residential south-shore area, a 15-minute drive from the north-shore beaches. If you head east you come to the laid-back community of Coral Bay, where there are growing numbers of villas and cottages. A stay outside of Coral Bay will be peaceful and quiet.

If you're looking for West Indian village charm, there are a few inns in Cruz Bay. Just know that when bands play at any of the town's bars (some of which stay open until the wee hours), the noise can be a problem. Your choice of accommodations also includes condominiums and cottages near town; two campgrounds, both at the edges of beautiful beaches (bring bug repellent); ecoresorts; and luxurious villas, often with a pool or a hot tub (sometimes both) and a stunning view.

If your lodging comes with a fully equipped kitchen, you'll be happy to know that St. John's handful of grocery stores sell everything from the basics to sun-dried tomatoes and green chilies—though the prices will

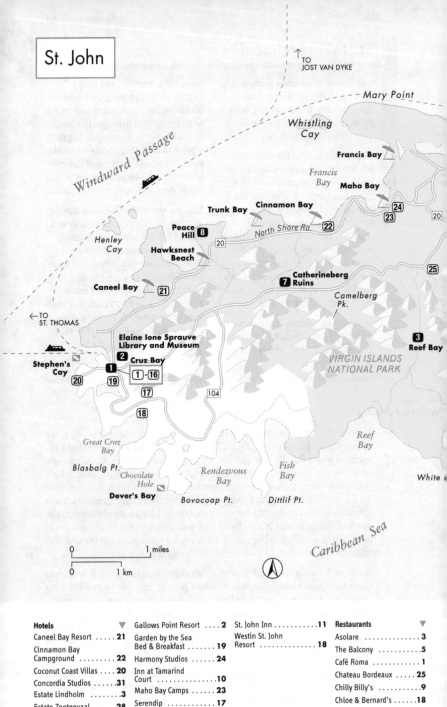

St. John

TO
JOST VAN DYKE

Mary Point

Whistling
Cay

Windward Passage

Francis Bay

Francis
Bay

Maho Bay

24

23

20

Trunk Bay Cinnamon Bay

22

Peace
Hill **8** North Shore Rd.

Hawksnest
Beach

25

Henley
Cay

Catherineberg
Ruins **7**

Caneel Bay **21**

Camelberg
Pk.

TO
ST. THOMAS

Elaine Ione Sprauve
Library and Museum

2 Cruz Bay

Reef Bay **3**

1 - **16**

VIRGIN ISLANDS
NATIONAL PARK

Stephen's
Cay

1

19

20 **17**

104

18

Great Cruz
Bay

Reef
Bay

Blasbalg Pt.

Chocolate
Hole Rendezvous
Bay Fish
Bay

Dever's Bay Bovocoap Pt. Dittlif Pt.

White

Caribbean Sea

0 ——————— 1 miles

0 ——————— 1 km

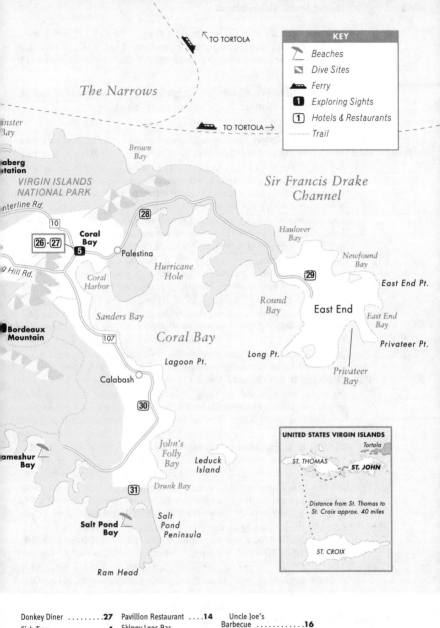

KEY

- ☆ Beaches
- ◹ Dive Sites
- 🚢 Ferry
- ❶ Exploring Sights
- ① Hotels & Restaurants
- ⋯⋯ Trail

TO TORTOLA

The Narrows

TO TORTOLA →

inster Bay

Brown Bay

aberg tation

VIRGIN ISLANDS NATIONAL PARK

Sir Francis Drake Channel

nterline Rd.

10

28

Haulover Bay

Coral Bay

26 - 27

Newfound Bay

5

Palestina

29

East End Pt.

9 Hill Rd.

Hurricane Hole

Coral Harbor

East End

East End Bay

Sanders Bay

Round Bay

Bordeaux Mountain

107

Coral Bay

Long Pt.

Privateer Pt.

Lagoon Pt.

Privateer Bay

Calabash

30

ameshur Bay

John's Folly Bay

Leduck Island

UNITED STATES VIRGIN ISLANDS

Tortola

Drunk Bay

ST. THOMAS

ST. JOHN

31

Distance from St. Thomas to St. Croix approx. 40 miles

Salt Pond Bay

Salt Pond Peninsula

ST. CROIX

Ram Head

take your breath away. If you're on a budget, consider bringing some staples (pasta, canned goods, paper products) from home. Hotel rates throughout the island, though considered expensive by some, do include endless privacy and access to most water sports.

For approximate costs, *see* the dining and lodging price chart on the U.S. Virgin Islands Planner, at the beginning of this chapter.

Hotels & Inns

$$$$
Fodor'sChoice
★

Caneel Bay Resort. Well-heeled honeymooners, couples celebrating anniversaries, and extended families all enjoy Caneel Bay Resort's laid-back luxury. If you want to spend your days sunning on any one of its seven gorgeous beaches, taking a kayak out for a paddle, or enjoying lingering dinners at its fine restaurants, you'll find no finer resort on St. John. Your room, which has air-conditioning or can be opened to the breezes, won't come with a TV or even a telephone (though management will loan you a cellular)—all the better to get away from it all. Rooms look as if they're modeled right out of a magazine; if you opt for one of the beachfront rooms, you can get out of bed and stumble a few steps across the sand to the Caribbean. Otherwise, you can look out on the gardens or the tennis courts. Nightlife runs to steel-pan music or an easy-listening combo; if you want lots of action, go elsewhere. ⊠ *Rte. 20, Caneel Bay* ⊕ *Box 720, Cruz Bay 00830* ☎ *340/776–6111 or 888/767–3966* 🖷 *340/693–8280* ⊕ *www.caneelbay.com* 🛏 *166 rooms* ⚬ *In-room: no phone, no TV. In-hotel: 4 restaurants, tennis courts, pool, spa, beachfront, diving, water sports, no elevator, children's programs (ages 4–12), public Wi-Fi, no-smoking rooms* ▤ *AE, DC, MC, V* ⦿l *CP.*

$$$$
Westin St. John Resort & Villas. Other than Caneel Bay, this is the only big resort on the island. Although it doesn't provide the same casual luxury, it does have a nice beachfront location and enough activities to make you never want to leave. That said, most guests rent a car for at least a couple of days to explore the many lovely beaches and the nearby town of Cruz Bay. The hotel is spread over 47 beachfront acres adjacent to Great Cruz Bay, with lushly planted gardens, a white sandy beach that beckons sunbathers, and nice—but not luxurious—rooms with tropical touches. Those strung out behind the beach put you closest to the water, but even the hillside villas are only a seven-minute stroll to the sand. You can keep very busy here with tennis and water sports, or you can idle the day away at the pool or beach. ⊠ *Rte. 104, Great Cruz Bay* ⊕ *Box 8310, Cruz Bay 00831* ☎ *340/693–8000 or 800/808–5020* 🖷 *340/779–4985* ⊕ *www.westinresortstjohn.com* 🛏 *174 rooms, 144 villas* ⚬ *In-room: safe, refrigerator, ethernet. In-hotel: 4 restaurants, tennis courts, pool, gym, beachfront, diving, water sports, no elevator, children's programs (ages 3–12), public Wi-Fi, no-smoking rooms* ▤ *AE, D, DC, MC, V* ⦿l *EP.*

$$–$$$$
Estate Lindholm Bed & Breakfast. Built among old stone ruins on a lushly planted hill overlooking Cruz Bay, Estate Lindholm provides a charming setting, with the convenience of being close to Cruz Bay's restaurants, shopping, and nightlife. You'll feel as if you're out of the fray but still near enough to run into town when you want. Rooms are sophisticated, with crisp white spreads accented by teak furniture. Although you can

easily walk to Cruz Bay, the return trip is up a big hill. To get out and about, rent a car. The sunset views from Asolare restaurant, on the property, provide a stunning end to your day. ⌂ *Box 1360, Cruz Bay 00831* ☎ *340/776–6121* 🖷 *800/322–6335* ⊕ *www.estatelindholm.com* ⇖ *10 rooms* ⚹ *In-room: refrigerator. In-hotel: restaurant, pool, gym, no elevator, no kids under 18, no-smoking rooms* ⊟ *AE, D, MC, V* ⧫⦶ *CP.*

$$ ⊡ **Garden by the Sea Bed & Breakfast.** A stay here will allow you to live like a local in a middle-class residential neighborhood near a bird-filled salt pond. This cozy B&B is also an easy walk from Cruz Bay, which makes it convenient. White spreads and curtains provide pristine counterpoints to the blue-and-green hues in your room. Your hosts serve a delightful breakfast—piña colada French toast is a specialty—on the front deck. It's perfect for folks who enjoy peace and quiet: there are no phones or TVs in the rooms. ⊠ *Enighed* ⌂ *5004A Enighed 87, Cruz Bay 00830* ☎🖷 *340/779–4731* ⊕ *www.gardenbythesea.com* ⇖ *3 rooms* ⚹ *In-room: no a/c, no phone, no TV. In-hotel: no elevator, no-smoking rooms* ⊟ *No credit cards* ⧫⦶ *BP.*

$$ ⊡ **St. John Inn.** A stay here gives you a bit of style at what passes for budget prices in St. John. You might find a four-poster bed or an old-fashioned armoire in rooms painted in lush hues. Tucked down a side street off a busy major thoroughfare, this cozy inn puts you an easy walk from Cruz Bay's shops, restaurants, and even the ferry dock (if you don't have much luggage). ⊠ *Off Rte. 104, Box 37, Cruz Bay 00831* ☎ *340/693–8688 or 800/666–7688* 🖷 *340/693–9900* ⊕ *www.stjohninn.com* ⇖ *11 units* ⚹ *In-room: kitchen (some), refrigerator. In-hotel: pool, no elevator* ⊟ *AE, MC, V* ⧫⦶ *CP.*

$ ⊡ **Inn at Tamarind Court.** If money is an object—and you don't want to camp at Maho—opt for the Inn at Tamarind Court. The rooms have rather pedestrian decor, but they're clean, and you can't beat the location, a five-minute walk from the heart of Cruz Bay's action. If you're up for a bit of a hike, you can even walk to the beach at Salomon Bay; the trip takes you about a mile up and down hill, but you'll be rewarded with a swim at the end. Ask at the national park visitor center for directions. Single rooms share a bath, but the rest have private baths. The hotel's courtyard restaurant, filled with umbrella-covered tables, is popular with locals. ⊠ *Rte. 104, Box 350, Cruz Bay 00831* ☎ *340/776–6378 or 800/221–1637* 🖷 *340/776–6722* ⊕ *www.tamarindcourt.com* ⇖ *20 rooms* ⚹ *In-room: kitchen (some), refrigerator. In-hotel: restaurant, no elevator* ⊟ *AE, D, MC, V* ⧫⦶ *CP.*

WHERE TO CAMP ⛰ **Cinnamon Bay Campground.** Cinnamon Bay Campground sits in the heart of Virgin Islands National Park, a stellar location right at the beach. Tents and rustic cottages are nestled in the trees that stretch behind the shore, and you have easy access to hiking, water sports, and ranger-led evening programs. The amenities are basic but include propane stoves, cooking equipment, and bed linens; reserve early if you'd like a cottage right behind the beach. Only the screened cottages have electric lights; tenters depend on propane lanterns. If you have your own gear, the tent sites are a steal at $27 per night. Showers and flush toilets, as well as a restaurant and a small store, are a short walk away from the camping area. ⚹ *Flush toilets, drinking water, showers (cold), picnic tables, food* *service, electricity (some), public telephone, general store, swimming (ocean) ➥ 55 tents, 40 cottages, 31 tent sites ⊠ Rte. 20, Cinnamon Bay ⌂ Box 720, Cruz Bay 00830-0720 ☎ 340/776–6330 or 800/ 539–9998 🖨 340/776–6458 ⊕ www.cinnamonbay.com ✉ $27 tent sites, $80 tents, $110–$140 cottages ⚐ Reservations essential ▭ AE, MC, V ☉ Closed Aug.–Oct.*

☾ ⚠ **Maho Bay Camps.** Tucked into the greenery along the island's north
FodorsChoice shore, Maho Bay Camps is particularly ecoconscious, and it attracts a
★ sociable crowd that likes to explore the undersea world off the campground's beach or attend on-site seminars. The "tents" (wooden plat-
forms protected from the elements by canvas and screening) are linked
by wooden stairs, ramps, and walkways—all of them elevated—so that
you can trek around camp, down to the beach, and to the unheated,
coolish public showers without disturbing the terrain. Although the tents
have some amenities like real beds and electricity, there are no refrigerators; ice-filled coolers keep your food from spoiling. ⚐ *Flush toilets,
drinking water, showers (cold), picnic tables, food service, electricity,
public telephone, general store, swimming (beach) ➥ 114 tent cottages
⊠ Maho Bay ⌂ Box 310, Cruz Bay 00830 ☎ 340/776–6240 or 800/
392–9004 🖨 340/776–6504 ⊕ www.maho.org ✉ $130 ⚐ Reserva-
tions essential ▭ AE, MC, V.*

Condominiums & Cottages

Many of the island's condos are just minutes from the hustle and bustle of Cruz Bay, but you'll find more scattered around the island.

$$$$ 🏨 **Gallows Point Resort.** Gallows Point Resort has an excellent waterfront
location just outside Cruz Bay's center. You're a short walk to restaurants and shops, but once you step into your condo, the hustle and bustle are left behind. The upper-level apartments have loft bedrooms and
the best views. The harborside villas get better trade winds, but they're
a tad noisier. Tropical rooms have wicker furniture, tile floors, and
brightly colored spreads in colors that reflect the sea and sky. Zozo's Ristorante, a popular spot for sunset watching, serves northern Italian cuisine above the lobby. ⊠ *Gallows Point, Bay St., Box 58, Cruz Bay
00831 ☎ 340/776–6434 or 800/323–7229 🖨 340/776–6520 ⊕ www.
gallowspointresort.com ➥ 60 units ⚐ In-room: kitchen. In-hotel: restaurant, pool, beachfront, water sports, no elevator, public Internet ▭ AE,
MC, V ⊙ EP.*

$$$–$$$$ 🏨 **Estate Zootenvaal.** Comfortable and casual, this small cottage colony
gives you the perfect place to relax. They are certainly out of the way,
along the island's East End Road. Though you'll feel that you're get-
ting away from it all, a five-minute drive will bring you to Coral Bay's
few restaurants, a handful of shops, and tiny grocery store. The small
but very private beach across the road is a major plus. ⊠ *Rte. 10, Hur-
ricane Hole, Zootenvaal 00830 ☎ 340/776–6321 ⊕ www.
estatezootenvaal.com ➥ 4 units ⚐ In-room: no a/c, no phone (some),
kitchen, no TV. In-hotel: beachfront, no elevator ▭ No credit cards
⊙ EP.*

$$$ 🏨 **Coconut Coast Villas.** This small condominium complex with studio,
two-, and three-bedroom apartments is a 10-minute walk from Cruz Bay,

but is insulated from the town's noise in a sleepy suburban neighborhood. You can swim and snorkel at the small beach or relax poolside and catch some rays. Rooms have a fresh feel; each is a little bit different in decor, with whites, blues, and greens predominating in the color scheme. Colorful artwork by the owner's mother, St. John artist Elaine Estern, graces the walls. ⊠ *Turner Bay* 🕮 *Box 618, Cruz Bay 00831* ☎ *340/693–9100 or 800/858–7989* 🖷 *340/779–4157* 🌐 *www.coconutcoast.com* 🗭 *9 units* ♿ *In-room: kitchen. In-hotel: pool, beachfront, no elevator* ⊟ *MC, V* ¶⊙¶ *EP.*

$$ 🏨 **Harmony Studios.** These condominium-style units sit hillside at Maho Bay, giving you more of the comforts of home than at the Maho Bay Camp tents just below. An ecologically correct environment is one of the draws here. Entryway mats are made of recycled tires, the pristine white walls of recycled newspapers, and your electricity comes from the wind and the sun. Best of all, you share access to interesting evening programs and a nice beach at Maho. Be prepared to hike up and down long flights of steep, wooden stairs. ⊠ *Maho Bay* 🕮 *Box 310, Cruz Bay 00830* ☎ *340/776–6240 or 800/392–9004* 🖷 *340/776–6504* 🌐 *www.maho.org* 🗭 *12 units* ♿ *In-room: no a/c, no phone, kitchen, no TV. In-hotel: restaurant, beachfront, water sports, no elevator, children's programs (ages 8–16), public Internet, no-smoking rooms* ⊟ *AE, MC, V* ¶⊙¶ *EP.*

$$ 🏨 **Serendip.** We'd pick Serendip for a budget vacation in a residential locale. This complex offers modern apartments on lush grounds with lovely views. Although this is a property from the 1960s, the units don't feel dated. There are colorful spreads, fully equipped kitchens, and bookshelves filled with good vacation reads. You definitely need a car if you stay here, though; it's about 1 mi (1½ km) up a steep hill out of Cruz Bay. ⊠ *Enighed* 🕮 *Box 273, Cruz Bay 00831* ☎ *340/776–6646 or 888/800–6445* 🌐 *www.serendipstjohn.com* 🗭 *10 apartments* ♿ *In-room: kitchen, Wi-Fi. In-hotel: no elevator* ⊟ *MC, V* ¶⊙¶ *EP.*

$–$$ 🏨 **Concordia Studios and Eco-tents.** This off-the-beaten-path resort—under the same management as Maho Bay Camps—is on the remote Salt Pond peninsula. It shares the back-to-nature bent of its sister resorts but with a decent level of comfort. The spacious condominium units are casually comfortable, with tile floors, kitchens, and lovely sea views. Next door are 25 "eco-tents," upscale camping structures made of environmentally friendly materials but also equipped with solar power, composting toilets, and kitchenettes. ⊠ *20–27 Estate Concordia, Concordia 00830* ☎ *340/693–5855 or 800/392–9004* 🖷 *340/693–5960* 🌐 *www.maho.org* 🗭 *9 studios, 25 tents* ♿ *In-room: no a/c, no phone, kitchen (some), no TV. In-hotel: pool, no elevator, no-smoking rooms* ⊟ *AE, MC, V* ¶⊙¶ *EP.*

Private Condos & Villas

Tucked here and there between Cruz Bay and Coral Bay are about 350 private villas and condos (prices range from $ to $$$$). With pools or hot tubs, full kitchens, and living areas, these lodgings provide a fully functional home away from home. They're perfect for couples and extended groups of family or friends. You need a car, since most lodgings are in the hills and very few are at the beach. Villa managers usually pick you up at the dock, arrange for your rental car, and answer questions upon arrival as well as during your stay. Prices drop in the summer season, which is generally after April 15. Some companies begin off-season pricing a week or two later, so be sure to ask.

If you want to be close to Cruz Bay's restaurants and boutiques, a villa in the Chocolate Hole and Great Cruz Bay areas will put you just a few minutes away. The Coral Bay area has a growing number of villas, but you'll be about 20 minutes from Cruz Bay. Beaches string out along the North Shore, so you won't be more than 15 minutes from the water no matter where you stay.

Book-It VI (⌂ 5000 Estate Enighed, PMB 15, Cruz Bay 00830 ☎ 340/693–8555 or 800/416–1205 ᵬ 340/693–8480 ⊕ www.bookitvi.com) handles villas all across St. John. **Carefree Get-Aways** (⌂ Box 1626, Cruz Bay 00831 ☎ 340/779–4070 or 888/643–6002 ᵬ 340/774–6000 ⊕ www.carefreegetaways.com) manages vacation villas on the island's southern and western edges. **Caribbean Villas & Resorts** (⌂ Box 458, Cruz Bay 00831 ☎ 340/776–6152 or 800/338–0987 ᵬ 340/779–4044 ⊕ www.caribbeanvilla.com) handles condo rentals for Cruz Views and Gallow's Point Resort, as well as for many private villas. **Catered to Vacation Homes** (⊠ Marketplace Suite 206, 5206 Enighed, Cruz Bay 00830 ☎ 340/776–6641 or 800/424–6641 ᵬ 340/693–8191 ⊕ www.cateredto.com) has luxury homes, mainly mid-island and on the western edge. **Destination St. John** (⌂ Box 8306, Cruz Bay 00831 ☎ 340/779–4647 or 800/562–1901 ᵬ 340/715–0073 ⊕ www.destinationstjohn.com) manages villas across the island. **Great Caribbean Getaways** (⌂ Box 8317, Cruz Bay 00831 ☎ 340/693–8692 or 800/341–2532 ᵬ 340/693–9112 ⊕ www.greatcaribbeangetaways.com) handles private villas from Cruz Bay to Coral Bay. **Island Getaways** (⌂ Box 1504, Cruz Bay 00831 ☎ 340/693–7676 or 888/693–7676 ᵬ 340/693–8923 ⊕ www.islandgetaways.net) has villas in the Great Cruz Bay–Chocolate Hole area, with a few others scattered around the island.

On-Line Vacations (⌂ Box 9901, Emmaus 00830 ☎ 340/776–6036 or 888/842–6632 ᵬ 340/693–5357 ⊕ www.onlinevacations.com) books vacation villas around St. John. **Private Homes for Private Vacations** (⊠ 7605 Mamey Peak, Coral Bay 00830 ☎ᵬ 340/776–6876 ⊕ www.privatehomesvi.com) has homes across the island. **Seaview Vacation Homes** (⌂ Box 644, Cruz Bay 00831 ☎ 340/776–6805 or 888/625–2963 ᵬ 340/779–4349 ⊕ www.seaviewhomes.com) handles homes with views of the ocean in the Chocolate Hole, Great Cruz Bay, and Fish Bay areas. **Star Villas** (⌂ 1202 Gallows Point, Cruz Bay 00830 ☎ 340/776–6704 or 888/897–9759 ᵬ 340/776–6183 ⊕ www.starvillas.com) has cozy villas just outside Cruz Bay. **Vacation Vistas** (⌂ Box 476, Cruz Bay 00831 ☎ 340/776–6462 ⊕ www.vacationvistas.com) manages villas mainly in the Chocolate Hole, Great Cruz Bay, and Rendezvous areas. **Windspree** (⊠ 7924 Emmaus, Cruz Bay 00830 ☎ 340/693–5423 or 888/742–0357 ᵬ 340/693–5623 ⊕ www.windspree.com) handles villas mainly in the Coral Bay area.

Where to Eat

The cuisine on St. John seems to get better every year, with culinary-school-trained chefs vying to see who can come up with the most imaginative dishes. There are restaurants to suit every taste and budget—from the elegant establishments at Caneel Bay Resort (where men may be required to wear a jacket at dinner) to the casual in-town eateries of Cruz Bay. For quick lunches, try the West Indian food stands in Cruz Bay Park and across from the post office. The cooks prepare fried chicken legs, pates (meat- and fish-filled pastries), and callaloo.

Some restaurants close for vacation in September and even October. If you have your heart set on a special place, call ahead to make sure it's open during these months.

For approximate costs, *see* the dining and lodging price chart on the U.S. Virgin Islands Planner, at the beginning of this chapter.

Bordeaux

CONTINENTAL
★ $$$$

✕ **Chateau Bordeaux.** This rustic restaurant with a to-die-for view of Coral Bay is a bit out of the way, but worth the trip. Its interior is made elegant with lace tablecloths, glowing candles, and stylish dinner presentations. Start with sourdough bruschetta, a crisp bread topped with caramelized onions, goat cheese, and marinated tomatoes, then segue into seared sea scallops with sautéed spinach, wild mushrooms, and a potato galette, or rack of lamb with roasted corn and a raspberry sauce. Save room for dessert—the fresh berry cups with Chambord and caramel are wonderful. ⊠ *Rte. 10, Bordeaux* ☎ *340/776–6611* ⊟ *AE, MC, V* ☽ *No lunch.*

Coral Bay & Environs

AMERICAN
★ ¢–$

✕ **Skinny Legs Bar & Restaurant.** Sailors who live aboard boats anchored just offshore and an eclectic coterie of residents gather for lunch and dinner at this funky spot in the middle of a boatyard-cum-shopping complex. If owner Moe Chabuz is around, take a gander at his gams; you'll see where the restaurant got its name. It's a great place for burgers, fish sandwiches, and whatever sports event is on the satellite TV. ⊠ *Rte. 10, Coral Bay* ☎ *340/779–4982* ⊟ *AE, D, MC, V.*

CARIBBEAN
★ $$–$$$

✕ **Miss Lucy's Restaurant.** Sitting seaside at remote Friis Bay, Miss Lucy's dishes up Caribbean food with a contemporary flair. Dishes like tender conch fritters, a spicy West Indian stew called callaloo, and fried fish make up most of the menu, but you also find a generous paella filled with seafood, sausage, and chicken on the menu. Sunday brunches are legendary, and if you're around on the full moon, stop by for the monthly full-moon party. The handful of small tables near the water are the nicest, but if they're taken or the mosquitoes are bad, the indoor tables do nicely. ⊠ *Rte. 107, Friis Bay* ☎ *340/693–5244* ⊟ *AE, D, MC, V* ☽ *Closed Mon. No dinner Sun.*

★ ¢–$

✕ **Vie's Snack Shack.** Stop by Vie's when you're out exploring the island. Although it's just a shack by the side of the road, Vie's serves up some great cooking. The garlic chicken legs are crisp and tasty, and the conch fritters are really something to write home about. Plump and filled with fresh herbs, a plateful will keep you going for the rest of the afternoon. Save room for a wedge of coconut pie—called a tart in this neck of the woods. When you're done eating, a spectacular white-sand beach across the road beckons. ⊠ *Rte. 10, Hansen Bay* ☎ *340/693–5033* ▤ *No credit cards* ⊗ *Closed Sun. and Mon. No dinner.*

ECLECTIC
$$–$$$
✕ **Donkey Diner.** In an odd combination that works well for Coral Bay visitors and residents, this tiny spot along the main road through Coral Bay sells yummy breakfasts and pizza. Breakfasts can be as ordinary or as innovative as you like, with the menu running from fried eggs with bacon to blueberry pancakes to scrambled tofu served with home fries. Pizzas are equally eclectic, with toppings that include everything from the usual pepperoni and mushrooms to more exotic corn, raisins, and kalamata olives. ⊠ *Rte. 10, Coral Bay* ☎ *340/693–5240* ▤ *No credit cards* ⊗ *Closed Mon. and Tues.*

☾ **$$**
✕ **Pavillion Restaurant.** At the end of a long, partially paved road at Maho Bay Camps, this casual open-air restaurant is worth the drive. The menu changes daily, but there's always a handful of seafood, chicken, and vegetarian entrées. Give your order at the counter. While you wait for it to be cooked—the chef calls your name when it's done—help yourself to the salad bar, rolls, and iced tea included with your dinner. Arrive early to enjoy the spectacular sunset views. ⊠ *Maho Bay Camps, off Rte. 20* ☎ *340/776–6226* ▤ *AE, MC, V* ⊗ *No lunch.*

Cruz Bay & Environs

BARBECUE
☾ **$–$$**
✕ **Uncle Joe's Barbecue.** Juicy ribs and tasty chicken legs dripping with the house barbecue sauce make for one of St. John's best dining deals. An ear of corn, rice, and a generous scoop of macaroni salad or coleslaw round out the plate. This casual spot crowds the edge of a busy sidewalk in the heart of Cruz Bay. Even though there are a few open-air tables for dining "in," the ambience is more than a tad on the pedestrian side, so take-out is a better bet. ⊠ *North Shore Rd., across from post office* ☎ *340/693–8806* ▤ *No credit cards.*

CONTINENTAL
$$$–$$$$
✕ **Chloe & Bernard's.** With a cuisine that draws from all corners of the globe, Chloe & Bernard's is always delightful. The menu changes regularly, but you might start with a tasty bowl of mussels in a white wine and garlic sauce, or a salad of wild field greens with grapes and candied walnuts drizzled with a roasted apple vinaigrette. Dinner might be grilled tuna served with potatoes, andouille sausage, and a green bean salad. ⊠ *Westin St. John Resort & Villas, Rte. 104* ☎ *340/693–8000* ▤ *AE, MC, V* ⊗ *No lunch.*

★ **$$$–$$$$**
✕ **Stone Terrace Restaurant.** A delightful harbor view, soft lantern light, and white-linen tablecloths provide the backdrop for this restaurant's imaginative cuisine. To standards like rack of lamb, the chef adds a crisp Dijon mustard–onion crust, a few savory carrot gnocchi, and a Stilton cheese cream sauce and rosemary glaze. The salad is jazzed up with a confit of duck perched on arugula, figs, and plantain chips drizzled with a tamarind-balsamic dressing. The desserts change daily but are always as intriguing as the other courses. ⊠ *Bay St.* ☎ *340/693–9370* ▤ *D, MC, V* ⊗ *Closed Mon. No lunch.*

★ **$$$–$$$$** ✕ **Tage.** This place gets rave reviews from locals and visitors alike for its imaginative cuisine. The menu isn't large but changes seasonally; look for dishes like pan-seared yellowfin tuna served with olive ratatouille, basil butter, and lavender rice. Save room for desserts such as almond and lemon pound cake topped with a passion fruit–caramel sauce. Although you may be tempted to eat outside, resist the urge—it's much quieter indoors. ✉ *Rte. 104, across from Julius E. Sprauve School* ☎ *340/715–4270* ▭ *AE, MC, V* ⊘ *Closed Mon. No lunch.*

$$–$$$ ✕ **Lime Inn.** Vacationers and mainland transplants who call St. John home flock to this alfresco spot for the congenial hospitality and good food, including all-you-can-eat shrimp on Wednesday nights. Fresh lobster is the specialty, and the menu also includes shrimp-and-steak dishes and such specials as coconut-encrusted chicken breast with plantains and a Thai curry–cream sauce. ✉ *Lemon Tree Mall, King St.* ☎ *340/776–6425* ▭ *AE, MC, V* ⊘ *Closed Sun. No lunch Sat.*

$–$$$ ✕ **Morgan's Mango.** A visit to this alfresco eatery requires you to climb a long flight of stairs, but the food is well worth the effort. Although fish is the specialty—try the voodoo snapper topped with a many-fruit salsa— the chef also creates a vegetarian platter with black beans, fried plantains, and even an ear of corn. ✉ *North Shore Rd., across from V. I. National Park Visitors Center* ☎ *340/693–8141* ▭ *AE, MC, V* ⊘ *No lunch.*

ECLECTIC ✕ **The Balcony.** If you arrive early enough, you'll catch the sunset along **$$$–$$$$** with the lovely harbor view from this aptly-named restaurant. Start with a serving of tasty lobster crepes or a Stilton chesse and pear salad served with a raspberry vinaigrette before moving on to the main course. The pecan and almond encrusted Chilean sea bass is especially tasty, but beef eaters might enjoy the mango glazed baby back ribs served with garlic mashed potatoes. ✉ *Wharfside Village, Strand St.* ☎ *340/774–8470* ▭ *AE, MC, V.*

♻ **$$–$$$$** ✕ **Fish Trap.** The rooms here all open to the breezes and buzz with a mix of locals and visitors. Start with a tasty appetizer like conch fritters and fish chowder (a creamy combination of snapper, white wine, paprika, and secret spices). You can always find steak and chicken dishes, as well as an interesting pasta of the day. ✉ *Bay and Strand Sts., next to Our Lady of Mount Carmel Church* ☎ *340/693–9994* ▭ *D, MC, V* ⊘ *Closed Mon. No lunch.*

♻ **$$–$$$$** ✕ **High Tide.** This casual spot right at Cruz Bay Beach serves everything from hamburgers and mahimahi sandwiches to a fish of the day with sauces like mango chutney or island salsa. The kids' menu includes favorites like chicken tenders and grilled cheese sandwiches. ✉ *Wharfside Village, Strand St.* ☎ *340/714–6169* ▭ *AE, MC, V.*

$–$$$ ✕ **Inn at Tamarind Court Restaurant.** There's a different chef—each with a unique style—every night, which makes for an eclectic menu. On Monday, schoolteacher Val serves up gyros and spanokapita from her native Greece; Wednesday is stir fry night. On other nights you might find Mexican, West Indian, or down-home American cooking, depending on who's in the kitchen. ✉ *Rte. 104* ☎ *340/776–6378* ▭ *D, MC, V* ⊘ *No lunch.*

$ ✕ **Sun Dog Cafe.** There's an unusual assortment of dishes at this charming alfresco restaurant, which you'll find tucked into a courtyard in the upper reaches of the Mongoose Junction shopping center. Kudos to the white pizza with artichoke hearts, roasted garlic, mozzarella cheese, and capers. The Jamaican jerk chicken sub and the black-bean quesadilla are also good choices. ⊠ *Mongoose Junction, North Shore Rd.* ☎ *340/ 693–8340* ⊟ *AE, MC, V* ⊗ *No dinner.*

¢–$ ✗ **Chilly Billy's.** Although you might stop by this restaurant at lunchtime for a heartburn-inducing St. John Reuben (with turkey, cheese, sauerkraut, and mustard on rye), this restaurant's claim to fame is breakfast. The stuffed French toast is one step this side of heaven: before it's fried, the bread is soaked in a mixture of eggs and Bailey's. If you're not one for morning sweets, try a savory breakfast burrito filled with eggs and jalepeño jack cheese. ⊠ *Lumberyard Shopping Center, Boulon Center Rd.* ☎ *340/693–8708* ⊟ *MC, V* ⊗ *No dinner.*

ITALIAN   ✗ **Zozo's Ristorante.** Creative takes on old standards coupled with lovely
$$$–$$$$ presentations draw the crowds to this restaurant at Gallows Point Re-
Fodor'sChoice sort. Start with crispy fried calamari served with a pesto mayonnaise.
★ The chef dresses up roasted grouper with a pistachio crust and serves it with a warm goat cheese and arugula salad. The grilled veal chop comes with a pancetta and spinach gratin and crisp fried potatoes. The sunset views will take your breath away. ⊠ *Gallows Point Resort, Bay St.* ☎ *340/ 693–9200* ⊟ *AE, MC, V* ⊗ *No lunch.*

☼ **$$–$$$** ✗ **Café Roma.** This second-floor restaurant in the heart of Cruz Bay is *the* place for traditional Italian cuisine: lasagna, spaghetti and meatballs, and seafood puttanesca. Small pizzas are available at the table, but larger ones are for takeout only. Rum-caramel bread pudding is a dessert specialty. This casual eatery can get crowded in the winter, so show up early. ⊠ *Vesta Gade* ☎ *340/776–6524* ⊟ *MC, V* ⊗ *No lunch.*

PAN-ASIAN   ✗ **Asolare.** Contemporary Asian cuisine dominates the menu at this el-
★ **$$$–$$$$** egant open-air eatery in an old St. John house. Come early and relax over drinks while you enjoy the sunset lighting up the harbor. Start with an appetizer such as pork dumplings served with a glass noodle salad, then move on to entrées such as beef fillet served with roasted haystack potatoes and napa cabbage, or seared tuna served with an apple-and-greens salad. If you still have room for dessert, try the chocolate pyramid, a luscious cake with homemade ice cream melting in the middle. ⊠ *Estate Lindholm, Rte. 20 on Caneel Hill* ☎ *340/779–4747* ⊟ *AE, MC, V* ⊗ *No lunch.*

Beaches

St. John is blessed with many beaches, and all of them fall into the good, great, and don't-tell-anyone-else-about-this-place categories. Those along the north shore are all within the national park. Some are more developed than others—and many are crowded on weekends, holidays, and in high season—but by and large they're still pristine. Beaches along the south and eastern shores are quiet and isolated.

Cinnamon Bay Beach. This long, sandy beach faces beautiful cays and abuts the national park campground. The facilities are open to the public and include cool showers, toilets, a commissary, and a restaurant. You can rent water-sports equipment here—a good thing, because there's excellent snorkeling off the point to the right; look for the big angelfish and large schools of purple triggerfish. Afternoons on Cinnamon Bay can be windy—a boon for windsurfers but an annoyance for sunbathers—so arrive early to beat the gusts. The Cinnamon Bay hiking trail begins across the road from the beach parking lot; ruins mark the trailhead. There are actually two paths here: a level nature trail (signs along it identify the flora) that loops through the woods and passes an old Danish cemetery, and a steep trail that starts where the road bends past the ruins and heads straight up to Route 10. Restrooms are located on the main path from the commissary to the beach and scattered around the campground. ⊠ *North Shore Rd., Rte. 20, about 4 mi (6 km) east of Cruz Bay.*

Francis Bay Beach. Because there's little shade, this beach gets toasty warm in the afternoon when the sun comes around to the west, but the rest of the day, it's a delightful stretch of white sand. The only facilities are a few picnic tables tucked among the trees and a portable bathroom, but folks come here to watch the birds that live in the swampy area behind the beach. The park offers bird-watching hikes here on Sunday morning; sign up at the visitor center in Cruz Bay. To get here, turn left at the Annaberg intersection. ⊠ *North Shore Rd., Rte. 20, ¼ mi (½ km) from Annaberg intersection.*

Hawksnest Beach. Sea grape and waving palm trees line this narrow beach, and there are restrooms, cooking grills, and a covered shed for picnicking. A patchy reef just offshore near the middle of the beach offers snorkeling an easy swim away, but the best underwater views are reserved for ambitious snorkelers who head farther to the east along the bay's fringes. Watch out for boat traffic—a channel guides dinghies to the beach, but the occasional boater strays into the swim area. It's the closest drivable beach to Cruz Bay, so it's often crowded with locals and visitors. ⊠ *North Shore Rd., Rte. 20, about 2 mi (3 km) east of Cruz Bay.*

Lameshur Bay Beach. This sea grape–fringed beach is toward the end of a very long, partially paved road on the southeast coast. The reward for your long drive is solitude, good snorkeling, and a chance to spy on some pelicans. The beach has a couple of picnic tables, rusting barbecue grills, and a portable restroom. The ruins of the old plantation are a five-minute walk down the road past the beach. The area has good hiking trails, including a trek (more than a mile) up Bordeaux Mountain before an easy walk to Yawzi Point. ⊠ *Off Rte. 107, about 1½ mi (2½ km) from Salt Pond.*

Maho Bay Beach. This popular beach is below Maho Bay Camps—a wonderful hillside enclave of tent cabins. The campground offers breakfast and dinner at its Pavillion Restaurant, water-sports equipment rentals at the beach, and restrooms. After a five-minute hike down a long flight of stairs to the beach, snorkelers head off along rocky outcroppings for a look at all manner of colorful fish. Watch for a sea turtle or two to cross your path. Another lovely strip of sand with the same name sits right along the North Shore Road. Turn left at the Annaberg intersection and follow the signs about 1 mi (1½ km) for Maho Bay Camps. ⊠ *Off North Shore Rd., Rte. 20, Maho Bay.*

Salt Pond Bay Beach. If you're adventurous, this rocky beach on the scenic southeastern coast—next to Coral Bay and rugged Drunk Bay—is worth exploring. It's a short hike down a hill from the parking lot, and the only facilities are an outhouse and a few picnic tables scattered about. Tide pools are filled with all sorts of marine creatures, and the snorkeling is good, particularly along the bay's edges. A short walk takes you to a salt pond, where salt crystals collect around the edges. Hike farther uphill past cactus gardens to Ram Head for see-forever views. Leave nothing valuable in your car; reports of thefts are common. ⊠ *Rte. 107, about 3 mi (5 km) south of Coral Bay.*

Fodor'sChoice   **Trunk Bay Beach.** St. John's most-photographed beach is also the preferred
★   spot for beginning snorkelers because of its underwater trail. (Cruise-ship passengers interested in snorkeling for a day flock here, so if you're looking for seclusion, arrive early or later in the day.) Crowded or not, this stunning beach is one of the island's most beautiful. There are changing rooms with showers, bathrooms, a snack bar, picnic tables, a gift shop, phones, lockers, and snorkeling-equipment rentals. The parking lot often overflows, but you can park along the road. ⊠ *North Shore Rd., Rte. 20, about 2½ mi (4 km) east of Cruz Bay.*

Sports & the Outdoors

BOATING &   If you're staying at a hotel or campground, your activities desk will usu-
SAILING   ally be able to help you arrange a sailing excursion aboard a nearby boat.
★   Most day sails leaving Cruz Bay head out along St. John's north coast. Those that depart Coral Bay might drop anchor at some remote cay off the island's east end or even in the nearby British Virgin Islands. Your trip usually includes lunch, beverages, and at least one snorkeling stop. Keep in mind that inclement weather could interfere with your plans, though most boats will still go out if rain isn't too heavy. If you're staying in a villa, or if your hotel or campground doesn't have an affiliated charter sailboat, contact **St. John Concierge Services** (⊠ Across from the post office, Cruz Bay ☎ 340/777–2665 or 800/808–6025 ⊕ www.adventuresstjohn.com). The very capable staff can find a boat that fits your style and pocketbook. The company also books fishing and scuba trips.

For a speedier trip to the cays and remote beaches off St. John, you can rent a power boat from **Ocean Runner** (⊠ On the waterfront, Cruz Bay ☎ 340/693–8809 ⊕ www.oceanrunner.vi). The company rents one- and two-engine boats for $275 to $300 per day. Gas and oil will run you $100 to $300 a day extra, depending on how far you're going. It's a good idea to have some skill with power boats for this self-drive adventure, but if you don't, you can hire a captain to go along to instruct you.

Even novice sailors can take off in a small sailboat from Cruz Bay Beach with **Sail Safaris** (☎ 340/626–8181 or 866/820–6906 ⊕ www.sailsafaris.net) to one of the small islands off St. John. Guided half-day tours, rentals, and lessons each run $70 per person.

DIVING &   Although just about every beach has nice snorkeling—Trunk Bay, Cin-
SNORKELING   namon Bay, and Waterlemon Cay at Leinster Bay get the most praise—you need a boat to head out to the more remote snorkeling locations

and the best scuba spots. Sign on with any of the island's water-sports operators to get to spots farther from St. John. If you use the one at your hotel, just stroll down to the dock to hop aboard. Their boats will take you to hot spots between St. John and St. Thomas, including the tunnels at **Thatch Cay,** the ledges at **Congo Cay,** and the wreck of the *General Rogers.* Dive off St. John at **Stephens Cay,** a short boat ride out of Cruz Bay, where fish swim around the reefs as you float downward. At **Devers Bay,** on St. John's south shore, fish dart about in colorful schools. **Carval Rock,** shaped somewhat like an old-time ship, has gorgeous rock formations, coral gardens, and lots of fish. It can be too rough here in the winter, though. Count on paying $75 for a one-tank dive and $90 for a two-tank dive. Rates include equipment and a tour. If you've never dived before, try an introductory course, called a resort course. Or if certification is in your vacation plans, the island's dive shops can help you get your card.

Cruz Bay Watersports (☎ 340/776–6234 ⊕ www.divestjohn.com) has two locations: in Cruz Bay at the Lumberyard Shopping Complex and at the Westin St. John Resort. Owners Marcus and Patty Johnston offer regular reef, wreck, and night dives and USVI and BVI snorkel tours. The company holds both PADI five-star facility and NAUI Dream Resort status. **Low Key Watersports** (☎ 340/693–8999 or 800/835–7718 ⊕ www.divelowkey.com), at Wharfside Village, offers one- and two-tank dives and specialty courses. It's certified as a PADI five-star training facility.

FISHING Well-kept charter boats—approved by the U.S. Coast Guard—head out to the north and south drops or troll along the inshore reefs, depending on the season and what's biting. The captains usually provide bait, drinks, and lunch, but you need to bring your own hat and sunscreen. Fishing charters run between $550 and $750 per half day for the boat. **Capt. Byron Oliver** (☎ 340/693–8339) takes you out to the north and south drops or closer in to St. John. **Gone Ketchin'** (☎ 340/714–1175 ⊕ www.goneketchin.com), in St. John, arranges trips with old salt Captain Grizz.

HIKING Although it's fun to go hiking with a Virgin Islands National Park guide, don't be afraid to head out on your own. To find a hike that suits your ability, stop by the park's visitor center in Cruz Bay and pick up the free trail guide; it details points of interest, trail lengths, and estimated hiking times, as well as any dangers you might encounter. Although the park staff recommends long pants to protect against thorns and insects, most people hike in shorts because it can get very hot. Wear sturdy shoes or hiking boots even if you're hiking to the beach. Don't forget to bring water and insect repellent.

Fodor'sChoice The **Virgin Islands National Park** (✉ 1300 Cruz Bay Creek, St. John ★ ☎ 340/776–6201 ⊕ www.nps.gov/viis) maintains more than 20 trails on the north and south shores and offers guided hikes along popular routes. A full-day trip to Reef Bay is a must; it's an easy hike through lush and dry forest, past the ruins of an old plantation, and to a sugar factory adjacent to the beach. It can be a bit arduous for young kids, however. Take the $6 safari bus from the park's visitor center to the trailhead, where you can meet a ranger who'll serve as your guide. The park provides a boat ride back to Cruz Bay for $15 to save you the walk back up the mountain. The schedule changes from season to season; call for times and reservations, which are essential.

HORSEBACK RIDING Clip-clop along the island's byways for a slower-pace tour of St. John. **Carolina Corral** (☎ 340/693–5778) offers horseback trips and wagon rides down scenic roads with owner Dana Barlett. She has a way with horses and calms even the most novice riders. Rates start at $75 for a 1½-hour horseback ride and $12 for a 45-minute wagon ride.

SEA KAYAKING Poke around crystal bays and explore undersea life from a sea kayak. Rates run about $70 for a full day in a double kayak. Tours start at $50 for a half day. On the Cruz Bay side of the island, **Arawak Expeditions** (☎ 340/693–8312 or 800/238–8687 ⊕ www.arawakexp.com), which operates out of Low Key Watersports in Cruz Bay's Wharfside Village, has professional guides who use traditional and sit-on-top kayaks to ply coastal waters. The company also rents single and double kayaks, so you can head independently to nearby islands like Stephen's Cay. Explore Coral Bay Harbor and Hurricane Hole on the eastern end of the island in a sea kayak from **Crabby's Watersports** (⊠ Rte. 107, outside Coral Bay ☎ 340/714–2415 ⊕ www.crabbyswatersports.com). If you don't want to paddle into the wind to get out of Coral Bay Harbor, the staff will drop you off in Hurricane Hole so you can paddle downwind back to Coral Bay. Crabby's also rents snorkel gear, dinghies, and fishing tackle.

SIGHTSEEING TOURS In St. John, taxi drivers provide tours of the island, making stops at various sites, including Trunk Bay and Annaberg Plantation. Prices run around $15 a person. The taxi drivers congregate near the ferry in Cruz Bay. The dispatcher will find you a driver for your tour.

WALKING TOURS Along with providing trail maps and brochures about Virgin Islands National Park, the park service also gives several guided tours on- and off-shore. Some are only offered during particular times of the year, and some require reservations. For more information, contact the **V. I. National Park Visitors Center** (⊠ Cruz Bay ☎ 340/776–6201 ⊕ www.nps.gov/viis).

WINDSURFING Steady breezes and expert instruction make learning to windsurf a snap. Try **Cinnamon Bay Campground** (⊠ Rte. 20, Cinnamon Bay ☎ 340/693–5902 or 340/626–4769), where rentals are $30 to $70 per hour. Lessons are available right at the waterfront; just look for the Windsurfers stacked up on the beach. The cost for a one-hour lesson starts at $70. You can also rent kayaks, boogie boards, and surfboards.

Shopping

Areas & Malls

Luxury goods and handicrafts can be found on St. John. Most shops carry a little of this and a bit of that, so it pays to poke around. The Cruz Bay shopping district runs from **Wharfside Village,** just around the corner from the ferry dock, to **Mongoose Junction,** an inviting shopping center on North Shore Road. (The name of this upscale shopping mall, by the way, is a holdover from a time when those furry island creatures gathered at a nearby garbage bin.) Out on Route 104, stop in at the **Marketplace** to explore its gift and crafts shops. At the island's other end, there are a few stores—selling clothes, jewelry, and artwork—here and there from the village of **Coral Bay** to the small complex at **Shipwreck Landing.**

On St. John, store hours run from 9 or 10 to 5 or 6. Wharfside Village and Mongoose Junction shops in Cruz Bay are often open into the evening.

Specialty Items

ART **Bajo el Sol.** Bajo el Sol sells works by owner Livy Hitchcock, plus those from a roster of the island's best artists. Shop for oil and acrylics, sculptures, and ceramics. ☒ *Mongoose Junction, North Shore Rd., Cruz Bay* ☎ *340/693–7070.*

Coconut Coast Studios. This waterside shop, a five-minute walk from Cruz Bay, showcases the work of Elaine Estern. She specializes in undersea scenes. ☒ *Frank Bay, Cruz Bay* ☎ *340/776–6944.*

BOOKS **National Park Headquarters.** The headquarters sells several good histories of St. John, including *St. John Back Time,* by Ruth Hull Low and Rafael Lito Valls, and, for linguists, Valls's *What a Pistarckle!*—an explanation of the colloquialisms that make up the local version of English (*pistarckle* is a Dutch Creole word that means "noise" or "din," which pretty much sums up the language here). ☒ *Cruz Bay* ☎ *340/ 776–6201.*

CLOTHING **Big Planet Adventure Outfitters.** You knew when you arrived that some place on St. John would cater to the outdoor enthusiasts who hike up and down the island's trails. Well, this outdoor-clothing store is where you can find the popular Naot sandals and Reef footware, along with colorful and durable cotton clothing and accessories by Billabong. The store also sells children's clothes. ☒ *Mongoose Junction, North Shore Rd., Cruz Bay* ☎ *340/776–6638.*

Bougainvillea Boutique. If you want to look as if you stepped out of the pages of the resort-wear spread in an upscale travel magazine, try this store. Owner Susan Stair carries *very* chic men's and women's resort wear, straw hats, leather handbags, and fine gifts. ☒ *Mongoose Junction, North Shore Rd., Cruz Bay* ☎ *340/693–7190.*

Jolly Dog. Stock up on the stuff you forgot to pack at this store. Sarongs in cotton and rayon, beach towels with tropical motifs, and hats and T-shirts sporting the Jolly Dog logo fill the shelves. ☒ *Shipwreck Landing, Rte. 107, Sanders Bay* ☎ *340/693–5333* ☒ *Skinny Legs Shopping Complex, Rte. 10, Coral Bay* ☎ *340/693–5900.*

Sloop Jones. It's worth the trip all the way out to the island's east end to shop for made-on-the-premises clothing, pillows, and fabrics by the yard splashed with tropical bright colors. Fabrics are in cotton, linen, and rayon and are supremely comfortable. ☒ *Off Rte. 10, East End* ☎ *340/779–4001.*

St. John Editions. Shop here for nifty cotton dresses that go from beach to dinner with a change of shoes and accessories. Owner Molly Soper also carries attractive straw hats and inexpensive jewelry. ☒ *North Shore Rd., Cruz Bay* ☎ *340/693–8444.*

FOODSTUFFS If you're renting a villa, condo, or cottage and doing your own cooking, there are several good places to shop for food; just be aware that prices are much higher than those at home.

Love City Mini Mart. This market doesn't look like much, but it's just about the only place to shop in Coral Bay and has a surprising selection of items. ✉ *Off Rte. 107, Coral Bay* ☎ *340/693–5790.*

Starfish Market. The island's largest store usually has the best selection of meat, fish, and produce. ✉ *The Marketplace, Rte. 104, Cruz Bay* ☎ *340/779–4949.*

GIFTS **Bamboula.** Owner Jo Sterling travels the Caribbean and the world to find unusual housewares, art, rugs, bedspreads, accessories, and men's and women's clothes and shoes for this multicultural boutique. ✉ *Mongoose Junction, North Shore Rd., Cruz Bay* ☎ *340/693–8699.*

Best of Both Worlds. Pricy metal sculptures and attractive artworks hang from this shop's walls; the nicest are small glass decorations shaped like shells and seahorses. ✉ *Mongoose Junction, North Shore Rd., Cruz Bay* ☎ *340/693–7005.*

The Canvas Factory. If you're a true shopper who needs an extra bag to carry home all your treasures, this store offers every kind of tote and carrier imaginable, from simple bags to suitcases with numerous zippered compartments. All are made of canvas, naturally. It also sells great canvas hats. ✉ *Mongoose Junction, North Shore Rd., Cruz Bay* ☎ *340/776–6196.*

Donald Schnell Studio. In addition to pottery, this place sells unusual hand-blown glass, wind chimes, kaleidoscopes, fanciful fountains, and more. Your purchases can be shipped worldwide. ✉ *Amore Center, Rte. 108 near the Texaco, Cruz Bay* ☎ *340/776–6420.*

Every Ting. As its name implies, this store has a bit of this and a bit of that. Shop for Caribbean books and CDs, picture frames decorated with shells, and T-shirts with tropical motifs. Residents and visitors also drop by to have a cup of espresso. ✉ *Gallows Point Resort, Bay St., Cruz Bay* ☎ *340/693–5820.*

Fabric Mill. Shop here for women's clothing in tropical brights, as well as place mats, napkins, and batik wraps. Or take home a brilliant-hued bolt from the upholstery-fabric selection. ✉ *Mongoose Junction, North Shore Rd., Cruz Bay* ☎ *340/776–6194.*

Mumbo Jumbo. With what may be the best prices in St. John, this cozy shop carries everything from tropical clothing to stuffed sea creatures to gift items. ✉ *Skinny Legs Shopping Complex, Rte. 10, Coral Bay* ☎ *340/779–4277.*

Nest and Company. In colors that reflect the sea, this cozy store carries perfect take-home gifts. Shop here for soaps in tropical scents, dinnerware, and much more. ✉ *Marketplace Shopping Center, Rte. 108, Cruz Bay* ☎ *340/715–2522.*

★ **Pink Papaya.** This store is where you can find the well-known work of longtime Virgin Islands resident M. L. Etre, plus a huge collection of one-of-a-kind gifts, including bright tablecloths, unusual trays, and unique tropical jewelry. ✉ *Lemon Tree Mall, King St., Cruz Bay* ☎ *340/693–8535.*

Wicker, Wood and Shells. Shop the second floor of this store for lovely sculptures and other objets d'art, all with a tropical theme. The first floor houses the island's best selection of greeting cards, notepaper, and other interesting gifts to tuck in your suitcase for friends back home. ⊠ *Mongoose Junction, North Shore Rd., Cruz Bay* ☎ *340/776–6909.*

JEWELRY **Caravan Gallery.** Owner Radha Speer travels the world to find much of the unusual jewelry she sells here. And the more you look, the more you see—folk art, tribal art, and masks for sale cover the walls and tables, making this a great place to browse. ⊠ *Mongoose Junction, North Shore Rd., Cruz Bay* ☎ *340/779–4566.*

Free Bird Creations. Head here for special handcrafted jewelry—earrings, bracelets, pendants, chains—as well as the good selection of water-resistant watches for your excursions to the beach. ⊠ *Wharfside Village, Strand St., Cruz Bay* ☎ *340/693–8625.*

Jewels. This branch of a St. Thomas store carries emeralds, diamonds, and other jewels in attractive yellow- and white-gold settings as well as strings of creamy pearls, watches, and other designer jewelry. ⊠ *Mongoose Junction, North Shore Rd., Cruz Bay* ☎ *340/776–6007.*

R&I Patton Goldsmiths. Rudy and Irene Patton design most of the lovely silver and gold jewelry displayed in this shop. The rest comes from various designer friends. Sea fans (those large, lacy plants that sway with the ocean's currents) in filigreed silver, lapis lazuli set in gold, starfish and hibiscus pendants in silver or gold, and gold sand-dollar-shape charms and earrings are choice selections. ⊠ *Mongoose Junction, North Shore Rd., Cruz Bay* ☎ *340/776–6548.*

Verace. Jewelry from such well-known designers as John Bagley and Patrick Murphy fill the shelves. Murphy's stunning silver sailboats with gems for hulls will catch your attention. ⊠ *Wharfside Village, Strand St., Cruz Bay* ☎ *340/693–7599.*

PHOTO **Cruz Bay Photo.** Pick up disposable cameras, film, and other photo needs,
DEVELOPING or when your memory card fills up, download your digital photos to a disk or print them out. Shop here also for good-quality sunglasses, a must for your tropical vacation. ⊠ *Wharfside Village, Strand St., Cruz Bay* ☎ *340/779–4313.*

Nightlife

St. John isn't the place to go for glitter and all-night partying. Still, after-hours Cruz Bay can be a lively little town in which to dine, drink, dance, chat, or flirt. Notices posted on the bulletin board outside the Connections telephone center—up the street from the ferry dock in Cruz Bay—or listings in the island's two small newspapers (the *St. John Sun Times* and *Tradewinds*) will keep you apprised of special events, comedy nights, movies, and the like.

After a sunset drink at **Zozo's Ristorante** (⊠ Gallows Point Resort, Bay St., Cruz Bay ☎ 340/693–9200), up the hill from Cruz Bay, you can stroll around town (much is clustered around the small waterfront park). Many of the young people from the U.S. mainland who live and work on St. John will be out sipping and socializing, too.

Lizard's Landing (⊠ Veste Gade, Cruz Bay ☎ 340/774–0800) is the wild and crazy place. Loud music and drinks like the Sunburned Lizard make this Cruz Bay's hottest late-night spot. There's calypso and reggae on Friday night at **Fred's** (⊠ King St., Cruz Bay ☎ 340/776–6363). Young folks like to gather at **Woody's** (⊠ Near ferry dock, across from Subway restaurant, Cruz Bay ☎ 340/779–4625), where sidewalk tables provide a close-up view of Cruz Bay's action.

On the far side of the island, landlubbers and old salts listen to music and swap stories at **Skinny Legs Bar & Restaurant** (⊠ Rte. 10, Coral Bay ☎ 340/779–4982).

As its name implies, **Island Blues** (⊠ Rte. 107, Coral Bay ☎ 340/776–6800) is the hot place to go for music at the eastern end of the island.

Exploring St. John

St. John is an easy place to explore. One road runs along the northern shore, another across the center of the mountains. There are a few roads that branch off here and there, but it's hard to get lost. Pick up a map at the visitor center before you start out and you'll have no problems. Few residents remember the route numbers, so have your map in hand if you stop to ask for directions. Bring along a swimsuit for stops at some of the most beautiful beaches in the world. You can spend all day or just a couple of hours exploring, but be advised that the roads are narrow and wind up and down steep hills, so don't expect to get anywhere in a hurry. There are lunch spots at Cinnamon Bay and in Coral Bay, or you can do what the locals do—find a secluded spot for a picnic. The grocery stores in Cruz Bay sell Styrofoam coolers just for this purpose.

If you plan to do a lot of touring, renting a car will be cheaper and will give you much more freedom than relying on taxis; on St. John, taxis are shared safari vans, and drivers are reluctant to go anywhere until they have a full load of passengers. Although you may be tempted by an open-air Suzuki or Jeep, a conventional car can get you just about everywhere on the paved roads, and you'll be able to lock up your valuables. You may be able to share a van or open-air vehicle (called a safari bus) with other passengers on a tour of scenic mountain trails, secret coves, and eerie bush-covered ruins.

Numbers in the margin correspond to points of interest on the St. John map.

★ ➏ **Annaberg Plantation.** In the 18th century, sugar plantations dotted the steep hills of this island. Slaves and free Danes and Dutchmen toiled to harvest the cane that was used to create sugar, molasses, and rum for export. Built in the 1780s, the partially restored plantation at Leinster Bay was once an important sugar mill. Although there are no official visiting hours, the National Park Service has regular tours, and some well-informed taxi drivers will show you around. Occasionally you may see a living-history demonstration—someone making johnnycake or weaving baskets. For information on tours and cultural events, contact the St. John National Park Service Visitors Center. ⊠ *Leinster Bay*

1

Rd., Annaberg ☎ *340/776–6201* ⊕ *www.nps.gov/viis* 🎟 *Free* ☉ *Daily sunrise–sunset.*

★ ❹ **Bordeaux Mountain.** St. John's highest peak rises to 1,277 feet. Route 10 passes near enough to the top to offer breathtaking views. Don't stray into the road here—cars whiz by at a good clip along this section. Instead, drive nearly to the end of the dirt road that heads off next to the restaurant and gift shop for spectacular views at Picture Point and the trailhead of the hike downhill to Lameshur. Get a trail map from the park service before you start. ⊠ *Rte. 10.*

❼ **Catherineberg Ruins.** At this fine example of an 18th-century sugar and rum factory, there's a storage vault beneath the windmill. Across the road, look for the round mill, which was later used to hold water. In the 1733 slave revolt, Catherineberg served as headquarters for the Amina warriors, a tribe of Africans captured into slavery. ⊠ *Rte. 10, Catherineberg.*

❺ **Coral Bay.** This laid-back community at the island's dry, eastern end is named for its shape rather than for its underwater life—the word *coral* comes from *krawl,* Dutch for "corral." It's a small, quiet, neighborhoody settlement—a place to get away from it all. You'll need a four-wheel-drive vehicle if you plan to stay at this end of the island, as some of the rental houses are up unpaved roads that wind around the mountain. If you come just for lunch, a regular car will be fine.

❶ **Cruz Bay.** St. John's main town may be compact (it consists of only several blocks), but it's definitely a hub: the ferries from St. Thomas and the BVI pull in here, and it's where you can get a taxi or rent a car to travel around the island. There are plenty of shops in which to browse, a number of watering holes where you can stop for a breather, many restaurants, and a grassy square with benches where you can sit back and take everything in. Look for the current edition of the handy, amusing "St. John Map" featuring Max the Mongoose. To pick up a useful guide to St. John's hiking trails, see various large maps of the island, and find out about current park service programs, including guided walks and cultural demonstrations, stop by the **V. I. National Park Visitors Center** (⊠ Near the baseball field, Cruz Bay ☎ 340/776–6201 ⊕ www.nps. gov/viis). It's open daily from 8 to 4:30.

❷ **Elaine Ione Sprauve Library.** On the hill just above Cruz Bay is the Enighed Estate greathouse, built in 1757. *Enighed* is the Danish word for "concord" (unity or peace). The greathouse and its outbuildings (a sugar factory and horse-driven mill) were destroyed by fire and hurricanes, and the house sat in ruins until 1982. The library offers Internet access for $2 an hour. ⊠ *Rte. 104, make a right past Texaco station, Cruz Bay* ☎ *340/776–6359* 🎟 *Free* ☉ *Weekdays 9–5.*

❽ **Peace Hill.** It's worth stopping at this spot just past the Hawksnest Bay overlook for great views of St. John, St. Thomas, and the BVI. On the flat promontory is an old sugar mill. ⊠ *Off Rte. 20, Denis Bay.*

★ ❸ **Reef Bay Trail.** Although this is one of the most interesting hikes on St. John, unless you're a rugged individualist who wants a physical challenge (and that describes a lot of people who stay on St. John), you can probably get the most out of the trip if you join a hike led by a park service ranger who can identify the trees and plants on the hike down, fill you in on the history of the Reef Bay Plantation, and tell you about the petroglyphs on the rocks at the bottom of the trail. A side trail takes you to the plantation's greathouse, a gutted but mostly intact structure that maintains vestiges of its former beauty. Take the safari bus from the park's visitor center. A boat takes you from the beach at Reef Bay back to the visitor center, saving you the uphill climb. ⊠ *Rte. 10, Reef Bay* ☎ *340/776–6201 Ext. 238 reservations* ⊕ *www.nps.gov/viis* ⊠ *Free, safari bus $6, return boat trip to Cruz Bay $15* ⊗ *Tours at 9:30 AM, days change seasonally.*

ST. CROIX

By Lynda Lohr

As my seaplane skimmed St. Croix's north coast on the flight from St. Thomas, the island's agrarian past played out below. Stone windmills left over from the days when sugar ruled stood like sentinels in the fields. As we closed in on Christiansted, the big yellow Fort Christiansvaern loomed on the waterfront, and the city's red roofs created a colorful counterpoint to the turquoise harbor. A visit to St. Croix, once a Danish colony, always puts me in touch with my Danish roots (my grandmother was a Poulsen). Indeed, history is so popular in St. Croix that planes are filled with Danish visitors who, like other vacationers, come to sun at the island's powdery beaches, enjoy pampering at the hotels, and dine at interesting restaurants, but mainly wish to explore the island's colonial history.

Until 1917 Denmark owned St. Croix and her sister Virgin Islands, an aspect of the island's past that is reflected in street names in the main towns of Christiansted and Frederiksted as well as in the surnames of many island residents. Those early Danish settlers, as well as those from other European nations, left behind slews of 18th- and 19th-century ruins, all of them once worked by slaves brought over on ships from Africa, by their descendants, and by white indentured servants lured to St. Croix to pay off their debt to society. Some—such as the Christiansted National Historic site, Whim Plantation, the ruins at St. George Village Botanical Garden, the Nature Conservancy's property at Estate Princess, and the ruins at Estate Mount Washington and Judith's Fancy—are open for easy exploration. Others are on private land, but a drive around the island reveals the ruins of 100 plantations here and there on St. Croix's 84 square mi. Their windmills, greathouses, and factories are all that's left of the 224 plantations that once grew sugarcane, tobacco, and other agricultural products at the height of the island's plantation glory.

The downturn began in 1801 when the British occupied the island. The demise of the slave trade in 1803, another British occupation from 1807 to 1815, droughts, the development of the sugar beet industry in Europe, political upheaval, and a depression sent the island on a downward spiral.

St. Croix never recovered from these blows. The end of slavery in 1848, followed by labor riots, fires, hurricanes, and an earthquake during the

CLOSE UP

Turtles on St. Croix

1

Like creatures from the earth's prehistoric past, green, leatherback, and hawksbill turtles crawl ashore during the annual April-to-November turtle nesting season to lay their eggs. They return from their life at sea every two to seven years to the beach where they were born. Since turtles can live for up to 100 years, they may return many times to nest in St. Croix.

The leatherbacks like Sandy Point National Wildlife Refuge and other spots on St. Croix's western end, but the hawksbills prefer Buck Island and the East End. Green turtles are also found primarily on the East End.

All are endangered species that face numerous natural and man-made predators. Particularly in the Frederiksted area, dogs and cats prey on the nests and eat the hatchlings.

Occasionally a dog will attack a turtle about to lay its eggs, and cats train their kittens to hunt at turtle nests, creating successive generations of turtle-egg hunters. In addition, turtles have often been hit by fast-moving boats that leave large gashes in their shells if they don't kill them outright.

The leatherbacks are the subject of a project by the international group Earthwatch. Each summer, teams arrive at Sandy Point National Wildlife Refuge to ensure that poachers, both natural and human, don't attack the turtles as they crawl up the beach. The teams also relocate nests that are laid in areas prone to erosion. When the eggs hatch, teams stand by to make sure the turtles make it safely to the sea, and scientists tag them so they can monitor their return to St. Croix.

---

last half of the 19th century, brought what was left of the island's economy to its knees. The start of prohibition in 1922 called a halt to the island's rum industry, further crippling the economy. The situation remained dire—so bad that President Herbert Hoover called the territory an "effective poorhouse" during a 1931 visit—until the rise of tourism in the late 1950s and 1960s. With tourism came economic improvements coupled with an influx of residents from other Caribbean islands and the mainland, but St. Croix depends partly on industries like the huge oil refinery outside Frederiksted to provide employment.

Today, suburban subdivisions fill the fields where sugarcane once waved in the tropical breeze. Condominium complexes line the beaches along the north coast outside Christiansted. Homes that are more elaborate dot the rolling hillsides. Modern strip malls and shopping centers sit along major roads, and it's as easy to find a McDonald's as it is Caribbean fare.

Although St. Croix sits definitely in the 21st century, with only a little effort you can easily step back into the island's past.

Where to Stay

You can find everything from plush resorts to simple beachfront digs in St. Croix. If you sleep in either the Christiansted or Frederiksted area, you'll be closest to shopping, restaurants, and nightlife. Most of the is-

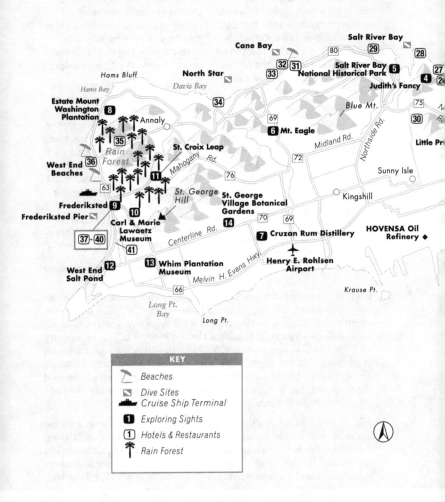

St. Croix

↑
TO
ST. THOMAS

Cane Bay

Salt River Bay

Salt River Bay
National Historical Park

Judith's Fancy

Hams Bluff

North Star

Hams Bay

Davis Bay

Blue Mt.

Estate Mount
Washington
Plantation **8**

Annaly

6 Mt. Eagle

Little Pr

35

34

Midland Rd.

Rain
Forest

St. Croix Leap

Mahogany Rd.

76

Northside Rd.

30

West End
Beaches **36**

11

Sunny Isle

63

St. George
Hill

St. George
Village Botanical
Gardens

Kingshill

Frederiksted **9**

Frederiksted Pier

10

14

Cruzan Rum Distillery **7**

HOVENSA Oil
Refinery ◆

Carl & Marie
Lawaetz
Museum

37–**40**

41

Centerline Rd.

70

69

12

13 Whim Plantation
Museum

Henry E. Rohlsen
Airport

West End
Salt Pond

Melvin H. Evans Hwy.

Krause Pt.

66

Long Pt.
Bay

Long Pt.

KEY

- Beaches
- Dive Sites
- Cruise Ship Terminal
- **1** Exploring Sights
- **1** Hotels & Restaurants
- Rain Forest

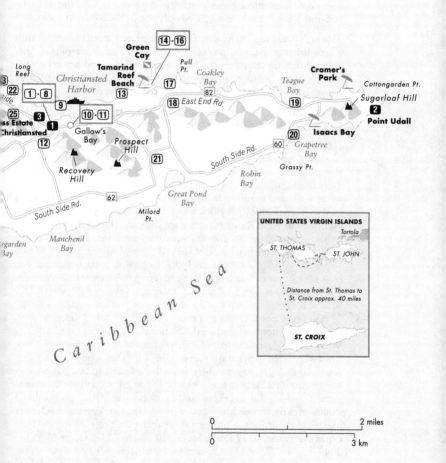

Buck
Island

Buck Island Reef
National Monument

Long
Reef

Christiansted
Harbor

Green
Cay

Tamarind
Reef Beach

Pull
Pt.

Coakley
Bay

Teague
Bay

Cramer's
Park

Cottongarden Pt.

Sugarloaf Hill

Point Udall

82

East End Rd.

Isaacs Bay

Estate
Christiansted

Gallow's
Bay

Prospect
Hill

South Side Rd.

60

Grapetree
Bay

Grassy Pt.

Recovery
Hill

Robin
Bay

62

Great Pond
Bay

South Side Rd.

Milord
Pt.

Manchenil
Bay

garden
ay

Caribbean Sea

UNITED STATES VIRGIN ISLANDS

Tortola

ST. THOMAS   ST. JOHN

Distance from St. Thomas to
St. Croix approx. 40 miles

ST. CROIX

0   2 miles

0   3 km

land's other hotels will put you just steps from the beach. St. Croix has several small but special properties that offer personalized service. If you like all the comforts of home, you may prefer to stay in a condominium or villa. Room rates on St. Croix are competitive with those on other islands, and if you travel off-season, you'll find substantially reduced prices. Many properties offer money-saving honeymoon and dive packages. Whether you stay in a hotel, a condominium, or a villa, you'll enjoy up-to-date amenities. Most properties have room TVs, but at some bed-and-breakfasts there might be only one in the common room.

Although a stay right in historic Christiansted may mean putting up with a little urban noise, you probably won't have trouble sleeping. Christiansted rolls up the sidewalks fairly early, and air-conditioners drown out any noise. Solitude is guaranteed at hotels and inns outside Christiansted and those on the outskirts of sleepy Frederiksted.

For approximate costs, *see* the dining and lodging price chart on the U.S. Virgin Islands Planner, at the beginning of this chapter.

Hotels

CHRISTIANSTED
$$
Hotel Caravelle. Near the harbor, at the waterfront end of a pleasant shopping arcade, the Caravelle's in-town location puts you just steps away from shops and restaurants. Rooms are tasteful and tropical, with white walls and floral-print bedspreads and curtains; most have ocean views. A small pool provides a swimming and sunning option. The ever-popular Rum Runners restaurant sits just off the lobby. Although its location provides city conveniences, use your normal prudence when walking back to the hotel at night. ⊠ *44A Queen Cross St., 00820* ☎ *340/ 773–0687 or 800/524–0410* 🖷 *340/778–7004* ⊕ *www.hotelcaravelle. com* ⤶ *43 rooms, 1 suite* 🖒 *In-room: refrigerator, ethernet, Wi-Fi. In-hotel: restaurant, bar, pool, public Internet, no elevator* ⊟ *AE, D, DC, MC, V* ¶◎¶ *EP.*

$–$$
Pink Fancy Hotel. Offering a connection to the island's elegant past, the venerable hotel is listed on the National Register of Historic Places. While the building dates from 1780, it did not become a hotel until 1948. Rooms are filled with antiques, mahogany furnishings, and Oriental carpets, and lush gardens meander around the fenced-in compound, creating a comfortable base for folks who like to get out and about. Guests gather poolside for breakfast and conversation. Although the hotel shines brightly, its neighborhood is run-down, so take a taxi back after nighttime excursions. Continental breakfast isn't offered for the least expensive rooms. ⊠ *27 Prince St., 00820* ☎ *340/773–8460 or 800/524– 2045* 🖷 *340/773–6448* ⊕ *www.pinkfancy.com* ⤶ *12 rooms* 🖒 *In-room: kitchen, dial-up. In-hotel: no elevator, public Wi-Fi, no-smoking rooms* ⊟ *AE, MC, V* ¶◎¶ *CP.*

$
Hotel on the Cay. Hop on the free ferry to reach this casual spot on an island in the middle of Christiansted Harbor. Although the location sounds a bit inconvenient, the ferry ride takes no time at all. The captain zips over to the waterfront whenever he sees someone waiting. Rooms are pleasantly furnished and have harbor views, balconies or patios, and kitchenettes for times when you don't want to eat at the hotel's restaurant. In addition to sunning at the small beach and strolling

the lushly planted grounds, you can try windsurfing and other water sports. Keep an eye out for one of the endangered St. Croix ground lizards that call the island home. ⊠ *Protestant Cay 00820-4441* ☎ *340/773–2035 or 800/524–2035* ⎙ *340/773–7046* ⊕ *www.hotelonthecay. com* ⇆ *53 rooms* ♨ *In-room: kitchen, In-hotel: restaurant, pool, beachfront, water sports, no elevator, public Internet, public Wi-Fi* ▭ *AE, D, MC, V* ℩◉℩ *EP.*

$ ▥ **King Christian Hotel.** A stay at the King Christian puts you right in the heart of Christiansted's historic district. Parts of the building date back to the mid-1700s, but numerous additions and refurbishments have brought it up to modern standards. Rooms are a bit on the pedestrian side, but floral spreads and pastel walls brighten things up considerably. We recommend this hotel for its location. You can hop a ferry to nearby Protestant Cay for an afternoon at the beach when you tire of the pool. Out the front door and you're a quick walk to restaurants, shops, and water-sports excursions. ⊠ *57 King St., Box 24467, 00824-0467* ☎ *340/773–6330 or 800/524–2012* ⎙ *340/773–9411* ⊕ *www.kingchristian. com* ⇆ *39 rooms* ♨ *In-room: safe (some), refrigerator. In-hotel: pool, diving* ▭ *AE, MC, V* ℩◉℩ *EP.*

OUTSIDE
CHRISTIANSTED
$
Fodor'sChoice
★

▥ **Carringtons Inn.** Hands-on owners Claudia and Roger Carrington are the real reason to stay here, and they conjure up delicious breakfasts—rum-soaked French toast is a house specialty—dole out advice, and make you feel right at home. Formerly a private home, the comfy bed-and-breakfast is a 10-minute drive from Christiansted. Each room is different, with a decorating theme that reflects a namesake flower. Wicker furniture, handwoven carpets, and balconies in some rooms, colorful spreads, and sea or pool views create an inviting atmosphere. The hillside suburban location means you need a rental car if you stay. ⊠ *4001 Estate Hermon Hill, Christiansted 00820* ☎ *340/713–0508 or 877/658–0508* ⎙ *340/719–0841* ⊕ *www.carringtonsinn.com* ⇆ *5 rooms* ♨ *In-room: kitchen (some), refrigerator, no TV. In-hotel: pool, no elevator, public Internet, no-smoking rooms* ▭ *AE, MC, V* ℩◉℩ *BP.*

EAST END
♨ $$$–$$$$

▥ **The Buccaneer.** Offering a total resort experience just outside of Christiansted, this property has sandy beaches, swimming pools, and extensive sports facilities. A palm-tree-lined main drive leads to the large, pink main building atop a hill; the rest of the resort sits on the grounds of a 300-acre former sugar plantation, where shops, restaurants, and guest quarters are scattered about the manicured lawns. Spacious rooms are Mediterranean in style, with tile floors, four-poster beds, massive wardrobes of pale wood, marble baths, and local works of art. Beachside doubloon rooms are the largest and are steps from the beach, but you can be perfectly comfortable no matter where you stay. All rooms are stocked with hair dryers, irons, and a nice selection of toiletries. ⊠ *Rte. 82, Box 25200, Shoys 00824* ☎ *340/712–2100 or 800/255–3881* ⎙ *340/712–2104* ⊕ *www.thebuccaneer.com* ⇆ *138 rooms* ♨ *In-room: safe, refrigerator, Wi-Fi (some). In-hotel: 4 restaurants, bar, golf course, tennis courts, pools, gym, spa, beachfront, water sports, children's programs (ages 4–12), no elevator, public Internet, no-smoking rooms* ▭ *AE, D, MC, V* ℩◉℩ *BP.*

⏱ **$$$–$$$$** 🏨 **Chenay Bay Beach Resort.** The beachfront location and complimentary tennis and water-sports equipment make this resort a real find, particularly for families with active kids. Refurbishment projects have upgraded nearly all the rooms, which have ceramic-tile floors, bright peach or yellow walls, rattan furnishings, and front porches. Gravel paths meander among terraced wood or stucco cottages. Other facilities include a large L-shape pool, a protected beach, a picnic area, and a casual restaurant. There's also a shuttle to grocery stores and shopping areas for a reasonable fee. ⊠ *Rte. 82, Green Cay* ⊕ *Box 24600, Christiansted 00824* ☎ *340/773–2918 or 800/548–4457* 🖷 *340/773–6665* ⊕ *www.chenaybay.com* 🛏 *50 rooms* ⟐ *In-room: kitchen, dial-up. In-hotel: restaurant, bar, tennis courts, pool, beachfront, water sports, no elevator, children's programs (ages 4–12), public Wi-Fi* ⊟ *AE, D, MC, V* ⧖ *EP.*

$$$–$$$$ 🏨 **Divi Carina Bay Resort.** An oceanfront location puts most rooms at the Divi Carina Bay Resort close to the beach, but the villas are across the road, behind the main building. Because it has the island's only casino and regular evening entertainment, this resort is your best choice if you enjoy nonstop nightlife. The rooms have rattan and wicker furniture, white-tile floors, sapphire-and-teal linens, and accessories that complement the creamy white walls. Although its location way out on the island's East End puts you a long way from anywhere, the hotel provides a fair amount of activities to keep you busy. If you still have some energy left after dancing the night away, you'll need a car for treks around the island. ⊠ *25 Rte. 60, Estate Turner Hole 00820* ☎ *340/773–9700 or 877/773–9700* 🖷 *340/773–9479* ⊕ *www.divicarina.com* 🛏 *146 rooms, 2 suites, 20 villas* ⟐ *In-room: safe, refrigerator, dial-up, Wi-Fi (some). In-hotel: 2 restaurants, bars, tennis courts, pool, gym, beachfront, water sports, public Internet, public Wi-Fi* ⊟ *AE, D, DC, MC, V* ⧖ *EP.*

$–$$$$ 🏨 **Tamarind Reef Hotel.** Spread out along a small, sandy beach, these motel-like buildings offer casual comfort. Independent travelers who want the option to eat in or out will enjoy the rooms with basic kitchenettes. The spacious modern rooms have rattan furniture, tropical-print fabrics, and either a terrace or a deck with views of St. Croix's sister islands to the north. Snorkelers can explore a nearby reef, but shallow water makes serious swimming difficult. There's a snack bar just off the beach, and the Galleon Restaurant is next door at Green Cay Marina. ⊠ *5001 Tamarind Reef, off Rte. 82, Annas Hope 00820* ☎ *340/773–4455 or 800/619–0014* 🖷 *340/773–3989* ⊕ *www.usvi.net/hotel/tamarind* 🛏 *39 rooms* ⟐ *In-room: refrigerator, Wi-Fi. In-hotel: restaurant, pool, water sports, no elevator, no-smoking rooms* ⊟ *AE, DC, MC, V* ⧖ *EP.*

FREDERIKSTED 🏨 **Sandcastle on the Beach.** Right on a gorgeous stretch of white beach,
$–$$$$ this hotel caters primarily to gay men and lesbians, but anyone is welcome. The hotel has a tropical charm that harks back to a simpler time in the Caribbean; proximity to Frederiksted's interesting dining scene is also a plus. Rooms, which have contemporary decor, tile floors, and bright fabrics, come in several sizes and locations. All have kitchens or kitchenettes, and most have sea views. Packages that include a car and bar privileges are a good value. Although some people bring their kids, the hotel caters more to singles and couples, especially during the win-

ter season. ✉ *127 Smithfield, Rte. 71, Frederiksted 00840* ☎ *340/772–1205 or 800/524–2018* 🖷 *340/772–1757* ⊕ *www.sandcastleonthebeach.com* 🛏 *8 rooms, 8 suites, 5 villas* ♿ *In-room: no phone, safe, kitchen (some), VCRs (some). In-hotel: restaurant, pools, gym, beachfront, water sports, no elevator, laundry facilities, public Internet, public Wi-Fi* ▭ *AE, D, MC, V* ⦿ *CP.*

$ 🏨 **Frederiksted Hotel.** The Frederiksted Hotel offers basic but comfortable waterfront rooms in this sleepy town. If you want a laid-back atmosphere steps from a handful of interesting restaurants and a shop or two, it's a decent choice. Rooms along Strand Street have lovely water views; others overlook the pool. Although the area is perfect for strolling during the day, a few streets inland the neighborhood turns seedy, so use caution at night. Lovely beaches are a short drive away. ✉ *442 Strand St., Frederiksted 00840* ☎ *340/772–0500* ☎ *800/595–9519* ⊕ *www.frederikstedhotel.com* 🛏 *40 rooms* ♿ *In-room: refrigerator, Wi-Fi (some). In-hotel: restaurant, pool, no elevator.* ▭ *AE, D, DC, MC, V.*

NORTH SHORE   🏨 **Villa Greenleaf.** This spacious B&B is all about the details—four-poster
$$$ beds with elegant duvets, towels folded just so, hand-stenciled trim on
Fodor's Choice   the walls, and gardens tastefully planted. Staying here is like visiting a
★   well-heeled relative who happens to have a home in the Caribbean. The house was built in the 1950s but was totally renovated in 2004. You'll want to spend your days gazing at the lovely view of St. Croix's north shore or relaxing beside the sparkling pool, but a car is included in the rates for trips around the island. ✉ *Island Center Rd., Montpelier* ⊡ *Box 675, Christiansted 00821* ☎ *340/719–1958 or 888/282–1001* 🖷 *340/772–5425* ⊕ *www.villagreenleaf.com* 🛏 *6 rooms* ♿ *In-room: refrigerator, no TV, Wi-Fi. In-hotel: pool, no elevator, public Wi-Fi* ▭ *AE, D, MC, V* ⦿ *BP.*

$$–$$$ 🏨 **The Palms at Pelican Cove.** A 10-minute drive from Christiansted's interesting shopping and eclectic restaurants, this resort has a gorgeous strand of white sand at its doorstep. The rooms are fresh with floral accents that reflect the tropics. You need a car if you plan to venture beyond the hotel's gates, but the Hibiscus Beach Hotel, next door, gives you a nearby dinner option besides the excellent Elizabeth's Restaurant at the hotel. ✉ *Off Rte. 752, La Grande Princesse 00820* ☎ *340/778–8920 or 800/548–4460* 🖷 *340/778–9218* ⊕ *www.palmsatpelicancove.com* 🛏 *40 rooms* ♿ *In-room: safe, refrigerator, dial-up. In-hotel: restaurant, tennis courts, pool, beachfront, water sports, no elevator, public Wi-Fi* ▭ *AE, MC, V* ⦿ *EP.*

$$ 🏨 **Cane Bay Reef Club.** These modestly sized lodgings sit seaside in the peaceful community of Cane Bay. They're perfect for folks who don't need every amenity but want to be right at the water's edge. All the rooms in the two-story buildings have no-frills kitchenettes, the usual rattan furniture with tropical accents, and balconies or porches that put you almost on the beach. You can rent dive gear nearby to explore St. Croix's famous Cane Bay Wall. ✉ *Rte. 80, Cane Bay* ⊡ *Box 1407, Kingshill 00851* ☎ *340/778–2966* ☎ *800/253–8534* ⊕ *www.canebay.com* 🛏 *9 units* ♿ *In-room: kitchen. In-hotel: restaurant, pool, no elevator, public Internet* ▭ *AE, D, DC, MC, V* ⦿ *EP.*

$$ ⊞ **Hibiscus Beach Hotel.** This hotel is on a lovely beach, which is the best reason to stay here. Rooms, each named for a tropical flower, show obvious wear and tear, but all have spacious balconies and are decorated with brightly colored fabrics. Bathrooms are clean but nondescript—both the shower stalls and the vanity mirrors are on the small side. You'll need a car to get around, as the surrounding neighborhood isn't a great place for walking. ⊠ *4131 Estate La Grande Princesse, off Rte. 752, La Grande Princesse 00820-4441* ☎ *340/773–4042 or 800/442–0121* 🖷 *340/773–7668* ⊕ *www.hibiscusbeachresort.com* ➲ *37 rooms* ⌂ *In-room: safe, refrigerator, dial-up. In-hotel: restaurant, pool, beachfront, water sports, no elevator, public Internet, public Wi-Fi* ⊟ *AE, D, MC, V* ⦿| *CP.*

$$ ⊞ **Renaissance Carambola Beach Resort.** We like this resort's stellar beachfront setting and peaceful ambience. As of this writing the hotel has just finished a massive renovation and was being reflagged under the Renaissance brand. The refurbished rooms are lovely, with attractive palm-themed accessories that match the resort's atmosphere. Rooms are spread over 25 two-story red-roof villas with ocean or garden views. All have terra-cotta floors, ceramic lamps, mahogany ceilings and furnishings, and rocking chairs. Each has a patio and a huge bath (shower only). Lushly planted walkways connect the rooms and the hotel's restaurants and pool. ⊠ *Rte. 80, Davis Bay* ⬧ *Box 3031, Kingshill 00851* ☎ *340/778–3800 or 888/503–8760* 🖷 *340/778–1682* ⊕ *www.marriott.com* ➲ *151 rooms* ⌂ *In-room: safe, kitchen (some), dial-up. In-hotel: 3 restaurants, tennis courts, pool, gym, beachfront, diving, water sports, no elevator, public Internet, public Wi-Fi* ⊟ *AE, D, DC, MC, V* ⦿| *EP.*

$–$$ ⊞ **Inn at Pelican Heights.** If you don't mind renting a car to explore the island, a stay at this comfortable B&B will make you feel as if you're leaving the rest of the world far behind. The buildings ramble over the hillside, providing sea views and a comfortable ambience. Each room is a bit different, though all have typical tropical decor—brightly colored spreads and wicker or rattan furniture. Enjoy elaborate breakfasts that might include anything from breakfast lasagna to pancakes with fruit and sausage. You can walk to the spacious beach at Pelican Cove in 10 minutes. If you need a dose of civilization, Christiansted is a 15-minute drive away. ⊠ *Off Rte. 751, 4201 Estate St. John, Christiansted 00820-4491* ☎ *340/713–8022 or 888/445–9458* 🖷 *340/713–8526* ⊕ *www.innatpelicanheights.com* ➲ *5 rooms* ⌂ *In-room: kitchen. In-hotel: pool, no elevator, public Internet* ⊟ *MC, V* ⦿| *BP.*

$–$$ ⊞ **Villa Margarita.** This quiet retreat is along a tranquil north-shore beach, about 20 minutes from Christiansted's shops and restaurants. It provides a particularly good base if you want to admire the dramatic views of the windswept coast. You'll want to rent a car to explore the island, as the resort's amenities are limited. Units vary in size but come complete with kitchenettes, tropical furnishings, private balconies, and those spectacular views. Swimming in front of the hotel is a bit difficult because of shallow water, but sandy beaches are steps away. The snorkeling nearby is excellent. ⊠ *Off Rte. 80, Salt River* ⬧ *9024 Salt River, Christiansted 00820* ☎ *340/713–1930 or 866/274–8811* 🖷 *340/719–3389* ⊕ *www.villamargarita.com* ➲ *3 units* ⌂ *In-room: no phone,* *kitchen, refrigerator. In-hotel: pool, no elevator, no kids under 17* 🚪 *MC, V* ⦿ *EP.*

$–$$ 🏨 **Waves at Cane Bay.** St. Croix's famed Cane Bay Wall is just offshore from this resort, giving it an enviable location. It's a good bet for divers, as there's a dive shop just down the road. Although the hotel's stretch of beach is rocky, you can sunbathe at a small patch of sand beside the pool, which has been carved from the coral along the shore. Two peach-and-mint-green buildings house large, balconied rooms decorated with soft pastel prints. The only drawback is the isolation; you definitely need a car if you stay here. ⊠ *Rte. 80, Cane Bay* 🖃 *Box 1749, Kingshill 00851* ☎ *340/778–1805 or 800/545–0603* 🖷 *340/778–4945* ⊕ *www. canebaystcroix.com* 🛏 *12 rooms* △ *In-room: safe, kitchen, Wi-Fi. In-hotel: restaurant, bar, pool, water sports, no elevator* 🚪*AE, MC, V* ⦿*EP.*

Condominiums & Villas

In addition to several condo and villa complexes, you can also rent a private home—usually for a week or more. Renting a house gives you the convenience of home as well as top-notch amenities. Many have pools, hot tubs, and deluxe furnishings. Most companies meet you at the airport, arrange for a rental car, and provide helpful information.

If you want to be close to the island's restaurants and shopping, look for a villa or condominium in the hills above Christiansted or on either side of the town. An East End location gets you out of Christiansted's hustle and bustle, but you're still only 15 minutes from town. North Shore locations are lovely, with gorgeous sea views and lots of peace and quiet.

Caribbean Property Management (☎ 340/778–8782 or 800/496–7379 ⊕ www.enjoystcroix.com) has a supply of villas on the east end. **Rent A Villa** (☎ 800/533–6863 ⊕ www.rentavillavacations.com) specializes in villas on the island's east end. **Vacation St. Croix** (☎ 340/778–0361 or 877/ 788–0361 ⊕ www.vacationstcroix.com) has villas all around the island.

🛎 $$–$$$$ 🏨 **Sugar Beach.** With all the conveniences of home, Sugar Beach has apartments that are immaculate and breezy. Each has a full kitchen and a large patio or balcony with an ocean view; larger units have washers and dryers. Though the exteriors of these condos are drab beige stucco, the interiors are white with tropical furnishings. The pool occupies the ruins of a 250-year-old sugar mill. A lovely beach is just steps away, and Christiansted's conveniences are an easy 10-minute drive. It's one of a string of condominium complexes near a public-housing project, so don't walk in the neighborhood at night. ⊠ *Rte. 752, Estate Golden Rock 00820* ☎ *340/773–5345 or 800/524–2049* 🖷 *340/773–1359* ⊕ *www. sugarbeachstcroix.com* 🛏 *46 apartments* △ *In-room: kitchen. In-hotel: tennis courts, pool, beachfront, no elevator, public Internet, public Wi-Fi* 🚪 *AE, D, MC, V* ⦿ *EP.*

🛎 $$–$$$ 🏨 **Club St. Croix.** Sitting beachfront just outside Christiansted, this modern condominium complex faces a lovely sandy beach. You have easy access to shopping and restaurants in nearby Christiansted, but you need a car to get there. Breezes restaurant provides full meal service if you tire of cooking in your fully equipped kitchen. Spacious condos come in different sizes: studios, one-, and two-bedrooms; all have balconies or patios. Rooms are modern, with rattan furniture and bright accents. The location near public housing doesn't encourage strolls through the neighborhood. ⊠ *Rte. 752, Estate Golden Rock 00824* ☎ *340/773–9150 or 800/524–2025* 🖷 *340/778–4009* ⊕ *www.antillesresorts.com* ⇱ *53 apartments* ⚘ *In-room: kitchen, dial-up, Wi-Fi. In-hotel: restaurant, tennis courts, pool, beachfront, no elevator, public Internet, public Wi-Fi* ☱ *AE, MC, V* ⑩ *EP.*

★ $$–$$$ 🏠 **Villa Madeleine.** If you like privacy and lovely accommodations, we think you'll like Villa Madeline. The two-story units flow downhill from this condominium resort's centerpiece, a West Indian plantation greathouse. Each villa has a full kitchen and a private pool. The decor evokes the property's natural surroundings: rattan furniture with plush cushions, rocking chairs, and, in some, bamboo four-poster beds. Special touches include pink-marble showers and hand-painted floral wall borders. You definitely need a car for sightseeing and dining out. ⊠ *Off Rte. 82, Teague Bay* 🕾 *Box 24212, Christiansted 00822* ☎ *340/277–3303 or 888/786–8784* ⊕ *www.villamadeleine-stcroix.com* ⇱ *43 villas* ⚘ *In-room: kitchen. In-hotel: tennis court, pools, no elevator* ☱ *AE, MC, V* ⑩ *EP.*

☝ $$ 🏠 **Colony Cove.** In a string of condominium complexes, Colony Cove lets you experience comfortable beachfront living. Units all have two bedrooms, two bathrooms, and washer/dryer combos, making it a good choice for families. They have typical tropical furnishings with most furniture made of rattan and wicker. Floors are tile. The neighborhood isn't the best, so don't plan on strolling too far at night. ⊠ *Rte. 752, Estate Golden Rock 00824* ☎ *340/773–1965 or 800/524–2025* ⊕ *www.antillesresorts.com* ⇱ *62 apartments* ⚘ *In-room: kitchen, dial-up, Wi-Fi. In-hotel: pool, beachfront, no elevator, public Wi-Fi* ☱ *AE, MC, V* ⑩ *EP.*

WHERE TO CAMP ⛰ **Mount Victory Camp.** A remarkable quietude distinguishes this out-of-the-way spread on 8 acres in the island's rain forest. If you really want to commune with nature, you'll be hard-pressed to find a better way to do it on St. Croix. Hosts Bruce and Mathilde Wilson are on hand to explain the environment. You sleep in screened-in tent–cottages perched on a raised platform and covered by a roof. Each has electricity and a rudimentary outdoor kitchen. The shared, spotlessly clean bathhouse is an easy stroll away. The location feels remote, but a lovely sand beach and the Sunset Grill restaurant are a 2-mi (3-km) drive down the hill. In another 10 minutes you're in Frederiksted. ⚘ *Flush toilets, drinking water, showers, picnic tables, public telephone* ⇱ *5 tents* ⊠ *Creque Dam Rd., Frederiksted 00841* ☎ *340/772–1651 or 866/772–1651* ⊕ *www.mtvictorycamp.com* 🛏 *$85–$95* 🕾 *Reservations essential* ☱ *No credit cards.*

Where to Eat

Seven flags have flown over St. Croix, and each has left its legacy in the island's cuisine. You can feast on Italian, French, and American dishes; there are even Chinese and Mexican restaurants in Christiansted. Fresh local seafood is plentiful and always good; wahoo, mahimahi, and conch are most popular. Island chefs often add Caribbean twists to familiar dishes. For a true island experience, stop at a local restaurant for goat stew, curried chicken, or fried pork chops. Regardless of where you eat, your meal will be an informal affair. As is the case everywhere in the Caribbean, prices are higher than you'd pay on the mainland. Some restaurants may close for a week or two in September or October, so if you are traveling during these months it's best to call ahead.

For approximate costs, *see* the dining and lodging price chart on the U.S. Virgin Islands Planner, at the beginning of this chapter.

Christiansted

CARIBBEAN
¢–$$
✕ **Harvey's.** The dining room is plain, even dowdy, and plastic lace tablecloths constitute the sole attempt at decor—but who cares? The food is delicious. Daily specials, such as mouthwatering goat stew and tender whelks in butter, served with big helpings of rice, fungi, and vegetables, are listed on the blackboard. Genial owner Sarah Harvey takes great pride in her kitchen, bustling out from behind the stove to chat and urge you to eat up. ⊠ *11B Company St.* ☎ *340/773–3433* ▤ *No credit cards* ◷ *Closed Sun. No dinner.*

CONTINENTAL
★ $$$–$$$$
✕ **Kendricks.** The chef at this open-air restaurant—a longtime favorite among locals—conjures up creative contemporary cuisine. To start, try the Alaskan king crab cakes with lemon–black pepper aioli or the warm chipotle pepper with garlic and onion soup. Move on to the house specialty: pecan-crusted roast pork loin with ginger mayonnaise. ⊠ *21–32 Company St.* ☎ *340/773–9199* ▤ *MC, V* ◷ *Closed Sun. No lunch.*

★ ☺
$$–$$$$
✕ **Rum Runners.** The view is as stellar as the food at this highly popular local standby. Sitting right on Christiansted Boardwalk, Rum Runners serves everything, including a to-die-for salad of crispy romaine lettuce and tender grilled lobster drizzled with a lemongrass vinaigrette. More hearty fare includes baby back ribs cooked with the restaurant's special spice blend and Guinness stout. ⊠ *Hotel Caravelle, 44A Queen Cross St.* ☎ *340/773–6585* ▤ *AE, MC, V.*

★ $$–$$$$
✕ **Savant.** Savant is one of those small but special spots that locals love. The cuisine is a fusion of Mexican, Thai, and Caribbean—an unusual combination that works surprisingly well. You can find anything from vegetables in a red curry sauce to enchiladas stuffed with chicken to maple-teriyaki pork tenderloin coming out of the kitchen. With 20 tables crammed into the indoor area and small courtyard, this little place can get crowded. Call early for reservations. ⊠ *4C Hospital St.* ☎ *340/713–8666* ▤ *AE, DC, MC, V* ◷ *No lunch. Closed Sun.*

★ $$–$$$
✕ **Restaurant Bacchus.** On the chic side, this restaurant is as notable for its extensive wine list as it is for its food. The menu changes regularly but often includes favorites like chopped tuna in a soy-sesame dressing served over crispy wontons. Entrées include local lobster and fresh fish, steak swimming in mushroom sauce, and pasta with Parmesan cheese and truffle oil. For dessert, try the rum-drenched sourdough-bread pudding. ⊠ *Queen Cross St., off King St.* ☎ *340/692–9922* ▤ *AE, D, DC, MC, V* ◷ *Closed Mon. No lunch.*

ECLECTIC
¢–$
✕ **Anna's Café.** Stop by this cozy spot in a popular shopping center for light fare. Lunch runs to wraps and sandwiches filled with veggies, cheeses, and sliced meats. If you can't decide, try the restaurant's famous

chicken salad, or a personal-sized pizza. For breakfast, the chef cooks up waffles, croissants, and eggs cooked any way you like. Smoothies are a house specialty. ☒ *Gallows Bay Market Pl.* ☎ *340/773–6620* ▭ *No credit cards* ☉ *Closed Sun. No dinner.*

¢–$ ✕ **Avocado Pitt.** Locals gather at this Christiansted waterfront spot for the breakfast and lunch specials as well as for a bit of gossip. Breakfast runs to stick-to-the-ribs dishes like oatmeal and pancakes. Lunches include such dressed-up basics as the Yard Bird on a Bun, a chicken breast sandwich tarted up with a liberal dose of hot sauce. The yellowfin tuna sandwich is made from fresh fish and gives a new taste to a standard lunchtime favorite. ☒ *King Christian Hotel, 59 Kings Wharf* ☎ *340/ 773–9843* ▭ *AE, D, MC, V* ☉ *No dinner.*

FRENCH   ✕ **Café Christine.** A favorite with the professionals who work in down-
★ $–$$ town Christiansted, Café Christine's presentation is as dazzling as the food. The small menu changes daily, but look for dishes like shrimp salad drizzled with a lovely vinaigrette or a vegetarian plate with quiche, salad, and lentils. Desserts are perfection. If the pear pie topped with chocolate is on the menu, don't hesitate. This tiny restaurant has both air-conditioned indoor tables and an outside porch that overlooks historic buildings. ☒ *Apothecary Hall Courtyard, 4 Company St.* ☎ *340/ 713–1500* ▭ *No credit cards* ☉ *Closed weekends. No dinner.*

ITALIAN   ✕ **Tutto Bene.** Its muraled walls, brightly striped cushions, and painted
$$–$$$$ trompe-l'oeil tables make Tutto Bene look more like a sophisticated Mexican cantina than an Italian cucina. One bite of the food, however, will clear up any confusion. Written on hanging mirrors is the daily menu, which includes such specialties as veal saltimbocca, a scallopine of veal with prosciutto and sage, all topped with mozzarella and Parmesan cheeses. Desserts, including a decadent tiramisu, are on the menu as well. ☒ *Hospital St. in Boardwalk shopping center* ☎ *340/773–5229* ▭ *AE, MC, V* ☉ *No lunch.*

Outside Christiansted

ECLECTIC   ✕ **Breezez.** This aptly named restaurant is poolside at Club St. Croix
☾ $$–$$$$ condominiums. Visitors and locals are drawn by its reasonable prices and good food. This is *the* place on the island to be for Sunday brunch, where the menu includes Caesar salad, burgers, and blackened prime rib with Cajun seasonings and a horseradish sauce. For dessert, try the flourless chocolate torte—a wedge of rich chocolate served with a river of chocolate sauce. ☒ *Club St. Croix, 3220 Golden Rock, off Rte. 752, Golden Rock* ☎ *340/773–7077* ▭ *AE, D, MC, V.*

$$–$$$ ✕ **Elizabeth's.** With a lovely beachfront location and stellar food, this
FodorsChoice   restaurant has developed quite a following. Dinner entrées include a tasty
★   vegetable napolean filled with grilled vegetables and drizzled with an herb cream sauce. Lunch brings out lots of locals for the generous helping of curried chicken salad and a crab cake wrapped in a flavorful tortilla. The piquant horseradish sauce adds a tasty touch. ☒ *The Palms at Pelican Cove, Off Rte. 752, Estate Princesse* ☝ *4126 La Grand Princesse, Christiansted, St. Croix* ☎ *340/719–0735* ▭ *AE, D, MC, V* ☉ *No lunch weekends.*

East End

AMERICAN-
CASUAL
☺ $-$$

✕ **Cheeseburgers in Paradise.** A perennial favorite with local and visiting families, this open-air restaurant in the middle of a field serves up terrific ribs smothered in a spicy house sauce, burgers with toppings that run from mushrooms to fried onions, and, of course, cheeseburgers. There's room for kids to run around before dinner. ✉ *Rte. 82, Southgate* ☎ *340/773–1119* ▭ *MC, V.*

ECLECTIC
$$$-$$$$

✕ **The Galleon.** This popular dockside restaurant is always busy. Start with the Caesar salad or perhaps a flaky layered duck napoleon. The chef's signature dish is a tender filet mignon topped with fresh local lobster. Pasta lovers should sample the linguine with grilled salmon, toasted hazelnuts, cherry tomatoes, and a Frangelico cream sauce. Take Route 82 out of Christiansted; then turn left at the sign for Green Cay Marina. ✉ *Annas Hope* ☎ *340/773–9949* ▭ *MC, V.*

$$-$$$

✕ **The Deep End.** A favorite with locals and vacationers, this poolside restaurant serves up terrific crab-cake sandwiches, London broil with onions and mushrooms, fresh local fish, and delicious pasta in various styles. To get here from Christiansted, take Route 82 and turn left at the sign for Green Cay Marina. ✉ *Tamarind Reef Hotel, Annas Hope* ☎ *340/713–7071* ▭ *MC, V.*

$$-$$$

✕ **South Shore Café.** This casual bistro, popular with locals for its good food, sits on the island's south shore near the Great Salt Pond. The restaurant's menu includes dishes drawn from several different cuisines. Meat lovers and vegetarians can find common ground with a menu that ranges from handmade pasta to prime rib. The selection isn't extensive, but the chef puts together a blackboard full of specials every day. ✉ *Southside Rd. near Great Pond* ☎ *340/773–9311* ▭ *MC, V* ☉ *Closed Mon. and Tues. No lunch.*

Frederiksted

ECLECTIC
★ $$$-$$$$

✕ **Blue Moon.** This terrific little bistro, which has a loyal local following, offers a changing menu that draws on Cajun and Caribbean flavors. Try the spicy gumbo with andouille sausage or crab cakes with a spicy aioli for your appetizer. Chicken, shrimp, sausage, and peppers served over pasta makes a good entrée. The Almond Joy sundae should be your choice for dessert. There's live jazz on Friday. ✉ *7 Strand St.* ☎ *340/772–2222* ▭ *AE, D, MC, V* ☉ *Closed Mon.*

☺ ¢-$

✕ **Turtles Deli.** Eat outside at this tiny spot just as you enter downtown Frederiksted. Lunches are as basic as a corned beef on rye or as imaginative as "The Raven" (turkey breast with bacon, tomato, and melted cheddar cheese on French bread). Also good is "The Beast," named after the grueling hill that challenges bikers in the annual triathlon. It's piled high with hot roast beef, raw onion, and melted Swiss cheese with horseradish and mayonnaise. Early risers stop by for cinnamon buns and espresso. ✉ *625 Strand St., at Prince Passage* ☎ *340/772–3676* ▭ *No credit cards* ☉ *Closed Sun. No dinner.*

FRENCH
$$-$$$$

✕ **Le St. Tropez.** A ceramic-tile bar and soft lighting set the mood at this Mediterranean-style bistro tucked into a courtyard one street from the waterfront. Seated either inside or on the adjoining patio, you can enjoy grilled meats in delicate sauces. The menu changes daily, often taking advantage of local seafood. The fresh basil, tomato, and mozzarella salad is heavenly. ⊠ *227 King St.* ☎ *340/772–3000* ▭ *AE, MC, V* ⊙ *Closed Sun. No lunch Sat.*

Outside Frederiksted

🖐 **$$$** ✕ **Sunset Grill.** As you would expect, this alfresco restaurant is a hot spot for sunset watchers, as well as a social hub for locals. The ever-changing menu features fish, fish, and more fish. Try the almond-crusted grouper in a soy-butter sauce or whatever else the chef whipped up that day. Those who aren't fond of fish can pick from dishes like a rib-eye steak for dinner; on the lunch menu is a buffalo burger. Desserts might include fresh blueberries and strawberries in a rum sauce. It's about 2 km (1 mi) north of Frederiksted. ⊠ *Rte. 63* ☎ *340/772–5855* ▭ *MC, V* ⊙ *Closed Mon.*

North Shore

ECLECTIC ✕ **Off the Wall.** Divers fresh from a plunge at the north shore's popular
¢–$$$ Cane Bay Wall gather at this breezy spot on the beach. If you want to sit a spell before you order, a hammock beckons. Burgers, deli sandwiches, and steak sandwiches make up most of the menu. ⊠ *Rte. 80, Cane Bay* ☎ *340/778–4771* ▭ *AE, MC, V.*

Beaches

★ **Buck Island.** A visit to this island beach, part of Buck Island Reef National Monument, is a must. The beach is beautiful, but its finest treasures are those you can see when you plop off the boat and adjust your mask, snorkel, and fins to swim over colorful coral and darting fish. Exceptionally warm water in the summer of 2005 damaged the coral, so you won't see it at its finest for some years to come. To get here you have to charter a boat or go on an organized trip. Don't know how to snorkel? No problem—the boat crew will have you outfitted and in the water in no time. Take care not to step on those black-pointed spiny sea urchins or touch the mustard-color fire coral, which can cause a nasty burn. Most charter-boat trips start with a snorkel over the lovely reef before a stop at the island's beach. An easy 20-minute hike leads uphill to an overlook for a bird's-eye view of the reef below. Find restrooms at the beach. Buck Island is 5 mi (8 km) north of St. Croix.

Cane Bay. The waters aren't always gentle at this breezy north-shore beach, but there are seldom many people around, and the scuba diving and snorkeling are wondrous. You can see elkhorn and brain corals, and less than 200 yards out is the drop-off called Cane Bay Wall. Cane Bay can be an all-day destination. You can rent kayaks and snorkeling and scuba gear at water-sports shops across the road, and a couple of very casual restaurants beckon when the sun gets too hot. The beach has no public restrooms. ⊠ *Rte. 80, about 4 mi (6 km) west of Salt River.*

West End Beaches. There are several unnamed beaches along the coast road north of Frederiksted, but it's best if you don't stray too far from civilization. For safety's sake, most vacationers plop down their towel near one of the very casual restaurants spread out along Route 63. The beachfront Sunset Grill makes a nice spot for lunch. The beach at the Rainbow Beach Club, a five-minute drive outside Frederiksted, has a bar, a casual restaurant, water sports, and volleyball. If you want to be close to the cruise-ship pier, just stroll on over to the adjacent sandy beach in front of Fort Frederik. On the way south out of Frederiksted, the stretch near Sandcastle on the Beach hotel is also lovely. ⊠ *Rte. 63, north and south of Frederiksted.*

Sports & the Outdoors

BOAT TOURS   Almost everyone takes a day trip to Buck Island aboard a charter boat. Most leave from the Christiansted waterfront or from Green Cay Marina and stop for a snorkel at the island's eastern end before dropping anchor off a gorgeous sandy beach for a swim, a hike, and lunch. Sailboats can often stop right at the beach; a larger boat might have to anchor a bit farther offshore. A full-day sail runs about $90, with lunch included on most trips. A half-day sail costs about $60. **Big Beard's Adventure Tours** (☎ 340/773–4482 ⊕ www.bigbeards.com) takes you on catamarans, either the *Renegade* or the *Flyer,* from the Christiansted waterfront to Buck Island for snorkeling before dropping anchor at a private beach for a barbecue lunch. **Caribbean Sea Adventures** (☎ 340/773–2628 ⊕ www.caribbeanseaadventures.com) departs from the Christiansted waterfront for half- and full-day trips on various boats. The **Teroro Charters** (☎ 340/773–3161 ⊕ www.visitstcroix.com/captainheinz.html) trimaran *Teroro II* leaves Green Cay Marina for full- or half-day sails. Bring your own lunch.

DIVING &   At **Buck Island,** a short boat ride from Christiansted or Green Cay Marina, the reef is so nice that it's been named a national monument. You
SNORKELING   can dive right off the beach at **Cane Bay,** which has a spectacular drop-off called the Cane Bay Wall. Dive operators also do boat trips along the Wall, usually leaving from Salt River or Christiansted. **Frederiksted Pier** is home to a colony of sea horses, creatures seldom seen in the waters of the Virgin Islands. At **Green Cay,** just outside Green Cay Marina in the east end, you can see colorful fish swimming around the reefs and rocks. Two exceptional north-shore sites are **North Star** and **Salt River,** which you can reach only by boat. At Salt River you can float downward through a canyon filled with colorful fish and coral.

The island's dive shops take you out for one- or two-tank dives. Plan to pay about $65 for a one-tank dive and $85 for a two-tank dive, including equipment and an underwater tour. All companies offer certification and introductory courses called resort dives for novices.

Which dive outfit you pick usually depends on where you're staying. Your hotel may have one on-site. If not, others are located close by. If you use the hotel's dive operation, you're just a short stroll away from the dock. Where the dive boat goes on a particular day depends on the weather, but in any case, all St. Croix's dive sites are special. All shops are affiliated with PADI, the Professional Association of Diving Instructors.

If you're staying in Christiansted, **Dive Experience** (⊠ 1111 Strand St., Christiansted ☎ 340/773–3307 or 800/235–9047 ⊕ www.divexp.com) has PADI five-star status and runs trips to the north-shore walls and reefs in addition to offering the usual certification and introductory classes.

St. Croix Ultimate Bluewater Adventures (✉ Queen Cross St., Christiansted ☎ 340/773–5994 or 877/567–1367 ⊕ www.stcroixscuba.com) can take you to your choice of more than 75 sites; it also offers a variety of packages that include hotel stays.

Folks staying in the Judith's Fancy area are closest to **Anchor Dive Center** (✉ Salt River Marina, Rte. 801, Salt River ☎ 340/778–1522 or 800/532–3483 ⊕ www.anchordivestcroix.com). The company also has facilities at the Buccaneer hotel. Anchor takes divers to more than 35 sites, including the wall at Salt River Canyon.

Cane Bay Dive Shop (✉ Rte. 80, Cane Bay ☎ 340/773–9913 or 800/338–3843 ⊕ www.canebayscuba.com) is the place to go if you want to do a beach dive or boat dive along the north shore. The famed Cane Bay Wall is 150 yards from the five-star PADI facility. This company also has shops at Pan Am Pavilion in Christiansted, on Strand Street in Frederiksted, at the Carambola Beach Resort, and at the Divi Carina Bay hotel.

In Frederiksted, **Scuba Shack** (✉ Frederiksted Beach, Rte. 631, Frederiksted ☎ 340/772–3483 or 888/789–3483 ⊕ www.stcroixscubashack.com) takes divers right off the beach near the Changes in Latitude restaurant, on night dives off the Frederiksted Pier, or on boat trips to wrecks and reefs. **Scuba West** (✉ 330 Strand St., Frederiksted ☎ 340/772–3701 or 800/352–0107 ⊕ www.divescubawest.com) runs trips to reefs and wrecks from its base in Frederiksted but specializes in showing divers the sea horses that live around the Frederiksted Pier.

FISHING Since the early 1980s, some 20 world records—many for blue marlin—have been set in these waters. Sailfish, skipjack, bonito, tuna (allison, blackfin, and yellowfin), and wahoo are abundant. A charter runs about $100 an hour per person, with most boats going out for four-, six-, or eight-hour trips. **Caribbean Sea Adventures** (✉ 59 Kings Wharf, Christiansted ☎ 340/773–2628 ⊕ www.caribbeanseaadventures.com) will take you out on a 38-foot powerboat called the *Fantasy.*

GOLF St. Croix's courses welcome you with spectacular vistas and well-kept greens. Check with your hotel or the tourist board to determine when major celebrity tournaments will be held. There's often an opportunity to play with the pros. The **Buccaneer** (✉ Rte. 82, Shoys ☎ 340/712–2144 ⊕ www.thebuccaneer.com) has an 18-hole course that is close to Christiansted and is the centerpiece of the hotel. Greens fees are $70, not including $20 for a cart rental. The spectacular 18-hole course at **Carambola Golf Club** (✉ Rte. 80, Davis Bay ☎ 340/778–5638 ⊕ www.golfcarambola.com), in the northwest valley, was designed by Robert Trent Jones, Sr. It sits near Carambola Beach Resort. Greens fees are $79 for 18 holes, which includes the use of a golf cart. The **Reef Golf Course** (✉ Teague Bay ☎ 340/773–8844), a public course on the island's east end, has 9 holes. Greens fees are $20, and cart rental is $15.

HIKING Although you can set off by yourself on a hike through a rain forest or along a shore, a guide will point out what's important and tell you why. **Ay-Ay Eco Hike & Tours Association** (✉ Box 2435, Kingshill 00851 ☎ 340/772–4079), run by Ras Lumumba Corriette, takes hikers up hill and down dale in some of St. Croix's most remote places, including the rain

1

forest and Mount Victory. Some hikes include stops at places like the Carl and Marie Lawaetz Museum and old ruins. The cost is $40 to $50 per person for a three- or four-hour hike. There's a three-person minimum. A jeep tour through the rain forest runs $120 per person.

HORSEBACK RIDING Well-kept roads and expert guides make horseback riding on St. Croix pleasurable. At Sprat Hall, just north of Frederiksted, Jill Hurd runs **Paul & Jill's Equestrian Stables** (⊠ Rte. 58, Frederiksted ☎ 340/772–2880 or 340/772–2627 ⊕ www.paulandjills.com). She will take you clip-clop-ping through the rain forest, across the pastures, along the beaches, and over the hilltops—explaining the flora, fauna, and ruins on the way. A 1½-hour ride costs $75.

KAYAKING **Caribbean Adventure Tours** (⊠ Columbus Cove Marina, Rte. 80, Salt River ☎ 340/778–1522 ⊕ www.stcroixkayak.com) takes you on trips through Salt River Bay National Historical Park and Ecological Preserve, one of the island's most pristine areas. All tours run $45. **Virgin Kayak Tours** (⊠ Rte. 80, Cane Bay ☎ 340/778–0071) runs guided kayak trips through the Salt River and rents kayaks so you can tour around the Cane Bay area by yourself. All tours run $45. Kayak rentals are $15 an hour or $40 for the entire day.

SIGHTSEEING TOURS **St. Croix Safari Tours** (☎ 340/773–6700 ⊕ www.gotostcroix.com/safaritours) offers van tours of St. Croix. Excursions depart from Christiansted and last about five hours. Costs run from $45 per person, including admission fees to attractions.

St. Croix Transit (☎ 340/772–3333) offers van tours of St. Croix. Tours depart from Carambola Beach Resort, last about three hours, and cost from $35 per person plus admission fees to attractions.

TENNIS The public courts in Frederiksted and out east at Cramer Park are in questionable shape. It's better to pay a fee and play at one of the hotel courts. Costs vary by resort, but count on paying up to $8 an hour per person. The **Buccaneer** (⊠ Rte. 82, Shoys ☎ 340/773–3036) has eight courts (two lighted), plus a pro and a full tennis shop. **Carambola Beach Resort** (⊠ Rte. 80, Davis Bay ☎ 340/778–3800) has four lighted courts. **Chenay Bay Beach Resort** (⊠ Rte. 82, Green Cay ☎ 340/773–2918) has two lighted courts. **Club St. Croix** (⊠ Rte. 752, Estate Golden Rock ☎ 340/773–4800) has three lighted courts.

WINDSURFING St. Croix's trade winds make windsurfing a breeze. Most hotels rent Wind-surfers and other water-sports equipment to nonguests. **St. Croix Water-sports** (⊠ Hotel on the Cay, Protestant Cay, Christiansted ☎ 340/773–7060 ⊕ www.stcroixwatersports.com) offers Windsurfer rentals, sales, and rides; parasailing; and water-sports equipment such as kayaks. Renting a Windsurfer runs about $25 an hour.

Shopping

Areas & Malls

Although the shopping on St. Croix isn't as varied or extensive as that on St. Thomas, the island does have several small stores with unusual merchandise. In Christiansted the best shopping areas are the **Pan Am**

Pavilion and **Caravelle Arcade,** off Strand Street, and along **King** and **Company streets.** These streets give way to arcades filled with boutiques. **Gallows Bay** has a blossoming shopping area in a quiet neighborhood. St. Croix shop hours are usually Monday through Saturday 9 to 5, but there are some shops in Christiansted open in the evening. Stores are often closed on Sunday.

The best shopping in Frederiksted is along **Strand Street** and in the side streets and alleyways that connect it with **King Street.** Most stores close Sunday except when a cruise ship is in port. One caveat: Frederiksted has a reputation for muggings, so for safety's sake stick to populated areas of Strand and King streets, where there are few—if any—problems.

Specialty Items

ART   **Maria Henle Studio.** Stunning paintings by Maria Henle hang on the walls, but you can also find prints by her father, the late Fritz Henle. He was an acclaimed St. Croix photographer, whose works chronicle St. Croix's recent history. ⊠ *55 Company St., Christiansted* ☎ *340/773-7376.*

BOOKS   **Undercover Books.** For Caribbean books or the latest good read, try this bookstore across from the post office in the Gallows Bay shopping area. ⊠ *5030 Anchor Way, Gallows Bay* ☎ *340/719-1567.*

CLOTHING   **Coconut Vine.** Pop into this store at the start of your vacation, and you'll
Fodor'sChoice   leave with enough comfy cotton or rayon batik men's and women's clothes
★   to make you look like a local. Although the tropical designs and colors originated in Indonesia, they're perfect for the Caribbean. ⊠ *1111 Strand St., Christiansted* ☎ *340/773-1991.*

From the Gecko. Come here for the hippest clothes on St. Croix, including superb hand-painted sarongs and other items. ⊠ *1233 Queen Cross St., Christiansted* ☎ *340/778-9433.*

Hot Heads. Hats, hats, and more hats perch on top of cotton shifts, comfortable shirts, and other tropical wear at this small store. If you forgot your bathing suit, this store has a good selection. ⊠ *Kings Alley Walk, Christiansted* ☎ *340/773-7888.*

Pacificotton. Round out your tropical wardrobe with something from this store. Shifts, tops, and pants in Caribbean colors as well as bags and hats fill the racks. ⊠ *1110 Strand St., Christiansted* ☎ *340/773-2125.*

Quiet Storm. With brands that include Tommy Bahama, Tori Richard, Roxy, and Quick Silver, shop here for upmarket resort wear and beach accessories. ⊠ *1108 King St., Christiansted* ☎ *340/773-7703.*

FOODSTUFFS   If you've rented a condominium or a villa, you'll appreciate St. Croix's excellent stateside-style supermarkets. Fresh vegetables, fruits, and meats arrive frequently. Try the open-air stands strung out along Route 70 for island produce.

Cost-U-Less. This warehouse-type store doesn't charge a membership fee. It's east of Sunny Isle Shopping Center. ⊠ *Rte. 70, Sunny Isle* ☎ *340/719-4442.*

Plaza Extra. Shop here for Middle Eastern foods in addition to the usual grocery-store items. ⊠ *United Shopping Plaza, Rte. 70, Sion Farm* ☎ *340/778-6240* ⊠ *Rte. 70, Mount Pleasant* ☎ *340/719-1870.*

Pueblo. This stateside-style market has branches all over the island. ✉ *Orange Grove Shopping Center, Rte. 75, Christiansted* ☎ *340/773–0118* ✉ *Villa La Reine Shopping Center, Rte. 75, La Reine* ☎ *340/778–1272.*

Schooner Bay Market. Although it's on the smallish side, Schooner Bay has good-quality deli items. ✉ *Rte. 82, Mount Welcome* ☎ *340/773–3232.*

GIFTS **Gone Tropical.** Whether you're looking for inexpensive souvenirs of your trip or a special gift, you can probably find it here. On her travels about the world, Margo Meacham keeps her eye out for special delights for her shop—from tablecloths and napkins in bright Caribbean colors to carefully crafted wooden birds. ✉ *5 Company St., Christiansted* ☎ *340/773–4696.*

Many Hands. Pottery in cool and bright colors, paintings of St. Croix and the Caribbean, prints, and maps—all made by local artists—make perfect take-home gifts. The owners ship all over the world if your purchase is too cumbersome to carry. ✉ *21 Pan Am Pavilion, Strand St., Christiansted* ☎ *340/773–1990.*

Mitchell-Larsen Studio. Carefully crafted glass plates, sun-catchers, and more grace the shelves of this interesting store. All made on-site by two St. Croix glassmakers, the pieces are often whimsically adorned with tropical fish, flora, and fauna. ✉ *58 Company St., Christiansted* ☎ *340/719–1000.*

Fodor'sChoice **Royal Poinciana.** This attractive shop is filled with island seasonings and
★ hot sauces, West Indian crafts, bath gels, and herbal teas. Shop here for tablecloths and paper goods in tropical brights. ✉ *1111 Strand St., Christiansted* ☎ *340/773–9892.*

Tesoro. The colors are bold and the merchandise eclectic at this crowded store. Shop for metal sculptures made from retired steel pans, mahogany bowls, and hand-painted place mats in bright tropical colors. ✉ *36C Strand St., Christiansted* ☎ *340/773–1212.*

Tradewinds Shop. Whatever the wind blew in seems to land here. Glass sailboats glide across the shelves while metal fish sculptures swim nearby. Candles with tropical motifs, note cards, and costume jewelry jostle for space with Naot sandals. ✉ *53 King St., Christiansted* ☎ *340/719–3918.*

HOUSEWARES **St. Croix Landmarks Museum Store.** If a mahogany armoire or cane-back rocker catches your fancy, the staff will arrange to have it shipped to your home at no charge from its mainland warehouse. Furniture aside, this store has one of the largest selections of local art, along with Caribbean-inspired bric-a-brac in all price ranges. ✉ *6 Company St., Christiansted* ☎ *340/713–8102.*

JEWELRY **Crucian Gold.** This store carries the unique gold creations of St. Croix native Brian Bishop. His trademark piece is the Turk's Head ring (a knot of interwoven gold strands), but the chess sets with Caribbean motifs as the playing pieces are just lovely. ✉ *59 Kings Wharf, Christiansted* ☎ *340/773–5241.*

Gold Worker. In silver and gold, the handcrafted jewelry at this tiny store will remind you of the Caribbean. Hummingbirds dangle from silver chains, and sand dollars adorn gold necklaces. The sugar mills in silver and gold speak of St. Croix's past. ✉ *3 Company St., Christiansted* ☎ *340/773–5167.*

ib Designs. This small shop showcases the handcrafted jewelry of local craftsman Whealan Massicott. In silver and gold, the designs are simply elegant. ⊠ *Company St. at Queen Cross St., Christiansted* ☎ *340/773–4322.*

Nelthropp and Low. Specializing in gold jewelry, this store also carries diamonds, emeralds, rubies, and sapphires. Jewelers will create one-of-a-kind pieces to your design. ⊠ *1102 Strand St., Christiansted* ☎ *340/773–0365 or 800/416–9078.*

Sonya's. Sonya Hough invented the hook bracelet, popular among locals as well as visitors. With hurricanes hitting the island so frequently, she has added an interesting decoration to these bracelets: the swirling symbol used in weather forecasts to indicate these storms. ⊠ *1 Company St., Christiansted* ☎ *340/778–8605.*

LIQUOR & TOBACCO **Baci Duty Free Liquor and Tobacco.** A walk-in humidor with a good selection of Arturo Fuente, Partagas, and Macanudo cigars is the centerpiece of this store, which also carries sleek Danish-made watches and Lladró figurines. ⊠ *1235 Queen Cross St., Christiansted* ☎ *340/773–5040.*

Kmart. The two branches of this discount department store—a large one in the Sunshine Mall and a smaller one mid-island at Sunny Isle Shopping Center—carry a huge line of discounted, duty-free liquor. ⊠ *Sunshine Mall, Rte. 70, Frederiksted* ☎ *340/692–5848* ⊠ *Sunny Isle Shopping Center, Rte. 70, Sunny Isle* ☎ *340/719–9190.*

PERFUMES **Violette Boutique.** Perfumes, cosmetics, and skin-care products are the draws here. ⊠ *Caravelle Arcade, 38 Strand St., Christiansted* ☎ *340/773–2148.*

Nightlife & the Arts

The island's nightlife is ever-changing, and its arts scene is eclectic—ranging from Christmastime performances of *The Nutcracker* to any locally organized shows. Folk-art traditions, such as quadrille dancers, are making a comeback. To find out what's happening, pick up the local newspapers—*V. I. Daily News* and *St. Croix Avis*—available at newsstands. Christiansted has a lively and eminently casual club scene near the waterfront. Frederiksted has a couple of restaurants and clubs offering weekend entertainment.

Nightlife

Hotel on the Cay (⊠ Protestant Cay, Christiansted ☎ 340/773–2035) has a West Indian buffet on Tuesday nights in the winter season, when you can watch a broken-bottle dancer (a dancer who braves a carpet of shattered glass) and mocko jumbie characters. Although you can gamble at the island's only casino, it's the nightly music that draws big crowds to **Divi Carina Bay Casino** (⊠ Rte. 60, Estate Turner Hole ☎ 340/773–9700). The **Moonraker** (⊠ 43A Queen Cross St., Christiansted ☎ 340/713–8025) attracts a youthful crowd for DJ music on Wednesday through Saturday night.

Blue Moon (⊠ 7 Strand St., Frederiksted ☎ 340/772–2222), a waterfront restaurant, is the place to be for live jazz on Friday from 9 PM to 1 AM.

The Arts

Sunset Jazz (⊠ Waterfront, Frederiksted ☎ 340/277–0692), has become the hot event in Frederiksted, drawing crowds of both visitors and locals at 6 PM on the third Friday of every month to watch the sun go down and hear good music.

The **Whim Plantation Museum** (⊠ Rte. 70, Estate Whim ☎ 340/772–0598), outside of Frederiksted, hosts classical music concerts in winter.

Exploring St. Croix

Though there are things to see and do in St. Croix's two towns, Christiansted and Frederiksted (both named after Danish kings), there are lots of interesting spots in between them and to the east of Christiansted. Just be sure you have a map in hand (pick one up at rental-car agencies, or stop by the tourist office for an excellent one that's free). Many secondary roads remain unmarked; if you get confused, ask for help.

Numbers in the margin correspond to points of interest on the St. Croix map.

Christiansted & the East

Christiansted is a historic Danish-style town that always served as St. Croix's commercial center. Your best bet is to see the historic sights in the morning, when it's still cool. This two-hour endeavor won't tax your walking shoes and will leave you with energy to poke around the town's eclectic shops. Break for lunch at an open-air restaurant before spending as much time as you like shopping.

An easy drive (roads are flat and well marked) to St. Croix's eastern end takes you through some choice real estate. Ruins of old sugar estates dot the landscape. You can make the entire loop on the road that circles the island in about an hour, a good way to end the day. If you want to spend a full day exploring, you can find some nice beaches and easy walks with places to stop for lunch.

❶ Fodor's Choice ★ **Christiansted.** In the 1700s and 1800s this town was a trading center for sugar, rum, and molasses. Today there are law offices, tourist shops, and restaurants, but many of the buildings, which start at the harbor and go up the gently sloped hillsides, still date from the 18th century. You can't get lost. All streets lead back downhill to the water. If you want some friendly advice, stop by the **Visitor Center** (⊠ 53A Company St. ☎ 340/773–0495) weekdays between 8 and 5 for maps and brochures.

♻ Large, yellow **Fort Christiansvaern** (⊠ Hospital St. ☎ 340/773–1460 ⊕ www.nps.gov/chri) dominates the waterfront. Because it's so easy to spot, it makes a good place to begin a walking tour. In 1749 the Danish built the fort to protect the harbor, but the structure was repeatedly damaged by hurricane-force winds and had to be partially rebuilt in 1771. It's now a national historic site, the best preserved of the few remaining Danish-built forts in the Virgin Islands. The park's visitor center is here. The $3 admission includes the Steeple Building. Rangers are on hand to answer questions. Hours are weekdays 8 to 4:45 and weekends 9 to 4:45.

When you're tired of sightseeing, stop at **D. Hamilton Jackson Park** (⊠ Between Fort Christiansvaern and Danish Customs House)—on the street side of Fort Christiansvaern—for a rest. It's named for a famed labor leader, judge, and journalist who started the first newspaper not under the thumb of the Danish crown (his birthday, November 1, is a territorial holiday celebrated with much fanfare in St. Croix).

Built in 1830 on foundations that date from 1734, the **Danish Customs House** (⊠ King St. ☎ 340/773–1460 ⊕ www.nps.gov/chri), near Fort Christiansvaern, originally served as both a customs house and a post office. In 1926 it became the Christiansted Library, and it's been a national park facility since 1972. It's closed to the public, but the sweeping front steps make a nice place to take a break.

Constructed in 1856, the **Scale House** (⊠ King St. ☎ 340/773–1460 ⊕ www.nps.gov/chri) was once the spot where goods passing through the port were weighed and inspected. Park staffers now sell a good selection of books about St. Croix history and its flora and fauna. The Scale House is open weekdays 8 to 4:30 and weekends 9 to 4:30.

Built by the Danes in 1753, the **Steeple Building** (⊠ Church St. ☎ 340/773–1460) was the first Danish Lutheran church on St. Croix. It's now a national park museum and contains exhibits that document the island's Indian inhabitants. It's worth the short walk to see the building's collection of archaeological artifacts, displays on plantation life, and exhibits on the architectural development of Christiansted, the early history of the church, and Alexander Hamilton, the first secretary of the U.S. Treasury, who grew up in St. Croix. Hours are irregular, so ask at the visitor center. The $3 admission includes Fort Christiansvaern.

The **Post Office Building** (⊠ Church St.), built in 1749, was once the Danish West India & Guinea Company warehouse. It now serves as the park's administrative building. One of the town's most elegant structures, **Government House** (⊠ King St. ☎ 340/773–1404) was built as a home for a Danish merchant in 1747. Today it houses offices. If you're here weekdays from 8 to 4:30, slip into the peaceful inner courtyard to admire the still pools and gardens. A sweeping staircase leads you to a second-story ballroom, still used for official government functions.

★ **Buck Island Reef National Monument** (⊠ Off the north shore of St. Croix ☎ 340/773–1460 ⊕ www.nps.gov/buis) has pristine beaches that are just right for sunbathing, but there's also some shade for those who don't want to fry. The snorkeling trail set in the reef allows close-up study of coral formations and tropical fish. After recovering from the spate of hurricanes that started in 1989, the coral now suffers from a condition called bleaching that leaves the coral white. Exceptionally warm water in 2005 further damaged the reefs. The reefs are expected to recover, but how long it will take is anyone's guess. There's an easy hiking trail to the island's highest point, where you'll be rewarded for your efforts by spectacular views of the reef and St. John. Charter-boat trips leave daily from the Christiansted waterfront or from Green Cay Marina, about 2 mi (3 km) east of Christiansted. Check with your hotel for recommendations.

2 Point Udall. This rocky promontory, the easternmost point in the United States, is about a half-hour drive from Christiansted. A paved road takes you to an overlook with glorious views. More adventurous folks can hike down to the pristine beach below. On the way back, look for the castle, an enormous mansion that can only be described as a cross between a Moorish mosque and the Taj Mahal. It was built by an extravagant recluse known only as the Contessa. It's sometimes a popular spot for vandals. Residents advise taking your valuables with you and leaving your car unlocked so they won't break into your car to look inside. ⌧ *Rte. 82, Et Stykkeland.*

Between Christiansted & Frederiksted

A drive through the countryside between these two towns will take you past ruins of old plantations, many bearing whimsical names (Morningstar, Solitude, Upper Love) bestowed by early owners. The traffic moves quickly—by island standards—on the main roads, but you can pause and poke around if you head down some side lanes. It's easy to find your way west, but driving from north to south requires good navigation. Don't leave your hotel without a map. Allow an entire day for this trip, so you'll have enough time for a swim at a north-shore beach. Although you can find lots of casual eateries on the main roads, pick up a picnic lunch if you plan to head off the beaten path.

7 Cruzan Rum Distillery. A tour of the company's factory, established in 1760, culminates in a tasting of its products, all sold here at bargain prices. It's worth a stop to look at the distillery's charming old buildings even if you're not a rum connoisseur. ⌧ *West Airport Rd., Estate Diamond* ☎ *340/692–2280* ⊕ *www.cruzanrum.com* ☜ *$4* ☾ *Weekdays 9–11:30 and 1–4:15.*

4 Judith's Fancy. In this upscale neighborhood are the ruins of an old greathouse and tower of the same name, both remnants of a circa-1750 Danish sugar plantation. The "Judith" comes from the first name of a woman buried on the property. From the guardhouse at the neighborhood entrance, follow Hamilton Drive past some of St. Croix's loveliest homes. At the end of Hamilton Drive the road overlooks Salt River Bay, where Christopher Columbus anchored in 1493. On the way back, make a detour left off Hamilton Drive onto Caribe Road for a close look at the ruins. The million-dollar villas are something to behold, too. ⌧ *Turn north onto Rte. 751, off Rte. 75.*

3 Little Princess Estate. If the old plantation ruins decaying here and there around St. Croix intrigue you, a visit to this Nature Conservancy project will give you even more of a glimpse into the past. The staff has carved walking paths out of the bush that surrounds what's left of a 19th-century plantation. It's easy to stroll among well-labeled fruit trees and see the ruins of the windmill, the sugar and rum factory, and the laborers' village. This is the perfect place to reflect on St. Croix's agrarian past fueled by the labor of African slaves. ⌧ *Off Rte. 75; turn north at Five Corners traffic light* ☎ *340/773–5575* ☜ *Donations accepted* ☾ *Weekdays 9–5.*

6 Mt. Eagle. At 1,165 feet, this is St. Croix's highest peak. Leaving Cane Bay and passing North Star Beach, follow the coastal road that dips briefly into a forest; then turn left on Route 69. Just after you make the turn, the pavement is marked with the words THE BEAST and a set of giant paw prints. The hill you're about to climb is the famous Beast of the St. Croix Half Ironman Triathlon, an annual event during which participants must cycle up this intimidating slope. ⊠ *Rte. 69.*

5 **Salt River Bay National Historical Park & Ecological Preserve.** This joint national and local park commemorates the area where Christopher Columbus's men skirmished with the Carib Indians in 1493 on his second visit to the New World. The peninsula on the bay's east side is named for the event: Cabo de las Flechas (Cape of the Arrows). Although the park is just in the developing stages, it has several sights with cultural significance. A ball court, used by the Caribs in religious ceremonies, was discovered at the spot where the taxis park. Take a short hike up the dirt road to the ruins of an old earthen fort for great views of Salt River Bay and the surrounding countryside. The area also encompasses a coastal estuary with the largest remaining mangrove forest in the region, a submarine canyon, and several endangered species, including the hawksbill turtle and the roseate tern. A visitor center sits just uphill to the west, but it has irregular hours. The water at the beach can be on the rough side, but it's a nice place for sunning. ⊠ *Rte. 75 to Rte. 80, Salt River* ☎ *340/773–1460* ⊕ *www.nps.gov/sari.*

Frederiksted & Environs

St. Croix's second-largest town, Frederiksted, was founded in 1751. A stroll around its historic sights will take you no more than an hour. Allow a little more time if you want to browse in the few small shops. The area just outside town has old plantations, some of which have been preserved as homes or historic structures that are open to the public.

Caribbean Museum Center for the Arts. Sitting across from the waterfront in a historic building, this small museum hosts an always-changing roster of exhibits. Many are cutting-edge multimedia efforts that you might be surprised to find in such an out-of-the-way location. The openings are popular events, and visitors are welcome. ⊠ *10 Strand St.* ☎ *340/ 772–2622* ⊕ *www.cmcarts.org* ⊠ *$8* ⊙ *Weekdays 10–6, Sat. 10–4.*

☾ On July 3, 1848, 8,000 slaves marched on the red-brick **Fort Frederik** (⊠ Waterfront ☎ 340/772–2021) to demand their freedom. Danish governor Peter von Scholten, fearing they would burn the town to the ground, stood up in his carriage parked in front of the fort and granted their wish. The fort, completed in 1760, houses a number of interesting historical exhibits as well as an art gallery and a display of police memorabilia. It's within earshot of the visitor center. Admission is $3; it's open weekdays 8:30 to 4.

10 **Carl & Marie Lawaetz Museum.** For a trip back in time, tour this circa-1750 farm. Owned by the prominent Lawaetz family since 1896, just after Carl Lawaetz arrived from Denmark, the lovely two-story house is in a valley at La Grange. A Lawaetz family member shows you the four-poster mahogany bed Carl and Marie shared, the china Marie painted, the family portraits, and the fruit trees that fed the family for several generations. Initially a sugar plantation, it was subsequently used to raise cattle and grow produce. ⊠ *Rte. 76, Mahogany Rd., Estate Lit-*

tle La Grange ☎ *340/772–1539* ⊕ *www.stcroixlandmarks.com* ✉ *$8* ⊙ *Tues., Thurs., and Sat. 10–4.*

8 **Estate Mount Washington Plantation.** Several years ago, while surveying the property, the owners discovered the ruins of a sugar plantation beneath the rain-forest brush. The grounds have since been cleared and opened to the public. You can take a self-guided walking tour of the mill, the rum factory, and other ruins. ⊠ *Rte. 63, Mount Washington* ☎ *340/772–1026* ⊙ *Ruins open daily dawn–dusk.*

9 **Frederiksted.** The town is noted less for its Danish than for its Victorian architecture, which dates from after the slave uprising and the great fire of 1878. One long cruise-ship pier juts into the sparkling sea. It's the perfect place to start a tour of this quaint city. The **Visitor Center** (⊠ 200 Strand St. ☎ 340/772–0357), across from the pier, has brochures from numerous St. Croix businesses. You can stop in weekdays from 8 to 5 to view exhibits on St. Croix.

⑪ **St. Croix Leap.** This workshop sits in the heart of the rain forest, about a 15-minute drive from Frederiksted. It sells mirrors, tables, bread boards, and mahogany jewelry boxes crafted by local artisans. ⊠ *Rte. 76, Brooks Hill* ☎ *340/772–0421* ⊙ *Weekdays 9–5, Sat. 10–5.*

⑭ **St. George Village Botanical Gardens.** At this 17-acre estate, lush, fragrant flora grows amid the ruins of a 19th-century sugarcane plantation village. There are miniature versions of each ecosystem on St. Croix, from a semiarid cactus grove to a verdant rain forest. ⊠ *Rte. 70, turn north at sign, St. George* ☎ *340/692–2874* ⊕ *www.sgvbg.org* ✉ *$8* ⊙ *Daily 9–5.*

⑫ **West End Salt Pond.** A bird-watcher's delight, this salt pond attracts a large number of winged creatures, including flamingos. ⊠ *Veteran's Shore Dr., Hesselberg.*

★ ☾ **⑬** **Whim Plantation Museum.** The lovingly restored estate, with a windmill, cook house, and other buildings, will give you a sense of what life was like on St. Croix's sugar plantations in the 1800s. The oval-shape greathouse has high ceilings and antique furniture and utensils. Notice its fresh, airy atmosphere—the waterless stone moat around the greathouse was used not for defense but for gathering cooling air. If you have kids, the grounds are the perfect place for them to stretch their legs, perhaps while you browse in the museum gift shop. It's just outside of Frederiksted. ⊠ *Rte. 70, Estate Whim* ☎ *340/772–0598* ⊕ *www.stcroixlandmarks. com* ✉ *$8* ⊙ *Mon.–Sat. 10–4.*

U.S. VIRGIN ISLANDS ESSENTIALS

To research prices, get advice from other travelers, and book travel arrangements, visit www.fodors.com.

Transportation

BY AIR

One advantage to visiting the USVI is the abundance of nonstop and connecting flights to St. Thomas and St. Croix that can have you at the beach in three to four hours from East Coast airports. Small island-hopper planes and a seaplane connect St. Thomas and St. Croix, and a ferry takes you from St. Thomas to St. John.

American, Continental, Delta, Spirit, United, and US Airways fly to the islands; some flights connect through San Juan, Puerto Rico. Cape Air flies from San Juan; Cape Air has code-share arrangements with all major airlines, so your luggage can transfer seamlessly. Seaborne Airlines flies between St. Thomas, St. Croix, and San Juan.

✈ Airlines **American/American Eagle** ☎ 340/776-2560 in St. Thomas, 340/778-2000 in St. Croix. **Cape Air** ☎ 800/352-0714 ⊕ www.flycapeair.com. **Continental** ☎ 800/231-0856. **Delta** ☎ 340/777-4177. **Seaborne** ☎ 340/773-6442 ⊕ www.seaborneairlines.com. **Spirit** ☎ 800/772-7117 ⊕ www.spiritairlines.com. **United** ☎ 340/774-9190. **US Airways** ☎ 800/622-1015.

✈ Airports **Cyril E. King Airport** ✉ St. Thomas ☎ 340/774-5100 ⊕ www.viport.com. **Henry Rohlsen Airport** ✉ St. Croix ☎ 340/778-1012 ⊕ www.viport.com.

BY BOAT & FERRY

Ferries are a great way to travel around the islands. There's frequent service between St. Thomas and St. John and their neighbors, the BVI. There's something special about spending a day on St. John and then joining your fellow passengers—a mix of tourists, local families, and construction workers on their way home—for a peaceful sundown ride back to St. Thomas.

Ferries to Cruz Bay, St. John, leave St. Thomas from either the Charlotte Amalie waterfront west of the U.S. Coast Guard dock or from Red Hook. From Charlotte Amalie ferries depart at 9, 11, 1, 3, 4, and 5:30. Ferries from Cruz Bay to Charlotte Amalie leave at 7:15, 9:15, 11:15, 1:15, 2:15, and 3:45. The one-way fare for the 45-minute ride is $10. From Red Hook, ferries to Cruz Bay leave at 6:30 AM and 7:30 AM. Starting at 8 AM, they leave hourly until midnight. Returning from Cruz Bay, ferries leave hourly starting at 6 AM until 11 PM. The 15- to 20-minute ferry ride is $5. There is an additional charge of $2 for each piece of luggage.

Car ferries, called barges, run about every hour between Red Hook, St. Thomas, and Cruz Bay, St. John. The ride costs $52 round-trip. Plan to arrive at least 15 minutes before departure.

Reefer is the name given to both of the brightly colored 26-passenger skiffs that run between the Charlotte Amalie waterfront and Marriott Frenchman's Reef hotel every day on the half hour from 8 to 5. It's a good way to beat the traffic (and is about the same price as a taxi) to Morning Star Beach, which adjoins the hotel. And you get a great view of the harbor as you bob along in the shadow of the giant cruise ships anchored in the harbor. The captain may be persuaded to drop you at Yacht Haven, but check first. The one-way fare is $6 per person, and the trip takes about 15 minutes.

There's daily service between either Charlotte Amalie or Red Hook, on St. Thomas, and West End or Road Town, Tortola, BVI, by either Smith's Ferry or Native Son, and to Virgin Gorda, BVI, by Smith's Ferry. The times and days the ferries run change, so it's best to call for schedules once you're in the islands. The fare is $22 one way or $40 round-trip, and the trip from Charlotte Amalie takes 45 minutes to an hour to West End, up to 1½ hours to Road Town; from Red Hook the trip is only a half hour. The twice-weekly 2¼-hour trip from Charlotte Amalie to Virgin Gorda costs $28 one way and $50 round-trip. From Red Hook and Cruz Bay, the boat goes Thursday and Sunday. Prices vary by barge company, but the most you'll pay is $55 round-trip. Three days a week (Friday, Saturday, and Sunday) a ferry operates between Red Hook, Cruz Bay, and Jost Van Dyke in the BVI; the trip takes 45 minutes and costs $50 per person round-trip.

There's also daily service between Cruz Bay, St. John, and West End, Tortola, aboard an Inter-Island Boat Service ferry. The half-hour trip costs $45 round-trip. You need to present proof of citizenship upon entering the BVI; a passport is best, but a birth certificate with a raised seal in addition to a government-issue photo ID will suffice.

🚢 **Inter-Island Boat Service** ☎ 340/776–6597. **Native Son** ☎ 340/774–8685 ⊕ www.nativesonbvi.com. *Reefer* ☎ 340/776–8500 Ext. 6814 ⊕ www.marriottfrenchmansreef.com. **Smith's Ferry** ☎ 340/775–7292 ⊕ www.smithsferry.com.

BY BUS

On St. Thomas, the island's large buses make public transportation a very comfortable—though slow—way to get from east and west to Charlotte Amalie and back (service to the north is limited). Buses run about every 30 minutes from stops that are clearly marked with VITRAN signs. Fares are $1 between outlying areas and town and 75¢ in town.

Privately owned taxi vans crisscross St. Croix regularly, providing reliable service between Frederiksted and Christiansted along Route 70. This inexpensive ($1.50 one way) mode of transportation is favored by locals, and though the many stops on the 20-mi (32-km) drive between the two main towns make the ride slow, it's never dull. Vitran public buses aren't the quickest way to get around the island, but they're comfortable and affordable. The fare is $1 between Christiansted and Frederiksted or to places in between.

Modern Vitran buses on St. John run from the Cruz Bay ferry dock through Coral Bay to the far eastern end of the island at Salt Pond, making numerous stops in between. The fare is $1 to any point.

BY CAR

Even at a sedate speed of 20 mph (30 kph), driving can be an adventure—for example, you may find yourself slogging behind a slow tourist-packed safari bus at a steep hairpin turn. It's a good idea to give a little beep at blind turns. Note that the general speed limit on these islands is only 25 to 35 mph (40 to 55 kph), which will seem fast enough for you on most roads. A Jeep or Suzuki with four-wheel drive will make it easier to navigate potholed side roads and to get up slick hills when it rains. All the major roads are paved.

Driving is on the left side of the road, British-style (although your steering wheel will be on the left side of the car, American-style). The law requires *everyone* in a car to wear a seat belt: many of the roads are narrow, and the islands are dotted with hills, so there's ample reason to put safety first.

In St. Thomas traffic can get pretty bad, especially in Charlotte Amalie at rush hour (7 to 9 and 4:30 to 6). Cars often line up bumper to bumper along the waterfront. If you need to get from an East End resort to the airport during these times, find the alternate route (starting from the East End, Route 38 to 42 to 40 to 33) that goes up the mountain and then drops you back onto Veterans Highway. If you plan to explore by car, be sure to pick up the latest edition of "Road Map St. Thomas–St. John," which includes the route numbers *and* the names of the roads that are used by locals. It's available anywhere you find maps and guidebooks.

Unlike St. Thomas and St. John, where narrow roads wind through hillsides, St. Croix is relatively flat, and it even has a four-lane highway. The speed limit on the Melvin H. Evans Highway is 55 mph (88 kph) and between 35 to 40 mph (55 to 65 kph) elsewhere. Roads are often unmarked, so be patient—sometimes getting lost is half the fun.

In St. John, use caution. The terrain is very hilly, the roads winding, and the blind curves numerous. You may suddenly come upon a huge safari bus careening around a corner or a couple of hikers strolling along the side of the road. Major roads are well paved, but once you get off a specific route, dirt roads filled with potholes are common. For such driving, a four-wheel-drive vehicle is your best bet.

Gas is expensive on St. Thomas and St. John; expect to pay considerably more than in the United States. But on St. Croix, where the big HOVENSA refinery is located, the prices are much closer to what you might expect to pay stateside.

ST. THOMAS Avis, Budget, and Hertz all have counters at Cyril E. King Airport. Dependable Car Rental offers pickups and drop-offs at the airport and to and from major hotels. Cowpet Rent-a-Car is on the east end of the island. Discount has a location at Bluebeard's Castle hotel. Avis is at the Marriott Frenchman's Reef, Havensight Mall (adjacent to the cruise-ship dock), and Seaborn Airlines terminal on the Charlotte Amalie waterfront; Budget has branches at the Sapphire Beach Resort & Marina and at the Havensight Mall, adjacent to the main cruise-ship dock.

Avis ☎ 340/774-1468. **Budget** ☎ 340/776-5774. **Cowpet Rent-a-Car** ☎ 340/775-7376. **Dependable Car Rental** ☎ 340/774-2253 or 800/522-3076. **Discount** ☎ 340/776-4858. **Hertz** ☎ 340/774-1879.

ST. CROIX Atlas is outside Christiansted but provides pickups at hotels. Avis is at Henry Rohlsen Airport and at the seaplane ramp in Christiansted. Budget has branches at the airport and in the King Christian Hotel in Christiansted. Judi of Croix delivers vehicles to your hotel. Midwest is outside Frederiksted but picks up at hotels. Olympic and Thrifty are outside Christiansted but will pick up at hotels.

Atlas ☎ 340/773-2886 or 800/426-6009. **Avis** ☎ 340/778-9355. **Budget** ☎ 340/778-9636 ⊕ www.budgetstcroix.com. **Judi of Croix** ☎ 340/773-2123 or 877/903-2123 ⊕ www.judiofcroix.com. **Midwest** ☎ 340/772-0438 or 877/772-0438 ⊕ www.

midwestautorental.com. **Olympic** ☎ 340/773-8000 or 888/878-4227 ⊕ www. stcroixcarrentals.com. **Thrifty** ☎ 340/773-7200.

ST. JOHN Best is just outside Cruz Bay near the public library, off Route 10. Cool Breeze is in Cruz Bay across from the Creek. Courtesy is in Cruz Bay next to the police station. Delbert Hill Taxi & Jeep Rental Service is in Cruz Bay across from Wharfside Village, just around the corner from the ferry dock. Denzil Clyne is across from the Creek. O'Connor Jeep is in Cruz Bay at the Texaco Station. St. John Car Rental is across from Wharfside Village shopping center on Bay Street in Cruz Bay. Spencer's Jeep is across from the Creek in Cruz Bay.

🚗 **Best** ☎ 340/693-8177. **Cool Breeze** ☎ 340/776-6588 ⊕ www.coolbreezecarrental. com. **Courtesy** ☎ 340/776-6650 ⊕ www.courtesycarrental.com. **Delbert Hill Taxi & Jeep Rental Service** ☎ 340/776-6637. **Denzil Clyne** ☎ 340/776-6715. **O'Connor Jeep** ☎ 340/776-6343 ⊕ www.oconnorcarrental.com. **St. John Car Rental** ☎ 340/776-6103 ⊕ www.stjohncarrental.com. **Spencer's Jeep** ☎ 340/693-8784 or 888/776-6628.

BY TAXI

USVI taxis don't have meters, but you needn't worry about fare gouging if you check a list of standard rates to popular destinations (required by law to be carried by each driver and often posted in hotel and airport lobbies and printed in free tourist periodicals, such as *St. Thomas–St. John This Week* and *St. Croix This Week*) and settle on the fare before you start out. Fares are per person, not per destination, but drivers taking multiple fares (which often happens, especially from the airport) will charge you a lower rate than if you're in the cab alone.

ST. THOMAS On St. Thomas, taxi vans line up along Havensight and Crown Bay docks when a cruise ship pulls in. If you booked a shore tour, the operator will lead you to a designated vehicle. Otherwise, there are plenty of air-conditioned vans and open-air safari buses to take you to Charlotte Amalie or the beach. The cab fare from Havensight to Charlotte Amalie is $6 if you ride alone or $5 per person if you share a cab; you can, however, make the 1½-mi (2½-km) walk into town in about 30 minutes along the beautiful waterfront. From Crown Bay to town the taxi fare is $5, or $4 per person if you share; it's a 1-mi (1½-km) walk, but the route passes along a busy highway, so it's not advisable. Transportation from Havensight to Magens Bay for swimming is $12 ($10 if you share).

Additionally, taxis of all shapes and sizes are available at various ferry, shopping, resort, and airport areas, and they also respond to phone calls. There are taxi stands in Charlotte Amalie across from Emancipation Garden (in front of Little Switzerland, behind the post office) and along the waterfront. But you probably won't have to look for a stand, as taxis are plentiful and routinely cruise the streets. Walking down Main Street, you'll be asked "Back to ship?" often enough to make you never want to carry another shopping bag.

🚕 **East End Taxi** ☎ 340/775-6974. **Islander Taxi** ☎ 340/774-4077. **VI Taxi Association** ☎ 340/774-4550.

ST. CROIX Taxis, generally station wagons or minivans, are a phone call away from most hotels and are available in downtown Christiansted, at the Henry E. Rohlsen Airport, and at the Frederiksted pier during cruise-ship arrivals.

In Frederiksted all the shops are a short walk away, and you can swim off the beach. Most ship passengers visit Christiansted on a tour; a taxi will cost $24 for one or two people.

Antilles Taxi Service ☎ 340/773-5020. **St. Croix Taxi Association** ☎ 340/778-1088.

ST. JOHN   Taxis meet ferries arriving in Cruz Bay. Most drivers use vans or open-air safari buses. You can find them congregated at the dock and at hotel parking lots. You can also hail them anywhere on the road. You're likely to travel with other tourists en route to their destinations. Paradise Taxi will pick you up if you call, but most of the drivers don't provide that service. If you need one to pick you up at your rental villa, ask the villa manager for suggestions on whom to call or arrange a ride in advance.

Some small cruise ships stop at St. John to let passengers disembark for a day. The main town of Cruz Bay is near the area where the ships drop off passengers. If you want to swim, the famous Trunk Bay is a $6 taxi ride per person from town.

Paradise Taxi ☎ 340/714-7913.

Contacts & Resources

BANKS & EXCHANGE SERVICES

The American dollar is used throughout the territory, just as in the neighboring BVI. If you need to exchange foreign currency, you need to go to the main branch of major banks. All major credit cards and traveler's checks are generally accepted. Some places will take Discover, though it's not as widely accepted as Visa, MasterCard, and American Express.

Each of the islands has several banks. On St. Thomas, First Bank has locations in Market Square, Waterfront, Estate Thomas, Port of $ale, Red Hook, and Tutu. There are waterfront locations for Banco Popular, as well as branches in Hibiscus Alley, Sugar Estate, Fort Mylner, Red Hook, and Altona, a mile east of the airport. Scotia Bank has branches at Havensight Mall, Nisky Center, Tutu Park Mall, and the Waterfront.

St. Croix has branches of Banco Popular in Orange Grove and Sunny Isle shopping centers. V. I. Community Bank is in Orange Grove Shopping Center and in downtown Christiansted. Scotia Bank has branches in Sunny Isle, Frederiksted, Christiansted, and Sunshine Mall.

St. John has two banks. First Bank is one block up from the ferry dock, and Scotia Bank is at the Marketplace on Route 104.

BUSINESS HOURS

Bank hours are generally Monday through Thursday 9 to 3 and Friday 9 to 5; a handful open Saturday 9 to noon. Walk-up windows open at 8:30 on weekdays. Hours vary slightly from branch to branch and island to island.

On St. Thomas, stores on Main Street in Charlotte Amalie are open weekdays and Saturday 9 to 5. The hours of the shops in the Havensight Mall (next to the cruise-ships dock) are the same, though occasionally some stay open until 9 on Friday, depending on how many cruise ships are at the dock. You may also find some shops open on Sunday if cruise ships are in port. Hotel shops are usually open evenings, as well.

St. Croix shop hours are usually Monday through Saturday 9 to 5, but there are some shops in Christiansted open in the evening.

On St. John, store hours run from 9 or 10 to 5 or 6. Wharfside Village and Mongoose Junction shops in Cruz Bay are often open into the evening.

ELECTRICITY

The USVI use the same current as the U.S. mainland—110 volts. European appliances will require adaptors. Since power fluctuations occasionally occur, bring a heavy-duty surge protector (available at hardware stores) if you plan to use your computer.

EMERGENCIES

📶 Coast Guard Marine Safety Detachment ☎ 340/776-3497 in St. Thomas and St. John, 340/772-5557 in St. Croix. Rescue Coordination Center ☎ 787/289-2041 in San Juan, PR.

📶 Emergency Services Air Ambulance Network ☎ 800/327-1966. Ambulance and fire emergencies ☎ 911. Medical Air Services ☎ 340/777-8580 or 800/643-9023. Police emergencies ☎ 911.

📶 Hospital on St. Thomas Roy L. Schneider Hospital & Community Health Center ✉ Sugar Estate, 1 mi [1½ km] east of Charlotte Amalie ☎ 340/776-8311.

📶 Hospitals on St. Croix Gov. Juan F. Luis Hospital and Health Center ✉ 6 Diamond Ruby, north of Sunny Isle Shopping Center on Rte. 79, Christiansted ☎ 340/778-6311. Ingeborg Nesbitt Clinic ✉ 516 Strand St., Frederiksted ☎ 340/772-0260.

📶 Hospital on St. John Myrah Keating Smith Community Health Center ✉ Rte. 10, about 7 mins east of Cruz Bay, Susannaberg ☎ 340/693-8900.

📶 Pharmacies on St. Thomas Doctor's Choice Pharmacy ✉ Wheatley Shopping Center, across from Roy L. Schneider Hospital, Sugar Estate ☎ 340/777-1400 ✉ Medical Arts Complex, off Rte. 30, 1½ mi [2½ km] east of Cyril E. King Airport ☎ 340/774-8988. Havensight Pharmacy ✉ Havensight Mall, Charlotte Amalie ☎ 340/776-1235. Kmart Pharmacy ✉ Tutu Park Mall, Tutu ☎ 340/777-3854.

📶 Pharmacy on St. Croix Kmart Pharmacy ✉ Sunshine Mall, Cane Estate ☎ 340/692-2622.

📶 Pharmacy on St. John Chelsea Drug Store ✉ The Marketplace, Rte. 104, Cruz Bay ☎ 340/776-4888.

📶 Scuba-Diving Emergencies Roy L. Schneider Hospital & Community Health Center ✉ Sugar Estate, 1 mi [1½ km] east of Charlotte Amalie ☎ 340/776-2686.

HOLIDAYS

Public holidays, in addition to the U.S. federal holidays, are: Three Kings Day (Jan. 6); Transfer Day (commemorates Denmark's 1917 sale of the territory to the United States, Mar. 31); Holy Thursday and Good Friday; Emancipation Day (when slavery was abolished in the Danish West Indies in 1848, July 3); Columbus Day and USVI–Puerto Rico Friendship Day (always on Columbus Day weekend); and Liberty Day (honoring David Hamilton Jackson, who secured freedom of the press and assembly from King Christian X of Denmark, Nov. 1).

INTERNET, MAIL & SHIPPING

The main U.S. Post Office on St. Thomas is near the hospital, with branches in Charlotte Amalie, Frenchtown, Havensight, and Tutu Mall;

there are post offices at Christiansted, Frederiksted, Gallows Bay, and Sunny Isle on St. Croix and at Cruz Bay on St. John. Postal rates are the same as if you were in the mainland United States, but Express Mail and Priority Mail aren't as quick.

On St. Thomas, FedEx offers overnight service if you get your package to the office before 5 PM. The FedEx office on St. Croix is in Peter's Rest Commercial Center; try to drop off your packages before 5:30 PM. Shipping services on St. Thomas are also available at Fast Shipping & Communications Nisky Mail Center and at Red Hook Mail Services. On St. John, call for Federal Express pickup.

On St. Thomas, Beans, Bytes & Websites is an Internet café in Charlotte Amalie. East End Secretarial Services offers long-distance dialing, copying, and fax services. At Little Switzerland, there's free Internet access along with an ATM, big-screen TV, telephones, and a bar with cold drinks. Near Havensight Mall, go to Soapy's Station or the Cyber Zone at Port of $ale, where there are 16 computers. Rates for Internet access range from $4 to $6 for 30 minutes to $8 to $12 per hour. On St. Croix, check your e-mail, make phone calls, and buy postage stamps at Strand Street Station Internet Café in Christiansted. Rates run $5 for a half hour of Internet time. On St. John the place to go to check your e-mail is Surf da Web in Cruz Bay and Keep Me Posted in Coral Bay. You'll pay $6 a half hour for Internet service.

Internet Cafes **Beans, Bytes & Websites** ⊠ Royal Dane Mall, behind Tavern on the Waterfront, Charlotte Amalie, St. Thomas ☎ 340/775-5262 ⊕ www.usvi.net/cybercafe. **Cyber Zone** ⊠ Port of $ale, Charlotte Amalie, St. Thomas ☎ 340/714-7743. **East End Secretarial Services** ⊠ Upstairs at Red Hook Plaza, Red Hook, St. Thomas ☎ 340/775-5262. **Keep Me Posted** ⊠ Cocoloba shopping center, Rte. 107, Coral Bay, St. John ☎ 340/775-1727. **Little Switzerland** ⊠ 5 Dronnigens Gade, across from Emancipation Garden, Charlotte Amalie, St. Thomas ☎ 340/776-2010. **Soapy's Station** ⊠ Havensight Mall, above Budget, Charlotte Amalie, St. Thomas ☎ 340/776-7170. **Strand Street Station** ⊠ Pan Am Pavilion, 1102 Strand St., Christiansted, St. Croix ☎ 340/719-6245. **Surf da Web** ⊠ St. John Marketplace, 2nd floor, Cruz Bay, St. John ☎ 340/693-9152 ⊕ www.surfdaweb.com.

Shipping **Fast Shipping & Communications** ⊠ Rte. 30, across from Havensight Mall, Charlotte Amalie, St. Thomas ☎ 340/714-7634. **FedEx** ⊠ Cyril E. King Airport, St. Thomas ☎ 340/777-4140 ⊕ www.fedex.com ⊠ Peter's Rest Commercial Center, Rte. 708, Peter's Rest, St. Croix ☎ 800/463-3339 ⊠ St. John ☎ 800/463-3339. **Nisky Mail Center** ⊠ Nisky Center, Rte. 30, Charlotte Amalie, St. Thomas ☎ 340/775-7055. **Red Hook Mail Services** ⊠ Red Hook Plaza, Rte. 32, 2nd fl., Red Hook, St. Thomas ☎ 340/779-1890.

PASSPORT REQUIREMENTS
Since the U.S. Virgin Islands are a U.S. territory, you won't pass through immigration on arrival if you are coming on a flight from the United States. However, you must still prove citizenship when you head back home regardless of where you are going. So long as you are a U.S. citizen, you will not have to carry a valid passport to visit the U.S. Virgin Islands unless you are flying from another country, including all other Caribbean islands except for St. Croix and Puerto Rico.

SAFETY

Vacationers tend to assume that normal precautions aren't necessary in paradise. They are. Though there isn't quite as much crime here as in large U.S. mainland cities, it does exist. To be safe, keep your hotel or vacation villa door locked at all times, stick to well-lighted streets at night, and use the same kind of street sense that you would in any unfamiliar territory. Don't wander the streets of Charlotte Amalie, Christiansted, or Frederiksted alone at night. If you plan to carry things around, rent a car—not an open-air vehicle—and lock possessions in the trunk. Keep your rental car locked wherever you park. Don't leave cameras, purses, and other valuables lying on the beach while you snorkel for an hour (or even for a minute), whether you're on the deserted beaches of St. John or the more crowded Magens and Coki beaches on St. Thomas. St. Croix has several good but remote beaches outside Frederiksted and on the East End; it's best to visit them with a group rather than on your own.

TAXES

There's no sales tax in the USVI, but there's an 8% hotel-room tax. Most hotels also add a 10% service charge to the bill. The St. John Accommodations Council members ask that hotel and villa guests voluntarily pay a $1 a day surcharge to help fund school and community projects and other good works. Many hotels add additional energy surcharges and the like, so please ask about any additional charges; these are not government-imposed taxes.

TELEPHONES

Phone service to and from the Virgin Islands is up-to-date and efficient. Phone cards are used throughout the islands; you can buy them in several denominations at many retail shops and convenience stores. They must be used in special card phones, which are widely available. Dialing a call to or from the USVI is exactly like dialing one in the rest of the United States. All U.S. calling cards work in the USVI, and most charge domestic long-distance rates. The area code for the USVI is 340.

Cell phones from the U.S. companies Cingular and Sprint work in most locations in the USVI if you have a roaming feature; if you are on St. John's north coast, you may have some difficulties with service, where you may find yourself connected to BoatPhone, a Tortola service. Phones from other companies may work, but only Cingular and Sprint have offices in the USVI. Many cell phone companies treat calls in the USVI just like any other calls in the United States, but be sure to ask; this is not always the case.

TIPPING

Many hotels in the USVI add a 10% to 15% service charge to cover the room maid and other staff. However, some hotels may use part of that money to fund their operations, passing on only a portion of it to the staff. Check with your maid or bellhop to determine the hotel's policy. If you discover you need to tip, give bellhops and porters 50¢ to $1 per bag and maids $1 or $2 per day. Special errands or requests of hotel staff always require an additional tip. At restaurants bartenders and waiters expect a 10%–15% tip, but always check your tab to see whether service is included. Taxi drivers in the USVI get a 15% tip.

VISITOR INFORMATION

🛈 **USVI Division of Tourism** ✉ 78-123 Estate Contant, Charlotte Amalie, St. Thomas 00804 ☎ 340/774-8784 or 800/372-8784 ✉ 53A Company St., Christiansted, St. Croix 00822 ☎ 340/773-0495 ✉ Strand St., Frederiksted, St. Croix 00840 ☎ 340/772-0357 ✉ Henry Samuel St. (next to post office), Cruz Bay, St. John ☎ 340/776-6450 ⊕ www.usvitourism.vi. **Virgin Islands Hotel & Tourism Association** ☎ 340/774-6835 ⊕ www.virgin-islands-hotels.com. **Virgin Islands National Park** ✉ At the Creek, Cruz Bay, St. John 00831 ☎ 340/776-6201 ⊕ www.nps.gov/viis.

WEDDINGS

The Virgin Islands provide a lovely backdrop for a wedding. Many couples opt to exchange vows on a white sandy beach or in a tropical garden. The process is easy but does require advance planning. The U.S. Virgin Islands Department of Tourism publishes a brochure with all the details and relevant contact information; you can also download marriage license applications from the Web site.

You must first apply for a marriage license at the Superior Court; there are offices in St. Thomas (which is also where you apply if you're getting married in St. John) and St. Croix. The fee is $50 for the application and $50 for the license. You have to wait eight days after the clerk receives the application to get married, and licenses must be picked up in person weekdays, though you can apply by mail. To make the process easier, most couples hire a wedding planner. If you plan to get married at a large hotel, most have planners on staff, but if you're staying in a villa, at a small hotel or inn, or are arriving on a cruise ship, you'll have to hire your own. Anne Marie Weddings, a wedding planner on St. John, provides a lovely service.

The wedding planner will help you organize your marriage license application as well as arrange for a location, flowers, music, refreshments, and whatever else you want to make your day special. The wedding planner will also hire a clergyman if you'd like a religious service or a nondenominational officiant if you prefer. Indeed, many wedding planners are licensed by the territory as nondenominational officiants and will preside at your wedding.

🛈 **Superior Court Offices In St. Croix** 🖉 Box 929, Christiansted 00821 ☎ 340/778-9750. **In St. Thomas** 🖉 Box 70, St. Thomas 00804 ☎ 340/774-6680.

🛈 **Wedding Planners Anne Marie Weddings** ✉ 5000 Enighed PMB 7, St. John 00830 ☎ 340/693-5153 or 888/676-5701 ⊕ www.stjohnweddings.com. **Weddings the Island Way** 🖉 Box 11694, St. Thomas 00801 ☎ 340/777-6505 or 800/582-4784 ⊕ www.weddingstheislandway.com.

British Virgin Islands

The Baths

WORD OF MOUTH

"You'll love Tortola. My best advice is to rent a really good Jeep so you can get around the island. The roads are really steep and if you're not used to it, it can be a bit scary at first."

—Coconut

"The Baths at Virgin Gorda are truly a magical spot, but only if you're not sharing them. . . . If you can, choose to go very early in the morning, or in the late afternoon—before and after the crowds."

—Callaloo

WELCOME TO THE BRITISH VIRGIN ISLANDS

NATURE'S LITTLE SECRETS

Most of the 50-some islands, islets, and cays that make up the British Virgin Islands (BVI) are remarkably hilly and volcanic in origin, having exploded from the depths of the sea some 25 million years ago. The exception is Anegada, which is a flat, coral-limestone atoll. Tortola (about 10 square mi/ 26 square km) is the largest member of the chain.

KEY	
🚢	Ferry
🚢	Cruise Ship Terminal

You can still find traces of a primeval rain forest at the top of Sage Mountain, the highest peak in the BVI.

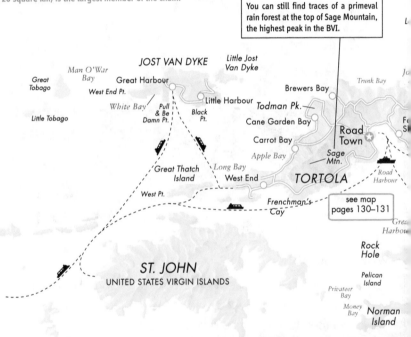

see map
pages 130–131

The British Virgin Islands are mostly quiet and casual, so don't expect to party 'til dawn, and definitely leave the tux at home. Luxury here means getting away from it all rather than getting the trendiest state-of-the-art amenities. And the jackpot is the chance to explore the many islets and cays by sailboat.

2

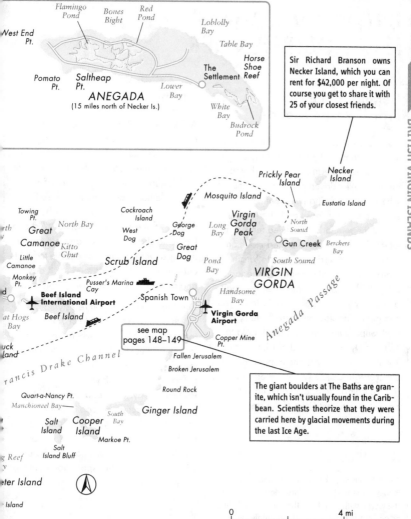

Sir Richard Branson owns Necker Island, which you can rent for $42,000 per night. Of course you get to share it with 25 of your closest friends.

see map
pages 148–149

The giant boulders at The Baths are granite, which isn't usually found in the Caribbean. Scientists theorize that they were carried here by glacial movements during the last Ice Age.

0   4 mi

0   4 km

TOP 4 REASONS TO VISIT THE BRITISH VIRGIN ISLANDS

1. With over 50 islands in the chain, sailors can drop anchor at a different, perfect beach every day.

2. Laid-back luxury resorts offer a full-scale retreat from your everyday life.

3. Diving and snorkeling doesn't get any easier than around Anegada, where vibrant reefs are often just feet from the shore.

4. Your trip isn't complete until you've chilled at the casual beach bars on Jost Van Dyke.

BRITISH VIRGIN ISLANDS PLANNER

Getting to the British Virgin Islands

There are no direct flights to the British Virgin Islands. To fly into Tortola (EIS), you must connect in San Juan or St. Thomas on a propeller-driven plane, regardless of where you are flying from. But it's sometimes just as easy and cheap to use one of the regularly scheduled ferries from either Charlotte Amalie or Red Hook on St. Thomas; these ferries also go to Virgin Gorda, but the only option for Anegada is a flight. The trip to Tortola takes less than an hour. If you're already in St. John, you can get to Tortola from there by ferry as well. Separate ferries go from Tortola to Jost Van Dyke and the other island retreats. You can take a tiny island-hopper flight to either Virgin Gorda (VIJ) or Anegada (NGD) from Tortola, but you'll have to book it directly with one of the small island-based airlines.

Hassle Factor: Medium to High

Activities

The BVI **sailing** scene is one of the best in the world, with Tortola as one of the major charter yacht centers of the Caribbean. It's no wonder that sailing is so popular; most of the best BVI **beaches** are on deserted islands and are accessible only by boat. The most famous beach in the chain is The Baths on Virgin Gorda, which is lined with giant, round boulders that provide for great off-the-beach snorkeling. The **nightlife** center of the region is actually a series of simple beach bars on Jost Van Dyke, but yachties in the know are happy to bop over for a drink and to hear Foxy Callwood sing at his eponymous bar and restaurant. **Diving** and **game-fishing** in these waters are also good.

On the Ground

At Tortola's Beef Island airport, taxis hover at the exit from customs. Fares are officially set but are lower per person for more than three passengers. Figure about $15 for up to three people and $5 for each additional passenger for the 20-minute ride to Road Town, and about $20 to $30 for the 45-minute ride to West End. Expect to share your taxi, and be patient if your driver searches for people to fill his cab—only a few flights land each day, and this could be your driver's only run.

On Virgin Gorda, if you're staying on North Sound, a taxi will take you from the airport to the dock, where your hotel launch will meet you, but be sure to make launch arrangements with your hotel before your arrival. If your destination is Leverick Bay, your land taxi will take you there directly. You can also take the North Sound Express directly from the Beef Island airport to Spanish Town or North Sound. On Anegada, your hotel will organize your transportation from the small airstrip.

Renting a Car

Both Tortola and Virgin Gorda have a number of car-rental agencies. Although taxi service is good, you may wish to rent a car to explore farther afield or try many different beaches (you may need to if you are staying at an isolated resort). On Anegada it's possible to rent a car, but most people rely on taxis for transportation. Jost Van Dyke has a single road, and visitors travel on foot or by local taxi.

Where to Stay

Pick your island carefully because each is different, as are the logistics of getting there. Tortola gives you a wider choice of restaurants, shopping, and resorts. Virgin Gorda has fewer off-resort places to eat and shop, but the resorts themselves are often better, and the beaches are exquisite. Anegada is remote and better suited for divers. Jost Van Dyke has some classic Caribbean beach bars, along with fairly basic accommodations. When you want to be pampered and pampered some more, select a remote resort reached only by ferry, or even one of the appealing outer-island resorts that are still somewhat affordable for mere mortals. If you want to enjoy everything the BVI have to offer, charter a sailboat so you can drop anchor where and when you want.

The largest resort in the British Virgin Islands has 120-some rooms, and most have considerably fewer. Luxury here is more about personal service than over-the-top amenities. The best places are certainly comfortable, but they aren't showy. You'll find villas and condos in abundance, and they are a good option for families.

Hotel & Restaurant Costs

Assume that hotels operate on the European Plan (**EP**—with no meals) unless we specify that they use either the Continental Plan (**CP**—with a Continental breakfast), Breakfast Plan (**BP**—with full breakfast), or the Modified American Plan (**MAP**—with breakfast and dinner). Other hotels may offer the Full American Plan (**FAP**—including all meals but no drinks) or may be All-Inclusive (**AI**—with all meals, drinks, and most activities).

WHAT IT COSTS in Dollars					
	$$$$	**$$$**	**$$**	**$**	**¢**
Restaurants	over $30	$20–$30	$12–$20	$8–$12	under $8
Hotels*	over $350	$250–$350	$150–$250	$80–$150	under $80
Hotels**	over $450	$350–$450	$250–$350	$125–$250	under $125

*EP, BP, CP   **AI, FAP, MAP
Restaurant prices are for a main course excluding 10% service charge. Hotel prices are for two people in a double room in high season and exclude 7% BVI hotel tax, 10% service charge, and meal plans (except at all-inclusives).

When to Go

2

High season doesn't really get into full swing until Christmas and ends sooner (usually by April 1) than on most Caribbean islands. In the off-season, rates can be a third less.

In April, glimpse the colorful spinnakers as sailing enthusiasts gather for the internationally known **BVI Spring Regatta**. In August, try your hand at sport fishing, as anglers compete to land the largest catch at the **BVI Sportfishing Tournament**.

Updated by
Carol M.
Bareuther and
Lynda Lohr

WITH THE SAILS DOWN AFTER A SMOOTH TRIP across Sir Francis Drake Channel, our boat glided into White Bay at Jost Van Dyke for an afternoon of snorkeling and sun. A fresh-from-the-sea lobster dinner followed at a shoreside restaurant. The next day we anchored at Cane Garden Bay on Tortola's north shore for a dinghy ride ashore to listen to some hot music, and the day after that at a remote bay where we were the only boat. Traveling by sea is the way to hop around this archipelago of small islands and tiny cays. If a sailing trip isn't on your horizon, take one of the ferries that connect all the islands except Anegada.

The British Virgin Islands (BVI) are in the midst of transition. Once a collection of about 50 sleepy islands and cays, the British Virgin Islands—particularly the main island of Tortola—now sees huge cruise ships crowding its dock outside Road Town. Shoppers clog the downtown area on busy cruise-ship days, and traffic occasionally comes to a standstill. Even the second-largest island, Virgin Gorda, gets its share of smaller ships anchored off the main village of Spanish Town. Despite this explosive growth in the territory's tourism industry, it's still easy to escape the hubbub. Hotels outside Road Town usually provide a quiet oasis, and those on the other islands can be downright serene.

Each island has a different flavor. Want access to lots of restaurants and shopping? Make Tortola your choice. The largest of the BVIs, it covers 10 square mi (26 square km) and sits only a mile from St. John in the United States Virgin Islands (USVI). If you want to kick back at a small hotel or posh resort, try Virgin Gorda. Sitting nearly at the end of the chain, the 8-square-mi (21-square-km) island offers stellar beaches and a laid-back atmosphere. If you really want to get away from it all, the outermost islands, including Anegada and Jost Van Dyke, will fill the bill. Some of the smallest—Norman, Peter, Cooper, and Necker—are home to just one resort or restaurant. Others remain uninhabited specks on the horizon.

No matter what your choice, the scenery is stunning, with lush mountains meeting sandy beaches on all but nearly flat and reef-fringed Anegada. The warm Caribbean Sea beckons no matter which island you choose. Visitors mainly come to relax, though the number of organized activities is growing. The territory stakes its reputation on sailing, and you will find a number of companies renting bare or crewed charter boats.

Visitors have long visited the BVI, starting with Christopher Columbus in 1493. He called the islands *Las Once Mil Virgines*—the 11,000 Virgins—in honor of the 11,000 virgin companions of St. Ursula, martyred in the 4th century AD. Pirates and buccaneers followed, and then came the British, who farmed the islands until slavery was abolished in 1834. The BVI are still politically tied to Britain, so the queen appoints a royal governor, but residents elect a local Legislative Council. Offshore banking and tourism share top billing in the territory's economy, but the majority of the islands' jobs are tourism-related. Despite the growth, you can usually find a welcoming smile.

TORTOLA

Updated by
Lynda Lohr

Once a sleepy backwater, Tortola is definitely busy these days, particularly when several cruise ships tie up at the Road Town dock. Passengers crowd the streets and shops, and open-air jitneys filled with cruise-ship passengers create bottlenecks on the island's byways. That said, most folks visit Tortola to relax on its deserted sands or linger over lunch at one of its many delightful restaurants. Beaches are never more than a few miles away, and the steep green hills that form Tortola's spine are fanned by gentle trade winds. The neighboring islands glimmer like emeralds in a sea of sapphire. It can be a world far removed from the hustle of modern life, but it simply doesn't compare to Virgin Gorda in terms of beautiful beaches—or even really nice resorts, for that matter.

Where to Stay

Luxury on Tortola is more about a certain state of mind—serenity, seclusion, gentility, and a bit of Britain in the Caribbean—than about state-of-the-art amenities and fabulous facilities. Indeed, don't let a bit of rust on the screen or a chip in the paint mar your appreciation of the ambience. Instead, enjoy getting to know your fellow guests at the island's cozy hotels. Hotels in Road Town don't have beaches, but they do have pools and are within walking distance of restaurants, nightspots, and shops. Accommodations outside Road Town are relatively isolated, but most are on beaches. The Tortola resorts are intimate—only a handful have more than 50 rooms. You will likely spend most of your time outside, so the location, size, or price of a hotel should be more of a factor to you than the decor. Guests are treated as more than just room numbers, and many return year after year. This can make booking a room at popular resorts difficult, even off-season, despite the fact that more than half the island's visitors stay aboard their own or chartered boats.

A few hotels lack air-conditioning, relying instead on ceiling fans to capture the almost constant trade winds. Nights are cool and breezy, even in midsummer, and never reach the temperatures or humidity levels that are common in much of the United States in summer. You may assume that all accommodations listed here have air-conditioning unless we mention otherwise. Remember that some places may be closed during the peak of hurricane season—August through October—to give their owners a much-needed break.

Villas

Renting a villa is growing in popularity. Vacationers like the privacy, the space to get comfortable, and the opportunity to cook their own meals. As everywhere, location counts, so if you want to be close to the beach, opt for a villa on the North Shore. If you want to dine out in Road Town every night, a villa closer to town may be a better bet.

Prices per week during the winter season run from around $2,000 for a one- or two-bedroom villa up to $10,000 for a five-room beachfront villa. Rates in summer are substantially less. Most, but not all, villa managers accept credit cards.

American or British?

Yes, the Union Jack flutters overhead in the tropical breeze, schools operate on the British system, place names have British spellings, Queen Elizabeth II appoints the governor—and the queen's picture hangs on many walls. Indeed, residents celebrate the queen's birthday every June with a public ceremony. You can overhear that charming English accent from a good handful of expats when you're lunching at Road Town restaurants, and you can buy British biscuits—which Americans call cookies—in the supermarkets.

But you can pay for your lunch and the biscuits with American money, because the U.S. dollar is legal tender here. The unusual circumstance is a matter of geography. The practice started in the mid-20th century, when BVI residents went to work in the nearby USVI. On trips home, they brought their U.S. dollars with them. Soon, they abandoned the barter system, and in 1959, the U.S. dollar became the official form of money. Interestingly, the government sells stamps for use only in the BVI that often carry pictures of Queen Elizabeth II and other royalty with the monetary value in U.S. dollars and cents.

The American influence continued to grow when Americans began to open businesses in the BVI because they preferred its quieter ambience to the hustle and bustle of St. Thomas. Inevitably, cable and satellite TV's U.S.-based programming, along with Hollywood-made movies, further influenced life in the BVI. And most goods are shipped from St. Thomas in the USVI, meaning you'll find more American-made Oreos than British-produced Peak Freens on the supermarket shelves.

Areana Villas (⌂ Box 263, Road Town ☎ 284/494–5864 🖷 284/494–7626 ⊕ www.areanavillas.com) represents top-of-the-line properties. Pastel-colored villas with one to six bedrooms can accommodate up to 10 guests. Many have pools, whirlpool tubs, and tiled courtyards.

The St. Thomas–based **McLaughlin-Anderson Luxury Villas** (⌂ 1000 Blackbeard's Hill, Suite 3, St. Thomas, USVI 00802-6739 ☎ 340/776–0635 or 800/537–6246 ⊕ www.mclaughlinanderson.com) manages nearly three dozen properties spread around Tortola. Villas range in size from one to six bedrooms and come with full kitchens and stellar views. Most have pools. The company can hire a chef and stock your kitchen with groceries.

Purple Pineapple Villa Rentals (⌂ 95167 Bermuda Dr., Fernandina Beach, FL 32034 ☎ 904/415–1231 or 866/867–8652 🖷 305/723–0855 ⊕ www.purplepineapple.com) manages seven luxury homes in locations all over the island. Most have pools, hot tubs, and other amenities. Villas range in size from one to six bedrooms.

Hotels & Inns

ROAD TOWN

$$–$$$

🏨 **Moorings-Mariner Inn.** If you enjoy the camaraderie of a busy marina, this inn on the edge of Road Town may appeal to you. It's a hot spot for charter boaters—usually a lively group—heading out for weeklong sails around the islands. Rooms are spacious and have balconies or porches that are perfect for an afternoon's relaxing. All have pastel accents that complement the peach exteriors. ⊠ *Waterfront Dr., Box 139* ☎ *284/ 494–2333 or 800/535–7289* 🖷 *284/494–2226* ➷ *36 rooms, 4 suites* ♨ *In-room: kitchen (some), refrigerator, dial-up. In-hotel: restaurant, bar, pool, diving, no elevator, public Internet* ☰ *MC, V* ⊚⊙ *EP.*

$–$$$ 🏨 **Fort Burt Hotel.** The Fort Burt Hotel surrounds the ruins of an old Dutch fort, giving you a sense of history along with a night's sleep. The hotel attracts many business travelers, who like its location on the fringes of Road Town and the two-line phones and fax machines in the suites and spacious deluxe rooms. Vacationers will enjoy it as well, especially those who think of it as a jumping-off place rather than a place to put down roots. A car will help a great deal in that regard. It's a bit of a hike to Road Town's shopping and restaurants, but there are a couple of stores and eating places right in the neighborhood. ⊠ *Waterfront Dr., Box 3380* ☎ *284/494–2587* 🖷 *284/494–2002* ➷ *11 rooms, 8 suites* ♨ *In-room: kitchen (some), refrigerator, dial-up (some). In-hotel: restaurant, bar, pool, no elevator, public Wi-Fi* ☰ *AE, MC, V* ⊚⊙ *EP.*

$$ 🏨 **Maria's Hotel by the Sea.** Sitting near the water in busy Road Town, Maria's Hotel by the Sea is perfect for budget travelers who want to be near shops and restaurants but who don't need many frills. The least expensive rooms don't have ocean views, but all have bright tropical fabrics and rattan furniture to remind you that you're on an island. ⊠ *Waterfront Dr., Box 2364* ☎ *284/494–2595* 🖷 *284/494–2420* ⊕ *www. mariasbythesea.com* ➷ *41 rooms* ♨ *In-room: refrigerator, dial-up. In-hotel: restaurant, bar, pool, public Wi-Fi* ☰ *AE, MC, V* ⊚⊙ *EP.*

$$ 🏨 **Village Cay Resort & Marina.** If you want to be able to walk to restaurants and shops, you simply can't beat the prime location in the heart of Road Town. It's perfect for charter-yachters who want a night or two in town before heading out to sea, but land-based vacationers like it equally well. Rooms and suites are done in tropical style with tile floors, rattan furniture, and town or marina views. If you're planning on seeing more than Road Town, you'll need a car to get to the beach. Otherwise, a tiny pool will have to suffice for your morning swim. ⊠ *Wickham's Cay I, Box 145* ☎ *284/494–2771* 🖷 *284/494–2773* ⊕ *www.villagecay.com* ➷ *21 rooms* ♨ *In-room: refrigerator, Ethernet. In-hotel: restaurant, bar, pool, spa, no elevator, public Internet, public Wi-Fi* ☰ *AE, MC, V* ⊚⊙ *EP.*

OUTSIDE ROAD TOWN

$$$$ 🏨 **Long Bay Beach Resort.** Although the service draws complaints, the management has been addressing the frosty attitude of some staff members. Long Bay Beach Resort is still Tortola's only choice if you want all the resort amenities, including a beach, scads of water sports, tennis courts, and even a pitch-and-putt golf course. Accommodations range from traditional hotel rooms to three-bedroom villas, with lots of choices in between. All have a modern tropical feel with rattan furniture and brightly colored fabrics. Given its relative isolation on the northwest shore, you may not be inclined to make many excursions. Luckily, the Garden Restaurant serves romantic dinners. ⊠ *Long Bay* 🖃 *Box 433, Road Town* ☎ *284/495–4252 or 800/345–0271* 🖷 *284/495–4677* ⊕ *www.*

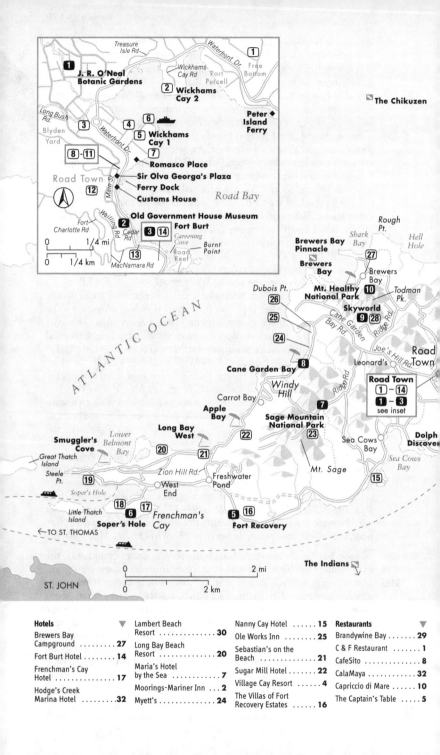

Road Town (see inset):

1. J. R. O'Neal Botanic Gardens
2. Wickhams Cay 2
3.
4.
5. Wickhams Cay 1
6.
7. Romasco Place
   Sir Olva Georga's Plaza
   Ferry Docks
   Customs House
8 - 11
12
13
2. Old Government House Museum
3. 14. Fort Burt

Map locations (main map):

- The Chikuzen
- Peter Island Ferry
- Brewers Bay Pinnacle
- Brewers Bay — 27
- Mt. Healthy National Park — 10
- Skyworld — 9, 28
- Dubois Pt. — 26
- 25
- 24
- Cane Garden Bay — 8
- Carrot Bay
- Apple Bay
- Long Bay West — 20, 21
- Sage Mountain National Park — 23, 22
- Smuggler's Cove
- 19
- 18, 6, 17
- Soper's Hole
- Frenchman's Cay
- Fort Recovery — 5, 16
- Sea Cows Bay — 15
- Dolphin Discovery
- The Indians

Road Town
1 – 14
1 – 3
see inset

← TO ST. THOMAS

ST. JOHN

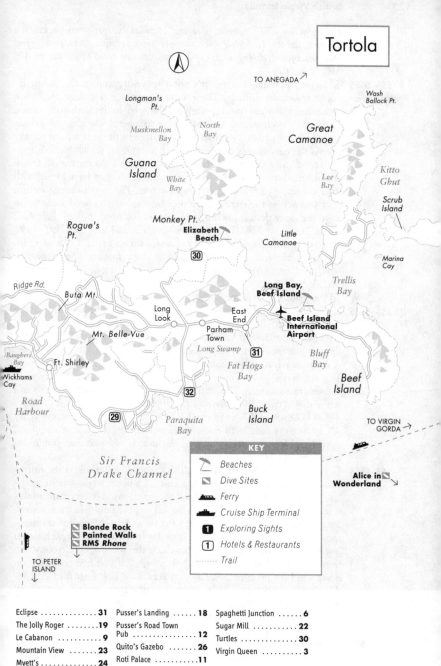

Tortola

TO ANEGADA ↗

Longman's Pt.

Muskmellon Bay

North Bay

Wash Ballock Pt.

Guana Island

White Bay

Great Camanoe

Kitto Ghut

Lee Bay

Scrub Island

Rogue's Pt.

Monkey Pt.

Elizabeth Beach

Little Camanoe

Marina Cay

Ridge Rd.

Buta Mt.

[30]

Trellis Bay

Long Bay, Beef Island

Mt. Belle-Vue

Long Look

Long Swamp

Parham Town

East End

Beef Island International Airport

[31]

Bluff Bay

Baughers Bay

Ft. Shirley

Wickhams Cay

Fat Hogs Bay

Beef Island

[32]

Road Harbour

[29]

Paraquita Bay

Buck Island

TO VIRGIN GORDA →

Sir Francis Drake Channel

Alice in Wonderland

KEY

Beaches	
Dive Sites	
Ferry	
Cruise Ship Terminal	
1 Exploring Sights	
(1) Hotels & Restaurants	
.... Trail	

Blonde Rock
Painted Walls
RMS Rhone

TO PETER ISLAND ↓

longbay.com ⟿ *53 rooms, 37 suites, 26 villas* 🖒 *In-room: safe, kitchen (some), dial-up. In-hotel: 3 restaurants, bars, tennis courts, pool, gym, spa, beachfront, diving, water sports, no elevator, public Internet* ☰ *AE, MC, V* ⫯ᵉ⫯ *EP.*

$$$–$$$$
FodorsChoice
★

🏨 **Sugar Mill Hotel.** Though it's not a sprawling resort, this is our favorite resort on Tortola. The rooms are attractively decorated with more than the usual floral spreads and have balconies with good views, kitchens or kitchenettes, and even some sofa beds. The grounds get accolades for their lovely gardens, but many say the real reason to stay here is the easy access to the excellent restaurant, which has both superb food and a stunning setting in the property's old sugar mill. Owners and food-and-travel writers Jeff and Jinx Morgan have brought all their expertise to this well-run small resort. The north-shore location puts you across the road from a nice beach, but you need a car to do anything more than enjoy the sun and sand. ⊠ *Apple Bay* ⌂ *Box 425, Road Town* ☎ *284/495–4355 or 800/462–8834* 🖶 *284/495–4696* ⊕ *www.sugarmillhotel.com* ⟿ *19 rooms, 2 suites, 1 villa, 1 cottage* 🖒 *Inroom: kitchen (some), no TV (some), dial-up. In-hotel: 2 restaurants, bars, pool, beachfront, water sports, no elevator, public Internet* ☰ *AE, MC, V* ⫯ᵉ⫯ *EP.*

★
⏱ **$$$–$$$$**

🏨 **The Villas of Fort Recovery Estates.** This is one of those small but special properties, distinguished by friendly service and the chance to get to know your fellow guests rather than the poshness of the rooms and the upscale amenities. Villas come in several sizes, and all are quaint—though not fancy—and have good views of St. John across the water. A sandy beach stretches seaside, providing calm waters perfect for kids. The emphasis on wellness is a welcome touch, and beachside yoga classes are a specialty. The staff is helpful and will arrange day sails and scuba-diving trips. ⊠ *Waterfront Dr., Box 239, Pockwood Pond* ☎ *284/495–4354 or 800/367–8455* 🖶 *284/495–4036* ⊕ *www.fortrecovery.com* ⟿ *29 suites, 1 villa* 🖒 *In-room: kitchen, dial-up, Wi-Fi. In-hotel: pool, gym, beachfront, water sports, no elevator, laundry service, public Internet* ☰ *AE, MC, V* ⫯ᵉ⫯ *EP.*

$$–$$$$

🏨 **Lambert Beach Resort.** Although this isolated location on the northeast coast puts you far from Road Town, Lambert Bay is one of the island's loveliest stretches of sand and the main reason to recommend this resort. Rooms are tucked back in the foliage, but you're just a few steps away from an afternoon of sunning and swimming. A handful of restaurants in and around nearby Fat Hogs Bay are within easy reach if you just have to get off that gorgeous beach. At this writing, condo construction was set to begin; ask about their progress if you fear construction noise will be a problem. ⊠ *Lambert Bay, Box 534, East End* ☎ *284/495–2877* 🖶 *284/495–2876* ⊕ *www.lambertbeachresort.com* ⟿ *38 rooms, 2 villas, 27 condos* 🖒 *In-room: kitchen (some), refrigerator, dial-up (some). In-hotel: restaurant, bar, tennis court, pool, spa, beachfront, water sports, no elevator, public Internet* ☰ *AE, D, MC, V* ⫯ᵉ⫯ *EP.*

$$$

🏨 **Frenchman's Cay Hotel.** Tucked away down a narrow road near busy Soper's Hole, Frenchman's Cay provides a quiet oasis for folks who want the option of eating in or out and a bit more space than you'd find in a typical hotel room. All accommodations are villa style, with separate bedrooms and kitchens. We like this place for its get-away-from-it-all feel. That said, you can easily walk to Soper's Hole to expand your dining horizons and to do some shopping. ⊠ *Frenchman's Cay, Box 1054, West End* ☎*284/495–4844 or 800/235–4077* 🖷*284/495–4056* ⊕*www.frenchmans.com* 🛏*9 villas* ♿ *In-room: kitchen, no TV. In-hotel: restaurant, bar, tennis court, pool, beachfront, water sports, no elevator* ▭ *AE, D, MC, V* ⎮⊚⎮ *EP.*

$–$$$ 🏨 **Sebastian's on the Beach.** Sitting on the island's north coast, Sebastian's definitely has a beachy feel, and that's its primary charm. Rooms vary in amenities and price, with the remodeled beachfront rooms a bit more up-to-date than those that the hotel calls "beach rear." The beachfront rooms have the best views and put you right on the sand. The less expensive rooms are basic, across the street from the ocean, and lack views. Those nearest the intersection of North Coast Road and Zion Hill Road suffer from traffic noise. Although you can eat all your meals at the resort's enjoyable restaurant, the wonderful Sugar Mill Restaurant is just a short drive east. ⊠ *Apple Bay* 📬 *Box 441, Road Town* ☎ *284/495–4212 or 800/336–4870* 🖷 *284/495–4466* ⊕ *www.sebastiansbvi.com* 🛏 *26 rooms, 9 villas* ♿ *In-room: refrigerator, no TV (some), dial-up (some). In-hotel: restaurant, bar, beachfront, no elevator, public Internet* ▭ *AE, D, MC, V* ⎮⊚⎮ *MAP.*

$$ 🏨 **Hodge's Creek Marina Hotel.** Sitting marina-side out on the island's East End, this hotel puts you in the middle of the nautical action. If you're heading out on a chartered sailboat or if you especially enjoy the marine scene, this is definitely the place for you. Rooms are carpeted and have tiny balconies, but brightly colored spreads and curtains give them a tropical feel. There's a small pool and the CalaMaya Restaurant in the complex, but you need a car to get out and about. ⊠ *Hodge's Creek* 📬 *Box 663, Road Town* ☎ *284/494–5000* 🖷 *284/494–7676* ⊕ *www.hodgescreek.com* 🛏 *24 rooms* ♿ *In-hotel: restaurant, pool, no elevator, public Internet* ▭ *AE, MC, V* ⎮⊚⎮ *EP.*

$$ 🏨 **Myett's.** Tucked away in a beachfront garden, this tiny hotel puts you right in the middle of Cane Garden Bay's busy nightlife. The restaurant is one of the area's hottest spots. Rooms have a typical tropical feel, thanks to the tile floors and rattan furniture. Although you might be content to lounge at the beach and stroll around the bay, you'll need a car to get out and about. ⊠ *Cane Garden Bay* 📬 *Box 556, Cane Garden Bay* ☎ *284/495–9649* 🖷 *284/495–9579* ⊕ *www.myettent.com* 🛏 *6 rooms* ♿ *In-room: refrigerator. In-hotel: restaurant, beachfront, no elevator, public Internet, public Wi-Fi* ▭ *AE, MC, V* ⎮⊚⎮ *EP.*

$$ 🏨 **Nanny Cay Hotel.** This quiet oasis is far enough from Road Town to give it a secluded feel but close enough to make shops and restaurants convenient. You're just steps from the hotel's restaurant, boat charters, and the chance to stroll the busy boatyard to gawk at the yachts under repair, but you still have to drive a good 20 minutes to get to the closest beach at Cane Garden Bay. The cheerful rooms, which have tile floors, are enlivened by lots of bright Caribbean colors. ⊠ *Nanny Cay* 📬 *Box 281, Road Town* ☎ *284/494–2512* 🖷 *284/494–0555* ⊕ *www.nannycay.com* 🛏 *38 rooms* ♿ *In-room: refrigerator. In-hotel: 2 restaurants, tennis court, pool, diving, no elevator, public Internet* ▭ *MC, V* ⎮⊚⎮ *EP.*

$–$$ ⌂ **Ole Works Inn.** The small hotel's location on busy Cane Garden Bay and its ownership by Quito Rymer, one of the island's most popular musicians, guarantee that it's not a quiet retreat. If you don't mind strolling a short distance to the beach, want to eat in the nearby casual restaurants, and enjoy mixing and mingling with the locals at the village's numerous bars, this is a good choice. Rooms are dated, have modest decor, and most have carpeting rather than tile. Opt for a beach-facing room for the best views. ⊠ *Cane Garden Bay* ⌂ *Box 560, Road Town* ☎ *284/495–4837* 🖷 *284/495–9618* ⊕ *www.quitorymer.com* ⇰ *14 rooms, 3 suites* ⚭ *In-room: kitchen (some), refrigerator. In-hotel: pool, no elevator* ⊟ *AE, MC, V* ¶Ⓞ¶ *EP.*

WHERE TO CAMP ⛺ **Brewers Bay Campground.** If you want to escape to nature and don't mind a rather ramshackle look to where you camp, this is a very sociable place to pitch your tent. It's not a manicured national-park-type place, but you're right on the water and can meet the other campers at the small bar and restaurant. Tarps draped here and there provide privacy and keep the rain off your cooking area. It's a great deal, especially if you bring your own tent. You need a car unless you want to take expensive taxi rides to see other parts of the island. ⚭ *Restaurant, flush toilets, drinking water, showers, public telephone, swimming (ocean)* ⇰ *20 sites* ⊠ *Brewers Bay* ⌂ *Box 185, Road Town* ☎ *284/494–3463* ⊟ *$16–$43* ⊟ *No credit cards.*

Where to Eat

Local seafood is plentiful on Tortola, and although other fresh ingredients are scarce, the island's chefs are a creative lot who apply genius to whatever the supply boat delivers. Contemporary American dishes prepared with a Caribbean influence are very popular. The fancier, more expensive restaurants have dress codes: long pants and collared shirts for men and elegant, casual resort wear for women.

Road Town

AMERICAN/ ✗ **The Pub.** At this lively waterfront spot, tables are arranged along a
CASUAL   terrace facing a small marina and the harbor in Road Town. Hamburg-
$$$ ers, salads, and sandwiches are typical lunch offerings. In the evening you can also choose grilled fish, sautéed conch, sizzling steaks, or barbecued ribs. There's live entertainment on weekends, and locals gather here nightly for spirited games at the pool table. ⊠ *Waterfront Dr.* ☎ *284/494–2608* ⚭ *Reservations not accepted* ⊟ *AE, MC, V* ⊗ *No lunch Sun.*

⟲ $–$$ ✗ **Pusser's Road Town Pub.** Almost everyone who visits Tortola stops here at least once to have a bite to eat and to sample the famous Pusser's Rum Painkiller (fruit juices and rum). The nonthreatening menu includes cheesy pizza, shepherd's pie, fish-and-chips, and hamburgers. Dine inside in air-conditioned comfort or outside on the verandah, which looks out on the harbor. ⊠ *Waterfront Dr.* ☎ *284/494–3897* ⊟ *AE, D, MC, V.*

CARIBBEAN ✗ **C&F Restaurant.** Crowds head to this casual spot for the best barbe-
$$–$$$$ cue in town (chicken, fish, and ribs), fresh local fish and lobster, and excellent curries. Sometimes there's a wait for a table, but it's worth it.

The restaurant is just outside Road Town, on a side street past the Moorings and Riteway. ☒ *Off Canaan Rd., Purcell Estate* ☎ *284/ 494–4941* ⌖ *Reservations not accepted* ▭ *AE, D, MC, V* ⊘ *No lunch.*

$–$$$
Fodor'sChoice
★
✕ **Roti Palace.** You might be tempted to pass this tiny spot on Road Town's Main Street when you see the plastic tablecloths and fake flowers, but owner Jean Leonard's reputation for dishing up fantastic roti is known far and wide. This flatbread is filled with curried potatoes, onions and lobster, chicken, beef, conch, goat, or vegetables. Ask for the bone out if you order the chicken to save yourself the trouble of fishing them out of your mouth. ☒ *Main St., Road Town* ☎ *284/494–4196* ▭ *No credit cards* ⊘ *Closed Sun.*

ECLECTIC
$$–$$$
✕ **CafeSito.** Don't be put off by the pedestrian decor. The chef at this shopping-center spot conjures up delicious dishes that run the gamut from burgers to lobster to chicken Alfredo. It's the place to go for pizza smothered with everything from the standard cheese and tomato to the more unusual chicken and bacon. In winter, the staff will deliver anything from its menu straight to your hotel. ☒ *Wickham's Cay I, Waterfront Dr.* ☎ *284/494–7412* ▭ *MC, V.*

$$–$$$
✕ **Virgin Queen.** The sailing and rugby crowds head here to play darts, drink beer, and eat Queen's Pizza—a crusty, cheesy pie topped with sausage, onions, green peppers, and mushrooms. Also on the menu is excellent West Indian and English fare: barbecued ribs with beans and rice, bangers and mash, shepherd's pie, and grilled sirloin steak. ☒ *Fleming St.* ☎ *284/494–2310* ▭ *MC, V* ⊘ *Closed Sun. No lunch Sat.*

FRENCH
$$–$$$$
✕ **Le Cabanon.** Birds and bougainvillea brighten the patio of this breezy French restaurant and bar, a popular gathering spot for locals and visitors alike. French onion soup and herring salad are good appetizer choices. From there, move on to roasted pigeon, monkfish in rosemary sauce, or beef tenderloin with green peppercorn sauce. Save room for such tasty desserts as chocolate cake and crème brûlée, or opt for a platter of French cheeses. ☒ *Waterfront Dr.* ☎ *284/494–8660* ▭ *D, MC, V* ⊘ *Closed Sun.*

ITALIAN
★ **$$–$$$$**
✕ **Spaghetti Junction.** Popular with the boating crowd, this longtime favorite serves up delightful West Indian food like stewed lobster along with Italian favorites like penne smothered in a spicy tomato sauce, spinach-mushroom lasagna, and angel-hair pasta with shellfish. For something that combines a bit of both, try the spicy jambalaya pasta. ☒ *Blackburn Hwy., Baughers Bay* ☎ *284/494–4880* ▭ *AE, MC, V* ⊘ *Closed Sun.*

★ **¢–$$**
✕ **Capriccio di Mare.** The owners of the well-known Brandywine Bay restaurant also run this authentic Italian outdoor café. Stop by for an espresso, fresh pastry, a bowl of perfectly cooked penne, or a crispy tomato and mozzarella pizza. Drink specialties include a mango Bellini, an adaptation of the famous cocktail served at Harry's Bar in Venice. ☒ *Waterfront Dr.* ☎ *284/494–5369* ⌖ *Reservations not accepted* ▭ *MC, V* ⊘ *Closed Sun.*

SEAFOOD
$$–$$$
✕ **The Captain's Table.** Select the lobster you want from the pool, but be careful not to fall in—it's in the floor right in the middle of the dining room. The menu also includes traditional escargots, filet mignon with blue-

cheese sauce, duckling with berry sauce, and creative daily specials that usually include freshly caught fish. Ceiling fans keep the dining room cool, but there are also tables on a breezy terrace overlooking the harbor. ⊠ *Wickham's Cay I* ☎ *284/494–3885* ▤ *MC, V* ☺ *No lunch Sat.*

Outside Road Town

AMERICAN–
CASUAL
☺ $$$–$$$$

✕ **Pusser's Landing.** Yachters flock to this waterfront restaurant. Downstairs, from late morning to well into the evening, you can belly up to the outdoor mahogany bar or sit down for sandwiches, fish-and-chips, and pizzas. At dinnertime head upstairs for a harbor view and a quiet alfresco meal of grilled steak or local fish. ⊠ *Soper's Hole* ☎ *284/495–4554* ▤ *AE, MC, V.*

CARIBBEAN
$$$–$$$$

✕ **Quito's Gazebo.** This rustic beachside bar and restaurant is owned and operated by island native Quito Rymer, a multitalented recording star who plays and sings solo on Tuesday and Thursday and performs with his reggae band on Friday and Saturday. The menu is Caribbean, with an emphasis on fresh fish. Try the conch fritters or the chicken roti. ⊠ *Cane Garden Bay* ☎ *284/495–4837* ▤ *AE, MC, V* ☺ *Closed Mon.*

$$–$$$$

✕ **Myett's Garden & Grille.** Right on the beach, this bi-level restaurant and bar is hopping day and night. Chowder made with fresh conch is the specialty here, although the menu includes everything from vegetarian dishes to grilled shrimp, steak, and tuna. There's live entertainment every night during the winter. ⊠ *Cane Garden Bay* ☎ *284/495–9649* ▤ *AE, MC, V.*

CONTINENTAL
$$$

✕ **Palm Terrace Restaurant.** Relax over dinner in this open-air restaurant at Long Bay Beach Resort. Tables are well spaced, offering enough privacy for intimate conversation. The menu changes daily, but several dishes show up regularly. Good appetizers are garlicky escargots in a pastry shell, Caribbean-style fish chowder, and shrimp fritters. Entrées include tuna glazed with tamarind and honey, pan-roasted duck with a rosemary glaze, or a filet mignon served with mushrooms. There are always at least five desserts to choose from, which might include Belgianchocolate mousse, strawberry cheesecake, or a fluffy lemon and coconut cake. ⊠ *Long Bay Beach Resort, Long Bay* ☎ *284/495–4252* ▤ *AE, D, MC, V* ☺ *No lunch.*

☺ $$$

✕ **Skyworld.** The top of a mountain is the location for this casually elegant dining room. The menu changes constantly, but look for imaginative dishes such as pork tenderloin medallions on a bed of red onion marmalade and rabbit with roasted vegetables. Other specialties include grilled local fish, roast duck, rack of lamb with a sauce du jour, and key lime pie. The lunch menu runs to hamburgers and sandwiches with some interesting additions such as a goat cheese tartlet. The restaurant can be crowded at midday when cruise ships dock. ⊠ *Ridge Rd., Joe's Hill* ☎ *284/494–3567* ▤ *AE, D, DC, MC, V.*

ECLECTIC
★ $$$–$$$$

✕ **Eclipse.** This popular waterfront spot isn't much more than a terrace filled with tables, but you can be caressed by the soft ocean breezes while you are impressed with the cuisine. With dishes from all over the globe, the menu is certainly well traveled. The garden lounge serves lighter fare—try the coconut shrimp, the seafood linguine, or maybe a slice or two of freshly baked pizza. In the main dining room, you'll find dishes like an apple-ginger pork tenderloin, spice-rubbed New York strip steak, and tuna dusted with seaweed, soy, and ginger. ⊠ *Fat Hog's Bay, East End* ☎ *284/495–1646* ▭ *MC, V* ☺ *No lunch.*

$$$–$$$$
FodorsChoice
★
✕ **Sugar Mill Restaurant.** Candles gleam, and the background music is peaceful in this romantic restaurant inside a 17th-century sugar mill. Well-prepared selections on the à la carte menu, which changes nightly, include some pasta and vegetarian entrées. Lobster bisque with basil croutons and a curried lobster patty are good starters. Favorite entrées include grilled swordfish with caramelized pineapple, beef curry with *poppadoms* (Indian popovers), pan-seared roast duck, and barbecued shrimp. ⊠ *Sugar Mill Hotel, Apple Bay* ☎ *284/495–4355* ▭ *AE, MC, V* ☺ *No lunch.*

$$–$$$$
✕ **CalaMaya.** Casual fare is what you'll find at this waterfront restaurant. You can always order a burger or lobster salad; the grilled Kaiser sandwich—shrimp, cheese, and pineapple on a crisp roll—is a tasty alternative. For dinner, try the snapper with onions, peppers, and thyme. ⊠ *Hodge's Creek Marina, Blackburn Hwy.* ☎ *284/495–2126* ▭ *AE, MC, V.*

$$–$$$$
✕ **The Jolly Roger Restaurant.** This casual, open-air restaurant near the ferry terminal is as popular with locals as it is with visitors. The menu ranges from burgers to rib-eye steak to the island favorite, local lobster. Try the savory conch fritters filled with tender local conch and herbs for a good start to your dinner. End it with a slice of sweet key lime pie. ⊠ *West End* ☎ *284/495–4559* ▭ *D, MC, V.*

$$–$$$$
FodorsChoice
★
✕ **Mountain View.** It's worth the drive up Sage Mountain for lunch or dinner at this casual restaurant. The view is spectacular—one of the best on Tortola. The small menu includes dishes like veal with a ginger sauce and grilled mahimahi in a lime-onion sauce. The lobster salad sandwich is the house lunch specialty. If it's on the menu, don't pass up the chicken roti. ⊠ *Sage Mountain* ✆ *Box 4036, Road Town* ☎ *284/495–9536* ▭ *MC, V.*

$$–$$$$
✕ **Sebastian's Beach Bar & Restaurant.** The waves practically lap at your feet at this beachfront restaurant on Tortola's northern shore. The menu runs to seafood—especially lobster, conch, and local fish—but you can also find dishes like ginger chicken and filet mignon. It's a perfect spot to stop for lunch on your around-the-island tour. Try the grilled dolphinfish sandwich, served on a soft roll with an oniony tartar sauce. Finish off with a cup of Sebastian's coffee spiked with home-brewed rum. ⊠ *North Coast Rd., Apple Bay* ☎ *284/494–4212* ▭ *AE, D, MC, V.*

$$$
✕ **Turtles.** If you're touring the island, Turtles is a good place to stop for lunch or dinner. Sitting just back from the beach at Lambert Beach Resort, this casual place provides a relaxing respite from the rigors of navigating mountain roads. At dinner you might find tiger shrimp in a curry sauce or rack of lamb with a raspberry glaze. Lunch favorites include fried shrimp, fresh tuna on a bun, and pasta dishes. ⊠ *Lambert Beach Resort, Lambert Bay, East End* ☎ *284/495–2877* ▭ *AE, D, MC, V.*

ITALIAN
$$$–$$$$
FodorsChoice
★
✕ **Brandywine Bay.** At this restaurant in Brandywine Bay, candlelit outdoor tables have sweeping views of neighboring islands. Owner Davide Pugliese prepares foods the Tuscan way: grilled with lots of fresh herbs. The remarkable menu may include duck with a berry sauce, beef carpac-

cio, grilled swordfish, and veal chop with ricotta and sun-dried tomatoes. The homemade mozzarella is another standout. The wine list is excellent, and the lemon tart and the tiramisu are irresistible. ⊠ *Sir Francis Drake Hwy., east of Road Town, Brandywine Bay* ⌂ *Box 2914, East End* ☎ *284/495–2301* ⌂ *Reservations essential* ⊟ *AE, MC, V* ⊘ *Closed Sun. No lunch.*

Beaches

Beaches in the BVI are less developed than those on St. Thomas or St. Croix, but they are also less inviting. The best BVI beaches are on deserted islands reachable only by boats, so take a snorkeling or sailing trip at least once. Tortola's north side has several perfect palm-fringed, white-sand beaches that curl around turquoise bays and coves, but none really achieves greatness. Nearly all are accessible by car (preferably a four-wheel-drive vehicle), albeit down bumpy roads that corkscrew precipitously. Some of these beaches are lined with bars and restaurants as well as watersports equipment stalls; others have absolutely nothing.

Apple Bay. If you want to surf, the area including Little Apple Bay and Capoon's Bay is the spot—although the white, sandy beach itself is narrow. Sebastian's, a very casual hotel, caters to those in search of the perfect wave. The legendary Bomba's Surfside Shack—a landmark festooned with all manner of flotsam and jetsam—serves drinks and casual food. Otherwise, there's nothing else in the way of amenities. Good waves are never a sure thing, but you're more apt to find them in January and February. If you're swimming and the waves are up, take care not to get dashed on the rocks. ⊠ *North Shore Rd. at Zion Hill Rd.*

Brewers Bay. The water here is good for snorkeling, and you can find a campground with showers and bathrooms and beach bar tucked in the foliage right behind the beach. An old sugar mill and ruins of a rum distillery are off the beach along the road. The beach is easy to find, but the paved roads leading down the hill to it can be a bit daunting. You can get there from either Brewers Bay Road East or Brewers Bay Road West. ⊠ *Brewers Bay Rd. E off Cane Garden Bay Rd., or Brewers Bay Rd. W off Ridge Rd.*

Cane Garden Bay. This silky stretch of sand has exceptionally calm, crystalline waters—except when storms at sea turn the water murky. Snorkeling is good along the edges. Casual guesthouses, restaurants, bars, and even shops are just steps from the beach in the growing village of the same name. The beach is a laid-back, even somewhat funky place to put down your towel. It's the closest beach to Road Town—one steep uphill and downhill drive—and one of the BVI's best-known anchorages (unfortunately, it can be very crowded when cruise ships are in town). Water-sports shops rent equipment. ⊠ *Cane Garden Bay Rd. off Ridge Rd.*

Elizabeth Beach. Home to Lambert Beach Resort, the palm-lined, wide, and sandy beach has parking for nonguests on its steep downhill access road. Other than at the hotel, which welcomes nonguests to its restaurant, there are no amenities aside from peace and quiet. Turn at the sign for Lambert Beach Resort. If you miss it, you wind up at Her Majesty's Prison. ⊠ *Lambert Rd. off Ridge Rd., on the eastern end of island.*

2

Long Bay, Beef Island. The scenery here is superlative: the beach stretches seemingly forever, and you can catch a glimpse of Little Camanoe and Great Camanoe islands. If you walk around the bend to the right, you can see little Marina Cay and Scrub Island. Long Bay is also a good place to search for seashells. Swim out to wherever you see a dark patch for some nice snorkeling. There are no amenities, so come prepared with your own drinks and snacks. Turn left shortly after crossing the bridge to Beef Island. ⊠ *Beef Island Rd., Beef Island.*

Long Bay West. Have your camera ready to snap the breathtaking approach to this stunning, mile-long stretch of white sand. Although Long Bay Resort sprawls along part of it, the entire beach is open to the public. The water isn't as calm here as at Cane Garden or Brewers Bay, but it's still swimmable. Rent water-sports equipment and enjoy the beachfront restaurant at the resort. Turn left at Zion Hill Road; then travel about half a mile. ⊠ *Long Bay Rd.*

Smuggler's Cove. After bouncing your way down a pothole-filled dirt road to this beautiful, palm-fringed beach, you'll feel as if you've found a hidden piece of the island. You probably won't be alone on weekends, when the beach fills with snorkelers and sunbathers. There's a fine view of Jost Van Dyke from the shore. The beach is popular with Long Bay Resort guests who want a change of scenery, but there are no amenities. Follow Long Bay Road past Long Bay Resort, keeping to the roads nearest the water until you reach the beach. It's about a mile past the resort. ⊠ *Long Bay Rd.*

ports & the Outdoors

Boating

Rent a 23-, 25-, or 30-foot powerboat for a day trip to offshore cays. Prices range from $200 for a half day on a smaller boat to $850 for a full day on a larger boat. Count on paying about $80 for gas and oil. Call **Sunshine Pleasure Boats** (⊠ C Dock, Village Cay Marina ☎ 284/494–8813).

Cricket

Fans of this sport are fiercely loyal and exuberant. Matches are held at the New Recreation Grounds, next to the J. R. O'Neal Botanic Gardens, weekends from February to April. Check local newspapers or ask at your hotel front desk for information on times and teams.

Diving & Snorkeling

Clear waters and numerous reefs afford some wonderful opportunities for underwater exploration. In some spots visibility reaches 100 feet, but colorful reefs teeming with fish are often just a few feet below the sea surface. The BVI's system of marine parks means the underwater life visible through your mask will stay protected.

There are several popular dive spots around the islands. **Alice in Wonderland** is a deep dive south of Ginger Island with a wall that slopes gently from 15 feet to 100 feet. It's an area overrun with huge mushroom-shape coral, hence its name. Crabs, lobsters, and shimmering fan corals make their homes in the tunnels, ledges, and overhangs of **Blonde Rock**, a pinnacle that goes from just 15 feet below the surface to 60 feet deep. It's between Dead Chest and Salt Island. When the currents aren't too strong, **Brewers Bay Pinnacle** (20 to 90 feet down) teems with sea life. At the **Indians**, near Pelican Island, colorful corals decorate canyons and grottoes created by four large, jagged pinnacles that rise 50 feet from the ocean floor. The **Painted Walls** is a shallow dive site where corals and sponges create a kaleidoscope of colors on the walls of four long gullies. It's northeast of Dead Chest.

The *Chikuzen,* sunk northwest of Brewers Bay in 1981, is a 246-foot vessel in 75 feet of water; it's home to thousands of fish, colorful corals, and big rays. In 1867 the **RMS Rhone,** a 310-foot royal mail steamer, split in two when it sank in a devastating hurricane. It's so well preserved that it was used as an underwater prop in the movie *The Deep.* You can see the crow's nest and bowsprit, the cargo hold in the bow, and the engine and enormous propeller shaft in the stern. Its four parts are at various depths from 30 to 80 feet. Get yourself some snorkeling gear and hop aboard a dive boat to this wreck near Salt Island (across the channel from Road Town). Every dive outfit in the BVI runs scuba and snorkel tours to this part of the BVI National Parks Trust; if you only have time for one trip, make it this one. Rates start at around $60 for a one-tank dive and $90 for a two-tank dive.

Your hotel probably has a dive company located right on the premises. If not, the staff can recommend one nearby. Using your hotel's dive company makes a trip to the offshore dive and snorkel sites a breeze. Just stroll down to the dock and hop aboard. All dive companies are certified by PADI, the Professional Association of Diving Instructors, which ensures your instructors are qualified to safely take vacationers diving. The boats are also inspected to make sure they're seaworthy. If you've never dived, try a short introductory dive, often called a resort course, which teaches you enough to get you under water. In the unlikely event you get a case of the bends, a condition that can happen when you rise to the surface too fast, your dive team will whisk you to the decompression chamber at Roy L. Schneider Regional Medical Center Hospital in nearby St. Thomas.

Blue Waters Divers (⊠ Nanny Cay ☎ 284/494–2847 ⊠ Soper's Hole, West End ☎ 284/495–1200 ⊕ www.bluewaterdiversbvi.com) teaches resort, open-water, rescue, and advanced diving courses, and also makes daily dive trips. If you're chartering a sailboat, the company's boat will meet your boat at Peter, Salt, or Cooper Island for a rendezvous dive. Rates include all equipment as well as instruction. Make arrangements two days in advance. **Dive Tortola** (⊠ Prospect Reef ☎ 284/494–9200 ⊕ www.divetortola.com) offers beginner and advanced diving courses and daily dive trips. Trainers teach open-water, rescue, advanced diving, and resort courses. Dive Tortola also offers a rendezvous diving option for folks on charter sailboats.

Fishing

Most of the boats that take you deep-sea fishing for bluefish, wahoo, swordfish, and shark leave from nearby St. Thomas, but local anglers like to fish the shallower water for bonefish. A half day runs about $480, a full day around $850. Call **Caribbean Fly Fishing** (⊠ Nanny Cay ☎ 284/ 494–4797 ⊕ www.caribflyfishing.com).

Hiking

Sage Mountain National Park attacts hikers who enjoy the quiet trails that crisscross the island's loftiest peak. There are some lovely views and the chance to see rare species that grow only at higher elevations.

Sailing

The BVI are among the world's most popular sailing destinations. They're clustered together and surrounded by calm waters, so it's fairly easy to sail from one anchorage to the next. Most of the Caribbean's biggest sailboat charter companies have operations in Tortola. If you know how to sail, you can charter a bareboat (perhaps for your entire vacation); if you're unschooled, you can hire a boat with a captain. Prices vary depending on the type and size of the boat you wish to charter. In season, a weekly charter runs from $1,500 to $35,000. Book early to make sure you get the boat that fits you best. Most of Tortola's marinas have hotels, which give you a convenient place to spend the nights before and after your charter.

If a day sail to some secluded anchorage is more your spot of tea, the BVI have numerous boats of various sizes and styles that leave from many points around Tortola. Prices start at around $80 per person for a full-day sail, including lunch and snorkeling equipment.

BVI Yacht Charters (⊠ Inner Harbour Marina, Road Town ☎ 284/494–4289 or 888/615–4006 ⊕ www.bviyachtcharters.com) offers 31-foot to 71-foot sailboats for charter—with or without a captain and crew, whichever you prefer. **Catamaran Charters** (⊠ Nanny Cay Marina, Nanny Cay ☎ 284/494–6661 or 800/262-0308 ⊕ www.catamarans.com) charters catamarans with or without a captain. The **Moorings** (⊠ Wickham's Cay II, Road Town ☎ 284/494–2331 or 800/535–7289 ⊕ www.moorings.com), considered one of the best bareboat operations in the world, has a large fleet of well-maintained, mostly Beneteau sailing yachts. Hire a captain or sail the boat yourself. If you prefer a powerboat, call **Regency Yacht Vacations** (⊠ Wickham's Cay I, Road Town ☎ 284/495–1970 or 800/524–7676 ⊕ www.regencyvacations.com) for both bareboat and captained sail and powerboat charters. **Sunsail** (⊠ Hodge's Creek Marina, East End ☎ 284/495–4740 or 800/327–2276 ⊕ www.sunsail.com) offers a full fleet of boats to charter with or without a captain. **Voyages** (⊠ Soper's Hole Marina, West End ☎ 284/494–0740 or 888/869–2436 ⊕ www.voyagecharters.com) offers a variety of sailboats for charter with or without a captain and crew.

Aristocat Charters (⊠ West End ☎ 284/499–1249 ⊕ www.aristocatcharters.com) sets sail daily to the Indians and Peter Island aboard a 48-foot catamaran. **White Squall II** (⊠ Village Cay Marina, Road Town ☎ 284/494–2564 ⊕ www.whitesquall2.com) takes you on regularly scheduled day sails to the Baths at Virgin Gorda, Jost Van Dyke, or the Caves at Norman Island on an 80-foot schooner.

Surfing

Surfing is big on Tortola's north shore, particularly when the winter swells come in to Josiah's and Apple bays. Rent surfboards starting at $25 for a full day.

HIHO (⊠ Waterfront Dr., Road Town ☎ 284/494–7694 ⊕ www.go-hiho. com) has a good surfboard selection for sale or rent. The staff will give you advice on the best spots to put in your board.

TENNIS Tortola's tennis options range from simple, untended, concrete courts to professionally maintained facilities that host organized tournaments. Most hotels have at least one or two courts for guests. The courts listed below are all open to the public; some have restrictions for nonguests.

Long Bay Beach Resort (⊠ Long Bay ☎ 284/495–4252) has two lighted soft courts. Private lessons are $60 per hour. Nonguests may rent a court for $10 an hour during the day and $20 an hour at night. Tennis rackets can be rented for $7 an hour.

Windsurfing

Steady trade winds make windsurfing a breeze. Three of the best spots for sailboarding are Nanny Cay, Slaney Point, and Trellis Bay on Beef Island. Rates for sailboards start at about $25 an hour or $75 for a lesson.

Boardsailing BVI (⊠ Trellis Bay, Beef Island ☎ 284/495–2447 ⊕ www. windsurfing.vi) rents equipment and offers private and group lessons.

Shopping

The BVI aren't really a shopper's delight, but there are many shops showcasing original wares—from jams and spices to resort wear to excellent artwork.

Shopping Areas

Many shops and boutiques are clustered along and just off Road Town's **Main Street.** You can shop in Road Town's **Wickham's Cay I** adjacent to the marina. The **Crafts Alive Market** on the Road Town waterfront is a collection of colorful West Indian–style buildings with shops that carry items made in the BVI. You might find pretty baskets or interesting pottery or perhaps a bottle of home-brewed hot sauce. There's an ever-growing number of art and clothing stores at **Soper's Hole** in West End.

Specialty Stores

ART The **Gallery** (⊠ 102 Main St., Road Town ☎ 284/494–6680) carries art by owner Lisa Gray and paintings by other Tortola artists. **Sunny Caribbee** (⊠ Main St., Road Town ☎ 284/494–2178) has many paintings, prints, and watercolors by artists from around the Caribbean.

CLOTHES & **Arawak** (⊠ On the dock, Nanny Cay ☎ 284/494–5240 ⊠ Hodge's Creek
TEXTILES Marina, Hodge's Creek ☎ 284/495–1106 ⊠ Soper's Hole Marina, West End ☎ 284/495–4262) carries batik sundresses, sportswear, and resort wear for men and women. There's also a selection of children's clothing. **Hucksters** (⊠ Main St., Road Town ☎ 284/495–7165 ⊠ Soper's Hole Marina, West End ☎ 284/495–3087) carries nifty souvenirs as well as unusual items for the home. **Latitude 18°** (⊠ Main St., Road Town ⊠ Soper's Hole Marina, West End ☎ 284/494–7807 for both stores) sells Maui Jim, Smith, Oakley, and Revo sunglasses; Freestyle and Reactor watches; and a fine collection of beach towels, sandals, sundresses,

and sarongs. **Pusser's Company Store** (✉ Main St. at Waterfront Rd., Road Town ☎ 284/494–2467 ✉ Soper's Hole Marina, West End ☎ 284/495–4599) sells nautical memorabilia, ship models, and marine paintings. There's also an entire line of clothing for both men and women, handsome decorator bottles of Pusser's rum, and gift items bearing the Pusser's logo. **Zenaida's of West End** (✉ Soper's Hole Marina, West End ☎ 284/495–4867) displays the fabric finds of Argentine Vivian Jenik Helm, who travels through South America, Africa, and India in search of batiks, hand-painted and hand-blocked fabrics, and interesting weaves that can be made into pareus (women's wraps) or wall hangings. The shop also sells unusual bags, belts, sarongs, scarves, and ethnic jewelry.

FOODSTUFFS **Ample Hamper** (✉ Inner Harbour Marina, Road Town ☎ 284/494–2494 ✉ Frenchman's Cay Marina, West End ☎ 284/495–4684 ⊕ www.amplehamper.com) has an outstanding collection of cheeses, wines, fresh fruits, and canned goods from the United Kingdom and the United States. You can have the management here provision your yacht or rental villa. **Best of British** (✉ Wickham's Cay I, Road Town ☎ 284/494–3462) has lots of nifty British food sitting cheek by jowl with American fare. Shop here for Marmite, Vegemite, shortbread, frozen meat pies, and delightful Christmas crackers filled with surprises. **RiteWay** (✉ Waterfront Dr., at Pasea Estate, Road Town ☎ 284/494–2263 ✉ Fleming St., Road Town ☎ 284/494–2263 Ext. 180 ⊕ www.rtwbvi.com) carries a good selection of the usual supplies, but don't expect an inventory like your hometown supermarket. RiteWay also provisions villas and yachts.

GIFTS **Bamboushay** (✉ Nanny Cay Marina, Nanny Cay ☎ 284/494–0393) sells handcrafted Tortola-made pottery in shades that reflect the sea. In a brightly painted West Indian house, **Sunny Caribbee** (✉ Main St., Road Town ☎ 284/494–2178) packages its own herbs, teas, coffees, vinegars, hot sauces, soaps, skin and suntan lotions, and exotic concoctions—Arawak Love Potion and Island Hangover Cure, for example. There are also Caribbean books and art and hand-painted decorative accessories.

JEWELRY **Columbian Emeralds International** (✉ Wickham's Cay I, Road Town ☎ 284/494–7477), a Caribbean chain catering to the cruise-ship crowd, is the source for duty-free emeralds plus other gems, gold, crystal, and china. **D'Zandra's** (✉ Wickham's Cay I, Road Town ☎ 284/494–8330) carries mostly black coral items set in gold and silver. Many pieces reflect Caribbean and sea themes. **Samarkand** (✉ Main St., Road Town ☎ 284/494–6415) crafts charming gold-and-silver pendants, earrings, bracelets, and pins, many with island themes like seashells, lizards, pelicans, and palm trees. There are also reproduction Spanish pieces of eight (old Spanish coins worth eight reals) that were found on sunken galleons.

PERFUMES & **Flamboyance** (✉ Palm Grove Shopping Center, Waterfront Dr., Road Town
COSMETICS ☎ 284/494–4099) carries designer fragrances and upscale cosmetics.

STAMPS The **BVI Post Office** (✉ Main St., Road Town ☎ 284/494–3701) is a philatelist's dream. It has a worldwide reputation for exquisite stamps in all sorts of designs. Although the stamps carry U.S. monetary designations, they can be used for postage only in the BVI.

Nightlife & the Arts

Nightlife

Like any other good sailing destination, Tortola has watering holes that are popular with salty and not-so-salty dogs. Many offer entertainment; check the weekly *Limin' Times* for schedules and up-to-date information. Bands change like the weather, and what's hot today can be old news tomorrow. The local beverage is the Painkiller, an innocent-tasting mixture of fruit juices and rums. It goes down smoothly but packs quite a punch, so give yourself time to recover before you order another.

By day **Bomba's Surfside Shack** (⊠ Apple Bay ☎ 284/495–4148), which is covered with everything from crepe-paper leis to ancient license plates to spicy graffiti, looks like a pile of junk; by night it's one of Tortola's liveliest spots and one of the Caribbean's most famous beach bars. There's a fish fry and a live band every Wednesday and Sunday. People flock here from all over on the full moon, when bands play all night long. At the **Jolly Roger** (⊠ West End ☎ 284/495–4559) an ever-changing roster of local and down-island bands plays everything from rhythm and blues to reggae and rock every Friday and Saturday—and sometimes Sunday—starting at 8. Local bands play at **Myett's** (⊠ Cane Garden Bay ☎ 284/495–9649) most nights, and there's usually a lively dance crowd. At the **Pub** (⊠ Waterfront St., Road Town ☎ 284/494–2608) there's a happy hour from 5 to 7 every day and live blues on Thursday. Courage is what people are seeking at **Pusser's Road Town Pub** (⊠ Waterfront St., Road Town ☎ 284/494–3897)—John Courage by the pint. Other nights try Pusser's famous mixed drinks—Painkillers—and snack on the excellent pizza. BVI recording star Quito Rhymer sings island ballads and love songs at **Quito's Gazebo** (⊠ Cane Garden Bay ☎ 284/495–4837), his rustic beachside bar–restaurant. Solo shows are on Tuesday and Thursday at 8:30; on Friday and Saturday nights at 9:30 Quito performs with his band. There's often live music at **Sebastian's** (⊠ Apple Bay ☎ 284/495–4212) on Thursday and Sunday evenings, and you can dance under the stars.

The Arts

Musicians from around the world take to the stage during the **Performing Art Series** (⊠ H. Lavity Stoutt Community College, Paraquita Bay ☎ 284/494–4994 ⊕ www.hlscc.edu.vg), held from October to March each year. Past artists have included Britain's premier a cappella group, Black Voices; the Leipzig String Quartet; and Keith Lockhart and the Serenac Quartet (from the Boston Pops Symphony).

Every May, hordes of people head to Tortola for the three-day **BVI Music Festival** (⊠ Cane Garden Bay ☎ 284/495–3378 ⊕ www.bvimusicfest. net) to listen to reggae, gospel, blues, and salsa music by musicians from around the Caribbean and the U.S. mainland.

Exploring Tortola

Tortola doesn't have many historic sights, but it does have lots of beautiful natural scenery. Although you could explore the island's 10 square mi (26 square km) in a few hours, opting for such a whirlwind tour would be a mistake. There's no need to live in the fast lane when you're surrounded by some of the Caribbean's most breathtaking panoramas. Also, the roads are extraordinarily steep and twisting, making driving demanding. The best strategy is to explore a bit of the island at a time. For example, you might try Road Town (the island's tiny metropolis) one morning and a drive to Cane Garden Bay and West End (a little town on, of course, the island's west end) the next afternoon. Or consider a visit to East End, a *very* tiny town located exactly where its name suggests. The north shore is where all the best beaches are found.

Numbers in the margin correspond to points of interest on the Tortola map.

What to See in Road Town

The bustling capital of the BVI looks out over Road Harbour. It takes only an hour or so to stroll down Main Street and along the waterfront, checking out the traditional West Indian buildings painted in pastel colors and with pitched, corrugated-tin roofs, bright shutters, and delicate fretwork trim. For sightseeing brochures and the latest information on everything from taxi rates to ferry schedules, stop in the BVI Tourist Board office. Or just choose a seat on one of the benches in Sir Olva Georges Square, on Waterfront Drive, and watch the people come and go from the ferry dock and customs office across the street.

❸ **Fort Burt.** The most intact historic ruin on Tortola was built by the Dutch in the early 17th century to safeguard Road Harbour. It sits on a hill at the western edge of Road Town and is now the site of a small hotel and restaurant. The foundations and magazine remain, and the structure offers a commanding view of the harbor. ⊠ *Waterfront Dr., Road Town* ☎ *No phone* ☜ *Free* ⊙ *Daily dawn–dusk.*

★ ❶ **J. R. O'Neal Botanic Gardens.** Take a walk through this 4-acre showcase of lush plant life. There are sections devoted to prickly cacti and succulents, hothouses for ferns and orchids, gardens of medicinal herbs, and plants and trees indigenous to the seashore. From the tourist office in Road Town, cross Waterfront Drive and walk one block over to Main Street and turn right. Keep walking until you see the high school. The gardens are on your left. ⊠ *Botanic Station, Road Town* ☎ *284/494–3904* ☜ *$3* ⊙ *Mon.–Sat. 9–4:30.*

★ ❷ **Old Government House Museum.** The seat of government until 1987, this gracious building now displays a nice collection of items from Tortola's past. The rooms are filled with period furniture, hand-painted china, books signed by Queen Elizabeth II on her 1966 and 1977 visits, and numerous items reflecting Tortola's seafaring legacy. ⊠ *Waterfront Dr., Road Town* ☎ *284/494–3701* ☜ *Free* ⊙ *Weekdays 8:30–4:30.*

What to See Elsewhere on the Island

❽ **Cane Garden Bay.** Once a sleepy village, Cane Garden Bay is growing into one of Tortola's important destinations. Stay here at a small hotel or guesthouse or stop by for lunch, dinner, or drinks at a seaside restaurant. You can find a few small stores selling clothing and basics like suntan lotion, and, of course, one of Tortola's most popular beaches is at your feet. The roads in and out of this area are dauntingly steep, so use caution when driving.

★ ☺ ❹ **Dolphin Discovery.** Get up close and personal with dolphins as they swim in a spacious seaside pen. There are two different programs that provide a range of experiences. In the Royal Swim, dolphins tow participants around the pen. The less expensive Encounter allows you to touch the dolphins. ✉ *Prospect Reef Resort, Road Town* ☎ *284/494–7675* ⊕ *www.dolphindiscovery.com* ✆ *Royal Swim $139, Encounter $79* ☉ *Daily, by appointment only.*

❺ **Fort Recovery.** The unrestored ruins of a 17th-century Dutch fort, measuring 30 feet in diameter, sit amid a profusion of tropical greenery on the grounds of Villas of Fort Recovery Estates. There's not much to see here, and there are no guided tours, but you're welcome to stop by and poke around. ✉ *Waterfront Dr., Road Town* ☎ *284/485–4467* ✆ *Free.*

❿ **Mount Healthy National Park.** The remains of an 18th-century sugar plantation are here. The windmill structure has been restored, and you can see the ruins of a mill, a factory with boiling houses, storage areas, stables, a hospital, and many dwellings. It's a nice place to picnic. ✉ *Ridge Rd., Todman Peak* ☎ *No phone* ⊕ *www.bvinationalparkstrust. org* ✆ *Free* ☉ *Daily dawn–dusk.*

★ ❼ **Sage Mountain National Park.** At 1,716 feet, Sage Mountain is the highest peak in the BVI. From the parking area, a trail leads you in a loop not only to the peak itself (and extraordinary views) but also to a small rain forest that is sometimes shrouded in mist. Most of the forest was cut down over the centuries to clear land for sugarcane, cotton, and other crops; to create pastureland; or simply to utilize the stands of timber. In 1964 this park was established to preserve what remained. Up here you can see mahogany trees, white cedars, mountain guavas, elephant-ear vines, mamey trees, and giant bullet woods, to say nothing of such birds as mountain doves and thrushes. Take a taxi from Road Town or drive up Joe's Hill Road and make a left onto Ridge Road toward Chalwell and Doty villages. The road dead-ends at the park. ✉ *Ridge Rd., Sage Mountain* ☎ *284/494–3904* ⊕ *www.bvinationalparkstrust.org* ✆ *$3* ☉ *Daily dawn–dusk.*

★ ❾ **Skyworld.** Drive up here and climb the observation tower for a stunning 360-degree view of numerous islands and cays. On a clear day you can even see St. Croix (40 mi [64½ km] away) and Anegada (20 mi [32 km] away). ✉ *Ridge Rd., Joe's Hill* ☎ *No phone* ✆ *Free.*

❻ **Soper's Hole.** On this little island connected by a causeway to Tortola's western end, you can find a marina and a captivating complex of pastel West Indian–style buildings with shady balconies, shuttered windows, and gingerbread trim that house art galleries, boutiques, and restaurants. Pusser's Landing is a lively place to stop for a cold drink (many are made with Pusser's famous rum) and a sandwich and to watch the boats in harbor.

VIRGIN GORDA

Virgin Gorda, or "Fat Virgin," received its name from Christopher Columbus. The explorer envisioned the island as a pregnant woman in a languid recline with Gorda Peak being her big belly and the boulders of the Baths her toes. Different in topography from Tortola, with its arid landscape covered with scrub brush and cactus, Virgin Gorda has a slower pace of life, too. Goats and cattle own the right-of-way, and the unpretentious friendliness of the people is winning.

Where to Stay

Virgin Gorda's charming hostelries appeal to a select, appreciative clientele; repeat business is extremely high. Those who prefer Sheratons, Marriotts, and the like may feel they get more for their money on other islands, but the peace and pampering offered on Virgin Gorda are priceless to the discriminating traveler.

Hotels & Inns

$$$$ **Biras Creek Resort.** Although Biras Creek is tucked out of the way on the island's North Sound, the get-away-from-it-all feel is actually the major draw. Anyway, you're just a five-minute ferry ride from the dock at Gun Creek. There are a handful of other hotels in the area, but this resort's gourmet meal plan means you won't want to leave. A member of the exclusive Relais &Châteaux family of hotels, Biras Creek offers suites with separate bedroom and living areas, though only bedrooms have air-conditioning. Guests get around on complimentary bicycles. Rates are per couple, per night, and include everything but beverages. *Box 54, North Sound* 284/494–3555 *or* 800/223–1108 284/494–3557 *www.biras.com* 31 *suites In-room: safe, refrigerator, no TV, dial-up. In-hotel: 2 restaurants, bar, tennis courts, pool, spa, beachfront, water sports, bicycles, no elevator, public Internet, public Wi-Fi* AE, MC, V FAP.

$$$$ **Bitter End Yacht Club.** Sailing's the thing at this busy hotel and marina
Fodor'sChoice   in the nautically inclined North Sound, and since the use of everything
★   from small sailboats to Windsurfers to kayaks is included in the price, you have no reason not to get out on the water. If you're serious about taking to the high seas, sign up for lessons at the resort's sailing school. Of course, if you just want to lounge about on the beachfront chaises or on your balcony, that's okay, too. There's a busy social scene, with guests gathering to swap tales at the hotel's bars. Rooms are bright and cheery, with the decor leaning toward tropical colors. You can reach the Bitter End only by a free private ferry. *Box 46, North Sound* 284/494–2746 *or* 800/872–2392 284/494–4756 *www.beyc.com* 87 *rooms In-room: no a/c (some), no TV. In-hotel: 3 restaurants, bar, pool, beachfront, diving, water sports, no elevator, children's programs (ages 6–18), public Internet, public Wi-Fi* AE, MC, V AI.

★ **$$$$**   **Little Dix Bay.** This laid-back luxury resort offers something for everyone, which is why we like it. You can swim, sun, and snorkel on a gorgeous sandy crescent, play tennis or windsurf, or just relax with a good

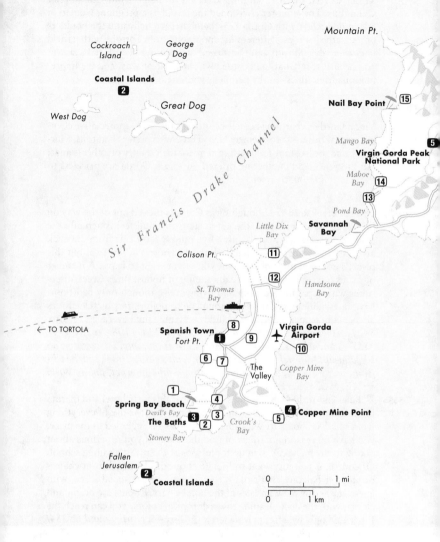

Virgin Gorda

Mountain Pt.

Cockroach Island

George Dog

Coastal Islands 2

Great Dog

West Dog

Nail Bay Point 15

Mango Bay 5

Virgin Gorda Peak National Park

Mahoe Bay 14

13

Pond Bay

Savannah Bay

Little Dix Bay 11

Sir Francis Drake Channel

Colison Pt.

12

Handsome Bay

St. Thomas Bay

← TO TORTOLA

8

Spanish Town 1

Fort Pt. 9

Virgin Gorda Airport

10

6 7

The Valley

Copper Mine Bay

1

4

3

2

Spring Bay Beach

Devil's Bay

The Baths 3

Crook's Bay

Stoney Bay

5

4 **Copper Mine Point**

Fallen Jerusalem 2 **Coastal Islands**

0   1 mi
0   1 km

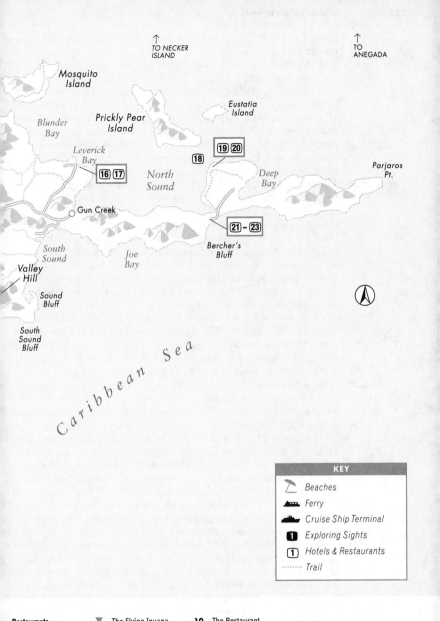

book. The hotel's restaurants serve stellar food, but you're only a five-minute drive from Spanish Town's less expensive restaurants and shopping. Rooms have rattan and wood furniture and a casual feel. The grounds are gorgeous, with lots of lush plantings kept snipped to perfection. Depending on when you visit, your fellow guests will be honeymooners or folks who've spent a week or two in the winter season for years. *Box 70, Little Dix Bay ☎ 284/495–5555 ᐸ 284/495–5661 ⊕ www. littledixbay.com ➟ 98 rooms, 8 suites, 2 villas ⅋ In-room: safe, refrigerator, no TV, dial-up, Wi-Fi. In-hotel: 3 restaurants, bars, tennis courts, pool, gym, spa, beachfront, water sports, no elevator, children's programs (ages 3–16), public Internet, public Wi-Fi ☰ AE, MC, V ⅋⅋ EP.*

★ **$$–$$$$**   🏨 **Nail Bay Resort.** Rambling up the hill above the coast, this resort offers a wide selection of rooms and suites to fit every need. The beach is just a short walk away from the units at lower elevations, but if you're staying higher up the hill, you might want to drive to avoid the uphill trek back to your room. You get cooking facilities (at least microwave, fridge, toaster oven, and coffeemaker) no matter how small your room. It's a bit of a drive down a miserable dirt road to reach the resort, but it offers lots of activities and a restaurant, so you won't need to leave unless you want to. The rooms and apartments have modern rattan furniture, tile floors, and nice views. There's some construction in the area, so check before you go if noise bothers you. *Box 69, Nail Bay ☎ 284/494–8000 or 800/871–3551 ᐸ 284/495–5875 ⊕ www.nailbay. com ➟ 9 rooms, 3 suites, 9 villas ⅋ In-room: kitchen (some), VCR (some). In-hotel: restaurant, bar, tennis court, beachfront, water sports, no elevator, public Internet, public Wi-Fi ☰ AE, MC, V ⅋⅋ EP.*

$$–$$$$ 🏨 **Saba Rock Resort.** Reachable only by a free ferry or by your own yacht, this resort on its own tiny cay isn't for everyone. However, it's good for folks who want to mix and mingle with the sailors who drop anchor for the night. The bar and restaurant are busy with yachters gathering for sundowners, lunch, and dinner. The rooms are spacious, each with a different decor. All have tile floors, rattan or wood furniture, and colorful spreads and drapes. A resort boat will drop you off at nearby North Sound resorts if you need a change of pace. *Box 67, North Sound ☎ 284/495–7711 or 284/495–9966 ᐸ 284/495–7373 ⊕ www.sabarock. com ➟ 7 1-bedroom suites, 1 2-bedroom suite ⅋ In-room: no phone (some), kitchen (some), refrigerator. In-hotel: restaurant, bar, beachfront, water sports, no elevator, public Wi-Fi ☰ MC, V ⅋⅋ CP.*

$$$ 🏨 **Olde Yard Village.** All the condos in this upscale complex have at least partial ocean views, and the location, a few minutes' drive from Spanish Town, is ideal: close enough so that you can easily pop out to dinner but far enough to make you feel as if you're more isolated than you are. You will need a car, though, to make those trips a breeze. The Olde Yard Village will be building new units over the next five years, but construction is a bit removed from the existing accommodations. *Box 26, The Valley ☎ 284/495–5544 or 800/653–9273 ᐸ 284/495–5986 ⊕ www. oldeyardvillage.com ➟ 26 condos ⅋ In-room: kitchen, refrigerator, dial-up, Wi-Fi. In-hotel: bar, pool, no elevator ☰ AE, MC, V ⅋⅋ EP.*

☾ **$–$$$**   🏨 **Fischer's Cove Beach Hotel.** The rooms are modest, the walls thin, and the owners in the midst of upgrading the chipped furniture and tired

2

bedspreads, but you can't beat the location. Budget travelers should consider this hotel if they want a good beach just steps away. If you plan to stay put, you won't even need to rent a car. Spanish Town's handful of restaurants and shopping at Virgin Gorda Yacht Harbor are an easy 15-minute walk away. For better views, opt for the beachfront rooms. ⌂ *Box 60, The Valley* ☎ *284/495–5252* 🖷 *284/495–5820* ⊕ *www. fischerscove.com* ⇄ *12 rooms, 8 cottages* ♿ *In-room: no a/c (some), kitchen (some), refrigerator, no TV (some), dial-up. In-hotel: restaurant, beachfront, no elevator* ⊟ *AE, MC, V* ¶⊙¶ *EP.*

$ 🏨 **Leverick Bay Resort & Marina.** With its colorful buildings and bustling marina, Leverick Bay is a good choice. The resort does not have a great beach, but with easy access to various water-sports activities, a tasty on-site restaurant, and comfortable and spacious rooms, it's still appealing. If you prefer an apartment, opt for one of the units stretching up the hillside above the marina. There's a one-week minimum stay in the apartments. All the accommodations have tile floors and pastel accents with a tropical feel. ⌂ *Box 63, Leverick Bay* ☎ *284/495–7421 or 800/848–7081* 🖷 *284/495–7367* ⊕ *www.leverickbay.com* ⇄ *14 rooms, 4 condos* ♿ *In-room: safe, kitchen (some), refrigerator. In-hotel: 2 restaurants, bar, tennis court, pool, spa, beachfront, diving, laundry facilities, public Internet* ⊟ *AE, MC, V* ¶⊙¶ *EP.*

Villas

Those craving seclusion would do well at a villa. Most have full kitchens and maid service. Prices per week in winter run from around $2,000 for a one- or two-bedroom villa up to $10,000 for a five-room beachfront villa. Rates in summer are substantially less.

On Virgin Gorda, a villa in the North Sound area means you'll pretty much stay put at night unless you want to make the drive on narrow roads to the Valley's restaurants. If you opt for a spot near the Baths, it's an easy drive to town.

The St. Thomas–based **McLaughlin-Anderson Luxury Villas** (⌂ 1000 Blackbeard's Hill, Suite 3, Charlotte Amalie, USVI 00802-6739 ☎ 340/776–0635 or 800/537–6246 ⊕ www.mclaughlinanderson.com) handles nearly two dozen properties all over Virgin Gorda. Villas range in size from two bedrooms to six bedrooms and come with many amenities, including full kitchens, pools, and stellar views. The company can hire a chef and stock your kitchen with groceries. A seven-night minimum is required during the winter season.

Virgin Gorda Villa Rentals (⌂ Box 63, The Valley ☎ 284/495–7421 or 800/848–7081 ⊕ www.virgingordabvi.com) manages more than 40 properties near Leverick Bay Resort and Mahoe Bay, so it's perfect for those who want to be close to activities. Many of the accommodations—from studios to six or more bedrooms—have private swimming pools and air-conditioning, at least in the bedrooms; all have full kitchens, are well maintained, and have spectacular views.

$–$$$$ 🏨 **Mango Bay Resort.** Sitting seaside on Virgin Gorda's north coast, this collection of contemporary duplex apartments will make you feel at home in the tropics. Each apartment is individually owned, so each has a different decor, but you can count on tile floors and tropical accents. The homes come with floats, kayaks, and snorkeling equipment, so you can find plenty to do when you're tired of lounging in the chaise. The popular Giorgio's Table restaurant is a short walk away. ⌂ *Box 1062, Mahoe Bay* ☎ *284/495–5672* 🖷 *284/495–5674* ⊕ *www.mangobayresort.com* ⇨ *18 condos, 2 villas* ⚒ *In-room: kitchen. In-hotel: beachfront, no elevator, public Wi-Fi* ▭ *MC, V* ⍾| *EP.*

★ **$$** 🏠 **Guavaberry Spring Bay Vacation Homes.** Rambling back from the beach, these hexagonal one- and two-bedroom villas give you all the comforts of home with the striking boulder-fringed beach just minutes away. The same company also manages 18 other villas in the vicinity. The villas are best for independent travelers who want to be able to cook or simply head 10 minutes to Spanish Town for a night out. The popular Baths are a short walk away, and snorkeling is excellent. The rooms have dark-wood or white walls, tile floors, and tropical bright spreads and curtains. Not all have sea views. ⌂ *Box 20, The Valley* ☎ *284/ 495–5227* 🖷 *284/495–5283* ⊕ *www.guavaberryspringbay.com* ⇨ *12 1-bedroom units, 6 2-bedroom units, 18 villas* ⚒ *In-room: no a/c, no phone, kitchen, no TV. In-hotel: beachfront, no elevator, public Internet, public Wi-Fi* ▭ *No credit cards* ⍾| *EP.*

Where to Eat

Restaurants range from simple to elegant. Hotels that are accessible only by boat will arrange transport in advance upon request from nonguests who wish to dine at their restaurants. It's wise to make dinner reservations almost everywhere except really casual spots.

AMERICAN–
CASUAL
$$$–$$$$
✕ **The Restaurant at Leverick Bay.** This bi-level restaurant looks out over North Sound. The fancier upstairs dining room is slightly more expensive, with a menu that includes steaks, pork chops, chicken, and fresh fish. There's a prime-rib special on Saturday nights. Below, the bar offers light fare all day—starting with breakfast and moving on to hamburgers, salads, and pizzas until well into the evening. There's a children's menu downstairs. ⊠ *Leverick Bay Resort & Marina, Leverick Bay* ☎ *284/495–7154* ▭ *AE, MC, V.*

⟳ **$$–$$$$** ✕ **The Flying Iguana Restaurant & Bar.** Local art is displayed in this charming restaurant's comfortable lounge. The open-air dining room looks past the island's tiny airport to the sea. Enjoy classic eggs and bacon for breakfast; for lunch there are sandwiches and juicy hamburgers. The dinner menu includes fresh seafood, grilled chicken, sizzling steaks, and a pasta special. ⊠ *Virgin Gorda Airport, The Valley* ☎ *284/495–5277* ▭ *MC, V.*

$$–$$$$ ✕ **The Mine Shaft Café.** Perched on a hilltop that offers a view of spectacular sunsets, this restaurant near Copper Mine Point serves simple yet well-prepared food, including grilled fish, chicken, steaks, and baby back ribs. Wednesday night features an all-you-can-eat Caribbean-style barbecue. The bar, as well as the monthly full-moon parties, draw a big local crowd. ⊠ *Copper Mine Point, The Valley* ☎ *284/495–5260* ▭ *MC, V.*

⟳ **$$$** ✕ **Top of the Baths.** At the entrance to the Baths, this popular restaurant starts serving at 8 AM. Tables are on an outdoor terrace or in an open-air pavilion; all have stunning views of the Sir Francis Drake Channel.

Hamburgers, sandwiches, and fish-and-chips are offered at lunch. Conch fritters and pumpkin soup are among the dinner appetizers. Entrées include fillet of yellowtail snapper, shrimp creole, and jerk chicken. For dessert, the mango raspberry cheesecake is excellent. The Sunday barbecue, with live music, is served from noon until 3 PM and is an island event. ✉ *The Valley* ☎ *284/495–5497* ▭ *AE, MC, V.*

$$–$$$ ✕ **LSL Restaurant.** An unpretentious place along the road to the Baths, this small restaurant with pedestrian decor is a local favorite. You'll always find fresh fish on the menu, but folks with a taste for other dishes won't be disappointed. Try the veal with mushrooms and herbs in a white wine sauce or the breast of chicken with rum cream and nuts. ✉ *Tower Rd., The Valley* ☎ *284/495–5151* ▭ *MC, V.*

$$ ✕ **The Bath & Turtle.** You can sit back and relax at this informal tavern with a friendly staff—although the noise from the television can sometimes be a bit much. Well-stuffed sandwiches, homemade pizzas, pasta dishes, and daily specials like conch soup round out the casual menu. Live musicians perform Wednesday night. ✉ *Virgin Gorda Yacht Harbour, Spanish Town* ☎ *284/495–5239* ▭ *AE, MC, V.*

$$ ✕ **The Fat Virgin's Café.** This casual beachfront eatery offers a straightforward menu of flying-fish sandwiches, baby back ribs, chicken roti, vegetable pasta, and fresh fish specials for lunch and dinner. Saturday nights there's a special Chinese menu. You'll find a good selection of Caribbean beer. ✉ *Biras Creek Resort, North Sound* ☎ *284/495–7052* ▭ *MC, V.*

¢ ✕ **Mad Dog's.** Piña coladas are *the* thing at this breezy bar just outside the entrance to the Baths. The menu includes great triple-decker sandwiches and hot dogs. ✉ *The Valley* ☎ *284/495–5830* ▭ *No credit cards* ⊙ *No dinner.*

CAJUN/CREOLE
$$–$$$$ ✕ **Chez Bamboo.** This pleasant little hideaway isn't difficult to find; look for the building with the purple and green latticework. Candles in the dining room and on the patio help make this a mellow place where you can enjoy a bowl of conch gumbo or one of the specialties like lobster curry. For dessert, try the chocolate cake or crème brûlée. Stop by Friday night for live music. ✉ *Across from and a little north of Virgin Gorda Yacht Harbour, Spanish Town* ☎ *284/495–5752* ▭ *AE, MC, V* ⊙ *No lunch.*

CONTINENTAL
$$$$ ✕ **Biras Creek Restaurant.** This hilltop restaurant at the Biras Creek Hotel has eye-popping views of North Sound. The four-course prix-fixe menu changes daily and includes several choices per course. For starters, there may be an artichoke, green bean, and wild mushroom salad with a balsamic vinaigrette, or cream of sweet potato soup topped with potato straws. Entrées may include pan-seared snapper over horseradish pearl pasta. The desserts, including a lemon ricotta cheesecake with a spicy passion-fruit sauce, are to die for. Dinner ends with Biras Creek's signature offering of cheese and port. ✉ *Biras Creek Hotel, North Sound* ☎ *284/494–3555 or 800/223–1108* ✍ *Reservations essential* ▭ *AE, D, MC, V* ⊙ *No lunch.*

$$$$ ✕ **Little Dix Bay Pavilion.** For an elegant evening, you can't do better than this—the candlelight in the open-air pavilion is enchanting, the daily chang-

ing menu sophisticated, the service attentive. The dinner menu always includes a fine selection of superbly prepared seafood, meat, and vegetarian entrées. Favorites include the pan-seared marinated tuna with sweet-chili sautéed spinach, rack of lamb with a garlic puree, and red snapper fillet with fennel served with sweet-potato tempura. The Monday breakfast, lunch, and evening buffets shine. ⊠ *Little Dix Bay Resort, Spanish Town* ☎ *284/495–5555* ⚑ *Reservations essential* ▤ *AE, D, MC, V.*

ITALIAN ✕ **Giorgio's Table.** Gaze up at the stars and listen to the water lap against
$$$$ the shore while dining on homemade ravioli, beef fillet in a brunello wine sauce, or truffle duck ragout served over pappardelle pasta. House specialties include fresh lobster that you choose from a 5,000-gallon seawater pool. There's also a selection of 120 different wines kept in a temperature-controlled cellar. Lunch is more casual and includes pizzas and sandwiches. ⊠ *Mahoe Bay* ☎ *284/495–5684* ▤ *AE, MC, V.*

$$–$$$ ✕ **The Rock Café.** Surprisingly good Italian cuisine is served among the waterfalls and giant boulders that form the famous Baths. For dinner at this open-air eatery, feast on spinach-and-ricotta gnocchi, spaghetti with lobster sauce, or fresh red snapper in a butter and caper sauce. For dessert, don't miss the chocolate mousse. For lunch there's more casual fare: pizza, burgers, and sandwiches. ⊠ *The Valley* ☎ *284/495–5482* ▤ *AE, D, MC, V.*

SEAFOOD ✕ **The Clubhouse.** The Bitter End Yacht Club's open-air waterfront
★ $$$$ restaurant is a favorite rendezvous for the sailing set, so it's busy day and night. You can find lavish buffets for breakfast, lunch, and dinner, as well as an à la carte menu. Dinner selections include grilled swordfish or tuna, local lobster, chopped sirloin, as well as veggie dishes. ⊠ *Bitter End Yacht Club, North Sound* ☎ *284/494–2745* ⚑ *Reservations essential* ▤ *AE, MC, V.*

Beaches

Although some of the best beaches are reachable only by boat, don't worry if you're a landlubber, because you can find plenty of places to sun and swim. Anybody going to Virgin Gorda must experience swimming or snorkeling among its unique boulder formations, which can be visited at several sites along Lee Road. The most popular is the Baths, but there are several other similar places nearby that are easily reached.

The Baths. Featuring a stunning maze of huge granite boulders that extend into the sea, this national-park beach is usually crowded midday with day-trippers. The snorkeling is good, and you're likely to see a wide variety of fish, but watch out for dinghies coming ashore from the numerous sailboats anchored just off the beach. Public bathrooms and a handful of bars and shops are close to the water and at the start of the path that leads to the beach. Lockers are available to keep belongings safe. ⊠ *About 1 mi (1½ km) west of Spanish Town ferry dock on Tower Rd., Spring Bay* ☎ *284/494–3904* ▥ *$3* ⊙ *Daily dawn–dusk.*

Nail Bay. Head to the island's north tip and you'll be rewarded with a trio of beaches within the Nail Bay Resort complex that are ideal for snorkeling. Mountain Trunk Bay is perfect for beginners, and Nail Bay and Long Bay beaches have coral caverns just offshore. The resort has a restaurant, which is an uphill walk but perfect for beach breaks. ⊠ *Nail Bay Resort, off Plum Tree Bay Rd., Nail Bay* ☎ *No phone* ☲ *Free* ☉ *Daily dawn–dusk.*

Savannah Bay. For a wonderfully private beach close to Spanish Town, try Savannah Bay. It may not always be completely deserted, but you'll find a spot to yourself on this long stretch of soft, white sand. Bring your own mask, fins, and snorkel, as there are no facilities. The view from above is a photographer's delight. ⊠ *Off North Sound Rd., ¾ mi (1¼ km) east of Spanish Town ferry dock, Savannah Bay* ☎ *No phone* ☲ *Free* ☉ *Daily dawn–dusk.*

Spring Bay Beach. Just off Tower Road, this national-park beach gets much less traffic than the nearby Baths, and has the similarly large, imposing boulders that create interesting grottoes for swimming. The snorkeling is excellent, and the grounds include swings and picnic tables. ⊠ *Off Tower Rd., 1 mi (1½ km) west of Spanish Town ferry dock, Spring Bay* ☎ *284/494–3904* ☲ *Free* ☉ *Daily dawn–dusk.*

ports & the Outdoors

Cricket

You can catch a match at the Recreation Grounds in Spanish Town February to April. The BVI Tourist Board at Virgin Gorda Yacht Harbor can give you information on game dates and times.

Diving & Snorkeling

Where you go snorkeling and what company you pick depend on where you're staying. Many hotels have on-site dive outfitters, but if they don't, one won't be far away. If your hotel does have a dive operation, just stroll down to the dock and hop aboard—no need to drive anywhere. The dive companies are all certified by PADI. Costs vary, but count on paying about $75 for a one-tank dive and $95 for a two-tank dive. All dive operators offer introductory courses as well as certification and advanced courses. Should you get an attack of the bends, which can happen when you ascend too rapidly, the nearest decompression chamber is at Roy L. Schneider Regional Medical Center in St. Thomas.

There are some terrific snorkel and dive sites off Virgin Gorda, including areas around the Baths, the North Sound, and the Dogs. The Chimney at Great Dog Island sports a coral archway and canyon covered with a wide variety of sponges. At Joe's Cave, an underwater cavern on West Dog Island, huge groupers, eagle rays, and other colorful fish accompany divers as they swim. At some sites you can see 100 feet down, but divers who don't want to go that deep and snorkelers will find plenty to look at just below the surface.

The **Bitter End Yacht Club** (⊠ North Sound ☎ 284/494–2746 ⊕ www. beyc.com) offers two snorkeling trips a day. **Dive BVI** (⊠ Virgin Gorda Yacht Harbour, Spanish Town ☎ 284/495–5513 or 800/848–7078 ⊠ Leverick Bay Resort and Marina, Leverick Bay ☎ 284/495–7328 ⊕ www.divebvi.com) offers expert instruction, certification, and day trips.

Sunchaser Scuba (⌧ Bitter End Yacht Club, North Sound ☎ 284/495–9638 or 800/932–4286 ⊕ www.sunchaserscuba.com) offers resort, advanced, and rescue courses.

Golf

The 9-hole minigolf course, **Golf Virgin Gorda** (⌧ Copper Mine Point, The Valley ☎ 284/495–5260), is next to the Mine Shaft Café, delightfully nestled between huge granite boulders.

Sailing & Boating

The BVI waters are calm, and terrific places to learn to sail. You can also rent sea kayaks, waterskiing equipment, dinghies, and powerboats, or take a parasailing trip.

Windsurfing

The North Sound is a good place to learn to windsurf: it's protected, so you can't be easily blown out to sea. The **Bitter End Yacht Club** (⌧ North Sound ☎ 284/494–2746 ⊕ www.beyc.com) gives lessons and rents equipment for $60 per hour for nonguests. A half-day Windsurfer rental runs $80 to $100.

Shopping

Most boutiques are within hotel complexes or at Virgin Gorda Yacht Harbour. Two of the best are at Biras Creek and Little Dix Bay. Other properties—the Bitter End and Leverick Bay—have small but equally select boutiques.

CLOTHING **Blue Banana** (⌧ Virgin Gorda Yacht Harbour, Spanish Town ☎ 284/495–5957) carries a large selection of gifts, clothing, and accessories. At **Dive BVI** (⌧ Virgin Gorda Yacht Harbour, Spanish Town ☎ 284/495–5513), you can find books about the islands as well as snorkeling equipment, sportswear, sunglasses, and beach bags. **Fat Virgin's Treasure** (⌧ Biras Creek Hotel, North Sound ☎ 284/495–7054) sells cool island-style clothing in tropical prints, a large selection of straw sun hats, and unusual gift items like island-made hot sauces, artistic cards, and locally fired pottery. **Margo's Boutique** (⌧ Virgin Gorda Yacht Harbour, Spanish Town ☎ 284/495–5237) is the place to buy handmade silver, pearl, and shell jewelry. The **Pavilion Gift Shop** (⌧ Little Dix Bay Hotel, Little Dix Bay ☎ 284/495–5555) has the latest in resort wear for men and women, as well as jewelry, books, housewares, and expensive T-shirts. **Pusser's Company Store** (⌧ Leverick Bay ☎ 284/495–7369) has a trademark line of sportswear, rum products, and gift items.

FOODSTUFFS The **Bitter End Emporium** (⌧ Bitter End Yacht Harbor, North Sound ☎ 284/494–2746) is the place for such edible treats as local fruits, cheeses, baked goods, and gourmet prepared food to take out. **Buck's Food Market** (⌧ Virgin Gorda Yacht Harbour, Spanish Town ☎ 284/495–5423 ⌧ Gun Creek, North Sound ☎ 284/495–7368) is the closest the island offers to a full-service supermarket and has everything from an in-store bakery and deli to fresh fish and produce departments. The **Chef's Pantry** (⌧ Leverick Bay ☎ 284/495–7677) has the fixings for an impromptu party in your villa or boat—fresh seafood, specialty meats, imported cheeses, daily baked breads and pastries, and an impressive wine and spirit selection. The **Wine Cellar & Bakery** (⊠ Virgin Gorda Yacht Harbour, Spanish Town ☎ 284/495–5250) sells bread, rolls, muffins, cookies, sandwiches, and sodas to go.

GIFTS **Flamboyance** (⊠ Virgin Gorda Yacht Harbour, Spanish Town ☎ 284/495–5946) has a large line of fragrances, including those inspired by tropical flowers. The **Palm Tree Gallery** (⊠ Leverick Bay ☎ 284/495–7479) sells attractive handcrafted jewelry, paintings, and one-of-a-kind gift items, as well as games and books about the Caribbean. **Reeftique** (⊠ Bitter End Yacht Harbor, North Sound ☎ 284/494–2746) carries island crafts and jewelry, clothing, and nautical odds and ends with the Bitter End logo.

Nightlife

Pick up a free copy of the *Limin' Times*—available at most resorts and restaurants—for the most current local entertainment schedule.

During high season, **The Bath & Turtle** (⊠ Virgin Gorda Yacht Harbour, Spanish Town ☎ 284/495–5239), one of the liveliest spots on Virgin Gorda, hosts island bands Wednesday from 8 PM until midnight. Local bands play several nights a week at **Bitter End Yacht Club** (⊠ North Sound ☎ 284/494–2746) during the winter season. **Chez Bamboo** (⊠ Across from Virgin Gorda Yacht Harbour, Spanish Town ☎ 284/495–5752) is the place for live jazz on Friday nights. The bar at **Little Dix Bay** (⊠ Little Dix Bay ☎ 284/495–5555) presents elegant live entertainment several nights a week in season. The **Mine Shaft Café** (⊠ Copper Mine Point, The Valley ☎ 284/495–5260) has live bands on Wednesday and Friday. The **Restaurant at Leverick Bay** (⊠ Leverick Bay Resort & Marina, Leverick Bay ☎ 284/495–7154) hosts live music on Saturday through Wednesday in season. The **Rock Café** (⊠ The Valley ☎ 284/495–5177) has live bands Friday.

Exploring Virgin Gorda

One of the most efficient ways to see Virgin Gorda is by sailboat. There are few roads, and most byways don't follow the scalloped shoreline. The main route sticks resolutely to the center of the island, linking the Baths at the tip of the southern extremity with Gun Creek and Leverick Bay at North Sound and providing exhilarating views. The craggy coast, scissored with grottoes and fringed by palms and boulders, has a primitive beauty. If you drive, you can hit all the sights in one day. The best plan is to explore the area near your hotel (either the Valley or North Sound) first, then take a day to drive to the other end. Stop to climb Gorda Peak, which is in the island's center.

Numbers in the margin correspond to points of interest on the Virgin Gorda map.

What to See

The Baths. At Virgin Gorda's most celebrated sight, giant boulders are scattered about the beach and in the water. Some are almost as large as houses and form remarkable grottoes. Climb between these rocks to swim in the many placid pools. Early morning and late afternoon are the best times to visit if you want to avoid crowds. If it's privacy you crave, follow the shore northward to quieter bays—Spring Bay, the Crawl, Little Trunk, and Valley Trunk—or head south to Devil's Bay. ⌧ *Off Tower Rd., The Baths* ☎ *284/494–3904* ⊕ *www.bvinationalparkstrust. org* ⌧ *$3* ⊙ *Daily dawn–dusk.*

Coastal Islands. You can easily reach the quaintly named Fallen Jerusalem Island and the Dog Islands by boat. They're all part of the BVI National Parks Trust, and their seductive beaches and unparalleled snorkeling display the BVI at their beachcombing, hedonistic best. ☎ *No phone* ⌧ *Free.*

Copper Mine Point. Here stand a tall stone shaft silhouetted against the sky and a small stone structure that overlooks the sea. These are the ruins of a copper mine established 400 years ago and worked first by the Spanish, then by the English, until the early 20th century. In April 2003 this historic site became the 20th park under the BVI National Parks Trust jurisdiction. ⌧ *Copper Mine Rd.* ☎ *No phone* ⊕ *www. bvinationalparkstrust.org* ⌧ *Free.*

Spanish Town. Virgin Gorda's peaceful main settlement, on the island's southern wing, is so tiny that it barely qualifies as a town at all. Also known as the Valley, Spanish Town has a marina, some shops, and a couple of car-rental agencies. Just north of town is the ferry slip. At the Virgin Gorda Yacht Harbour you can stroll along the dock and do a little shopping.

★ **Virgin Gorda Peak National Park.** There are two trails at this 265-acre park, which contains the island's highest point, at 1,359 feet. Small signs on North Sound Road mark both entrances; sometimes, however, the signs are missing, so keep your eyes open for a set of stairs that disappears into the trees. It's about a 15-minute hike from either entrance up to a small clearing, where you can climb a ladder to the platform of a wooden observation tower and a spectacular 360-degree view. ⌧ *North Sound Rd., Gorda Peak* ☎ *No phone* ⊕ *www.bvinationalparkstrust. org* ⌧ *Free.*

JOST VAN DYKE

Updated by
Carol M.
Bareuther

Named after an early Dutch settler, Jost Van Dyke is a small island northwest of Tortola and is *truly* a place to get away from it all. Mountainous and lush, the 4-mi-long (6½-km-long) island—with fewer than 200 full-time residents—has one tiny resort, some rental houses and villas, a campground, a handful of cars, and a single road. Life definitely rolls along on "island time," especially during the off-season from August to November, when finding a restaurant open for dinner can be a challenge. Water conservation is encouraged, as the source is rainwater col-

The Laid-Back Lifestyle at its Best

CLOSE UP

It's the laid-back attitude of Jost Van Dyke, which boasts a beach as its main street and has had electricity only since the 1990s, that makes the famous feel comfortable and everyday folk feel glorious. At no locale is this more so than at Foxy's Tamarind. Foxy Callwood, a seventh-generation Jost Van Dyker and calypsonian extraordinaire, is the star here, strumming and singing rib-tickling ditties full of lewd and laughable lyrics that attract a bevy of boaters and even celebrities like Tom Cruise, Kelsey Grammer, and Steven Spielberg.

What began in the 1970s as a lemonade-stand-size bar, albeit with "modern" fixtures like a galvanized roof and plywood walls, has evolved into a bona fide beach bar with sand floor, wattle walls, and thatched roof that defines the eastern end of the

beach at Great Harbour. Without the glitz of St. Thomas, glamour of St. John, or grace of Tortola, islanders like Foxy knew they needed to carve out their own unique niche—and have done so by appearing to have done nothing at all. Unhurried friendliness and a slice of quintessential Caribbean culture flow freely here.

Foxy, who fished for a living before he started singing for his supper, has traveled the world and has the world come to him for endless parties for Halloween, for Labor Day weekend, and for the New Year. The *New York Times* named Foxy's one of its three top picks to ring in the millennium. What's the appeal? Foxy sums it up himself: "It's the quantity of people and the quality of the party. You can dance on the tables and sleep on the beach. No one is going to bother you."

lected in basement-like cisterns. Most lodgings will ask you to follow the Caribbean golden rule: "In the land of sun and fun, we never flush for number one." Jost is one of the Caribbean's most popular anchorages, and there's a disproportionately large number of informal bars and restaurants, which have helped earn Jost its reputation as the "party island" of the BVI.

Where to Stay

For approximate costs, *see* the lodging price chart *in* Tortola.

$$–$$$$ **White Bay Villas & Seaside Cottages.** There's no missing the beautiful sea views from the verandahs of these hilltop one- to three-bedroom villas and cottages. Accommodations are open-air, with screenless doors and shuttered windows, although there's mosquito netting covering the beds. Almost everything is provided, from linens and beach towels to an occasional bunch of fresh bananas or a ripe papaya from the trees outside. Although there are some small markets on the island, it's a good idea to buy groceries on St. Thomas or Tortola before arriving. White Bay and five beach bars are a short, albeit steep and rocky, walk downhill. A mile farther down the beach there's a small supermarket, half a dozen beach bars and restaurants, a souvenir shop, and water-sports rental. ✉ *White Bay* 📭 *Box 3368, Annapolis, MD 21403* ☎ *410/571–6692*

or 800/778–8066 ⊕ *www.jostvandyke.com* ↪ *3 villas, 3 cottages* ⌂ *In-room: no a/c, kitchen, VCRs (some). In-hotel: beachfront, no elevator* ▭ *No credit cards* ❘❂❘ *EP.*

$$$ ▣ **Sandy Ground Estates.** Each of these privately owned one- and two-bedroom villas is distinct in decor, with interiors ranging from spartan to stylish. The settings are unique, too. The House on the Hill, 80 feet above sea level, is assured of a cool breeze, complete privacy, and spectacular views of Sandy Cay. The Little House has a private path to the beach, three minutes away. Sunfish and kayaks are available for rent. Foliage, ranging from native greenery to cacti, abounds on this eastern end of the island. The closest civilization is Foxy's Taboo, about a half-mile away. Your kitchen can be prestocked, or you can bring or buy your own groceries. To get here, you need to take a water taxi from St. Thomas or West End, Tortola, to the resort's private dock. ⊠ *Sandy Ground Estates* ⌂ *Box 594, West End* ☎ *284/494–3391* 🖷 *284/495–9379* ⊕ *www.sandyground.com* ↪ *7 houses* ⌂ *In-room: no a/c, no phone, kitchen, no TV. In-hotel: beachfront, no elevator* ▭ *MC, V* ❘❂❘ *EP.*

★ $$–$$$ ▣ **Sandcastle.** This six-cottage hideaway sits on a half-mile stretch of white-sand beach shared by a half dozen beach bars and restaurants. The peach-color cottages are simply furnished. Two-bedroom cottages have outdoor showers and no air-conditioning, but the one-bedroom cottages do have these conveniences. Either way, the Caribbean is no more than 20 feet from your doorstep. There's nothing to do here except relax in a hammock, read, walk the beach, swim, and snorkel. Unfortunately, you may find your serenity shattered between 11 AM and 3 PM by the charter-boat day-trippers who arrive on large catamarans for lunch and drinks at the Soggy Dollar Bar. At night, tuck into a casually elegant, four-course candlelight dinner at the Sandcastle Restaurant. For weeklong stays you have the option of a package that includes all breakfasts and most dinners. Owners Jerry and Tish O'Connell have maintained the same haven't-I-known-you-forever vibe for which original owners, Debby Pearce and Bruce Donath, were known. ⊠ *White Bay* ☎ *284/495–9888* 🖷 *284/495–9999* ⊕ *www.sandcastle-bvi.com* ↪ *4 1-bedroom cottages, 2 2-bedroom cottages* ⌂ *In-room: no a/c (some), no TV. In-hotel: restaurant, bar, beachfront, no elevator* ▭ *D, MC, V* ❘❂❘ *EP.*

$ ▣ **Sea Crest Inn.** Perched on the hillside at the far east end of Great Harbour, this two-story white building with red trim has four one-bedroom apartments, each equipped with a refrigerator, gas range, and microwave oven. All have wicker furnishings, tropical-print bedspreads and curtains, and cool tile floors. From the balconies you get a sweeping view of the beach, where a half dozen bars and restaurants are within walking distance. Great Harbour does rock, especially on weekend nights, and the thumping bass from live bands at the beach bars may keep you awake, or it may entice you to join the party. If you need tips on where to party, eat, or sightsee, just ask the charming proprietor, Jost native Ivy Chinnery Moses. ⊠ *Great Harbour* ☎ *284/495–9024* 🖷 *284/495–9034* ⊕ *www.bviwelcome.com/seacrestinn/seacrestinn.html* ↪ *4 1-bedroom apartments* ⌂ *In-room: kitchen. In-hotel: beachfront, no elevator* ▭ *MC, V* ❘❂❘ *EP.*

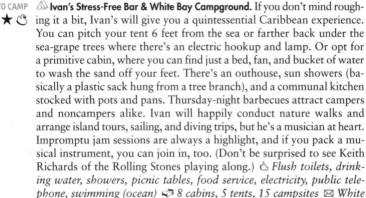 **Ivan's Stress-Free Bar & White Bay Campground.** If you don't mind rough-
★ ☾ ing it a bit, Ivan's will give you a quintessential Caribbean experience.
You can pitch your tent 6 feet from the sea or farther back under the
sea-grape trees where there's an electric hookup and lamp. Or opt for
a primitive cabin, where you can find just a bed, fan, and bucket of water
to wash the sand off your feet. There's an outhouse, sun showers (basically a plastic sack hung from a tree branch), and a communal kitchen
stocked with pots and pans. Thursday-night barbecues attract campers
and noncampers alike. Ivan will happily conduct nature walks and
arrange island tours, sailing, and diving trips, but he's a musician at heart.
Impromptu jam sessions are always a highlight, and if you pack a mu-
sical instrument, you can join in, too. (Don't be surprised to see Keith
Richards of the Rolling Stones playing along.) ☒ *Flush toilets, drinking water, showers, picnic tables, food service, electricity, public telephone, swimming (ocean)* ☝ *8 cabins, 5 tents, 15 campsites* ☒ *White
Bay* ☎ *284/495–9312* ⊕ *www.caribbeancruisingclub.com/ivan*
☒ *$25–$60* ☒ *Reservations essential* ⊟ *No credit cards.*

Where to Eat

Restaurants on Jost Van Dyke are informal (some serve meals family-
style at long tables) but charming. The island is a favorite charter-boat
stop, and you're bound to hear people exchanging stories about the previous night's anchoring adventures. Most restaurants don't take reservations, and in all cases dress is casual.

For approximate costs, *see* the dining price chart *in* Tortola.

$$$$ ✕ **Sandcastle.** Candles illuminate this tiny beachfront dining room during the four-course, prix-fixe affairs. The menu changes frequently but
can include West Indian pumpkin or curried-apple soup; curried shrimp
or three-mustard chicken; and, for dessert, rum bananas or key lime pie.
Reservations are required by 4 PM for the single dinner seating at 7 PM.
For lunch, you can get flying-fish sandwiches, hamburgers, and conch
fritters at the Soggy Dollar Bar, famous as the purported birthplace of
the lethal drink called the Painkiller. ☒ *Sandcastle, White Bay* ☎ *284/
495–9888* ☒ *Reservations essential* ⊟ *D, MC, V.*

☾ **$$–$$$$** ✕ **Foxy's Taboo.** An oasis in the middle of uninhabited marshland at Di-
amond Cay, this simple, open-air eatery has plastic chairs and tiled wooden
tables overlooking a "marina" (really a small dock). But the menu is
definitely more upscale here than at Foxy's place in Great Harbour. The
Taboo burger at lunch is a hand-formed mound of 100% beef, served
with mango chutney and pepper-jack cheese on ciabatta bread. House-
made pizzas have toppings ranging from jalapeño peppers to prosciutto
and kalamata olives. Dinner selections include mango-tamarind chicken.
There are a dozen or more wines available by the bottle or glass. Don't
miss the tiramisu for dessert. Dinner reservations are required by 5 PM.
☒ *Diamond Cay* ☎ *284/495–0218* ☒ *Reservations essential* ⊟ *AE,
MC, V* ☾ *Closed Mon. No dinner Sun.*

Fodor's Choice ✕ **Foxy's Tamarind.** One of the true hot spots in the BVI—and a must-
★ stop for yachties from the world over—Foxy's hosts the madcap Wooden
☾ **$$–$$$$** Boat Race every May and throws big parties on New Year's Eve, April

Fools' Day, and Halloween. This lively place serves local food, has terrific barbecue dinners on Friday and Saturday nights, mixes its own rum punch, and serves its own Foxy's brand beer. Famed calypso performer and owner Foxy Callwood plays the guitar and creates calypso ditties about diners. Reservations for dinner are required by 5 PM. ⊠ *Great Harbour* ☎ *284/495–9258* ⌕ *Reservations essential* ⊟ *AE, MC, V* ⊗ *No lunch weekends.*

$$–$$$$ ✕ **Sydney's Peace & Love.** Here you can find great lobster, caught aboard owner Sydney Hendrick's own fishing boat, as well as barbecue chicken and ribs. All are served on an open-air terrace or in an air-conditioned dining room at the water's edge. The find here is a sensational (by BVI standards) jukebox. The cognoscenti sail here for dinner, since there's no beach—meaning no irksome sand fleas. ⊠ *Little Harbour* ☎ *284/ 495–9271* ⊟ *D, MC, V.*

$$–$$$ ✕ **Abe's by the Sea.** Specialties at this popular, informal seaside spot include fresh lobster, conch, and spareribs. During the winter season there's a pig roast every Wednesday evening. ⊠ *Little Harbour* ☎ *284/ 495–9329* ⊟ *D, MC, V.*

★ ☺   ✕ **Ali Baba's.** This sandy-floor eatery offers beach-bar dining at its best.
$$–$$$ Lobster and grilled local fish, including swordfish, kingfish, and wahoo, are specialties. There's a pig roast on Monday night. Beware: Ali Baba's special rum punch is delicious but potent. Dinner reservations are required by 6 PM. ⊠ *Great Harbour* ☎ *284/495–9280* ⌕ *Reservations essential* ⊟ *AE, MC, V.*

☺ **$$–$$$**   ✕ **Corsairs Beach Bar & Restaurant.** This beach bar is easily recognized by the restored U.S. Army Jeep that adjoins the dining area. Tex-Mex and Caribbean foods star at lunch, with selections ranging from lobster quesadillas to jerk-chicken wings. Northern Italian takes over at night, when you can find seafood pomodoro, which is full of shrimp, fish, squid, and lobster. Live music and a great drink menu keep things moving at night. ⊠ *Great Harbour* ☎ *284/495–9294* ⊟ *MC, V.*

★ ☺   ✕ **Harris' Place.** Cynthia Harris is famous for her hospitality, along with
$$–$$$ her family's famous pig-roast buffets and Monday-night lobster specials. This is the hot spot to rub elbows with locals and the charter-boat crowd for breakfast, lunch, or dinner. ⊠ *Little Harbour* ☎ *284/495– 9302* ⊟ *AE, D, MC, V.*

$$–$$$ ✕ **Rudy's Mariner's Rendezvous.** Hamburgers, cheeseburgers, and barbecue ribs are the specialties at this beachfront spot at the extreme western end of Great Harbour. There's a lobster buffet every Thursday night in season. You'll also find a supermarket where you can buy basic groceries. ⊠ *Great Harbour* ☎ *284/495–9282* ⊟ *D, MC, V.*

☺ **$**   ✕ **Christine's Bakery.** The small porch of this two-story building, which is set back from the beach on Bun Road next to the icehouse, is a great spot to eat breakfast and watch the island come to life. The cinnamon buns are lush, especially if they've just come out of the oven. For lunch have a hearty sandwich on home-baked white or whole-wheat bread. The coconut cake, banana bread, and brownies are excellent, too. ⊠ *Great Harbour* ☎ *284/495–9281* ⊟ *No credit cards* ⊗ *No dinner.*

☺ **¢–$**   ✕ **Jewel's Snack Shack.** This little wooden shack sells the best—and only—hot dogs on the island. You will also find burgers, fries, and ice cream novelties. ⊠ *White Bay* ☎ *284/495–9286* ⊟ *No credit cards* ⊗ *No dinner.*

Beaches & Activities

Jost Van Dyke Safari Services. Native Jost Van Dyker Dorsey Chinnery is expert at navigating the steep roads here in his big, red, open-air safari cab. He knows all the best spots to visit on a sightseeing tour and can help you with everything from beach-hopping to barhopping. His tours cost $20 per person. ☎ *284/495–9267 or 284/443–3832* ⊕ *www.bviwelcome.com/jvdsafari.*

JVD Scuba and BVI Eco-Tours. See the undersea world around the island with divemaster Colin Aldridge. One of the most impressive dives in the area is off the north coast of Little Jost Van Dyke. Here you'll find the Twin Towers: a pair of rock formations rising an impressive 90 feet. A one-tank dive costs $60, two-tank dive $95, and four-hour beginner course $120. ⊠ *Great Harbour* ☎ *284/495–0271* ⊕ *www.jvdwatersports.com.*

Paradise Jeep Rentals. Even though Jost is a relatively small island, you really need to be in shape to walk from one bay to the next. Renting a jeep is an ideal way to tackle the steep, winding roads. This outfit rents four-door Suzukis for $50 per day and Grand Vitaras for $60. The vehicles are conveniently located at the gas station in Great Harbour, adjacent to Christine's Bakery. Reservations are a must. ⊠ *Great Harbour* ☎ *284/495–9477.*

Sandy Cay. Just offshore, the little islet known as Sandy Cay is a gleaming scimitar of white sand, with marvelous snorkeling.

★ ☺ **White Bay.** On the south shore, west of Great Harbour, this long stretch of white sand is especially popular with boaters who come ashore for a libation at one of the beach bars.

Nightlife

★ Jost Van Dyke is the most happening place to go barhopping in the BVI. In fact, yachties will sail over just to have a few drinks. All the spots are easy to find, congregated in two general locations: Great Harbour and White Bay (⇨ *see* Where to Eat, *above*). On the Great Harbour side you can find Foxy's, Rudy's, and Ali Baba's; on the White Bay side is the One Love Bar & Grill, where Seddy Callwood will entertain you with his sleight of hand, and the Soggy Dollar bar at the Sandcastle restaurant, where legend has it the famous Painkiller was first concocted. If you can't make it to Jost Van Dyke, you can have a Painkiller at almost any bar in the BVI.

ANEGADA

Updated by
Carol M.
Bareuther

Fodor's Choice

★

Anegada lies low on the horizon about 14 mi (22½ km) north of Virgin Gorda. Unlike the hilly volcanic islands in the chain, this is a flat coral-and-limestone atoll. Nine miles (14 km) long and 2 mi (3 km) wide, the island rises no more than 28 feet above sea level. In fact, by the time you're able to see it, you may have run your boat onto a reef. (More than 300 captains unfamiliar with the waters have done so since exploration days; note that bareboat charters don't allow their vessels to head here without a trained skipper.) Although the reefs are a sailor's nightmare, they (and the shipwrecks they've caused) are a scuba diver's dream. Snorkeling, especially in the waters around Loblolly Bay on the north shore, is a transcendent experience. You can float in shallow, calm water just a few feet from shore and see one coral formation after another, each shimmering with a rainbow of colorful fish. Such watery pleasures are complemented by ever-so-fine, ever-so-white sand (the northern and western shores have long stretches of the stuff) and the occasional beach bar (stop in for burgers, local lobster, or a frosty beer). The island's population of about 150 lives primarily in a small south-side village called the Settlement, which has two grocery stores, a bakery, and a general store. Many local captains are happy to take visitors out bonefishing.

Where to Stay

For approximate costs, *see* the lodging price chart *in* Tortola.

$$–$$$ 🏨 **Anegada Reef Hotel.** This may be the busiest place on sleepy Anegada. Although boaters drop anchor in sheltered waters inside the reef and guests from other hotels stop by for lobster salad lunches, the resort itself remains a serene spot. Head here if you want to relax in the shade on a beach that stretches forever, enjoy the company of like-minded folks, and do nothing more strenuous than heading out once or twice to fish the nearby waters. Rooms are simple but fresh with pastel fabrics. ⊠ *Setting Point* ☎ *284/495–8002* 🖷 *284/495–9362* ⊕ *www.anegadareef. com* 🛏 *16 rooms* ⚙ *In-room: no phone, no TV. In-hotel: restaurant, bar, beachfront, no elevator* ⊟ *MC, V* ⏹ *AI.*

☪ **$$** 🏨 **Anegada Seaside Villas.** This tiny resort is a good place if you really want to get away from it all. There isn't much to do except sun, swim, snorkel, stroll miles of gorgeous white-sand beaches, and catch up on all that reading you've always wanted to do. The modern villas have those tropical touches like wicker furniture and tile floors that you've come to expect. When you tire of cooking in your well-equipped kitchen, head out to one of the island's very casual restaurants for lunch or dinner. Pomato Point Restaurant is five minutes away by foot. ⊠ *Pomato Point* 🖷 *284/495–9466* ⊕ *www.anegadavillas.com* 🛏 *7 villas* ⚙ *In-room: no a/c, no phone, kitchen, no TV. In-hotel: beachfront, no elevator* ⊟ *MC, V* ⏹ *EP.*

☪ **$** 🏨 **Neptune's Treasure.** Basic beachside rooms with simple but squeaky-clean furnishings are the hallmark of this family-owned guesthouse. If you're happy with a simple place to rest your head (there aren't even TVs in the rooms) while you swim in crystal-clear waters, sun at the round-the-island beach, enjoy fresh-from-the-sea dinners at the hotel's restaurant, and watch the sun go down, this is the place. If you must move out of the hammock, the hotel will organize an island tour or a fishing expedition. ⊠ *Between Pomato and Saltheap points* ☎ *284/495–9439* 🖷 *284/495–8060* ⊕ *www.neptunestreasure.com* 🛏 *9 rooms* ⚙ *In-room: no TV. In-hotel: restaurant, beachfront, no elevator* ⊟ *MC, V* ⏹ *EP.*

Where to Eat

There are between 6 and 10 restaurants open at any one time, depending on the season and on whim. Check when you're on the island.

For approximate costs, *see* the dining price chart *in* Tortola.

AMERICAN-
CASUAL
★ $$–$$$$

✕ **Big Bamboo.** Ice-cold beer, fruity drinks, burgers, fresh fish, crab cakes, and grilled lobsters entice a steady stream of barefoot diners to this beach bar for lunch. Dinner is by request only. ⊠ *Loblolly Bay West* ☎ *284/495–2019* ▤ *MC, V.*

SEAFOOD
$$$–$$$$

✕ **Pomato Point Restaurant.** This relaxed restaurant–bar is on a narrow beach a short walk from the Anegada Reef Hotel. Entrées include steak, lobster, stewed conch, and freshly caught seafood. Owner Wilfred Creque displays various island artifacts, including shards of Arawak pottery and 17th-century coins, cannonballs, and bottles. ⊠ *Pomato Point* ☎ *284/495–9466* ⚓ *Reservations essential* ▤ *D, MC, V* ⊗ *Closed Sept.*

$$–$$$$

✕ **Anegada Reef Hotel Restaurant.** Seasoned yachters gather here nightly to share tales of the high seas. Dinner is by candlelight and always includes famous Anegada lobster, steaks, and succulent baby back ribs—all prepared on the large grill by the little open-air bar. ⊠ *Anegada Reef Hotel, Setting Point* ☎ *284/495–8002* ⚓ *Reservations essential* ▤ *MC, V.*

$$–$$$$

✕ **Cow Wreck Bar & Grill.** Named for the cow bones that once washed up on shore, this open-air beachside eatery is a fun place to watch the antics of surfers and kiteboarders skidding across the bay. Tuck into conch fritters or a lobster-salad sandwich for lunch and freshly grilled lobster for dinner. ⊠ *Loblolly Bay East* ☎ *284/495–8057* ▤ *MC, V.*

☾ $$–$$$$

✕ **Neptune's Treasure.** The owners catch, cook, and serve the seafood (lobster is a specialty, as is garlic-studded shark, in season) at this casual bar and restaurant in the Neptune's Treasure guesthouse. ⊠ *Between Pomato and Saltheap points* ☎ *284/495–9439* ▤ *MC, V.*

Shopping

Anegada Reef Hotel Boutique (⊠ Setting Point ☎ 284/495–8062) has a bit of everything: resort wear, hand-painted T-shirts, locally made jewelry, books, and one-of-a-kind gifts. At **Dotsy's Bakery** (⊠ The Settlement ☎ 284/495–9667) you can find a tempting array of fresh-baked breads, cookies, and desserts. Dotsy sells pizza and hamburgers too. **Pat's Pottery** (⊠ Nutmeg Point ☎ 284/495–8031) sells bowls, plates, cups, candlestick holders, and original watercolors.

OTHER BRITISH VIRGIN ISLANDS

For approximate costs, *see* the dining and lodging price charts *in* Tortola.

Cooper Island

This small, hilly island on the south side of the Sir Francis Drake Channel, about 8 mi (13 km) from Road Town, Tortola, is popular with the charter-boat crowd. There are no paved roads (which doesn't really matter, as there aren't any cars), but you can find a beach restaurant, a casual hotel, a few houses (some are available for rent), and great snorkeling at the south end of Manchioneel Bay.

$$
Fodor's Choice
★

✕⊡ **Cooper Island Beach Club.** Cooper Island is one of those Caribbean spots that hark back to an earlier era when frills were few but the peaceful atmosphere was sublime. You usually either love the quiet or hate the isolation. Once you arrive via a complimentary ferry ride from Prospect Reef, Tortola, there's nothing to do but relax, enjoy the sun and the sea, and visit with old and new friends. Rooms are really small suites with basic cooking facilities, but the hotel's restaurant is nearby if you don't want to lug groceries on the ferry. Don't pack your hair dryer or electric shaver, because the hotel's primitive electrical system can't handle it. Meals run to basics like fish, chicken, and steak. Reservations are essential for the restaurant if you're not a resort guest. ⊠ *Manchioneel Bay, Road Town* ⌂ *Box 512, Turner Falls, MA 01376* ☎ *413/863–3162 or 800/542–4624* 🖷 *413/863–3662* ⊕ *www.cooper-island.com* ⇨ *12 rooms* ⚬ *In-room: no a/c, no phone, kitchen, no TV. In-hotel: restaurant, bar, beachfront, diving, no elevator, public Wi-Fi* ▭ *MC, V* ⊟⊙ *EP.*

Guana Island

Guana Island sits off Tortola's northeast coast. Sailors often drop anchor at one of the island's bays for a day of snorkeling and sunning. The island is a designated wildlife sanctuary, and scientists often come here to study its flora and fauna. It's home to a back-to-nature resort that offers few activities other than relaxation. Unless you're a hotel guest or a sailor, there's no easy way to get here.

★ **$$$$**
⊡ **Guana Island Resort.** Guana Island is a nature lover's paradise, and it's a good resort if you want to stroll the hillsides, snorkel around the reefs, and swim at its six beaches, and still enjoy some degree of comfort. Rooms are simple but charming, with rattan furniture and tile or painted concrete floors, and are open to the tropical breezes. Once you're here, you're here. You can spend your time dining and socializing with the other guests or immersed in that book you never got around to reading. You can rent the entire 15-room resort if you'd like to vacation with a group of your friends or family. The hotel's launch picks you up near Terrence B. Lettsome Airport on Beef Island (Tortola's airport) for the short hop across the water to the resort. ⊠ *Guana Island* ⌂ *Box 32, Road Town, Tortola* ☎ *284/494–2354 or 800/544–8262* 🖷 *284/495–2900* ⊕ *www.guana.com* ⇨ *15 rooms, 1 cottage* ⚬ *In-room: no a/c, no phone, no TV, Wi-Fi. In-hotel: restaurant, beachfront, water sports, no elevator, public Internet, public Wi-Fi* ▭ *MC, V* ⊟⊙ *FAP.*

Necker Island

Necker Island sits off Virgin Gorda's northeast coast, reachable only by private ferry or helicopter. A mere speck in the British Virgin Islands, it's home to Sir Richard Branson's private estate. When he's not in residence, you and your friends are welcome to enjoy its gorgeous beaches and myriad amenities.

$$$$ ✕◫ **Necker Island.** You probably won't run into British magnate Sir Richard Branson, but you can live in his luxurious style when you rent his estate on Necker Island. If you're rich, famous, or well heeled enough to spend thousands a day to get away from it all, this would be the place to do it. Actually, it's not such a bad deal if you and 25 of your family and friends want to enjoy a vacation together. The island comes fully staffed, and all meals and activities are included. Rooms are spread out over the main house and a handful of cottages located around the island. Arrival is by helicopter or private launch from Terrence B. Lettsome Airport on Tortola. For two weeks every year (usually in the fall), couples can book individual rooms for a one-week stay. ⊠ *Necker Island* ☝ *Box 1091, The Valley, Virgin Gorda* ☎ *203/602–0300 or 800/ 557–4255* ⊕ *www.virgin.com/limitededition* ⤳ *10 rooms, 4 houses* ♿ *Inroom: no TV, Wi-Fi. In-hotel: tennis courts, pools, beachfront, water sports, no elevator, public Wi-Fi* ☰ *AE, MC, V* ❙◯❙ *FAP.*

arina Cay

☾ Beautiful little Marina Cay is in Trellis Bay, not far from Beef Island. Sometimes you can see it and its large J-shape coral reefs—a most dramatic sight—from the air soon after takeoff from the airport on Beef Island. Covering only 8 acres, this islet is considered small even by BVI standards. On it there's a restaurant, Pusser's Store, and a six-unit hotel. Ferry service is free from the dock on Beef Island.

Where to Stay & Eat

$$ ◫ **Pusser's Marina Cay Hotel & Restaurant.** If getting away from it all is your priority, this may be the place for you, because there's nothing to do on this beach-rimmed island other than swim, snorkel, and soak up the sun—there's not even a TV to distract you. Rooms, decorated in simple wicker and wood with floral-print fabrics, are on a hilltop facing the trade winds; two villas look right out to the morning sunrise. The laid-back tempo picks up at 4:30 PM, when charter boaters come ashore to hear local musicians entertain in the bar during happy hour. The restaurant, open for breakfast, lunch, and dinner, offers a menu that ranges from fish and lobster to steak, chicken, and barbecued ribs. Pusser's Painkiller Punch is the house specialty. There's free ferry service from the Beef Island dock for anyone visiting the island, though ferry times and frequency vary with the seasons. ⊠ *West side of Marina Cay* ☝ *Box 76, Road Town, Tortola* ☎ *284/494–2174* 🖷 *284/494–4775* ⊕ *www.pussers.com* ⤳ *4 rooms, 2 2-bedroom villas* ♿ *In-room: no a/c, no phone, no TV. In-hotel: restaurant, bar, beachfront, no elevator, public Wi-Fi* ☰ *AE, MC, V* ❙◯❙ *CP.*

Jorman Island

This uninhabited island is the supposed setting for Robert Louis Stevenson's *Treasure Island*. The famed caves at Treasure Point are popular with day sailors and power boaters. If you land ashore at the island's main anchorage in the Bight, you can find a small beach bar and behind it a trail that winds up the hillside and reaches a peak with a fantastic view of the Sir Francis Drake Channel to the north.

$$–$$$ ✕ *Willy T.* The ship, a former Baltic trader and today a floating bar and restaurant anchored to the north of the Bight, serves lunch and dinner in a party-hearty atmosphere. Try the jalapeño poppers for starters. For lunch and dinner, British-style fish-and-chips, West Indian roti sandwiches, and the barbecued chicken are winners. ⊠ *The Bight* ☎ *284/496–8603* ⌂ *Reservations essential* ▭ *MC, V.*

Peter Island

Although Peter Island is home to the resort of the same name, it's also a popular anchorage for charter boaters and a destination for Tortola vacationers. The scheduled ferry trip from Peter Island's shoreside base outside Road Town runs $15 round-trip for nonguests. The island is lush, with forested hillsides sloping seaward to meet white sandy beaches. There are no roads other than those at the resort, and there's nothing to do but relax at the lovely beach set aside for day-trippers. You're welcome to dine at the resort's restaurants.

$$$$ ✕🛏 **Peter Island Resort.** Total pampering and the prices to match are the ticket at this luxury resort. If you want to while away your days at the beach, enjoy a morning at the spa, stroll the lushly planted grounds, and relax over dinner with other like-minded guests—and have the money to afford the steep rates—this is a good place to do it. For more active types, there are tennis courts and water sports galore. Peter Island is a half-hour ferry ride from Tortola, but once you arrive, you're in another world. The rooms are gorgeous, with thoughtful touches like showers with a view. A couple of villas sit above the hotel rooms. ⊠ *Peter Island* ⌂ *Box 211, Road Town, Tortola* ☎ *284/495–2000 or 800/346–4451* 🖷 *284/495–2500* ⊕ *www.peterisland.com* ⇖ *52 rooms, 3 villas* ⌂ *In-room: safe, no TV. In-hotel: 2 restaurants, bar, pool, gym, spa, beachfront, diving, water sports, no elevator, public Internet, public Wi-Fi* ▭ *AE, MC, V* ❯◎❮ *FAP.*

BRITISH VIRGIN ISLANDS ESSENTIALS

To research prices, get advice from other travelers, and book travel arrangements, visit www.fodors.com.

Transportation

BY AIR

There's no nonstop service from the continental United States to the BVI; connections are usually made through San Juan, Puerto Rico, or St. Thomas. You can also fly to Anegada and Virgin Gorda; these flights may originate in San Juan, St. Thomas, or Tortola.

All three of the BVI's airports—on Tortola (TOV), Virgin Gorda (VIJ), and Anegada (no code)—are classic Caribbean and almost always sleepy. However, the Terrence B. Lettsome Airport terminal at Beef Island can get crowded when several departures are scheduled close together.

▮ Airline Contacts **Air Sunshine** ☎ 284/495-8900 ⊕ www.airsunshine.com. **American Eagle** ☎ 284/495-2559 ⊕ www.aa.com. **Cape Air** ☎ 284/495-2100 ⊕ www.

flycapeair.com. **Fly BVI** ☎ 284/495–1747 ⊕ www.fly-bvi.com. **LIAT** ☎ 284/495–1693 ⊕ www.liatairline.com.

⊠ **Airport Contacts BVI Taxi Association** ☎ 284/494–3942. **Mahogany Rentals & Taxi Service** ⊠ Virgin Gorda ☎ 284/495–5469.

BY BOAT & FERRY

Ferries connect the airport gateway of St. Thomas, USVI, with Tortola and Virgin Gorda. They leave from both Charlotte Amalie and Red Hook. Ferries also link St. John, USVI, with Tortola, Jost Van Dyke, and Virgin Gorda, as well as Tortola with Jost Van Dyke, Peter Island, and Virgin Gorda. Tortola has two ferry terminals—one at West End and one in Road Town—so make sure you hop a ferry that disembarks closest to where you want to go.

There's huge competition among the Tortola-based ferry companies on the St. Thomas–Tortola runs, with boats leaving close together. As you enter the ferry terminal to buy your ticket, crews may try to convince you to take their ferry. Ferries to Virgin Gorda land in the Valley. All ferries from the BVI to Red Hook, St. Thomas, stop in St. John to clear U.S. customs. Ferry schedules vary by day, and not all companies make daily trips. The BVI Tourist Board Web site (⇨ *see* Visitor Information, *below*) has links to all the ferry companies, which are the best up-to-date sources of information for specific routes and schedules.

⊠ **Inter-Island Boat Services** ☎ 284/495–4166. **Native Son** ☎ 284/495–4617 ⊕ www. nativesonbvi.com. **New Horizon Ferry Service** ☎284/495–9477 ⊕www.jostvandykeferry. com. **North Sound Express** ☎ 284/495–2138. *Nubian Princess* ☎ 284/495–4999. **Peter Island Ferry** ☎ 284/495–2000 ⊕ www.peterisland.com. **Smith's Ferry** ☎ 284/ 495–4495 ⊕ www.smithsferry.com. **Speedy's Ferries** ☎ 284/495–5240 ⊕ www. speedysbvi.com. **Tortola Fast Ferry** ☎ 284/494–2323 ⊕ www.tortolafastferry.com.

BY CAR

Driving in the BVI is on the left side of the road, British style—but your car will have left-hand drive like those used in the United States. Speed limits (rarely enforced) are 20 mph (30 kph) in town and 35 mph (55 kph) outside town. Gas tends to be expensive. Tortola's main roads are well paved, for the most part, but there are exceptionally steep hills and sharp curves; driving demands your complete attention. A main road circles the island, and several roads cross it, almost always through mountainous terrain. Virgin Gorda has a smaller road system, and a single, very steep road links the north and south ends of the island. Anegada's few roads are little more than sandy lanes.

You need a temporary BVI license, available at the rental-car company for $10 with a valid license from another country. The minimum age to rent a car is 25. Most agencies offer both four-wheel-drive vehicles and cars (often compacts).

⊠ **Avis** ⊠ Opposite Police Station, Road Town, Tortola ☎284/494–3322. **D&D** ⊠ Soper's Hole, West End, Tortola ☎ 284/495–4765. **D. W. Jeep Rentals** ⊠ The Settlement, Anegada ☎ 284/495–9677. **Hertz** ⊠ West End, Tortola ☎ 284/495–4405 ⊠ Airport, Tortola ☎ 284/495–2763 ⊠ Road Town, Tortola ☎ 284/494–6228. **Itgo Car Rental** ⊠ Wickham's Cay I, Road Town, Tortola ☎ 284/494–2639. **L&S Jeep Rental** ⊠ South Valley, Virgin Gorda ☎ 284/495–5297. **Mahogany Rentals & Taxi Service** ⊠ Spanish

Town, Virgin Gorda ☎ 284/495-5469. **Speedy's Car Rentals** ⊠ The Valley, Virgin Gorda ☎ 284/495-5240.

BY TAXI

Your hotel staff will be happy to summon a taxi for you. Rates aren't set, so you should negotiate the fare with your driver before you start your trip. It's cheaper to travel in groups because there's a minimum fare to each destination, which is the same whether you have one, two, or three passengers. The taxi number is also the license plate number. On Tortola, the BVI Taxi Association has stands in Road Town near Wickham's Cay I. The Waterfront Taxi Association picks up passengers from the Road Town ferry dock. The Beef Island Taxi Association operates at the Beef Island–Tortola airport. You can also usually find a West End Taxi Association ferry at the West End ferry dock.

Andy's Taxi & Jeep Rental offers service from one end of Virgin Gorda to the other. Mahogany Rentals & Taxi Service provides taxi service all over Virgin Gorda.

🚖 **Andy's Taxi & Jeep Rental** ⊠ The Valley, Virgin Gorda ☎ 284/495-5511. **Beef Island Taxi Association** ⊠ Beef Island Airport, Tortola ☎ 284/495-1982. **BVI Taxi Association** ⊠ Near the ferry dock, Road Town, Tortola ☎ 284/494-2322. **Mahogany Rentals & Taxi Service** ⊠ The Valley, Virgin Gorda ☎ 284/495-5469. **West End Taxi Association** ⊠ West End ferry terminal, Tortola ☎ 284/495-4934. **Waterfront Taxi Association** ⊠ Road Town ☎ 284/494-6362.

Contacts & Resources

BANKS & EXCHANGE SERVICES

The currency is the U.S. dollar. On Tortola, banks are near the Waterfront at Wickham's Cay I. All have ATM machines. Look for First Caribbean International Bank, First Bank, and Scotia Bank, among others. On Virgin Gorda, First Caribbean International isn't far from the ferry dock in Spanish Town.

BUSINESS HOURS

Banking hours are usually Monday through Thursday from 9 to 2:30 and Friday from 9 to 2:30 and 4:30 to 6. Post offices are open weekdays from 9 to 5 and Saturday from 9 to noon. Stores are generally open Monday through Saturday from 9 to 5. Some may be open on Sunday.

ELECTRICITY

Electricity is 110 volts, the same as in North America, so European appliances will require adapters. The electricity is quite reliable.

EMERGENCIES

🚑 Ambulance, Fire & Police **General emergencies** ☎ 999.

🏥 Hospitals & Clinics **Anegada Government Health Clinic** ☎ 284/495-8049. **Jost Van Dyke Government Health Clinic** ☎ 284/495-9239. **Peebles Hospital** ⊠ Road Town, Tortola ☎ 284/494-3497. **Virgin Gorda Government Health Clinic** ⊠ The Valley, Virgin Gorda ☎ 284/495-5337.

🚤 Marine Emergencies **VISAR** ☎ 767 from phone or Marine Radio Channel 16.

💊 Pharmacies **J. R. O'Neal Drug Store** ⊠ Road Town, Tortola ☎ 284/494-2292. **Medicure Pharmacy** ⊠ Road Town, Tortola ☎ 284/494-6189 ⊠ Spanish Town, Virgin Gorda ☎ 284/495-5479. **O'Neal's Drug Store** ✉ Spanish Town, Virgin Gorda ☎ 284/495-5449.

HOLIDAYS

The following public holidays are celebrated in the BVI: New Year's Day, Commonwealth Day (Mar. 14), Good Friday (Fri. before Easter), Easter Sunday (usually Mar. or Apr.), Easter Monday (day after Easter), Whit Monday (1st Mon. in May), Sovereign's Birthday (June 16), Territory Day (July 1), BVI August Festival Days (usually 1st 2 wks in Aug.), St. Ursula's Day (Oct. 21), Christmas, and Boxing Day (day after Christmas).

INTERNET, MAIL & SHIPPING

There are post offices in Road Town on Tortola and in Spanish Town on Virgin Gorda. Postage for a first-class letter to the United States and Canada is 50¢. Postcards to the United States and Canada are 35¢. For a small fee, Rush It, in Road Town and in Spanish Town, offers most U.S. mail and UPS services (via St. Thomas the next day). If you wish to write to an establishment in the BVI, be sure to include the specific island in the address.

Many hotels have Internet access for their guests. Internet cafés, however, are harder to find. On Tortola, try Trellis Bay Cybercafé.
🗓 **Rush It** ✉ Road Town, Tortola ☎ 284/494-4421 ✉ Spanish Town, Virgin Gorda ☎ 284/495-5821. **Trellis Bay Cybercafé** ✉ Trellis Bay, Tortola ☎ 284/495-2447.

PASSPORT REQUIREMENTS

U.S. and Canadian citizens, as well as citizens of all other countries, need a valid passport.

SAFETY

Although crime is rare, use common sense: don't leave your camera on the beach while you take a dip or your wallet on a hotel dresser when you go for a walk.

TAXES

The departure tax is $5 per person by boat and $20 per person by plane. There's a separate booth at the airport and ferry terminals to collect this tax, which must be paid in cash in U.S. currency. Most hotels add a service charge ranging from 5% to 18% to the bill. A few restaurants and some shops tack on an additional 10% charge if you use a credit card. There's no sales tax in the BVI. However, there's a 7% government tax on hotel rooms.

TELEPHONES

Your mobile phone may or may not work in the BVI. If you are on the south side of Tortola, you may be able to connect to Cingular and Sprint, but other islands are problematic. The BVI have local companies only. Even if your U.S. mainland company assures you that your phone will work, don't count on it.

The area code for the BVI is 284; when you make calls from North America, you need only dial the area code and the number. From the United Kingdom you must dial 001 and then the area code and the number.

From Australia and New Zealand you must dial 0011 followed by 1, the area code, and the number.

To call anywhere in the BVI once you've arrived, dial all seven digits. A local call from a pay phone costs 25¢, but such phones are sometimes on the blink. An alternative is a Caribbean phone card, available in $5, $10, and $20 denominations. They're sold at most major hotels and many stores and can be used to call within the BVI, as well as all over the Caribbean, and to access USADirect from special phone-card phones. For credit-card or collect long-distance calls to the United States, use a phone-card telephone or look for special USADirect phones, which are linked directly to an AT&T operator. USADirect and pay phones can be found at most hotels and in towns.

🔲 **USADirect** ☎ 800/872-2881, 111 from a pay phone.

TIPPING

Tip porters and bellhops $1 per bag. Sometimes a service charge (10%) is included on restaurant bills; it's customary to leave another 5% if you liked the service. If no charge is added, 15% is the norm. Cabbies normally aren't tipped because most own their cabs; add 10% to 15% if they exceed their duties.

TOUR OPTIONS

Romney Associates/Travel Plan Tours can arrange island tours, boat tours, snorkeling and scuba-diving trips, dolphin swims, and yacht charters from its Tortola and Virgin Gorda bases.

🔲 **Romney Associates/Travel Plan Tours** ☎ 284/494-4000.

VISITOR INFORMATION

🔲 **BVI Tourist Board** ✉ Ferry Terminal, Road Town, Tortola ☎ 284/494-3134 ⊕ www. bvitourism.com. **Virgin Gorda BVI Tourist Board** ✉ Virgin Gorda Yacht Harbour, Spanish Town, Virgin Gorda ☎ 284/495-5181.

WEDDINGS

Getting married in the BVI is a breeze, but you must make advance plans. To make things go smoother, hire a wedding planner to guide you through the ins and outs of the BVI system. Many hotels also have wedding planners on staff to help organize your event. Hotels often offer packages that include the ceremony; accommodations for you, your wedding party and your guests; and extras like massages, sailboat trips, and champagne dinners.

You must apply in person for your license ($110) weekdays at the attorney general's office in Road Town, Tortola. You must wait three days to pick it up at the registrar's office in Road Town. If you plan to be married in a church, announcements (called *banns* locally) must be published for three consecutive Sundays in the church bulletin. Only the registrar or clergy can perform ceremonies. The registrar charges $35 at the office and $100 at another location. No blood test is required.

🔲 **BVI Wedding Planners & Consultants** ☎ 284/494-5306 ⊕ www.bviweddings.com.

UNDERSTANDING THE VIRGIN ISLANDS

U.S. VIRGIN ISLANDS AT A GLANCE

Fast Facts

Capital: Charlotte Amalie, St. Thomas
National anthem: *The Virgin Islands March*
Type of government: Unincorporated territory of the U.S., with governor and lieutenant governor, unicameral senate, and one non-voting representative in the U.S. House of Representatives
Constitution: July 22, 1954
Legal system: U.S. District Court of the Virgin Islands under Third Circuit jurisdiction; Territorial Court (judges appointed by the governor for 10-year terms)
Suffrage: 18 years of age; universal; indigenous inhabitants are U.S. citizens but do not vote in U.S. presidential elections as long as they reside in the U.S. Virgin Islands
Legislature: Unicameral Senate (15 seats; members are elected by popular vote to serve two-year terms); one non-voting representative elected to the U.S. House of Representatives
Population: 124,778
Population density: 938 people per square mi
Median age: female 33.7, male 28.6
Life expectancy: female 82.7, male 74.7
Infant mortality rate: 9 deaths per 1,000 live births
Language: English (official), Spanish, Creole
Ethnic groups: West Indian 81% (49% born in the Virgin Islands and 32% born elsewhere in the West Indies); U.S. mainland 13%; Puerto Rican 4%; other 2%
Religion: Baptist 42%; Roman Catholic 34%; Episcopalian 17%; other 7%

Geography & Environment

Land area: 133 square mi, approximately twice the size of Washington, D.C.
Coastline: 116 mi
Terrain: Mostly hilly to rugged and mountainous with little level land (highest point: Crown Mountain 1,555 feet)
Islands: St. Croix, St. John, St. Thomas
Natural hazards: Hurricanes, frequent and severe droughts and floods, occasional earthquakes
Environmental issues: Lack of natural freshwater resources

Economy

Currency: U.S. Dollar
GDP: $2.4 billion
Per capita income: $13,139
Inflation: 2%
Unemployment: 4.9%
Work force: 49,000; services/tourism 79%; industry 20%; agriculture 1%
Major industries: Construction, electronics, petroleum refining, pharmaceuticals, rum distilling, textiles, tourism, watch assembly
Agricultural products: Fruit, Senepol cattle, sorghum, vegetables
Major export products: Refined petroleum products
Export partners: U.S., Puerto Rico
Major import products: Building materials, consumer goods, crude oil, foodstuffs
Import partners: U.S., Puerto Rico

Did You Know?

• On September 13, 2003, the world's largest underwater wedding took place off of Rainbow Beach in St. Croix. The bride, groom, minister, and more than 100 other guests in scuba equipment marked the matrimony in about 10 feet of water.

• The Hess Oil refinery on the south coast of St. Croix is one of the largest petroleum facilities in the world.

• If you're dying to drive on the wrong side of the road in America, this is your spot: The Virgin Islands are the only place in the U.S. where driving on the left side of the road is practiced.

• The marriage rate in the U.S. Virgin Islands is 35.1 per 1,000 people, the highest in the world.

• Point Udall on St. Croix is the far-thest point east that U.S. territory stretches.

• The large, red cattle on St. Croix are Senepol, a breed handpicked to thrive on the island. Originally from Senegal, they've been bred to have a high toler-ance for heat, no horns, and a strong immune system. After their success on the Virgin Islands, the cattle are now raised in the southern U.S.

• A leatherback turtle fitted with a depth recording device by scientists reached a depth of 3,973 feet off the Virgin Islands, a world record.

BRITISH VIRGIN ISLANDS AT A GLANCE

Fast Facts

Capital: Road Town, Tortola
National anthem: *God Save the Queen* (anthem of the United Kingdom)
Type of government: Overseas territory of the UK
Constitution: June 1, 1977
Legal system: English law
Suffrage: 18 years of age; universal
Legislature: Unicameral Legislative Council (13 seats; members are elected by direct popular vote, one member from each of 9 electoral districts, four at-large members; members serve four-year terms); next elections to be held in 2007
Population: 21,730

Population density: 229 people per square mi
Median age: female 30.4, male 31
Life expectancy: female 77.1, male 75.1
Infant mortality rate: 18.8 deaths per 1,000 live births
Literacy: 97.8%
Language: English (official)
Ethnic groups: Black 83%; white, Indian, Asian and mixed 17%
Religion: Methodist 33%; Anglican 17%; other Protestant 15%; Roman Catholic 10%; Church of God 9%; Seventh-Day Adventist 6%; Baptist 4%; Jehovah's Witnesses 2%; other 2%; unaffiliated 2%

Geography & Environment

Land area: The four major land masses are Tortola, Anegada, Virgin Gorda, and Jost Van Dyke, totaling 153 square km (59 square mi), about the size of Washington, D.C.
Coastline: 80 km (50 mi)
Terrain: Coral islands relatively flat; volcanic islands steep, hilly (highest point: Mount Sage 521 m [1,716 feet])

Islands: 60 islands and cays, including Tortola, Anegada, Virgin Gorda, and Jost Van Dyke
Natural hazards: Hurricanes and tropical storms (July to October)
Environmental issues: Limited natural fresh water resources (except for a few seasonal streams and springs on Tortola, most of the islands' water supply comes from wells and rainwater catchments)

Economy

Currency: U.S. Dollar
GDP: $320 million
Per capita income: $11,000
Inflation: 2.5%
Unemployment: 3%
Work force: 4,911
Debt: $36.1 million
Major industries: Concrete block, construction, finance, light industry, offshore, rum, tourism
Agricultural products: Fish, fruits, livestock, poultry, vegetables

Exports: $25.3 million
Major export products: Animals, fresh fish, fruits, gravel, rum, sand
Export partners: U.S. Virgin Islands, Puerto Rico, U.S.
Imports: $187 million
Major import products: Automobiles, building materials, foodstuffs, machinery
Import partners: U.S. Virgin Islands, Puerto Rico, U.S.

Did You Know?

• Almost half of BVI's economy is driven by tourism. An estimated 350,000 visit the islands each year, most from the United States.

• The world's smallest lizards live in this collection of islands. The *sphaerodactylus parthenopion* and *sphaerodactylus ariasiae* are about six-tenths of an inch long.

• This tiny nation has come up with big innovations for making money. An estimated 400,000 companies have taken advantage of a BVI offer allowing them to incorporate here to avoid paying taxes.

• There are five radio stations in the British Virgin Islands (one AM and four FM) and one TV station. The country does have a cable company.

• Pate here isn't the product of overfed ducks, it's a West Indian dish of pita bread filled with spiced meat, seafood, or vegetables.

• Watch for the misnamed "Century Plant," which blooms every eight years in the spring. Its yellow flowers can be seen in pods among its spiky leaves on a stalk that can reach 40 feet.

VIRGIN ISLANDS CUISINE

The bunch of bananas sitting on the roadside stand's plywood counter was bigger than my father had ever seen in New Jersey. Each fruit was nearly a foot long and thick as a summer sausage. Ripe black speckles burst over a sunny yellow peel. Money paid. Bunch in hand. He impatiently peeled the plumpest one and brought it to his mouth. A soft chuckle stopped him mid-bite. "Got to cook it first," said the market woman, grinning broadly. He set the plantain down, suddenly smarter. Foods in the Virgin Islands, he related to me later, weren't always as they seemed.

Take a mix of indigenous and imported ingredients, everything from papaya to salt cod. Blend this with the cooking styles of people like the ancient Amerindians, Africans, Europeans, East Indians, and Asians and you have the melting pot that is traditional Virgin Islands cuisine. The best places to sample these foods are at local restaurants and bakeries, mobile food vans and the many food fairs and political fish fries that take place throughout the year.

Start the day with dumb bread and bush tea. Dumb bread takes its name from a style of cooking native to India, where hot coals set around a kettle filled with dough cooks loaves to crusty perfection. You can nibble four-inch-thick pie-shaped wedges plain or filled with Cheddar cheese. In the local lingo, "bush" means herb. Parts of 420 different plants have been used to make tea in the Virgin Islands. Historically, these herbal blends have been touted as much for their medicinal value as for their taste. For example, there are bush teas like wormgrass, inflammation bush, and belly ache bush. When ordering bush tea in a restaurant, you'll most likely get lemongrass or mint.

You'll find bush for tea or seasoning at any of the roadside produce stands that dot the islands' roadways. While you're there, make sure to sample a mango, papaya, or finger-long fig banana. There are usually vegetables like small purple eggplants, green plantains, and gnarly root vegetables like tannia, cassava, and boniato. Elsewhere on the island you'll often find machete-wielding young men whacking the tops off of coconuts. They'll slip a straw into the nut's sturdy natural cup and hand it to you to drink the refreshing "coconut water" inside.

Pates are a popular snack, but don't envision goose or duck liver. Instead, these triangular-shaped fried pastries have an outer wrapping of bread and a spicy filling made from ground beef, conch, or salted fish. Do order a cup of mangoade, papaya punch, or soursop juice along with a pate. These tropical-fruit drinks make the perfect partner to the pates, as these pastries often boast a touch of fiery scotch bonnet peppers among their ingredients.

Fish and fungi ranks as the unofficial national dish for the Virgin Islands. It's a combination as common as a hamburger and french fries on the U.S. mainland. The fish is pot fish, so called for it being caught offshore by fishermen using pots or traps. Favorites include oldwife, snapper, grouper and grunt, served whole; the meat from the head and eyes are considered a delicacy. Don't expect the fish to be served with mushrooms, however. Fungi is a polenta-like dish of African origin that is made up of cornmeal studded with chunks of chopped fresh okra. The fungi sops up the buttery tomato, onion, garlic and thyme flecked gravy from the fish to perfection.

Fungi is often served with callaloo, a soupy stew made with spinach and okra, seasoned with fresh herbs, and made hearty with the addition of crab, fish, ham, or a pig part like ear, tail, or snout. Callaloo is traditionally eaten on the last evening of the year, known in these parts as Old Year's Night. The late Virgin Islands food writer and historian, Arona Petersen, once described how this tradition got its start: "By Old Year's Day, all that would be left of the ham served on Christmas day would be the bone. To make the kallaloo, someone would contribute the bone, another neighbor the fish or crab, and yet another person the greens." If you served kallaloo to your loved one on Old Year's Night, Petersen said, there would be a wedding by June.

Virgin Islanders love their kallaloo, as well as many other soups. Men especially enjoy spooning into a bowl of bullfoot soup or goat water, hearty dishes that are sworn to have aphrodisiac properties. Whether based of bull's feet, cow's heels, or some other type of meat, island soups are anything but anemic affairs. You'll find a full meal, for floating beside the namesake ingredient are a vast amount of vegetables and rib-stickers called dumplings.

Side dishes can be just as ambiguous in their names. For example, a plate of peas and rice is more likely to be made with red beans, kidney beans, black beans, or garbanzo beans than any type of pea. Potato stuffing, a mix of mashed white potatoes, tomato sauce, and seasonings, isn't used to stuff anything but it does accompany turkey at Thanksgiving. Boiled sweet potatoes, yams, and tannia are sliced and served with fish and poultry. On a menu, you'll find them referred to as "provisions," as these hearty root vegetables once sustained African slaves. Boiled green bananas and fried plantains are popular, too. Don't be surprised to find that a "plate of food," as a meal is called, includes an entrée, a green salad, and a choice of three starchy side dishes.

Dessert after a meal is more of an American than a West Indian convention, but Virgin Islanders do have their sweets. Tarts, filled with stewed sweetened coconut, guava, pineapple, or mango, are favorites—especially at Christmas. So is sweetbread, a dense fruitcake spiked with dried fruits that have been soaked for weeks in guavaberry rum. Coconut sugar cakes, a combination of shredded coconut and sugar boiled down into hard palm-sized rounds, more closely resemble candy than cake. Dundersloe, the Virgin Islands version of peanut brittle, is sold by ladies who have their "trays" set outside most of the islands' shopping centers.

For all its American flag status, with its abundant fast-food and Continental-style restaurants, Virgin Islands cuisine does hold its share of delicious surprises. It's no wonder that a favorite saying is: "Better belly bus' than good food waste."

BELOW THE WAVES

COLORFUL REEFS AND WRECKS rife with corals and tropical fish make the islands as interesting underwater as above. Bright blue tangs vie for your attention with darting blue-headed wrasses. Corals in wondrous shapes—some look like brains, others like elk antlers—live near colorful sponges. You might see a pink conch making its way along the ocean bottom in areas with seagrass beds. If you're really lucky, a turtle may swim into view, or a lobster may poke its antenna out of a hole in the reef or rocks. Scuba diving gets you up close and personal with the reefs and fish; snorkeling gives you a bird's-eye view of the underwater world as you meander along the sea's surface. Whether scuba diving or snorkeling, take along an underwater camera to capture memories of your exciting adventure. You can buy disposable ones at most dive shops, though usually not as cheaply as at the drugstore back home.

Scuba Diving

If you've never been diving, start with an introductory lesson—often called a "resort course"—run by any one of the Virgin Islands' dive shops. All meet stringent safety standards. If they didn't, they'd soon be out of business. If you're staying at a hotel, you'll often find the dive shop on-site; otherwise, your hotel probably has an arrangement with one nearby. If you're on a cruise, cruise-ship companies offer shore excursions that include transportation to and from the ship as well as the resort course.

The introductory course lasts a couple of hours and usually runs under $100. It starts with a video on the ins and outs of scuba diving. At the water's edge, you'll practice clearing your mask if it floods, breathing through the regulator, and learning to work your buoyancy compensator, which is called a "BC" in dive lingo. A shallow reef dive with the instructor practically holding your hand concludes the experi-

ence. This is the best way to learn if you'd like to take the plunge in to certification.

Certification, which requires much more study and practice, is required to rent air tanks, get air refills, and join others on guided dives virtually anywhere in the world. You can accomplish the entire 32- to 40-hour open-water certification course in as few as three days of vacation, but it's hard work. Assuming that you are fairly fit and able to swim, professionals suggest that you take a two-part approach: do the classroom study and pool exercises (basic swimming and equipment skills) through a dive school or a YMCA program at home, then, with a transfer form from your home instructor, certified Virgin Islands dive instructors will lead you through four open-water dives and check your qualifications for a certification card—called a "C card"—by the Professional Association of Diving Instructors (PADI) or the National Association of Underwater Instructors (NAUI). Most shops in the Virgin Islands offer certification from PADI, but you will find an occasional one that uses NAUI certification.

If you're really hooked, you can study further for advanced certification in fields such as night diving, wreck diving, search and recovery, underwater photography, and more. Who knows, you might like scuba diving so much, you'll go on to be a dive master or instructor so you can guide trips and teach others.

All certification courses stress diver safety. The basic rules for safe diving are simple, and fools ignore them at their own peril. Serious diving accidents are becoming increasingly rare these days, thanks to the high level of diver training. However, they *do* still occur occasionally. Surfacing too rapidly without exhaling—or going too deep for too long—can result in an air embolism or a case of the bends. Roy L. Schneider Hospital in St. Thomas has a decompression chamber that serves all the Virgin Islands. If you get the bends, you'll be whisked to the hospital for this necessary treatment.

Fauna is another concern. Though sharks, barracuda, and moray eels are on the most-feared list, more often it's sea urchins and fire coral that cause pain when you accidentally bump them. Part of any scuba-training program is a review of sea life and the importance of respecting the new world you're exploring. Dive professionals recognize the value of protecting fragile reefs and ecosystems in tropical waters, and instructors emphasize look-don't-touch diving (the unofficial motto is: take only pictures, leave only bubbles). Government control and protection of dive sites is increasing, especially in such heavily used areas as the Virgin Islands.

While you can scuba dive off a beach—and you'll find shops renting scuba equipment and providing airfills at the most popular beaches—a trip aboard a dive boat provides a more extensive glimpse into this wonderful undersea world. Since the dive shops can provide all equipment, there's no need to lug heavy weights and a bulky BC in your luggage. For the most comfort, you might want to bring your own regulator if you have one. The dive-boat captains and guides know the best dive locations, can find alternatives when the seas are rough, and will help you deal with heavy tanks and cumbersome equipment. Trips are easy to organize. Dive shops on all islands make frequent excursions to a wide variety of diving spots, and your hotel, vacation villa, or cruise-ship staff will help you make arrangements.

If you fly too soon after diving, you're at risk for decompression sickness, which occurs when nitrogen trapped in your bloodstream doesn't escape. This creates a painful and sometimes fatal condition called the bends, not a sickness you want to develop while you're winging your way home after a fun-filled beach vacation. Opinions vary, but as a rule of thumb, wait at least 12 hours after a single dive to fly. However, if you've made multiple dives or dived several days in a row, you should wait at least 18 hours. If you've made dives that required decompression stops, you should also wait at least 18 hours before flying. To be safe, consult with your physician.

Popular Dive Sites

The Virgin Islands offer a plethora of dive sites, and you'll be taken to some of the best if you sign on to a dive trip run by one of the many dive operations scattered around the islands.

The wreck of the **Rhone** tops the list for those who are willing to spend up to a few hours in a boat to reach the famous wreck. The mail ship *Rhone* went down off Salt Island in the British Virgin Islands in 1867 during a hurricane. It sits in two parts, one 15 feet down and the other 75 feet below the surface. The movie *The Deep* was filmed here in 1976.

St. Croix's Wall runs along that island's north shore. A boat trip with an operator makes reaching the dive site easy, but you can also swim out from Cane Bay Beach. Divers swim past coral, sponges, and numerous colorful fish. The wall drops off from about 30 feet to thousands of feet.

Grass and Mingo cays sit just a short boat ride off St. John. The water is usually calm, which makes for easier diving when winter swells come in from the north. Divers swim past colorful reefs that are studded with coral and home to many varieties of fish. You might even see a turtle or two.

Cow and Calf barely breaks water off the coast of St. Thomas. Divers swim through tunnels, overhangs, and archways only 40 feet below the surface. Colorful fish swim along with you, and you might even spot a harmless nurse shark.

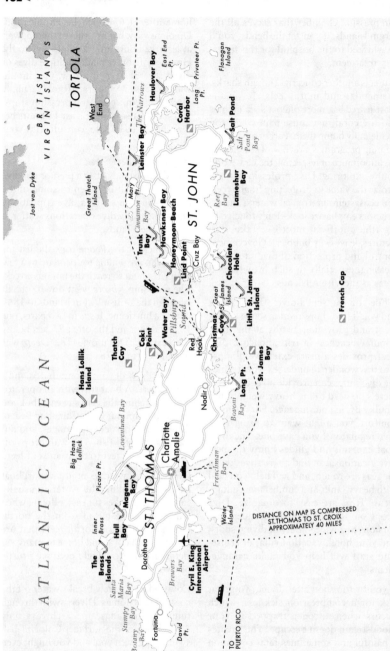

BRITISH
VIRGIN ISLANDS

TORTOLA

West End

Jost van Dyke

Great Thatch Island

ATLANTIC OCEAN

Haulover Bay

East End Pt.

Leinster Bay   The Narrows

Coral Harbor

Long Pt.

Privateer Pt.

Flanagan Island

Salt Pond

Salt Pond Bay

Mary Pt.

Cinnamon Bay

Trunk Bay

Hawksnest Bay

Honeymoon Beach

Lind Point

Cruz Bay

ST. JOHN

Reef Bay

Lameshur Bay

Chocolate Hole

Great St. James Island

Little St. James Island

French Cap

Hans Lollik Island

Big Hans Lollik

Thatch Cay

Coki Point

Red Hook

Christmas Cove

St. James Bay

Long Pt.

Pillsbury Sound

Loverland Bay

Picara Pt.

Nadir

Botany Bay

Inner Brass

The Brass Islands

Hull Bay

Magens Bay

ST. THOMAS

Charlotte Amalie

Water Island

Frenchman Bay

Dorothea

Brewers Bay

Cyril E. King International Airport

Santa Maria Bay

Stumpy Bay

Botany Bay

Fortuna

David Pt.

TO PUERTO RICO

DISTANCE ON MAP IS COMPRESSED
ST. THOMAS TO ST. CROIX
APPROXIMATELY 40 MILES

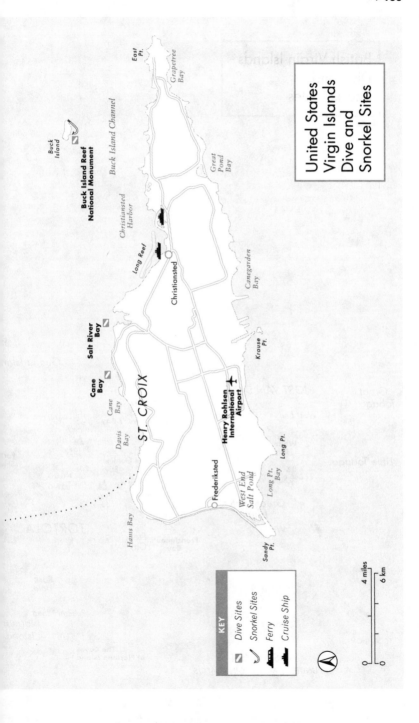

**United States
Virgin Islands
Dive and
Snorkel Sites**

East Pt.

Grapetree Bay

Buck Island Channel

Buck Island

**Buck Island Reef
National Monument**

Great Pond Bay

Christiansted Harbor

Long Reef

Christiansted

Canegarden Bay

Salt River Bay

Cane Bay

Krause Pt.

ST. CROIX

Cane Bay

Davis Bay

**Henry Rohlsen
International
Airport**

Frederiksted

Hans Bay

*West End
Salt Pond*

*Long Pt.
Bay*

Long Pt.

Sandy Pt.

KEY

	Dive Sites
	Snorkel Sites
	Ferry
	Cruise Ship

4 miles

6 km

0

0

British Virgin Islands
Dive and
Snorkel Sites

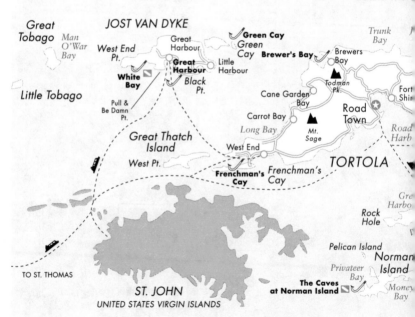

ATLANTIC

Guana Islan

*Great
Tobago* Man
O'War
Bay

Little Tobago

JOST VAN DYKE

West End
Pt.

Great
Harbour

Great
Harbour

**White
Bay**

Pull &
Be Damn
Pt.

*Black
Pt.*

Little
Harbour

*Green
Cay*

Green Cay

Brewer's Bay

Brewers
Bay

Trunk
Bay

Cane Garden
Bay

*Todman
Pk.*

Fort
Shir

Carrot Bay

Long Bay

*Mt.
Sage*

Road
Town

*Road
Harb*

*Great Thatch
Island*

West End

West Pt.

**Frenchman's
Cay**

*Frenchman's
Cay*

TORTOLA

*Gre
Harbo*

Rock
Hole

TO ST. THOMAS

ST. JOHN
UNITED STATES VIRGIN ISLANDS

Pelican Island

*Privateer
Bay*

**The Caves
at Norman Island**

Norman
Island

*Money
Bay*

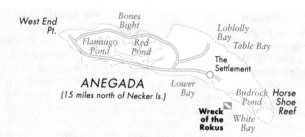

West End Pt.

Bones Bight

Flamingo Pond   Red Pond

Loblolly Bay

Table Bay

The Settlement

ANEGADA
(15 miles north of Necker Is.)

Lower Bay

Budrock Pond   **Horse Shoe Reef**

Wreck of the Rokus   White Bay

O C E A N

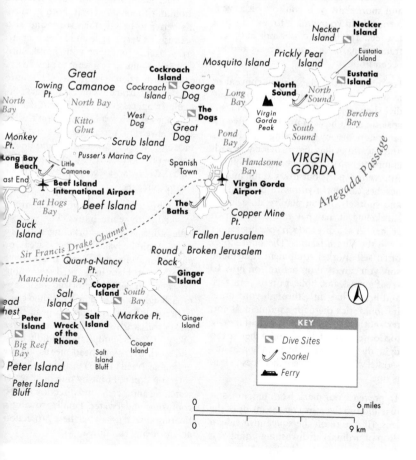

Necker Island   **Necker Island**

Prickly Pear Island   Eustatia Island

Mosquito Island   **Eustatia Island**

Great Camanoe

Cockroach Island

Towing Pt.   North Bay

Cockroach Island   George Dog

Long Bay

North Sound

North Sound

North Bay

Kitto Ghut

West Dog   **The Dogs**

Virgin Gorda Peak

Berchers Bay

Monkey Pt.

Scrub Island

Great Dog

Pond Bay

South Sound

Long Bay Beach   Little Camanoe

Pusser's Marina Cay

Spanish Town

Handsome Bay

VIRGIN GORDA

East End

Beef Island International Airport

Fat Hogs Bay   *Beef Island*

Virgin Gorda Airport

Anegada Passage

Buck Island

Sir Francis Drake Channel

The Baths

Copper Mine Pt.

Quart-a-Nancy Pt.

Fallen Jerusalem

Round Rock   Broken Jerusalem

Manchioneel Bay

Cooper Island

ead
hest

Salt Island

South Bay

Ginger Island

Peter Island   **Salt Island**   Markoe Pt.

Wreck of the Rhone

Ginger Island

Big Reef Bay

Salt Island Bluff

Cooper Island

Peter Island

Peter Island Bluff

KEY	
🔲	Dive Sites
✓	Snorkel
⛴	Ferry

0 ———————— 6 miles

0 ———————— 9 km

Snorkeling

Scuba diving always requires advance planning. Snorkeling, on the other hand, can be a far more casual affair. There's no heavy, expensive, complicated equipment involved. There's usually no need for a boat, since many of the finest snorkel sites are adjacent to a beach. Because lots of tropical marine life lives fairly near the water's surface, there's no link between the depth of a dive and your enjoyment. Many avid water-sports enthusiasts progress from swimming to snorkeling to scuba—and then gradually drift back to snorkeling. The silent world is even quieter without the hiss of a two-stage regulator. Just wade in, plop down on your stomach, and snorkel away. If you're a bit adventurous, hold your breath to dive down a few feet. You'll get a closer look at the entrancing marine life on the reefs and the ocean floor.

Few places on this planet are as convenient to snorkel as the Virgin Islands, and many dive shops rent snorkeling gear, provide instructions on how to use it, and give directions to nearby snorkeling sites. Hotels and vacation villas may provide you with complimentary gear or charge a small fee. And water-sports outfitters at the busiest beaches can outfit you with masks, fins, and snorkels. If you plan to do a lot of snorkeling, it may pay to buy your own gear either at a dive shop in your home area or in the Virgin Islands. Discount stores often sell snorkel equipment, but make sure you can try it on before you buy. To see if a mask fits, hold it up to your face and breath in gently through your nose. It should stick there for a moment. If not, try another. Fins should fit well: if they're too loose, they'll fall off, and if they're too tight, they'll give you blisters. Usually, any snorkel with a mouthpiece that doesn't leak is fine.

To prevent your mask from fogging, spit in it and rub the saliva on the inside of the lens. (If you're on the squeamish side, a drop of ordinary dishwashing liquid or a commercial "mask defogger" also works.) Warning: it's difficult to walk in fins. Some people walk into the water backwards with them; a better idea is to put them on while sitting in shallow water. Practice clearing your snorkel (with a sharp blow of air) in very shallow water, bracing yourself with your hands on clear sand. This will help you develop confidence before venturing into deeper waters.

The dangers of snorkeling are few and easily avoided. As when scuba diving, don't touch mustard-colored coral. It's fire coral, as its name implies, and can give you a burn. Avoid spiny sea urchins, which have long black spines; if you step on one, you'll feel it for days. But you shouldn't touch *any* coral, both because it's better to be safe than sorry and also because it's very fragile and takes years to grow back. Don't put your hands into dark holes—unless you want to play "patty cake" with a defensive moray eel. Ignore sharks and barracudas unless they act particularly aggressive. If so, retreat calmly without excessive splashing. Don't wear shiny jewelry; it attracts sharks and barracudas. Never snorkel alone, and unless you're on a guided trip, don't snorkel at night. Avoid areas with heavy surf or strong currents.

Most busy beaches have swim areas marked with white buoys. For safety's sake, confine your snorkeling to those areas. Avoid busy harbors, dock areas, or navigational channels. While boats aren't usually a problem in marked swimming areas, if you hear a motorized vessel approaching, resurface immediately and clasp both hands together over your head. This makes you clearly visible and means "Diver Okay." (Waving your hands rapidly back and forth over your head means "Diver in trouble. Need Help!") In addition, make sure you don't get hit by one boat while watching another. Sound direction can be confusing underwater. Finally, towing a floating dive flag is your best protection against being run down.

Popular Snorkeling Sites

Snorkel spots abound in the Virgin Islands. Indeed, just about every beach has a lovely spot to tempt you into the salty sea. However, Trunk Bay in St. John gets the most attention. The national park service has created an underwater trail that lets you know what you're seeing in terms of coral and other underwater features. And the beach is easy to reach; taxis leave on demand from the Cruz Bay ferry dock, and Trunk Bay is on every St. John tour.

Magens Bay, the most popular beach on St. Thomas, provides lovely snorkeling if you head along the edges. You're likely to see some colorful sponges, darting fish, and maybe even a turtle if you're lucky. Like Trunk Bay, Magens Bay is a stop on every island tour, and it's easy to reach by rental car or taxi from wherever you're staying.

Snorkeling at Buck Island Reef National Monument in St. Croix provides a variety of experiences. The only way to reach this offshore cay is by boat. Once there, just jump into the water for a float over colorful reefs teeming with coral and fish. There's also a marked snorkeling trail here.

The BVI is a snorkeler's paradise, but if you happen to be in Virgin Gorda, you're in luck. The Baths attracts numerous snorkelers who enjoy floating around the huge pools created by the huge rocks that created this natural attraction. You're sure to see some interesting fish.

–Lynda Lohr

TRY A YACHT CHARTER

SAVORING A FRESHLY BREWED MUG OF COF-FEE, I sat on the front deck of our chartered 43-foot catamaran and watched the morning show. Laser-like rays of sunlight streamed through a cottony cloudbank, bringing life to the emerald islands and turquoise seas surrounding our anchorage. My mind drifted back several centuries. What would it have been like to sail with Columbus and chart these waters for the first time? How would it feel to cast about the deserted beaches for the perfect place to bury plundered treasure? The aroma of freshly made banana pancakes roused me from my reverie. Our chef, Marcella, clad in khaki shorts and polo shirt with her blond hair tied back in a ponytail, playfully poured syrup over short stacks set on the cockpit table. The kids squealed in delight. My husband, who considered himself a confirmed landlubber, smiled and winked. As I scooted back to join him at the table, he whispered in my ear: "Let's tell everyone this trip was my idea."

Bareboat or Crewed?

Once considered an outward-bound adventure or exclusive domain of the rich and famous, chartering a boat is an affordable and attractive vacation alternative. It's ideal for everyone from young honeymoon couples to families with kids and active seniors. If you're already a sailor, perhaps you've always wanted to explore beyond your own lake, river, or bay, but didn't feel confident to take your own boat on a long-haul transit to your dream destination. Or maybe your idea of boat travel has always been a cruise ship, but now you're ready for a more intimate voyage. Or perhaps you've never sailed before, but you are now curious to cast off and explore a whole new world.

The first question to answer in planning a charter is whether you'd like to go bareboat or crewed. Bareboat means without any crew. You are the captain. You sail the boat, chart the course, and cook the meals. On a crewed charter, you sit back and relax while the crew provides for your every want and need. Captains are U.S. Coast Guard licensed or the equivalent in the British maritime system. Cooks—preferring to be called chefs—have skills that go far beyond peanut butter and jelly sandwiches. There's four meals a day and many chefs boast certificates from culinary school ranging from the Culinary Institute of America in New York to the Cordon Bleu in Paris.

If you'd like to bareboat, don't be intimidated. It's a myth that you must be a graduate of a sailing school in order to pilot your own charter boat. A bareboat company will ask you to fill out a resume. The company checks for prior boat handling experience, the type of craft you've sailed (whether power boat or sailboat), and in what type of waters. Real life experience, meaning all those day and weekend trips close to home, count as valuable know-how. If you've done a bit of boating, you may be more qualified than you think to take out a bareboat.

The advantage of a crewed yacht charter, with captain and cook, is that it takes every bit of stress out of the vacation. With a captain who knows the local waters, you get to see some of the coves and anchorages that are not necessarily in the guidebooks. Your meals are prepared, cabins cleaned, beds made up every day—and turned down at night, too. Plus, you can sail and take the helm as often as you like. But at the end of the day, the captain is the one who will take responsibility for anchoring safely for the night while the chef goes below and whips up a gourmet meal.

Costs can be very similar between a bareboat and crewed charter. For example, bareboats in the 50- to 55-foot range that carry six people start at $8,000 per week,

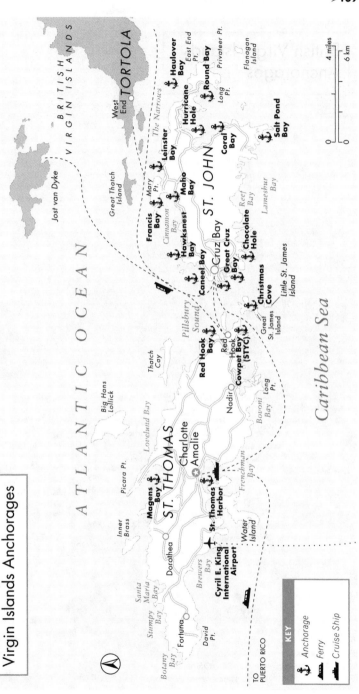

United States
Virgin Islands Anchorages

TORTOLA

BRITISH VIRGIN ISLANDS

West End

The Narrows

Haulover Bay
East End Pt.
Round Bay
Long Privateer Pt.
Flanagan Island

Hurricane Hole

Leinster Bay

Salt Pond Bay

Coral Bay

Mary Pt.
Maho Bay

ST. JOHN

Jost van Dyke

Great Thatch Island

Francis Bay

Cinnamon Bay
Hawksnest Bay
Caneel Bay

Cruz Bay

Great Cruz Bay

Chocolate Hole

Reef Bay
Lameshur Bay

Little St. James Island

Christmas Cove

ATLANTIC OCEAN

Pillsbury Sound

Red Hook Bay

Red Hook

Cowpet Bay (STYC)

Great St. James Island

Thatch Cay

Caribbean Sea

Big Hans Lollick

Nadir

Boroni Bay
Long Pt.

Loveland Bay

Picara Pt.

Charlotte Amalie

ST. THOMAS

Magens Bay

St. Thomas Harbor

Frenchman Bay

Inner Brass

Dorothea

Cyril E. King International Airport

Water Island

Santa Maria Bay

Brewers Bay

Fortuna

Stumpy Bay

David Pt.

Botany Bay

TO PUERTO RICO

4 miles
6 km

KEY

⚓ Anchorage
⛴ Ferry
🚢 Cruise Ship

British Virgin Islands Anchorages

ATLANTIC

La

Guana Islan

*Great
Tobago*

*Man
O'War
Bay*

JOST VAN DYKE

West End
Pt.

**Great
Harbour**

Great
Harbour

Little
Harbour

*Trunk
Bay*

Brewers
Bay

White Bay

White Bay

*Pull &
Be Damn
Pt.*

*Black
Pt.*

**Little
Harbour**

Cane
Garden
Bay

*Todman
Pk.*

Fort
Shirle

Little Tobago

**Cane
Garden
Bay**

**Road
Town**

**Baug
Bay**

Carrot Bay

Long Bay

West
End

Mt.
Sage

*Road
Harbc*

*Great Thatch
Island*

**Soper's
Hole**

TORTOLA

West Pt.

*Frenchman's
Cay*

*Grea
Harbou*

Rock
Hole

**Pete
Islan**

*Wh
B*

Pelican Island

*Privateer
Bay*

**Norman
Island**

*Mone
Bay*

TO ST. THOMAS

*Norman
Island*

ST. JOHN
UNITED STATES VIRGIN ISLANDS

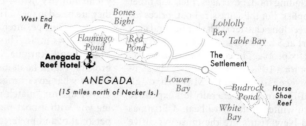

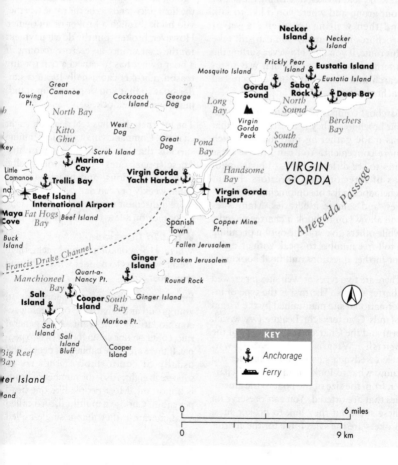

excluding food, beverages, fuel, and other supplies. For the same size boat, prices for a weeklong charter with skipper and chef start at $4,500 for a couple and $10,000 for six people. The cost is all-inclusive, except for a 10% to 15% gratuity. The summer season, from May through mid-December, is generally less expensive than winter in the Caribbean. Christmas and New Year's are the most expensive times to travel. Between the US and BVI, there are over 200 crewed yachts to choose from and well over 1,000 bareboats.

Choosing a Charter

A decade ago, choosing a charter would mean calling a bareboat company or crewed yacht broker, describing the size of your group and where you'd like to sail, and then waiting to receive a set of brochures in the mail. You can still take this route, if you like. However, surfing the Internet has become a popular way to research and book bareboat and crewed yacht charters.

Bareboat company Web sites are like online brochures. They're a research tool that has made gathering information much more convenient. You can browse these sites to see different types of boats, photos of interiors and exteriors, layout schematics, a list of equipment and amenities, and sample itineraries. Many sites will allow you to book a charter directly, while others give you the option of calling a toll-free number to speak with an agent for further questions and final booking.

There are two types of Web sites for crewed charter yachts. The first is the type of informational site maintained by the Virgin Islands Charteryacht League (www.vicl. org) and the Charter Yacht Society of the British Virgin Islands (www. bvicrewedyachts.com). These sites let you know what to look for in a crewed charter, from the size of the boat to the amenities that are offered. You can't reserve on these sites, but they link to broker sites. Brokers are the sales force for the charter

yacht industry. Most brokers, whether they are based in the Caribbean, the United States, or Europe, attend annual charter-yacht shows in St. Thomas, Tortola, St-Martin and Antigua. At these shows, brokers visit the boats and meet the crews. This is what gives brokers their depth of knowledge for "match-making," or linking you with a boat that will meet your personality and preferences.

The second form of Web site is for individual boat companies. About 30% of the crewed charter yachts based out of the U.S. and British Virgin Islands book directly. This saves the commission an owner has to pay to the broker. But while "going direct" might seem advantageous, the final price tends to be the same whether you book through a broker or an owner. However, brokers put the down payment for the charter into an escrow account. If a boat owner has to cancel a trip for any reason, a broker can usually locate a similar boat so that you don't end up standing alone at the dock.

The Internet often has real deals on yacht charters. Companies may offer last-minute specials that are available only online. These special rates—usually for specific dates, destinations, and boats—are updated weekly or even daily. You can often score a discount off the cost of the charter or tack on a few free days to your trip.

What to Consider

Whether bareboat or a crewed yacht, there are a few points to ponder when selecting your boat.

First, consider how many people are in your group and what kind of sleeping accommodations you want. As a general rule, count on one cabin for every two people. If there are three cabins, six people will usually fit comfortably. Don't try to squeeze in eight. Also, the number of heads is important. Most people like one head per cabin. Choose a multihull, also called a catamaran, rather than a single-hulled

monohull yacht if you want to be more as-
sured everyone has cabins of equal size and
space.

Second, consider the type of boat. If you
want to do some good old traditional sailing, where you're heeling over with the seas
at your rails, monohulls are a good option.
On the other hand, multihulls are more stable, easier to board, and have a big salon
for families. They're also ideal if some
people in the group tend to get seasick or
aren't as gung-ho for the more traditional
style of sailing. If you'd like to cover more
ground, choose a power boat.

Third, be aware that some crewed charter boats specialize in certain types of
charters. Among these are learn-to-sail
excursions, honeymoon cruises, scuba-
diving adventures, and family-friendly
trips. Your broker can steer you to the
boats that fit your specific needs.

Fourth and finally, bear in mind standard
and optional equipment. Most charter
boats have satellite navigation systems and
autopilots, as well as regulation safety gear,
dinghies with motors, and even stereos
and entertainment systems. Generators
will keep foods colder than battery-driven
refrigeration systems. Air-conditioning
really isn't needed during the winter, but
can be a nice addition in the summer
months. Crewed charter yachts can provide sea-to-shore communication, although
phoning home is an extra charge and can
be an expensive proposition at $4 or more
per minute. For an added charge, you can
request water toys like kayaks, boogie
boards, and windsurfers. Many bareboat
companies monitor the VHF round-the-
clock to aid in case of breakdowns.

Now that you've decided on bareboat ver-
sus crewed charter and selected your craft,
all you need to do is confirm the availability
of the date with the company or broker
and pay a nonrefundable deposit equal to
50% of the charter price.

Preparing for Your Charter

Buying provisions is one key point you'll
need to plan for in advance of a bareboat
charter. You have three choices: choose a
provisioning option from the charter company, shop from a local grocery via a
faxed or e-mailed grocery list in advance
of your trip, or buy groceries once you arrive on island and before you get on board
the boat.

If you choose the company option, provisioning packages can cost from $30 to
$40 per person per day. This may or may
not include all three meals. Some companies have packages that include food for
only three or four dinners, making it necessary for you to eat out some nights.

Some British Virgin Island grocery stores,
like **Bobby's Market Place** (✉ Wickham's
Cay I, Road Town ☎ 284/494–2189
⊕ www.bobbysmarketplace.com) and
Ample Hamper (✉ Inner Harbour Marina, Road Town ☎ 284/494–2494
✉ Frenchmans Cay Marina, West End
☎ 284/495–4684 ⊕ www.amplehamper.
com) offer the option of provisioning via
the Internet. For example, Bobby's Market Place offers three different packages
that include all breakfasts and lunches: one
with no dinners included, a second with
four dinners included, and a third with all
seven dinners included. Prices for these
packages range from $15 to $23 per person per day. An 18-page list found on the
company's Web site lets you designate
the number in your party and preferences
for breakfast, lunch, dinner, and snacks.
On the Ample Hamper's Web site there
are more than 1,200 items divided into 33
categories ranging from prepared foods
to vegetarian items. You can treat this
just like a shopping list to check off a
customized order around menus you've
planned. It's a good idea to arrange this
type of provisioning at least a week in advance. Many groceries will arrange free
delivery to your boat.

If you want to provision before boarding your boat, be sure to arrive at your destination by midday. This will give you time to shop, unpack your groceries, and become familiar with the boat's kitchen while it is still daylight. There are several grocery stores, ranging from large mainland-style supermarkets to upscale gourmet groceries, on St. Thomas and Tortola, the two most common embarkation points. Beware of sticker shock, however. Food is about 30% more expensive than on the U.S. mainland. For example, a half-gallon of milk can range from $2.89 to $3.89, a loaf of whole-wheat sandwich bread costs $2.29, and a dozen large eggs is $2.29. The U.S. dollar is the legal tender in both the U.S. and British Virgin Islands, and traveler's checks and major credit cards are widely accepted. Remember that most of the larger grocery stores are located inland and require a taxi ride to and from major marinas. Still, if you stick with the basics from big supermarkets, this could be the most economical route.

On a crewed charter the chef does all the cooking, so it's important to let the crew know just what you'd like to eat. In advance of your trip, your broker will send a preference sheet. On this sheet you can list your favorite foods. Are you a meat eater or vegetarian? Have allergies? Special requests for birthdays or anniversaries? Do you want a big breakfast or just a Continental-style meal and coffee? There is an added charge for fine wines and premium liquors.

This sheet is also where you can describe your wish for the trip. Perhaps you'd like lazy days of sleeping late, sunning, and swimming. Or you might prefer active days scooting across the seas with sails billowing and stops for snorkeling and exploring ashore. If there's a special spot you'd like to visit—Charlotte Amalie for shopping, Jost Van Dyke to hear calypsonian Foxy Callwood sing, or the giant boulder filled grottos of The Baths at Virgin Gorda—list it so your captain can plan the itinerary accordingly.

Pack light for any type of charter. Bring soft-sided luggage, rather than hard suitcases, since space is limited and storage spots are usually odd shaped. Shorts, T-shirts and swimsuits are all you need for the bulk of your trip. Shoes are seldom required except ashore, but you might want beach shoes for exploring or snorkeling in areas that might be inhabited by sea urchins. If you'd like to dine out in a more formal restaurant, bring more formal clothing. This means a dress or skirt for women and long pants and collared shirts for men. There are a few upscale resort dining rooms that enforce this type of dress code. Most boats provide snorkel equipment, but double check before you go. Bring sunscreen, but a type that will not stain cockpit cushions and decks.

What You'll See in the USBVI

The U.S. and British Virgin Islands boast over 100 stepping-stone islands and cays within a 50-nautical-mile radius. This means easy line-of-sight navigation and island-hopping in protected waters, and it's rare that you'll spend more than a few hours moving from one anchorage to another.

Tortola, in the British Virgin Islands, is the crewed-charter and bareboat mecca of the Caribbean. This fact is plainly apparent from the forest of masts rising out of locales like Soper's Hole, Nanny Cay, and the capital of Road Town. The neighboring U.S. Virgin Islands fleet is based in St. Thomas' historic Charlotte Amalie and at the eastern end of the island in Red Hook. Direct flights from the mainland, luxurious accommodations, and duty-free shopping are drawing cards for departures from the U.S. Virgin Islands, whereas the British Virgins are closer to the prime cruising grounds.

On a typical weeklong charter, you could set sail from Red Hook, St. Thomas, then cross Pillsbury Sound to St. John's northshore anchorages in Honeymoon, Trunk or Francis bays. After clearing customs in West End, Tortola, many yachts hop along a series of smaller islands that run along the south side of the Sir Francis Drake Channel. Norman Island is the rumored site of Robert Louis Stevenson's Treasure Island. Further east, off Salt Island, is the wreck of the *Rhone*—considered the most magnificent dive site in the eastern Caribbean. Giant boulders form caves and grottoes called The Baths at Virgin Gorda's southern end, while the North Sound is home to several quiet anchorages as well as the Bitter End Yacht Club. A downwind run along Tortola's northshore ends at Jost Van Dyke, where that famous guitar-strumming calypsonian, Foxy Callwood, sings personalized ditties that make for a memorable finale.

If you're not sure whether a charter-yacht vacation is right for you, consider this: Would you enjoy a floating hotel room where the scenery outside your window changed according to your desires? A "yes" enticed my husband to try chartering. After a single one-week trip, I had him hooked.

FURTHER READING

If you have the time before your trip, read James Michener's *Caribbean;* it will enhance your visit. *Don't Stop the Carnival* by Herman Wouk is a classic Caribbean book, though some of its 1950s perspectives seem rather dated.

Once you get to the Virgin Islands, take time to book-shop; there are some prolific Virgin Islands writers and artists publishing on every subject from pirates to architecture. Look for books, art prints, and cards by Mapes de Monde, published by Virgin Islands native son Michael Paiewonsky, who splits his time between Rome and the USVI. Mapes de Monde also publishes *The Three Quarters of the Town of Charlotte Amalie* by local historian Edith Woods. It's richly printed and illustrated with Woods's fine pen-and-ink drawings. Photography buffs will want to look for the book of internationally known St. Croix photographer Fritz Henle. For BVI history buffs, Vernon Pickering's *Concise History of the British Virgin Islands* is a wordy but worthy guide to the events and personalities that shaped the region. Pickering also produces the *Official Tourist Handbook* for the BVI. Pick up a copy of *A Place Like This: Hugh Benjamin's Peter Island,* the charming and eloquent personal account of the Kittitian's past two decades in the British Virgin Islands. The book was written in collaboration with Richard Myers, a New York writer.

For children there's *Up Mountain One Time* by Willie Wilson, and a *St. John Historical Coloring Book.*

For linguists, *What a Pistarckle!* by Lito Valls gives the origins of the many expressions you'll be hearing, and historians will enjoy *St. John Backtime* by Ruth Hull Low and Rafael Valls, and *Eyewitness Accounts of Slavery in the Danish West Indies* by Isidor Paiewonsky. For sailors, Simon Scott has written a *Cruising Guide to the Virgin Islands.*

U.S. & British Virgin Islands Essentials

PLANNING TOOLS, EXPERT INSIGHT, GREAT CONTACTS

There are planners, and there are those who fly by the seat of their pants. We happily place ourselves among the planners. Our writers and editors try to anticipate all the issues you may face before and during any journey, and then they do their research. This section is the product of their efforts. Use it to get excited about your trip to the U.S. & British Virgin Islands, to inform your travel planning, or to guide you on the road should the seat of your pants start to feel threadbare.

GETTING STARTED

We're really proud of our Web site: Fodors.com is a great place to begin any journey. Scan Travel Wire for suggested itineraries, travel deals, restaurant and hotel openings, and other up-to-the-minute info. Check out Booking to research prices and book plane tickets, hotel rooms, rental cars, and vacation packages. Head to Talk for on-the-ground pointers from travelers who frequent our message boards. You can also link to loads of other travel-related resources.

▌ RESOURCES

ONLINE TRAVEL TOOLS
Information on the U.S. & British Virgin Islands is just a click away on the islands' respective tourism Web sites. And of course every Caribbean traveler should bookmark the Caribbean Tourism Organization's comprehensive site.

ALL ABOUT THE U.S.
& BRITISH VIRGIN ISLANDS
Web Sites USVI Department of Tourism ⊕ www.usvitourism.vi BVI Tourism Bureau ⊕ www.bvitouristboard.com Caribbean Tourism Organization ⊕ www.doitcaribbean.com

Safety Transportation Security Administration (TSA) ⊕ www.tsa.gov
Time Zones Timeanddate.com ⊕ www.timeanddate.com/worldclock can help you figure out the correct time anywhere.
Weather Accuweather.com ⊕ www.accuweather.com is an independent weather-forecasting service with good coverage of hurricanes. Weather.com ⊕ www.weather.com is the Web site for the Weather Channel.

WORD OF MOUTH

After your trip, be sure to rate the places you visited and share your experiences and travel tips with us and other Fodorites in Travel Ratings and Talk on www.fodors.com.

Other Resources CIA World Factbook ⊕ www.odci.gov/cia/publications/factbook/index.html has profiles of every country in the world. It's a good source if you need some quick facts and figures.

VISITOR INFORMATION
Stop by the Tourism Department's local offices for brochures on things to do and places to see. The offices are open only from 8 AM to 5 PM Monday through Friday, so if you need information on the weekend or on one of the territory's many holidays, you're out of luck. (For locations, see ⇨ Visitor Information in the Essentials section of each chapter.) For general information on the islands, contact these tourist offices before you go.
USVI: United States Virgin Islands Department of Tourism USVI Government Tourist Office ☎ 404/688-0906 in Atlanta ☎ 312/670-8784 in Chicago ☎ 213/739-0138 in Los Angeles ☎ 305/442-7200 in Florida ☎ 212/332-2222 in New York ☎ 202/624-3590 in Washington, DC ⊕ www.usvitourism.vi
BVI: British Virgin Islands Tourist Board BVI Tourist Board ☎ 212/696-0400 or 800/835-8530 in New York ☎ 770/874-5951 in Georgia ☎ 213/736-8931 in Los Angeles.

▌ THINGS TO CONSIDER

GOVERNMENT ADVISORIES
As different countries have different world views, look at travel advisories from a range of governments to get more of a sense of what's going on out there. And be sure to parse the language carefully. For example, a warning to "avoid all travel" carries more weight than one urging you to "avoid nonessential travel," and both are much stronger than a plea to "exercise caution." A U.S. government travel warning is more permanent (though not necessarily more serious) than a so-called public announcement, which carries an expiration date.

TIP→ Consider registering online with the ate Department (https://travelregistration. ate.gov/ibrs/), so the government will know look for you should a crisis occur in the untry you're visiting.

ae U.S. Department of State's Web site s more than just travel warnings and ad-sories. The consular information sheets ued for every country have general safety os, entry requirements (though be sure verify these with the country's em-ssy), and other useful details.

neral Information & Warnings Australian partment of Foreign Affairs & Trade ⊕ www.smartraveller.gov.au. **Consular fairs Bureau of Canada** ⊕ www.voyage.gc. . **U.K. Foreign & Commonwealth Office** ⊕ www.fco.gov.uk/travel. **U.S. Department State** ⊕ www.travel.state.gov.

EAR

he Virgin Islands are definitely laid-back estinations. If you're staying at a posh re-rt, you may need some dressier attire, irticularly during the winter months. es are never required, but jackets for en sometimes are. Sturdy shoes are a ust if you plan on hiking, and don't for-t to tuck a folding umbrella into your iitcase for those once-in-awhile rain iowers. You may need a light sweater or ng-sleeve T-shirt for breezy nights (or verly air-conditioned restaurants) or for ie ferry ride home after a day in the sun.

iarmacies, grocery and discount stores—irticularly Kmart on St. Thomas and St. roix—carry a large variety of sundries, it you may not find the brand you want, id most prices are higher. The selection the BVI, particulary on the out islands, definitely on the slim side. If you prefer have a certain brand of mosquito re-ellent or baby formula, for example, ing it from home. The larger islands ive pharmacies that can contact your ome drug store if you need a prescription led, but it will be easier and quicker to ing what you need from home.

nless you just have to have a certain cut meat, think breakfast isn't breakfast without one particular brand of cereal, or must have a specific type of coffee, there's really no need to bring food on your USBVI vacation. After all, the folks who live there year-round find plenty to fill their refrigerators. You'll find stateside brands in both the USBVI as well as other unfamiliar labels. There are occasional shortages of some goods, but do like the islanders do and substitute. No bananas at the supermarket? Eat papayas instead.

There are no prohibitions about bringing any food items to the USVI, but you can't bring meat into the BVI without a $25 agricultural permit. You need to apply in advance at the Agriculture Department, but it's hardly worth the effort when you can buy what you'll need at the island's grocery stores. You can't take most meat and agricultural products back to the U.S. mainland, so don't plan on taking unused food back home.

But we know that frugal folks will still bring some staples from home. If you don't want to buy an entire jar of spices or plan to make something that needs just a cup of flour, take only what you think you'll need. Film cans make perfect spice containers, and anything else can go in plastic bags. Double-bag bottled liquids to make sure you don't have leaks. To bring your favorite cut of meat, freeze it thoroughly, pack it in a cooler with ice packs, and tape the cooler shut with duct tape. Unless the cooler is small enough to fit in the overhead compartment of the airplane, you'll have to check it as luggage.

Remember to pack light. There are no luggage carts at USVI or BVI airports, and porters can be scarce. Small interisland planes have very limited carry-on space. Suitcases that fit under seats on major carriers just won't fit in these tiny planes, so you'll probably have to check some luggage. If you do, pack some toiletries, a change of clothes, and perhaps a bathing suit in your carry-on bag—just in case your checked luggage arrives on a later flight (which may be the next day).

PASSPORTS & VISAS

Upon entering the USVI from the U.S., there are no immigration procedures to face. If you're arriving from an international destination—even from the BVI—you'll have to clear customs as well as immigration. When you depart for the U.S. or if you're connecting in San Juan, you'll clear customs and immigration at the USVI airport. If you arrive in the USVI by ferry from the BVI, you must also go through customs and immigration procedures. If you're arriving by air or ferry in the BVI from the USVI or San Juan, you must go through customs and immigration. There are no special procedures for departure from the BVI.

Passports are not required for travel to or from the USVI, but proof of citizenship is. Even though one is not required for travel to or from the USVI, a passport works best for this purpose; however, officials will still accept a birth or citizenship certificate. In the BVI, U.S. citizens must have a valid passport, but Canadians may be able to use a certified birth certificate and government-issued photo I.D.

PASSPORTS

We're always surprised at how few Americans have passports—only 25% at this writing. This number is expected to grow in coming years, when it becomes impossible to re-enter the United States from trips to neighboring Canada or Mexico without one. Remember this: A passport verifies both your identity and nationality—a great reason to have one.

U.S. passports are valid for 10 years. You must apply in person if you're getting a passport for the first time; if your previous passport was lost, stolen, or damaged; or if your previous passport has expired and was issued more than 15 years ago or when you were under 16. All children under 18 must appear in person to apply for or renew a passport. Both parents must accompany any child under 14 (or send a notarized statement with their permission) and provide proof of their relationship to the child.

■ TIP→ Before your trip, make two copies of your passport's data page (one for someone at home and another for you to carry separately). Or scan the page and e-mail it to someone at home and/or yourself.

There are 13 regional passport offices, as well as 7,000 passport acceptance facilities in post offices, public libraries, and other governmental offices. If you're renewing a passport, you can do so by mail. Forms are available at passport acceptance facilities and online.

The cost to apply for a new passport is $97 for adults, $82 for children under 16; renewals are $67. Allow six weeks for processing, both for first-time passports and renewals. For an expediting fee of $60 you can reduce this time to about two weeks. If your trip is less than two weeks away, you can get a passport even more rapidly by going to a passport office with the necessary documentation. Private expediters can get things done in as little as 48 hours, but charge hefty fees for their services.

VISAS

A visa is essentially formal permission to enter a country. Visas allow countries to keep track of you and other visitors—and generate revenue (from application fees). You *always* need a visa to enter a foreign country; however, many countries routinely issue tourist visas on arrival, particularly to U.S. citizens. When your passport is stamped or scanned in the immigration line, you're actually being issued a visa. Sometimes you have to stand in a separate line and pay a small fee to get your stamp before going through immigration, but you can still do this at the airport on arrival.

Getting a visa isn't always that easy. Some countries require that you arrange for one in advance of your trip. There's usually—but not always—a fee involved, and said fee may be nominal ($10 or less) or substantial ($100 or more).

If you must apply for a visa in advance, you can usually do it in person or by mail. When you apply by mail, you send your

PACKING 101

Why do some people travel with a convoy of huge suitcases yet never have a thing to wear? How do others pack a duffle with a week's worth of outfits *and* supplies for every contingency? We realize that packing is a matter of style, but there's a lot to be said for traveling light. These tips help fight the battle of the bulging bag.

MAKE A LIST. In a recent Fodor's survey, 29% of respondents said they make lists (and often pack) a week before a trip. You can use your list to pack and to repack at the end of your trip. It can also serve as record of the contents of your suitcase—in case it disappears in transit.

THINK IT THROUGH. What's the weather like? Is this a business trip? A cruise? Going abroad? In some places dress may be more or less conservative than you're used to. As you create your itinerary, note outfits next to each activity (don't forget accessories).

EDIT YOUR WARDROBE. Plan to wear everything twice (better yet, thrice) and to do laundry along the way. Stick to one basic look—urban chic, sporty casual, etc. Build around one or two neutrals and an accent e.g., black, white, and olive green). Women can freshen looks by changing scarves or jewelry. For a week's trip, you can look smashing with three bottoms, four or five tops, a sweater, and a jacket.

BE PRACTICAL. Put comfortable shoes atop your list. (Did we need to say this?) Pack lightweight, wrinkle-resistent, compact, washable items. (Or this?) Stack and roll clothes, so they'll wrinkle less. Unless you're on a guided tour or a cruise, select luggage you can readily carry. Porters, like good butlers, are hard to find these days.

CHECK WEIGHT AND SIZE LIMITATIONS. In the United States you may be charged extra for checked bags weighing more than 50 pounds. Abroad some airlines don't allow you to check bags over 60 to 70 pounds at all, or they charge outrageous fees for every excess pound—or bag. Carry-on size limitations can be stringent, too.

CHECK CARRY-ON RESTRICTIONS. Research restrictions with the TSA. Rules vary abroad, so check them with your airline if you're traveling overseas on a foreign carrier. Consider packing all but essentials (travel documents, prescription meds, wallet) in checked luggage. This leads to a "pack only what you can afford to lose" approach that might help you streamline.

RETHINK VALUABLES. On U.S. flights, airlines are liable for only about $2,800 per person for bags. On international flights, the liability limit is around $635 per bag. But items like computers, cameras, and jewelry aren't covered, and as gadgetry can go on and off the list of carry-on no-no's, you can't count on keeping things safe by keeping them close. Although comprehensive travel policies may cover luggage, the liability limit is often a pittance. Your home-owner's policy may cover you sufficiently when you travel—or not.

LOCK IT UP. If you must pack valuables, use TSA-approved locks (about $10) that can be unlocked by all U.S. security personnel.

TAG IT. Always tag your luggage; use your business address if you don't want people to know your home address. Put the same information (and a copy of your itinerary) inside your luggage, too.

REPORT PROBLEMS IMMEDIATELY. If your bags—or things in them—are damaged or go astray, file a written claim with your airline *before leaving the airport*. If the airline is at fault, it may give you money for essentials until your luggage arrives. Most lost bags are found within 48 hours, so alert the airline to your whereabouts for two or three days. If your bag was opened for security reasons in the States and something is missing, file a claim with the TSA.

passport to a designated consulate, where your passport will be examined and the visa issued. Expediters—usually the same ones who handle expedited passport applications—can do all the work of obtaining your visa for you; however, there's always an additional cost (often more than $50 per visa).

Most visas limit you to a single trip—basically during the actual dates of your planned vacation. Other visas allow you to visit as many times as you wish for a specific period of time. Remember that requirements change, sometimes at the drop of a hat, and the burden is on you to make sure that you have the appropriate visas. Otherwise, you'll be turned away at the airport or, worse, deported after you arrive in the country. No company or travel insurer gives refunds if your travel plans are disrupted because you didn't have the correct visa.

U.S. Passport Information U.S. Department of State ☎ 877/487-2778 ⊕ http://travel. state.gov/passport.

U.S. Passport & Visa Expediters A. Briggs Passport & Visa Expeditors ☎ 800/806-0581 or 202/464-3000 ⊕ www.abriggs.com. **American Passport Express** ☎ 800/455-5166 or 603/559-9888 ⊕ www.americanpassport.com. **Passport Express** ☎ 800/362-8196 or 401/ 272-4612 ⊕ www.passportexpress.com. **Travel Document Systems** ☎ 800/874-5100 or 202/ 638-3800 ⊕ www.traveldocs.com. **Travel the World Visas** ☎ 866/886-8472 or 301/495-7700 ⊕ www.world-visa.com.

GENERAL REQUIREMENTS FOR US VIRGIN ISLANDS	
Passport	Not required for entry from U.S.; required for entry from BVI and other foreign locations.
Visa	Depends on nationality. Most visitors do not need a visa.
Vaccinations	None required.
Driving	Home driver's license ok.
Departure Tax	None.

GENERAL REQUIREMENTS FOR BRITISH VIRGIN ISLANDS	
Passport	Required for all visitors.
Visa	Depends on nationality. Most do not need a visa.
Vaccinations	None required.
Driving	Drivers required to buy local driver's license for $10. Available at car rental agencies.
Departure Tax	US$20 by air, $5 by sea.

SHOTS & MEDICATIONS

You won't have to worry about diseases like malaria and Lyme disease when visiting the USBVI, but there are occasional outbreaks of dengue fever after long spates of heavy rains increase the mosquito population. The best defense is a liberal application of mosquito repellent. If you're traveling with young children, bring a mosquito net to cover the crib.

■ TIP→ If you travel a lot internationally—particularly to developing nations—refer to the CDC's *Health Information for International Travel* (aka Traveler's Health Yellow Book). Info from it is posted on the CDC Web site (www.cdc.gov/travel/yb), or you can buy a copy from your local bookstore for $24.95.

For more information *see* Health *under* On the Ground in the U.S. & British Virgin Islands, *below.*

Health Warnings National Centers for Disease Control & Prevention (CDC) ☎ 877/ 394-8747 international travelers' health line ⊕ www.cdc.gov/travel. **World Health Organization** (WHO) ⊕ www.who.int.

TRIP INSURANCE

What kind of coverage do you honestly need? Do you even need trip insurance at all? Take a deep breath and read on.

We believe that comprehensive trip insurance is especially valuable if you're booking a very expensive or complicated trip (particularly to an isolated region) or if you're booking far in advance. Who knows what could happen six months down the ad? But whether or not you get insurance ...s more to do with how comfortable you ...e assuming all that risk yourself.

...omprehensive travel policies typically ...ver trip-cancellation and interruption, ...tting you cancel or cut your trip short ...cause of a personal emergency, illness, ..., in some cases, acts of terrorism in your ...stination. Such policies also cover evac-...ition and medical care. Some also cover ...u for trip delays because of bad weather ... mechanical problems as well as for lost ... delayed baggage. Another type of cov-...age to look for is financial default—...at is, when your trip is disrupted because ...our operator, airline, or cruise line goes ...t of business. Generally you must buy ...is when you book your trip or shortly ...ereafter, and it's only available to you ...your operator isn't on a list of excluded ...mpanies.

...you're going abroad, consider buying ...edical-only coverage at the very least. ...either Medicare nor some private in-...rers cover medical expenses anywhere ...utside of the United States besides Mex-...o and Canada (including time aboard a

cruise ship, even if it leaves from a U.S. port). Medical-only policies typically re-imburse you for medical care (excluding that related to pre-existing conditions) and hospitalization abroad, and provide for evacuation. You still have to pay the bills and await reimbursement from the in-surer, though.

Expect comprehensive travel insurance policies to cost about 4% to 7% of the total price of your trip (it's more like 12% if you're over age 70). A medical-only policy may or may not be cheaper than a comprehensive policy. Always read the fine print of your policy to make sure that you are covered for the risks that are of most concern to you. Compare several policies to make sure you're getting the best price and range of coverage available.

■ TIP→ OK. You know you can save a bundle on trips to warm-weather destinations by trav-eling during the hurricane season. But there's also a chance that a severe storm will disrupt your plans. The solution? Look for hotels and resorts that offer storm/hurricane guarantees. Although they rarely allow refunds, most guar-antees do let you rebook later if a storm strikes.

rip Insurance Resources

NSURANCE COMPARISON SITES		
...sure My Trip.com		www.insuremytrip.com.
...quare Mouth.com		www.quotetravelinsurance.com.
OMPREHENSIVE TRAVEL INSURERS		
...ccess America	866/807-3982	www.accessamerica.com.
...SA Travel Protection	800/873-9855	www.csatravelprotection.com.
...TH Worldwide	610/254-8700 or 888/243-2358	www.hthworldwide.com.
...avelex Insurance	888/457-4602	www.travelex-insurance.com.
...avel Guard International	715/345-0505 or 800/826-4919	www.travelguard.com.
...avel Insured International	800/243-3174	www.travelinsured.com.
EDICAL-ONLY INSURERS		
...ternational Medical Group	800/628-4664	www.imglobal.com.
...ternational SOS	215/942-8000 or 713/521-7611	www.internationalsos.com.
...allach & Company	800/237-6615 or 504/687-3166	www.wallach.com.

BOOKING YOUR TRIP

Unless your cousin is a travel agent, you're probably among the millions of people who make most of their travel arrangements online.

But have you ever wondered just what the differences are between an online travel agent (a Web site through which you make reservations instead of going directly to the airline, hotel, or car-rental company), a discounter (a firm that does a high volume of business with a hotel chain or airline and accordingly gets good prices), a wholesaler (one that makes cheap reservations in bulk and then re-sells them to people like you), and an aggregator (one that compares all the offerings so you don't have to)?

Is it truly better to book directly on an airline or hotel Web site? And when does a real live travel agent come in handy?

▮ ONLINE

You really have to shop around. A travel wholesaler such as Hotels.com or Hotel-Club.net can be a source of good rates, as can discounters such as Hotwire or Priceline, particularly if you can bid for your hotel room or airfare. Indeed, such sites sometimes have deals that are unavailable elsewhere. They do, however, tend to work only with hotel chains (which makes them just plain useless for getting hotel reservations outside of major cities) or big airlines (so that often leaves out upstarts like jetBlue and some foreign carriers like Air India).

Also, with discounters and wholesalers you must generally prepay, and everything is nonrefundable. And before you fork over the dough, be sure to check the terms and conditions, so you know what a given company will do for you if there's a problem and what you'll have to deal with on your own.

▮ TIP ➡ To be absolutely sure everything was processed correctly, confirm reservations made through online travel agents, discounters, and wholesalers directly with your hotel before leaving home.

Booking engines like Expedia, Travelocity, and Orbitz are actually travel agents, albeit high-volume, online ones. And airline travel packagers like American Airlines Vacations and Virgin Vacations—well, they're travel agents, too. But they may still not work with all the world's hotels.

An aggregator site will search many sites and pull the best prices for airfares, hotels, and rental cars from them. Most aggregators compare the major travel-booking sites such as Expedia, Travelocity, and Orbitz; some also look at airline Web sites, though rarely the sites of smaller budget airlines. Some aggregators also compare other travel products, including complex packages—a good thing, as you can sometimes get the best overall deal by booking an air-and-hotel package.

▮ WITH A TRAVEL AGENT

If you use an agent—brick-and-mortar or virtual—you'll usually pay a fee for the service. And know that the service you get from some online agents isn't comprehensive. For example Expedia and Travelocity don't search for prices on budget airlines like jetBlue, Southwest, or small foreign carriers. That said, some agents (online or not) *do* have access to fares that are difficult to find otherwise, and the savings can more than make up for any surcharge.

A knowledgeable brick-and-mortar travel agent can be a godsend if you're booking a cruise, a package trip that's not available to you directly, an air pass, or a complicated itinerary including several overseas flights. What's more, travel agents that specialize in a destination may have exclusive access to certain deals and insider information on things such as charter flights. Agents who specialize in types of

Online Booking Resources

AGGREGATORS

Kayak	www.kayak.com	looks at cruises and vacation packages.
Mobissimo	www.mobissimo.com.	
Qixo	www.qixo.com	compares cruises, vacation packages, and even travel insurance.
Sidestep	www.sidestep.com	compares vacation packages and lists travel deals.
Travelgrove	www.travelgrove.com	compares cruises and vacation packages.

BOOKING ENGINES

Cheap Tickets	www.cheaptickets.com	discounter.
Expedia	www.expedia.com	large online agency that charges a booking fee for airline tickets.
Hotwire	www.hotwire.com	discounter.
Lastminute.com	www.lastminute.com	specializes in last-minute travel; the main site is for the U.K., but it has a link to a U.S. site.
Luxury Link	www.luxurylink.com	has auctions (surprisingly good deals) as well as offers on the high-end side of travel.
Onetravel.com	www.onetravel.com	discounter for hotels, car rentals, airfares, and packages.
Orbitz	www.orbitz.com	charges a booking fee for airline tickets, but gives a clear breakdown of fees and taxes before you book.
Priceline.com	www.priceline.com	discounter that also allows bidding.
Travel.com	www.travel.com	allows you to compare its rates with those of other booking engines.
Travelocity	www.travelocity.com	charges a booking fee for airline tickets, but promises good problem resolution.

ONLINE ACCOMMODATIONS

Hotelbook.com	www.hotelbook.com	focuses on independent hotels worldwide.
Hotel Club	www.hotelclub.net	good for major cities worldwide.
Hotels.com	www.hotels.com	big Expedia-owned wholesaler that offers rooms in hotels all over the world.
Quikbook	www.quikbook.com	offers "pay when you stay" reservations that allow you to settle your bill when you check out, not when you book.

OTHER RESOURCES

Bidding For Travel	www.biddingfortravel.com	good place to figure out what you can get and for how much before you start bidding on, say, Priceline.

travelers (senior citizens, gays and lesbians, naturists) or types of trips (cruises, luxury travel, safaris) can also be invaluable.

■ TIP➡ Remember that Expedia, Travelocity, and Orbitz are travel agents, not just booking engines. To resolve any problems with a reservation made through these companies, contact them first.

A top-notch agent planning your cruise may get you a cabin upgrade or arrange to have a bottle of champagne chilling in your cabin when you embark. And complain about the surcharges all you like, but when things don't work out the way you'd hoped, it's nice to have an agent to put things right.

If you have the least little bit of computer ability, you can book just about everywhere in the USBVI online. Even the major consolidators now have Web sites that make booking a breeze, and those small, but special bed-and-breakfasts are also online.

Agent Resources **American Society of Travel Agents** ☎ 703/739-2782 ⊕ www.travelsense. org.

■ ACCOMMODATIONS

Decide whether you want to pay the extra price for a room overlooking the ocean or pool. At less expensive properties, location may mean a difference in price of only $10 to $20 per night; at luxury resorts, however, it could amount to as much as $100 per night. Also find out how close the property is to a beach. At some hotels you can walk barefoot from your room onto the sand; others are across a road or a 10-minute drive away.

Nighttime entertainment is often alfresco in the USBVI, so if you go to sleep early or are a light sleeper, ask for a room away from the dance floor. Air-conditioning isn't a necessity on all islands, many of which are cooled by trade winds, but it can be a plus if you enjoy an afternoon snooze or are bothered by humidity. Breezes are best on upper floors, particularly corner rooms. If you like to sleep without air-conditioning, make sure that windows can be opened and have screens; also make sure there are no security issues with leaving your windows open. If you're staying away from the water, make sure the room has a ceiling fan and that it works. In even the most luxurious resorts, there are times when things simply *don't* work; it's a fact of Caribbean life. No matter how diligent the upkeep, humidity and salt air take their toll, and cracked tiles and chipped paint are common everywhere.

The lodgings we list are the cream of the crop in each price category. We always list the facilities that are available, but we don't specify whether they cost extra; when pricing accommodations, always ask what's included and what costs extra. Properties are assigned price categories based on the range between their least and most expensive standard double room at high season (excluding holidays).

Most hotels and other lodgings require you to give your credit-card details before they will confirm your reservation. If you don't feel comfortable e-mailing this information, ask if you can fax it (some places even prefer faxes). However you book, get confirmation in writing and have a copy of it handy when you check in.

Be sure you understand the hotel's cancellation policy. Some places allow you to cancel without any kind of penalty—even if you prepaid to secure a discounted rate—if you cancel at least 24 hours in advance. Others require you to cancel a week in advance or penalize you the cost of one night. Small inns and B&Bs are most likely to require you to cancel far in advance. Most hotels allow children under a certain age to stay in their parents' room at no extra charge, but others charge for them as extra adults; find out the cutoff age for discounts.

■ TIP➡ Assume that hotels operate on the European Plan (EP, no meals) unless we specify that they use the Breakfast Plan (BP, with full breakfast), Continental Plan (CP, Continental breakfast), Full American Plan (FAP, all meals)

‣dified American Plan (**MAP**, breakfast and ‣ner) or are **all-inclusive** (**AI**, all meals and ‣st activities).

‣ARTMENT & VILLA RENTALS

‣llas—whether luxurious or modest—‣ popular lodging options on all the ‣rgin Islands.

‣nting a villa lets you settle in. You'll have ‣om to spread out, you can cook any or ‣ of your meals, and you will have all the ‣vacy you desire. Since most villas are ‣ated in residential neighborhoods, your ‣ighbors probably won't appreciate late-‣ht parties. And you may be disturbed ‣ your neighbor's weekend yard main-‣ance. That said, there's no better way ‣experience life in the USBVI.

‣any villas are set up specifically for the ‣tal market with bedrooms at opposite ‣ds of the house. This makes them per-‣t for two couples who want to share an ‣ommodation but still prefer some pri-‣cy. Others with more bedrooms are ‣ed right for families. Ask about the villa ‣out to make sure young children won't ‣ve to sleep too far away from their par-‣ts. Villas with separate bedroom build-‣gs, called pods, are probably not a good ‣a unless your children are in their teens.

‣ost villas are owned by people who live ‣mewhere else but hire a local manage-‣nt company to attend to the details. De-‣nding on the island and the rental, the ‣nager will either meet you at the ferry ‣ airport or will give you directions to ‣ur villa. Most of the companies offer the ‣ne services with similar degrees of effi-‣ncy.

‣u can book your villa through the nu-‣rous agencies that show up on the In-‣net, but they are usually not based on ‣ island you want to visit. Booking ‣ough an island-based manager means ‣t you can talk to a person who knows ‣ villa and can let you know whether it ‣ets your specifications. Your villa man-‣r can also arrange for a maid, a chef, ‣d other staffers to take care of the myr-‣ other details that make your vacation

10 WAYS TO SAVE

1. Join "frequent guest" programs. You may get preferential treatment in room choice and/or upgrades in your favorite chains.

2. Call direct. You can sometimes get a better price if you call a hotel's local toll-free number (if available) rather than a central reservations number.

3. Check online. Check hotel Web sites, as not all chains are represented on all travel sites.

4. Look for specials. Always inquire about packages and corporate rates.

5. Look for price guarantees. For overseas trips, look for guaranteed rates. With your rate locked in you won't pay more, even if the price goes up in the local currency.

6. Look for weekend deals at business hotels. High-end chains catering to business travelers are often busy only on weekdays; to fill rooms they often drop rates dramatically on weekends.

7. Ask about taxes. Verify whether local hotel taxes are included in quoted rates. In some places taxes can add 20% or more to your bill.

8. Read the fine print. Watch for add-ons, including resort fees, energy surcharges, and "convenience" fees for such things as unlimited local phone service you won't use or a free newspaper in a language you can't read.

9. Know when to go. If your destination's high season is December through April and you're trying to book, say, in late April, you might save money by changing your dates by a week or two. Ask when rates go down, though: if your dates straddle peak and non-peak seasons, a property may still charge peak-season rates for the entire stay.

10. Weigh your options (we can't say this enough). Weigh transportation times and costs against the savings of staying in a hotel that's cheaper because it's out of the way.

go smoothly. They're only a phone call away when something goes wrong or you have a question.

Villa Management Companies McLaughlin Anderson ⌂ 1000 Blackbeard's Hill, Suite 3, Charlotte Amalie St. Thomas, VI 00802-6739 ☎ 340/776-0635 or 800/537-6246 ⊕ www. mclaughlinanderson.com has rentals across the USBVI. **Catered To Vacation Homes** ✉ Marketplace Suite 206, 5206 Enighed, Cruz Bay St. John VI 00830 ☎ 340/776-6641 or 800/424-6641 ⎙ 340/693-8191 ⊕ www. cateredto.com focuses on St. John. **Vacation St. Croix** ⌂ Box 1150, Christiansted St. Croix, VI 00821 ☎ 340/778-0361 or 877/788-0361 ⊕ www.vacationstcroix.com is based on St. Croix.

CAMPING

Camping in the USBVI is limited to established campgrounds. Except for the National Park Service's Cinnamon Bay Campground on St. John, all are privately operated. Camping is a big draw on St. John, so be sure to make reservations as early as possible. Most campgrounds do not have hot showers, game rooms, or swimming pools; instead, your entertainment comes on the beach and along hiking trails.

Campgrounds Brewers Bay Campground ✉ Tortola ☎ 284/494-3463. **Cinnamon Bay Campground** ✉ St. John ☎ 340/776-6330 or 800/539-9998 ⊕ www.cinnamonbay.com. **Maho Bay Camps** ✉ St. John ☎ 340/776-6240 or 800/392-9004 ⊕ www.maho.org. **Mount Victory Camp** ✉ St. Croix ☎ 340/772-1651 or 866/772-1651 ⊕ www.

WORD OF MOUTH

Did the resort look as good in real life as it did in the photos? Did you sleep like a baby, or were the walls paper thin? Did you get your money's worth? Rate hotels and write your own reviews in Travel Ratings or start a discussion about your favorite places in Travel Talk on www.fodors.com. Your comments might even appear in our books. Yes, you, too, can be a correspondent!

---

mtvictorycamp.com. **White Bay Campground** ✉ Jost Van Dyke ☎ 284/495-9358 ⊕ www. caribbeancruisingclub.com/ivan.

HOME EXCHANGES

With a direct home exchange you stay in someone else's home while they stay in yours. Some outfits also deal with vacation homes, so you're not actually staying in someone's full-time residence, just their vacant weekend place.

Exchange Clubs Home Exchange.com ☎ 800/877-8723 ⊕ www.homeexchange. com; $59.95 for a 1-year online listing. **Home-Link International** ☎ 800/638-3841 ⊕ www. homelink.org; $80 yearly for Web-only membership; $125 includes Web access and two catalogs. **Intervac U.S.** ☎ 800/756-4663 ⊕ www.intervacus.com; $78.88 for Web-only membership; $126 includes Web access and a catalog.

■ AIRLINE TICKETS

Most domestic airline tickets are electronic; international tickets may be either electronic or paper. With an e-ticket the only thing you receive is an e-mailed receipt citing your itinerary and reservation and ticket numbers.

The greatest advantage of an e-ticket is that if you lose your receipt, you can simply print out another copy or ask the airline to do it for you at check-in. You usually pay a surcharge (up to $50) to get a paper ticket, if you can get one at all.

The sole advantage of a paper ticket is that it may be easier to endorse over to another airline if your flight is canceled and the airline with which you booked can't accommodate you on another flight.

■ RENTAL CARS

When you reserve a car, ask about cancellation penalties, taxes, drop-off charges (if you're planning to pick up the car in one city and leave it in another), and surcharges (for being under or over a certain age, for additional drivers, or for driving across state or country borders or beyond specific distance from your point of ntal). All these things can add substanally to your costs. Request car seats and ctras such as GPS when you book.

ates are sometimes—but not always—etter if you book in advance or reserve arough a rental agency's Web site. There e other reasons to book ahead, though: r popular destinations, during busy times f the year, or to ensure that you get cerin types of cars (vans, SUVs, exotic orts cars).

TIP→ Make sure that a confirmed reservaon guarantees you a car. Agencies somemes overbook, particularly for busy weekends d holiday periods.

nless you plan to spend all your days at resort or plan to take taxis everywhere, ou'll need a rental car at least for a few ays. While driving is on the left, you'll ive an American-style car with the steerg wheel on the left. Traffic doesn't move d that fast in most USBVI locations, so iving on the left is not that difficult to aster.

you're staying on St. Thomas or St. roix and don't plan to venture far off the ain roads, you won't need a four-wheel-ive vehicle. On St. John and in the BVI, four-wheel-drive vehicle is useful to get o steep roads when it rains. Many rental omes in St. John and the BVI are down apaved roads, so a four-wheel-drive vecle with high clearance may be a necesty if you rent a villa. While rental agencies

don't usually prohibit access to certain roads, use common sense. If the road looks too bad, turn around.

Most car-rental agencies won't rent to anyone under age 25 or over age 75.

Some car-rental agencies offer infant car seats for about $5 a day, but check and check again right before you leave for your trip to make sure one will be available. Their use isn't compulsary in the USBVI, but they are always a good idea if you have small children. You might consider bringing your own car seat from home.

Book your rental car well in advance during the winter season. Vehicles are particularly scarce around the busy President's Day holiday. If you don't reserve, you might find yourself with wheels. Prices will be higher during the winter season.

You usually won't find any long lines when picking up your car or dropping it off. If your rental agency is away from the airport or ferry terminal, you'll have to allot extra time to get there. Ask when you pick up your car how much time you should allot for returning it.

Rates range from $50 a day ($300 a week) for an economy car with air-conditioning, automatic transmission, and unlimited mileage; you may pay as much as $80 a day ($400 a week) for a four-wheel-drive vehicle. Both the USVI and the BVI have major companies (with airport locations) as well as numerous local companies (near the airports, in hotels, and in

Online Booking Resources

CONTACTS		
At Home Abroad	212/421-9165	www.athomeabroadinc.com.
Vacation Home Rentals Worldwide	201/767-9393 or 800/633-3284	www.vhrww.com.
Villanet	206/417-3444 or 800/964-1891	www.rentavilla.com.
Villas & Apartments Abroad	212/213-6435 or 800/433-3020	www.vaanyc.com.
Villas International	415/499-9490 or 800/221-2260	www.villasintl.com.
Villas of Distinction	707/778-1800 or 800/289-0900	www.villasofdistinction.com.
Wimco	800/449-1553	www.wimco.com.

10 WAYS TO SAVE

1. Nonrefundable is best. If saving money is more important than flexibility, then non-refundable tickets work. Just remember that you'll pay dearly (as much as $100) if you change your plans.

2. Comparison shop. Web sites and travel agents can have different arrangements with the airlines and offer different prices for exactly the same flights.

3. Beware those prices. Many airline Web sites—and most ads—show prices *without* taxes and surcharges. Don't buy until you know the full price.

4. Stay loyal. Stick with one or two frequent-flier programs. You'll rack up free trips faster and you'll accumulate more quickly the perks that make trips easier. On some airlines these include a special reservations number, early boarding, access to upgrades, and more roomy economy-class seating.

5. Watch those ticketing fees. Surcharges are usually added when you buy your ticket anywhere but on an airline Web site. (That includes by phone—even if you call the airline directly—and paper tickets regardless of how you book).

6. Check early and often. Start looking for cheap fares up to a year in advance. Keep looking till you find a price you like.

7. Don't work alone. Some Web sites have tracking features that will e-mail you immediately when good deals are posted.

8. Jump on the good deals. Waiting even a few minutes might mean paying more.

9. Be flexible. Look for departures on Tuesday, Wednesday, and Thursday, typically the cheapest days to travel. And check on prices for departures at different times and to and from alternative airports.

10. Weigh your options. What you get can be as important as what you save. A cheaper flight might have a long layover, or it might land at a secondary airport, where your ground transportation costs might be higher.

the main towns), which are sometimes cheaper. Most provide pick-up service; some ask that you take a taxi to their headquarters.

Your driver's license may not be recognized outside your home country. You may not be able to rent a car without an International Driving Permit (IDP), which can be used only in conjunction with a valid driver's license and which translates your license into 10 languages. Check the AAA Web site for more info as well as for IDPs ($10) themselves. A driver's license from the U.S. or other countries is fine in the USVI, but in the BVI you'll have to buy a temporary driver's license for $10.

CAR-RENTAL INSURANCE

Everyone who rents a car wonders whether the insurance that the rental companies offer is worth the expense. No one—including us—has a simple answer. It all depends on how much regular insurance you have, how comfortable you are with risk, and whether or not money is an issue.

If you own a car, your personal auto insurance may cover a rental to some degree, though not all policies protect you abroad; always read your policy's fine print. If you don't have auto insurance, then seriously consider buying the collision- or loss-damage waiver (CDW or LDW) from the car-rental company, which eliminates your liability for damage to the car. Some credit cards offer CDW coverage, but it's usually supplemental to your own insurance and rarely covers SUVs, minivans, luxury models, and the like. If your coverage is secondary, you may still be liable for loss-of-use costs from the car-rental company. But no credit-card insurance is valid unless you use that card for *all* transactions, from reserving to paying the final bill. All companies exclude car rental in some countries, so be sure to find out about the destination to which you are traveling.

■ TIP→ Diners Club offers primary CDW coverage on all rentals reserved and paid for with the card. This means that Diners Club's comany—not your own car insurance—pays in ase of an accident. It *doesn't* mean your car-surance company won't raise your rates once discovers you had an accident.

ome countries require you to purchase CDW coverage or require car-rental companies to include it in quoted rates. Ask our rental company about issues like hese in your destination. In most cases it's heaper to add a supplemental CDW plan o your comprehensive travel-insurance olicy (⇨ Trip Insurance *under* Things o Consider *in* Getting Started, *above*) han to purchase it from a rental company. That said, you don't want to pay for supplement if you're required to buy insurance from the rental company.

■ TIP→ You can decline the insurance from he rental company and purchase it through a hird-party provider such as Travel Guard www.travelguard.com)—$9 per day for $35,000 f coverage. That's sometimes just under half he price of the CDW offered by some car-ental companies.

▮ VACATION PACKAGES

Packages *are not* guided excursions. Packages combine airfare, accommodations, and perhaps a rental car or other extras (theater tickets, guided excursions, boat trips, reserved entry to popular museums, transit passes), but they let you do your own thing. During busy periods packages may be your only option, as flights and rooms may be sold out otherwise.

Packages will definitely save you time. They can also save you money, particularly in peak seasons, but—and this is a really big "but"—you should price each part of the package separately to be sure. And be aware that prices advertised on Web sites and in newspapers rarely include service charges or taxes, which can up your costs by hundreds of dollars.

■ TIP→ Some packages and cruises are sold only through travel agents. Don't always assume that you can get the best deal by booking everything yourself.

Car Rental Resources

AUTOMOBILE ASSOCIATIONS		
U.S.: American Automobile Association (AAA)	315/797-5000	www.aaa.com; most contact with the organization is through state and regional members.
National Automobile Club	650/294-7000	www.thenac.com; membership is open to California residents only.
LOCAL AGENCIES		
St. John Car Rental	340/776-6103	www.stjohncarrental.com.
Judi of Croix	340/773-2123 or 877/903-2123	www.judiofcroix.com.
Dependable Car Rental on St. Thomas	340/774-2253 or 800/522-3076	www.dependablecar.com.
Itgo Car Rental on Tortola	284/494-2639.	
L&S Jeep Rental on Virgin Gorda	284/495-5297.	
MAJOR AGENCIES		
Alamo	800/522-9696	www.alamo.com.
Avis	800/331-1084	www.avis.com.
Budget	800/472-3325	www.budget.com.
Hertz	800/654-3001	www.hertz.com.
National Car Rental	800/227-7368	www.nationalcar.com.

10 WAYS TO SAVE

1. Beware of cheap rates. Those great rates aren't so great when you add in taxes, surcharges, and insurance. Such extras can double or triple the initial quote.

2. Rent weekly. Weekly rates are usually better than daily ones. Even if you only want to rent for five or six days, ask for the weekly rate; it may very well be cheaper than the daily rate for that period of time.

3. Don't forget the locals. Price local companies as well as the majors.

4. Airport rentals can cost more. Airports often add surcharges, which you can sometimes avoid by renting from an agency whose office is just off airport property.

5. Wholesalers can help. Investigate wholesalers, which don't own fleets but rent in bulk from firms that do, and which frequently offer better rates (note that you must usually pay for such rentals before leaving home).

6. Look for rate guarantees. With your rate locked in, you won't pay more, even if the price goes up in the local currency.

7. Fill up farther away. Avoid hefty refueling fees by filling the tank at a station well away from where you plan to turn in the car.

8. Pump it yourself. Don't buy the tank of gas that's in the car when you rent it unless you plan to do a lot of driving.

9. Get all your discounts. Find out whether a credit card you carry or organization or frequent-renter program to which you belong has a discount program. And confirm that such discounts really are a deal. You can often do better with special weekend or weekly rates offered by a rental agency.

10. Check out packages. Adding a car rental onto your air/hotel vacation package may be cheaper than renting a car separately.

Each year consumers are stranded or lose their money when packagers—even large ones with excellent reputations—go out of business. How can you protect yourself?

First, always pay with a credit card; if you have a problem, your credit-card company may help you resolve it. Second, buy trip insurance that covers default. Third, choose a company that belongs to the United States Tour Operators Association, whose members must set aside funds to cover defaults. Finally, choose a company that also participates in the Tour Operator Program of the American Society of Travel Agents (ASTA), which will act as mediator in any disputes.

You can also check on the tour operator's reputation among travelers by posting an inquiry on one of the Fodors.com forums.

A package trip that includes airfare, hotel and some extras probably saves you money, but you're often limited to the larger properties. That quirky, off-the-beaten-path spot, particularly in the British Virgin Islands, probably doesn't work with the airlines or package companies.

Of the major U.S. airline packagers, only American Airlines Vacations offers packages in both the U.S. and British Virgin Islands. US Airways Vacations and Delta Vacations offer trips on all three U.S. Virgin Islands; Continental Vacations offers only St. Thomas.

You'll usually find the best deals on packages in the slower summer season, when hoteliers have lots of vacant rooms. Check with your travel agent, online, with the airlines, or in the pages of your local major newspaper for the best deals. The best packages for the USVI can often be found through Liberty/GoGo, Travel Impressions, and Apple Vacations. For the BVI, Liberty/GoGo Travel, Apple Vacations, and Classic Custom Vacations offer packages. They often tout last-minute specials, so late planning may save you money.

Online travel agencies such as Orbitz, Expedia, and Travelocity, also offer packages to the Virgin Islands.

Airline Vacation Packagers American Airlines Vacations ☎ 800/321-2121 ⊕ www.aavacations.com. **Continental Airlines Vacations** ☎ 800/301-3800 ⊕ www.covacations.com. **Delta Vacations** ☎ 800/654-6559 ⊕ www.deltavacations.com. **US Airways Vacations** ☎ 800/422-3861 ⊕ www.usairwaysvacations.com.

Large Agency Packagers Apple Vacations ⊕ www.applevacations.com. **Classic Custom Vacations** ☎ 800/635-1333 ⊕ www.classicvacations.com. **Liberty Travel** ☎ 888/271-1584 ⊕ www.libertytravel.com. **Travel Impressions** ⊕ www.travelimpressions.com.

Online Agency Packagers Cheap Tickets ⊕ www.cheaptickets.com. **Expedia** ⊕ www.expedia.com. **Orbitz** ⊕ www.orbitz.com. **Priceline** ⊕ www.priceline.com. **Travelocity** ⊕ www.travelocity.com.

Organizations American Society of Travel Agents (ASTA) ☎ 703/739-2782 or 800/965-7782 ⊕ www.astanet.com. **United States Tour Operators Association** (USTOA) ☎ 212/599-6599 ⊕ www.ustoa.com.

⫾ TIP➔ Local tourism boards can provide information about lesser-known and small-niche operators that sell packages to only a few destinations.

CRUISES

All the major cruise lines—Carnival, Celebrity, Holland America, Royal Caribbean, and many more—drop anchor in the USBVI. Except in St. Thomas and St. Croix, almost all ships have to anchor and then bring passengers ashore in tenders. Often, larger ships don't even go to St. John or the BVI. Smaller cruise lines like Windstar start out in St. Thomas, stopping at smaller islands like St. John and even Jost Van Dyke. With fewer passengers, you'll have a more intimate experience.

Cruising is a relaxing and convenient way to tour this beautiful part of the world. You get all of the amenities of a resort hotel and enough activities to guarantee fun, even on the occasional rainy day. All your important decisions are made long before you board. Your itinerary is set, and you know the basic cost of your vacation before-

hand. Ships usually call at several ports on a single voyage but are at each port for only one day. Thus, while you don't get much of a feel for any specific island, you get a taste of what several islands are like and can then choose to vacation on your favorite one for a longer time on a future trip. While cruises are never restricted solely to the USBVI, St. Thomas is one of the Caribbean's most popular cruise destinations, and ships also call at St. Croix, St. John, Tortola, and Virgin Gorda.

If you are planning a Caribbean cruise, consider Fodor's *The Complete Guide to Caribbean Cruises* (available in bookstores everywhere).

Cruise Lines Carnival Cruise Line ☎ 305/599-2600 or 800/227-6482 ⊕ www.carnival.com. **Celebrity Cruises** ☎ 305/539-6000 or 800/437-3111 ⊕ www.celebrity.com. **Costa Cruises** ☎ 954/266-5600 or 800/462-6782 ⊕ www.costacruise.com. **Crystal Cruises** ☎ 310/785-9300 or 800/446-6620 ⊕ www.crystalcruises.com. **Cunard Line** ☎ 661/753-1000 or 800/728-6273 ⊕ www.cunard.com. **Disney Cruise Line** ☎ 407/566-7000 or 800/939-2784 ⊕ www.disneycruise.com. **Holland America Line** ☎ 206/281-3535 or 877/932-4259 ⊕ www.hollandamerica.com. **MSC Cruises** ☎ 212/772-6262 or 800/666-9333 ⊕ www.msccruises.com. **Norwegian Cruise Line** ☎ 305/436-4000 or 800/327-7030 ⊕ www.ncl.com. **Oceania Cruises** ☎ 305/514-2300 or 800/531-5658 ⊕ www.oceaniacruises.com. **Princess Cruises** ☎ 661/753-0000 or 800/774-6237 ⊕ www.princess.com. **Regent Seven Seas Cruises** ☎ 402/501-5600 or 800/477-7500 ⊕ www.rssc.com. **Royal Caribbean International** ☎ 305/539-6000 or 800/327-6700 ⊕ www.royalcaribbean.com. **Seabourn Cruise Line** ☎ 305/463-3000 or 800/929-9595 ⊕ www.seabourn.com. **SeaDream Yacht Club** ☎ 305/631-6100 or 800/707-4911 ⊕ www.seadreamyachtclub.com. **Silversea Cruises** ☎ 954/522-4477 or 800/722-9955 ⊕ www.silversea.com. **Star Clippers** ☎ 305/442-0550 or 800/442-0551 ⊕ www.starclippers.com. **Windjammer Barefoot Cruises** ☎ 305/672-6453 or 800/327-2601 ⊕ www.windjammer.com. **Windstar Cruises** ☎ 206/281-3535 or 800/258-7245 ⊕ www.windstarcruises.com.

TRANSPORTATION

Ferries that connect St. Thomas, St. John, and the British Virgin Islands are the simplest ways of traveling among them. If you're heading between St. Thomas and St. Croix, you have your choice of a ferry, seaplane, or regular plane. The ferry takes longer; if you're pressed for time but still want an island experience, take the seaplane. You may find yourself sitting next to an island VIP. The seaplane leaves from downtown locations on both islands.

TRAVEL TIMES FROM ST. THOMAS BY AIR AND BY FERRY			
To	By Air	Ferry From Charlotte Amalie	Ferry From Red Hook
St. John	N/A	45 minutes	20 minutes
West End, Tortola	N/A	45 minutes	20 minutes
Road Town, Tortola	15 minutes	1 hour	45 minutes
Virgin Gorda	15 minutes	1 1/2 hours	2 hours
St. Croix	30 minutes	1 1/2 hours	N/A

■ TIP➔ Ask the local tourist board about hotel and local transportation packages that include tickets to major museum exhibits or other special events.

■ BY AIR

The nonstop flight from New York to St. Thomas or San Juan takes about 4 hours; from Miami to St. Thomas or San Juan it's about three hours. Nonstop flights from London to Miami are about 7 to 8 hours, then it's another three hours to the USBVI. Once you've arrived in the USBVI, hops between the islands take 10 to 20 minutes.

Reconfirming your flights on interisland carriers is not obsolete yet, as it is for major airlines, particularly when you're traveling to the smallest islands. You may be subjected to a carrier's whims: If no other passengers are booked on your flight, you may be asked (or told) to take another flight later in the day, or your plane may make unscheduled stops to pick up more passengers or cargo. It's all part of the excitement—and unpredictability—of travel in the Caribbean. In addition, regional carriers use small aircraft with limited baggage space, and they often impose weight restrictions; travel light, or you could be subject to outrageous surcharges or delays in getting very large or heavy luggage, which may have to follow on another flight.

■ TIP➔ If you travel frequently, look into TSA's Registered Traveler program. The program, which is still being tested in several U.S. airports, is designed to cut down on gridlock at security checkpoints by allowing pre-screened travelers to pass quickly through kiosks that scan an iris and/or a fingerprint. How sci-fi is that?

Airlines & Airports Airline and Airport Links.com ⊕ www.airlineandairportlinks.com has links to many of the world's airlines and airports.

Airline Security Issues Transportation Security Administration ⊕ www.tsa.gov has answers for almost every question that might come up.

AIRPORTS

The major airports are Terrence B. Lettsome International Airport on Beef Island, Tortola, Cyril E. King Airport on St. Thomas, and Henry Rohlsen Airport on St. Croix. There is a small airport (so small that it doesn't have a phone number) on Virgin Gorda.

Airport Information Terrence B. Lettsome International Airport ☎ 284/495-2525. Cyril E. King Airport ☎ 340/774-5100. Henry Rohlsen Airport ☎ 340/778-1012.

GROUND TRANSPORTATION

Ground transportation options are covered in the Essentials sections in individual island-group chapters.

FLYING 101

Flying may not be as carefree as it once was, but there are some things you can do to make your trip smoother.

MINIMIZE THE TIME SPENT STANDING IN LINE. Buy an e-ticket, check in at an electronic kiosk, or—even better—check in on your airline's Web site before leaving home. Pack light and limit carry-on items to only the essentials.

ARRIVE WHEN YOU NEED TO. Research your airline's policy. It's usually at least an hour before domestic flights and two to three hours before international flights. But airlines at some busy airports have more stringent requirements. Check the TSA Web site for estimated security waiting times at major airports.

GET TO THE GATE. If you aren't at the gate at least 10 minutes before your flight is scheduled to take off (sometimes earlier), you won't be allowed to board.

DOUBLE-CHECK YOUR FLIGHT TIMES. Do this especially if you reserved far in advance. Schedules change, and alerts may not reach you.

DON'T GO HUNGRY. Ask whether your airline offers anything to eat; even when it does, be prepared to pay.

GET THE SEAT YOU WANT. Often, you can pick a seat when you buy your ticket on an airline Web site. But it's not guaranteed; the airline could change the plane after you book, so double-check. You can also select a seat if you check in electronically. Avoid seats on the aisle directly across from the lavatories. Frequent fliers say those are even worse than back-row seats that don't recline.

GOT KIDS? GET INFO. Ask the airline about its children's menus, activities, and fares. Sometimes infants and toddlers fly free if they sit on a parent's lap, and older children fly for half price in their own seats. Also inquire about policies involving car seats; having one may limit seating options. Also ask about seat-belt extenders for car seats. And note that you can't count on a flight attendant to produce an extender; you may have to ask for one when you board.

CHECK YOUR SCHEDULING. Don't buy a ticket if there's less than an hour between connecting flights. Although schedules are padded, if anything goes wrong you might miss your connection. If you're traveling to an important function, depart a day early.

BRING PAPER. Even when using an e-ticket, always carry a hard copy of your receipt; you may need it to get your boarding pass, which most airports require to get past security.

COMPLAIN AT THE AIRPORT. If your baggage goes astray or your flight goes awry, complain before leaving the airport. Most carriers require this.

BEWARE OF OVERBOOKED FLIGHTS. If a flight is oversold, the gate agent will usually ask for volunteers and offer some sort of compensation for taking a different flight. If you're bumped from a flight *involuntarily*, the airline must give you some kind of compensation if an alternate flight can't be found within one hour.

KNOW YOUR RIGHTS. If your flight is delayed because of something within the airline's control (bad weather doesn't count), the airline must get you to your destination on the same day, even if they have to book you on another airline and in an upgraded class. Read the Contract of Carriage, which is usually buried on the airline's Web site.

BE PREPARED. The Boy Scout motto is especially important if you're traveling during a stormy season. To quickly adjust your plans, program a few numbers into your cell: your airline, an airport hotel or two, your destination hotel, your car service, and/or your travel agent.

FLIGHTS

There are nonstop and connecting flights, usually through San Juan, from the United States mainland to both St. Thomas and St. Croix, with connecting ferry service from St. Thomas to St. John. There are no nonstop flights to the BVI from the United States or from Europe; you must connect in San Juan or St. Thomas for the short hop over to Tortola or Virgin Gorda. To reach Anegada, take a ferry from Tortola. Several European airlines fly to other Caribbean destinations, such as Antigua or Barbados, where there are connections to the USVI and BVI. Canadians and Europeans must connect to flights in the U.S. or in San Juan. There are nonstop flights from London to Miami.

American Airlines and its subsidiary, American Eagle, are the biggest carriers to the USBVI. They operate several nonstop flights a day from New York and Miami to St. Thomas and connecting flights through San Juan. American also flies nonstop to St. Croix from Miami. The number of flights per day depends on the season, with more frequent flights during the winter. Continental flies nonstop daily to St. Thomas from Newark, and USAirways has nonstop flights from Philadelphia and Charlotte, N.C. Spirit Airlines flies nonstop everyday from Fort Lauderdale. Delta flies nonstop from Atlanta. Northwest Airlines has a winter Saturday flight from Detroit. United also flies non-stop from Chicago and Washington, D.C. While connecting through San Juan is your best bet for arriving by air on Tortola or Virgin Gorda, you can fly from St. Thomas and St. Croix to Tortola and Virgin Gorda on Air Sunshine.

Some airlines have codeshare partnerships with airlines that fly to the Caribbean. The codeshare agreement allows an airline to sell a certain number of seats on a flight operated by its partner. Bear in mind, however, that if the flight is canceled because of weather or for any reason not the fault of the operating airline, you'll be re-booked on the next flight that has available seats specifically designated to the codeshare partner that issued your tickets. This may not be the next flight out.

Some islands in the British Virgin Islands are accessible only by small planes operated by local or regional carriers. International carriers will sometimes book those flights for you as part of your overall travel arrangements, or you can confidently book directly with the local carrier, using a major credit card, either online or by phone.

Airline Contacts **American Airlines** ☎ 800/433-7300 ⊕ www.aa.com. **Continental Airlines** ☎ 800/523−3273 for U.S. and Mexico reservations, 800/231-0856 for international reservations ⊕ www.continental.com. **Delta Airlines** ☎ 800/221-1212 for U.S. reservations, 800/241-4141 for international reservations ⊕ www.delta.com. **jetBlue** ☎ 800/538-2583 ⊕ www.jetblue.com. **Northwest Airlines** ☎ 800/225-2525 ⊕ www.nwa.com. **Spirit Airlines** ☎ 800/772-7117 or 586/791-7300 ⊕ www.spiritair.com. **United Airlines** ☎ 800/864-8331 for U.S. reservations, 800/538-2929 for international reservations ⊕ www.united.com. **USAirways** ☎ 800/428-4322 for U.S. and Canada reservations, 800/622-1015 for international reservations ⊕ www.usairways.com.

Interisland carriers: **Air Sunshine** ☎ 800/327-8900, 800/435-8900 in Florida ⊕ www.airsunshine.com. **American Eagle** ☎ 800/433-7300 ⊕ www.aa.com. **Cape Air** ☎ 800/352-0714 ⊕ www.flycapeair.com. **LIAT** ☎ 888/844-5428 ⊕ www.liatairline.com. **Seaborne** ☎ 340/773-6442 ⊕ www.flyseaborne.com.

▌ BY BOAT

Ferries travel between St. Thomas and St. John. You can also travel by ferry from both St. Thomas and St. John to the British Virgin Islands, and between the British Virgin Islands themselves. The companies run regularly scheduled trips, departing from Charlotte Amalie or Red Hook on St. Thomas; Cruz Bay, St. John; Gallows ay, St. Croix; West End, Road Town, or eef Island on Tortola; The Valley or orth Sound on Virgin Gorda; and Jost an Dyke. Schedules change, so check ith your hotel or villa manager to find ut the latest. The ferry companies are all gulated by the U.S. Coast Guard, and ices are about the same, so there is no int in trying to organize your schedule take one company's ferries rather than other's. Just show up at the dock to y your ticket on the next ferry depart-g for your destination. If it all seems nfusing—and it can be very confusing r ferry travel to or around the BVI—just k a local resident who's also buying a ket. They've been doing it for years and ow the ropes.

hile you might save a few dollars flying to St. Thomas if you're headed to the /I, it's much easier to connect through n Juan for a flight to Tortola or Virgin orda. If you're headed to St. John or to ints like North Sound, Virgin Gorda Jost Van Dyke, you'll have to hop a ferry gardless. If you're splitting your vacation tween the U.S. and British Virgin Is-ds, ferries are the perfect way to get m one to another. You'll also get a nus—views of the many small islands at dot the ferry route.

hm's Water Taxi runs from St. Thomas St. John and any point in the BVI. You'll oid the often crowded ferries, the crew ll handle your luggage, and you'll arrive your destination feeling relaxed; how-er, you'll pay significantly more for the nvenience. For more information, *see* at Ferry Travel *in* the Essentials sec-n at the end of each chapter.

BY CAR

car gives you mobility. You'll be able to end an hour browsing at that cozy out--the-way shop instead of the 10 minutes otted by your tour guide. You can beach-p without searching for a ride, and you n sample that restaurant you've heard much about that's a half-hour (and an expensive taxi ride) away. On parts of some of the islands, you may need to rent a four-wheel-drive vehicle to really get out and about. Paved roads are generally good, but you may encounter a pothole or two or three or four. Except for one di-vided highway on St. Croix, roads are narrow, and in hilly locations, twist and turn with the hill's contours. The roads on the north side of Tortola are particularly twisty, with scary dropoffs that will send you plummeting down the hillside if you miss the turn. Drive slowly. Many villas are located on unpaved roads in St. John and the BVI. A four-wheel-drive could be a necessity if it rains. A higher clearance vehicle will help get safely over the rocks that may litter the road.

GASOLINE
Except in St. Croix, where it may be cheaper than in many parts of the U.S., gas is expensive throughout the Virgin Islands. Prices rise to as much as $4 a gallon on most islands. The USVI stations sell gas by the gallon; in the BVI, you'll buy it by the liter or the gallon, depending on the sta-tion. Most stations take major credit cards, but on St. John, only the Texaco in Cruz Bay accepts credit cards. Some stations offer a pump-it-yourself option, but it's still easy to find ones with attendants. There's no need to tip unless they change a tire or do some other quick mechanical chore. St. Croix has a few stations where you pay the cashier and pump it yourself. You'll have to ask for a handwritten receipt if you're not paying by credit card. Gas sta-tions are found along the main roads on St. Croix, St. Thomas, and Tortola; on Virgin Gorda, St. John, and other islands, be sure to fill up before you leave the main towns. Most stations are open from early morning until early evening. On smaller islands, they may be closed on Sunday.

PARKING
Parking can be very tight in towns across the USBVI. Workers grab up the street parking, sometimes arriving several hours

early to get prime spaces. It's particularly difficult to find parking in Cruz Bay, St. John. There are free public lots scattered around town, but they're usually filled early by folks taking the ferry to St. Thomas. Instead, your rental-car company probably will allow you to park in their lot. Charlotte Amalie, St. Thomas, has a paid-parking lot next to Fort Christian. A machine takes your money—$1 for the first hour and $5 for all day. In Christiansted, St. Croix, you'll find a public parking lot on Strand Street. Since the attendant booth isn't staffed, there is no charge. There's also a public lot near Fort Christianvaern, but that lot closes at 4:30 PM, and you won't be able to exit after that. It costs $1 for the first hour, and $6 for all time over an hour. Tortola has several free parking lots along and across the street from the waterfront. In Virgin Gorda, there's a free lot at Virgin Gorda Yacht Harbor. There are no parking meters anywhere in the USBVI. Even if you're desperate for a parking space in the USVI, don't park in a handicapped space without a sticker unless you want to pay a $1,000 fine.

ROAD CONDITIONS

Island roads, particularly in mountainous regions that experience heavy tropical rains, are often potholed and bumpy—as well as narrow, winding, and hilly. Streets in towns are narrow, a legacy of the days when islanders walked or used carts. Drive with extreme caution, especially if you venture out at night. You won't see guardrails on every hill and curve, although the drops can be frighteningly steep. And pedestrians (including children and the elderly) and livestock often share the roadway with vehicles.

You'll face rush-hour traffic in St. Thomas (especially in Charlotte Amalie); in St. Croix (especially in Christiansted and on Centerline Road); and in Tortola (especially around Road Town). All the main towns, as well as Cruz Bay in St. John, have one-way streets. Although they're marked, the signs may be obscured by overhanging trees and other obstacles.

Drivers are prone to stopping in the road to chat up a passerby, to let a passenger out, or to buy a newspaper from a vendor. Pay attention when entering curves because you might find a stopped car on the other side.

ROADSIDE EMERGENCIES

To reach police, fire, or ambulance, dial 911 in the USVI and 999 in the BVI. There are no emergency-service companies such as AAA in the USBVI. Before driving off into the countryside, check your rental car for tire-changing equipment, including an inflated spare.

RULES OF THE ROAD

Driving in the Virgin Islands can be tricky. Traffic moves on the left in *both* the USVI and BVI. (The BVI obviously followed the British tradition; no one knows why the USVI followed suit.) Except for the odd right-hand drive car in the BVI, cars on both the BVI and USVI have left-hand drive, the same as cars on the U.S. mainland. This means the driver sits on the side of the car next to the road's edge, a position that makes some people nervous. Note that you may turn left from the left-hand lane when the light is red.

Buckle up before you turn the key. Police in the USVI are notorious for giving $25 tickets to unbelted drivers and front-seat passengers. The police are a bit lax about drunk-driver enforcement, but why risk it? Take a taxi or appoint a designated driver when you're out on the town.

Traffic moves at about 10 mph in town; on major highways—in St. Croix, for example—you can fly along at 50 mph. On other roads, the speed limit may be less.

Main roads in the USVI carry route numbers, but locals may not know them, nor are they always marked. (Be prepared for such directions as "turn left at the big tree.") Few USVI secondary roads have signs; throughout the BVI, roads aren't very well marked either.

ON THE GROUND

DDRESSES

Whimsical" might best describe USBVI ddresses. Street names change for no ap-rent reason, and most buildings have no umbers. Streets in the main towns gen-ally have names, though they may not ve signs. Once you get out into the untry on all islands, street names are re. Areas are often known by their old antation or estate names; for example, tate Emmaus in St. John is found in hat's now the heart of Coral Bay. Some-nes the estate names appear on maps, d sometimes they don't. The smaller e island, the less chance there is of a lo-tion having a specific street address. ddresses throughout this guide may in-de cross streets, landmarks, and other rectionals. But to find your destination, u might have to ask a local—and be pre-red for such directions as, "Go past the s station, then take a right at the fish arket. Stay on that road past the church d take a left after the palm tree."

BUSINESS SERVICES & FACILITIES

fice Max at Tutu Park Mall on St. homas provides copying services, but re are also a handful of small business-vices places scattered around the USBVI. k at your hotel for the closest.

ice Max ✉ Tutu Park Shopping Mall, Rte. Estate Tutu, St. Thomas ☎ 340/775-5646.

COMMUNICATIONS

TERNET

any hotels now offer high-speed or dial-Internet service. In most cases, Inter-service is complimentary, but some orts do charge a fee. Some provide com-ters in their lobbies if you've left your nputer at home. You'll also find a few taurants, bars, and businesses that offer ernet service for a fee. Specific cover-

age of internet cafés can be found in the individual destination chapters.

Cybercafes ⊕ www.cybercafes.com lists over 4,000 Internet cafés worldwide.

PHONES

The good news is that you can now make a direct-dial telephone call from virtually any point on earth. The bad news? You can't always do so cheaply. Calling from a hotel is almost always the most expensive option; hotels usually add huge surcharges to all calls, particularly international ones. In some countries you can phone from call centers or even the post office. Calling cards usually keep costs to a minimum, but only if you purchase them locally. And then there are mobile phones (⇨ *below*), which are sometimes more prevalent—particularly in the developing world—than land lines; as expensive as mobile-phone calls can be, they are still usually a much cheaper option than calling from your hotel.

Phone service to and from the Virgin Islands is up-to-date and efficient. Phone cards are used throughout the islands for long-distance and international calling; you can buy them (in several denominations) at many retail shops and convenience stores. They must be used in special card phones, which are also widely available.

CALLING WITHIN THE USBVI

Local calls from USBVI pay phones run 25¢, although some privately owned phones are now charging 35¢. Calls from the USVI to the BVI and vice versa are charged as international toll calls. In the USVI and BVI, you dial just as if you were anywhere else in the U.S.

The area code for the USVI is 340; for the BVI, 284.

In the USVI, dial 913 to reach the operator. In the BVI, dial 119. In both locations, dial 0 for advice on how to place your call.

LOCAL DO'S & TABOOS

CUSTOMS OF THE COUNTRY
Events seldom start on time in the USBVI. You may find yourself standing for quite a while in the sun while you wait for events like a carnival parade to begin. Even music and theater productions are prone to running late, but it pays to arrive on schedule in case there's a rare on-time start. Use the waiting time to socialize with your neighbors.

Folks in the USBVI are keenly interested in local politics. If you want to know more about the local culture, ask your taxi driver or other local you may meet what's the latest on the political scene. There's always something intereting afoot.

GREETINGS
When passing strangers on the street, say good morning, good afternoon, or good evening. It's considered polite. When meeting new people, Virgin Islanders usually shake hands. No kissy-kissy needed here. But it's particularly important to take the time to greet shopkeepers and other service personnel. You'll get much better service if you do. Really, any interaction should start with some kind of pleasantry—whether you're doing business or not; it's considered rude if you don't. It's also important to try not to come on too strong; too much assertiveness is considered rude in any interaction, even when you are making a valid complaint.

SIGHTSEEING
Cover up when you're not at the beach; Virgin Islanders are modest folks. When passing people on hiking trails or when walking on narrow country roads, be sure to greet fellow hikers or walkers.

FORMALITY
Casual clothes are generally fine for most official interactions, but men should wear a tie and jacket and women summer business attire when going to government offices, insurance companies, and the like. Only wear shorts to the most casual of marine-related businesses. More and more visitors are seen wearing shorts to Sunday church services, but locals always wear their Sunday finery, including hats.

OTHER ISSUES
There isn't much of a problem with beggars, and most people just ignore them. Where there are traffic lights, use them to cross safely. Folks do jaywalk all the time, but it's safer to use the crosswalks.

OUT ON THE TOWN
If your check hasn't arrived by the time you're ready to leave a restaurant, just catch your waiter's eye as he or she goes by. Liquor is available at all meals, but local law prevents serving it until late in the day on Good Friday only. Since the USBVI is a vacation paradise, just about anything goes when it comes to drinking, but for safety's sake, don't drive when you've had too much to drink. How to dress when you're out on the town depends on where you're going. Heading down to that beachfront bar? Shorts and T-shirts are fine, but if you're planning to dance the night away at the resort's nightclub, you'll want to wear something nicer. Some resorts have a dress code, so check before you pack so you have the right clothes. Some restaurants have no-smoking sections, and the trade winds help blow away smoke at alfresco spots. That said, it's always polite to wait until you've left the restaurant to light up. If you happen to be invited to someone's home for dinner, a bottle of wine is a nice gift. If you know in advance, ask if there's anything special they'd like that they can't get in the USBVI.

ᴸLING OUTSIDE THE USBVI

ᵉe country code for the United States
1.

ᴵlling the United States and Canada from
ₑ USBVI is just like making a long dis-
ₙce call within those countries: dial 1,
ᵤs the area code. To reach Europe, Aus-
ᴵlia, and New Zealand, dial 011 fol-
ʷed by the country code.

ʸou are using a U.S.-based calling card,
ₑ U.S. access number should be on the
ᶜk of the card. If you are using a local
ᴵling card, the access number will be on
ₑ back of your calling card.

ᴼBILE PHONES

ʸou have a multiband phone (some
ₐntries use different frequencies than
ᴵat's used in the United States) and your
ʳvice provider uses the world-standard
ᶜM network (as do T-Mobile, Cingular,
ₐd Verizon), you can probably use your
ₒne abroad. Roaming fees can be steep,
ʷever: 99¢ a minute is considered rea-
ₙable. And overseas you normally pay
ₑ toll charges for incoming calls. Inter-
ᵗionally, it's almost always cheaper to
ₙd a text message than to make a call,
ᵢce text messages have a very low set fee
ᶠten less than 5¢).

ʸou just want to make local calls, con-
ᴵer buying a new SIM card (note that
ᵘr provider may have to unlock your
ₒne for you to use a different SIM card)
ₐd a prepaid service plan in the destina-
ₒn. You'll then have a local number and
ₙ make local calls at local rates. If your
ᵖ is extensive, you could also simply buy
ᵉw cell phone in your destination, as
ₑ initial cost will be offset over time.

ᵀIP→ If you travel internationally frequently,
ᵛe one of your old mobile phones or buy a
ᵉap one on the Internet; ask your cell phone
ᵐpany to unlock it for you, and take it with
ᵘ as a travel phone, buying a new SIM card
ᵗh pay-as-you-go service in each destina-
ₙ.

ᵉre are no cellphone rental companies
the USBVI. There are a few places that

CON OR CONCIERGE?

Good hotel concierges are invaluable—for
arranging transportation, getting reservations at the hottest restaurant, and scoring
tickets for a sold-out show or entree to an
exclusive nightclub. They're in the know
and well connected. That said, sometimes
you have to take their advice with a grain
of salt.

It's not uncommon for restaurants to ply
concierges with free food and drink in exchange for steering diners their way. Indeed, European concierges often receive
referral *fees*. Hotel chains usually have guidelines about what their concierges can accept.
The best concierges, however, are above re-
proach. This is particularly true of those who
belong to the prestigious international society of Les Clefs d'Or.

What can you expect of a concierge? At a typical tourist-class hotel you can expect him
or her to give you the basics: to show you
something on a map, make a standard restaurant reservation (particularly if you don't
speak the language), or help you book a tour
or airport transportation. In Asia concierges
perform the vital service of writing out the
name or address of your destination for you
to give to a cab driver.

Savvy concierges at the finest hotels and
resorts, can arrange for just about any good
or service imaginable—and do so quickly.
You should compensate them appropriately.
A $10 tip is enough to show appreciation for
a table at a hot restaurant. But the reward
should really be much greater for tickets to
that U2 concert that's been sold out for
months or for those last-minute sixth-row-
center seats for *The Lion King*.

sell cellphones, but the price is much higher than in the U.S. and other locations. It's best to bring your own. Cell phones from most U.S. companies, including Sprint, work in most locations in the USVI if you have a roaming feature; if you are on St. John's north coast, you may have some difficulties with service, where you may find yourself connected to BoatPhone, a Tortola service. If you are on the south side of Tortola, you may be able to connect to Cingular and Sprint, but other islands in the BVI are problematic. Phones from other companies may work, but only Cingular and Sprint have offices in the USVI. The BVI has local companies only. Even if your U.S. mainland company assures you that your phone will work in the USBVI, don't count on it. Both companies use GSM and TDMA networks with single- and dual-band phones.

Cellular Abroad ☎ 800/287-5072 ⊕ www.cellularabroad.com rents and sells GMS phones and sells SIM cards that work in many countries. **Mobal** ☎ 888/888-9162 ⊕ www.mobalrental.com rents mobiles and sells GSM phones (starting at $49) that will operate in 140 countries. Per-call rates vary throughout the world. **Planet Fone** ☎ 888/988-4777 ⊕ www.planetfone.com rents cell phones, but the per-minute rates are expensive. **Cingular** ☎ 340/777-7777. **Sprint** ☎ 340/715-5400.

▌CUSTOMS & DUTIES

You're always allowed to bring goods of a certain value back home without having to pay any duty or import tax. But there's a limit on the amount of tobacco and liquor you can bring back duty-free, and some countries have separate limits for perfumes; for exact figures, check with your customs department. The values of so-called "duty-free" goods are included in these amounts. When you shop abroad, save all your receipts, as customs inspectors may ask to see them as well as the items you purchased. If the total value of your goods is more than the duty-free limit, you'll have to pay a tax (most often

a flat percentage) on the value of everything beyond that limit.

As long as you're not bringing in meat, passing through BVI customs is usually a breeze. If you want to bring that special cut of steak from home, you'll need a $25 agriculture permit, but it's not worth the effort since you can buy meat all over the BVI. You don't clear customs entering the USVI if you're coming from the U.S., but rather on your way out. You can't take fruits and vegetables out of either the USVI or BVI, so eat up that apple on the way to the airport. You may travel with your pets to the USBVI without any special shots or paperwork.

U.S. Information U.S. Customs & Border Protection ⊕ www.cbp.gov.

▌EATING OUT

Everything from fast food to fine cuisine in elegant settings is available in the USBVI, and prices run about the same as what you'd pay in New York or any other major city. You'll find kid favorites McDonald's, Pizza Hut, KFC, and more on St. Thomas and St. Croix, but families will also find plenty of non-chain restaurants with kid-friendly menus. Resorts that cater to families always have a casual restaurant, but there are delis and other restaurants across the USBVI that offer something for everyone on their menus. Most chefs at top-of-the-line restaurants and even some small spots went to a major culinary school, which means innovative and interesting cuisine. Don't be afraid to sample local dishes at the roadside restaurants located on all the islands. More and more restaurants have vegetarian offerings on their menus, though true vegetarian restaurants are very hard to find. Throughout the book, the restaurants we list are the cream of the crop in each price category. For information on food-related health issues, *see* Health *below.*

MEALS & MEALTIMES

Your hotel is your best bet for breakfast in the USBVI, where you'll easily find Amer-

n-style food. Local restaurants serve fish
d other heavy dishes for breakfast. Other
als are similar to those in the U.S.

r fast food, island-style, try a pate (pro-
unced *patty*) from a roadside stand. It's
ried pastry filled with conch, salted
h, or hamburger, which islanders call
at. Maubi, made from tree bark, is a
ique drink popular in the USBVI.

ost restaurants open for lunch from
ound 11:30 AM to about 3 PM; they
ve dinner from around 6:30 PM to
out 10 PM.

less otherwise noted, the restaurants
ed in this guide are open daily for lunch
d dinner.

YING

ajor restaurants take at least two major
dit cards, most often MasterCard and
sa, but that off-the-beaten-path spot
u've heard so much about may accept
ly cash.

r guidelines on tipping *see* Tipping
ow.

SERVATIONS & DRESS

gardless of where you are, it's a good
a to make a reservation if you can. In
ny places in the Caribbean, it's ex-
cted, particularly at nicer restaurants. We
ly mention specifically when reservations
essential (there's no other way you'll
er get a table) or when they are not ac-
pted. For popular restaurants, book as
ahead as you can (often 30 days), and
confirm as soon as you arrive. (Large par-
s should always call ahead to check the
servations policy.) We mention dress
ly when men are required to wear a
cket or a jacket and tie. Beach attire is
iversally frowned upon in restaurants
roughout the Caribbean.

INES, BEER & SPIRITS

p-notch restaurants offer good selec-
ns of fine wines. Beer and spirits are
ailable on all islands at all kinds of
staurants and roadside stands, but you
ay not find the brand you prefer. Cruzan

Rum, manufactured in St. Croix, is available across the USBVI. Alcoholic beverages
are available from the smallest corner rum
shop to the fanciest resort at all hours of
the day and night. The only prohibition
comes during the day on Good Friday
when no one can sell drinks.

❚ ELECTRICITY

The USBVI use the same current as the U.S.
mainland—110 volts. European appliances will require adaptors. Since power
fluctuations occasionally occur, bring a
heavy-duty surge protector (available at
hardware stores) if you plan to use your
computer.

Steve Kropla's Help for World Traveler's
⊕ www.kropla.com has information on elec-
trical and telephone plugs around the world.
Walkabout Travel Gear ⊕ www.
walkabouttravelgear.com has a good coverage
of electricity under "adapters."

GAY & LESBIAN TRAVEL

Gay and lesbian travelers are generally
welcome in the USBVI, but some un-
friendly attitudes still exist. Ask at your
hotel for advice on places to go. St. Thomas
has a thriving gay community, and you'll
be made very welcome. St. Croix has several gay-friendly resorts perfect for couples as well as singles.

❚ HEALTH

The most common types of illnesses are
caused by contaminated food and water.

Especially in developing countries, drink only bottled, boiled, or purified water and drinks; don't drink from public fountains or use ice. You should even consider using bottled water to brush your teeth. Make sure food has been thoroughly cooked and is served to you fresh and hot; avoid vegetables and fruits that you haven't washed (in bottled or purified water) or peeled yourself. If you have problems, mild cases of traveler's diarrhea may respond to Imodium (known generically as loperamide) or Pepto-Bismol. Be sure to drink plenty of fluids; if you can't keep fluids down, seek medical help immediately.

Infectious diseases can be airborne or passed via mosquitoes and ticks and through direct or indirect physical contact with animals or people. Some, including Norwalk-like viruses that affect your digestive tract, can be passed along through contaminated food. If you are traveling in an area where malaria is prevalent, use a repellent containing DEET and take malaria-prevention medication before, during, and after your trip as directed by your physician. Condoms can help prevent most sexually transmitted diseases, but they aren't absolutely reliable and their quality varies from country to country. Speak with your physician and/or check the CDC or World Health Organization Web sites for health alerts, particularly if you're pregnant, traveling with children, or have a chronic illness.

For information on travel insurance, shots and medications, and medical-assistance companies *see* Shots & Medications *under* Things to Consider *in* Before You Go, *above.*

Water in the USBVI is generally safe to drink. Mosquitoes can be a problem here, particularly after a spate of showers. Off! insect repellent is readily available, but you may want to bring something stronger. Also a nuisance are the little pests from the sand-flea family known as no-see-ums.

You don't realize you're being had for dinner until it's too late, and these bites stay, and itch, and itch, and itch. No-see-ums start getting hungry around 3 PM and are out in force by sunset. They're always more numerous in shady and wooded areas (such as the campgrounds on St. John). Take a towel along for sitting on the beach, and keep reapplying insect repellent.

Beware of the manchineel tree, which grows near the beach and has green applelike fruit that is poisonous and bark and leaves that burn the skin.

Even if you've never been sunburned in your life, believe the warnings and use sunscreen in the USBVI. If you're dark-skinned, start with at least an SPF of 15 and keep it on. If you're fair-skinned, use a sunscreen with a higher SPF and stay out of the sun during the midday. Rays are most intense between 11 and 2, so move under a sea-grape tree (although you can still burn here) or, better yet, take a shady lunch break. You can also burn in this part of the world when it's cloudy, so putting sunscreen on every day no matter what the weather is the best strategy.

OVER-THE-COUNTER REMEDIES
Over-the-counter medications like aspirin, Tylenol, and Mylanta are readily available in the USBVI. Kmart on St. Thomas and St. Croix have cheaper prices, but you'll find a big selection of these products at grocery and drug stores across the USBVI. You'll find less of a selection (and considerably higher prices) on the smaller islands.

▍HOURS OF OPERATION

Bank hours are generally Monday through Thursday 9 to 3 and Friday 9 to 5; a handful open Saturday (9 to noon). Walk-up windows open at 8:30 on weekdays. Hours may vary slightly from branch to branch and island to island, but they are generally weekdays 7:30 or 8 to 4 or 5:30 and Saturday 7:30 or 8 to noon or 2:30.

ops, especially those in the heavily
urristed areas, are open Monday to Sat-
day 9 to 5. Those near the cruise ships
ay also be open on Sunday.

OLIDAYS

addition to the U.S. federal holidays, lo-
ls in the USVI celebrate Three Kings
ay (Jan. 6); Transfer Day (commemorates
enmark's 1917 sale of the territory to the
nited States, Mar. 31); Holy Thursday
d Good Friday; Emancipation Day
hen slavery was abolished in the Dan-
1 West Indies in 1848, July 3); Colum-
as Day and USVI–Puerto Rico Friendship
ay (always on Columbus Day weekend);
d Liberty Day (honoring David Hamil-
n Jackson, who secured freedom of the
ess and assembly from King Christian
of Denmark, Nov. 1).

although the government closes down for
3 days a year, most of these holidays
ve no effect on shopping hours. Unless
ere's a cruise-ship arrival, expect most
ores to close for Christmas and a few
ther holidays in the slower summer
onths.

he following public holidays are cele-
rated in the BVI: New Year's Day, Com-
onwealth Day (Mar. 14), Good Friday
ri. before Easter), Easter Sunday (usu-
ly Mar. or Apr.), Easter Monday (day
ter Easter), Whit Monday (1st Mon. in
1ay), Sovereign's Birthday (June 16), Ter-
tory Day (July 1), BVI August Festival
ays (usually 1st 2 wks in Aug.), St. Ur-
la's Day (Oct. 21), Christmas, and Box-
g Day (day after Christmas).

MAIL

irmail between the USBVI and cities in
ne United States or Canada takes 7 to
4 days; surface mail can take 4 to 6
eeks. For island-specific information
n post office locations, postal rates, and
pening hours, *see* Mail & Shipping *in*
ne Essentials sections of individual island
napters.

SHIPPING PACKAGES

Courier services (such as Airborne, DHL,
Federal Express, UPS, and others) operate
in the USBVI, although not every company
serves each island. "Overnight" service is
more likely to take two or more days, because of the limited number of flights on
which packages can be shipped. Service to
St. John and the smaller of the British Virgin Islands can take even longer.

■ MONEY

The U.S. dollar is the currency on both the
USVI and BVI.

ITEM	AVERAGE COST
Cup of Coffee	$2
Glass of Wine	$5
Glass of Beer	$3
Sandwich	$8
One-Mile Taxi Ride in Charlotte Amalie	$10
Museum Admission	$5–$10

*Prices throughout this guide are given for adults.
Reduced admission fees for seniors are hard to
come by in the USBVI.*

ATMS & BANKS

Your own bank will probably charge a fee
for using ATMs abroad; the foreign bank
you use may also charge a fee. Nevertheless, you'll usually get a better rate of exchange at an ATM than you will at a
currency-exchange office or even when
changing money in a bank. And extract-
ing funds as you need them is a safer option than carrying around a large amount
of cash.

■ TIP➔ PIN numbers with more than four
digits are not recognized at ATMs in many
countries. If yours has five or more, remember to change it before you leave.

You'll find ATMs at most banks in the
USBVI. The ATMs at FirstBank and Scotia Banks, the only two in St. John, sometimes run out of cash on long holiday
weekends.

CREDIT CARDS

Throughout this guide, the following abbreviations are used: **AE**, American Express; **D**, Discover; **DC**, Diners Club; **MC**, MasterCard; and **V**, Visa.

It's a good idea to inform your credit-card company before you travel, especially if you're going abroad and don't travel internationally very often. Otherwise, the credit-card company might put a hold on your card owing to unusual activity—not a good thing halfway through your trip. Record all your credit-card numbers—as well as the phone numbers to call if your cards are lost or stolen—in a safe place, so you're prepared should something go wrong. Both MasterCard and Visa have general numbers you can call (collect if you're abroad) if your card is lost, but you're better off calling the number of your issuing bank, since MasterCard and Visa usually just transfer you to your bank; your bank's number is usually printed on your card.

If you plan to use your credit card for cash advances, you'll need to apply for a PIN at least two weeks before your trip. Although it's usually cheaper (and safer) to use a credit card abroad for large purchases (so you can cancel payments or be reimbursed if there's a problem), note that some credit-card companies *and* the banks that issue them add substantial percentages to all foreign transactions, whether they're in a foreign currency or not. Check on these fees before leaving home, so there won't be any surprises when you get the bill.

■ TIP→ Before you charge something, ask the merchant whether or not he or she plans to do a dynamic currency conversion (DCC). In such a transaction the credit-card *processor* (shop, restaurant, or hotel, not Visa or MasterCard) converts the currency and charges you in dollars. In most cases you'll pay the merchant a 3% fee for this service in addition to any credit-card company and issuing-bank foreign-transaction surcharges.

Major credit cards are widely accepted at hotels, restaurants, shops, car-rental agencies, other service providers, and ATM machines throughout the Caribbean. The only places that might not accept them are open-air markets or tiny shops in out-of-the-way villages. Villa renters should be forewarned that some managers may not accept credit cards.

Reporting Lost Cards American Express ☎ 800/992-3404 in the U.S. or 336/393-1111 collect from abroad ⊕ www.americanexpress. com. **Diners Club** ☎ 800/234-6377 in the U.S. or 303/799-1504 collect from abroad ⊕ www.dinersclub.com. **Discover** ☎ 800/ 347-2683 in the U.S. or 801/902-3100 collect from abroad ⊕ www.discovercard.com. **MasterCard** ☎ 800/622-7747 in the U.S. or 636/ 722-7111 collect from abroad ⊕ www. mastercard.com. **Visa** ☎ 800/847-2911 in the U.S. or 410/581-9994 collect from abroad ⊕ www.visa.com.

TRAVELER'S CHECKS & CARDS

Some consider this the currency of the cave man, and it's true that fewer establishments accept traveler's checks these days. Nevertheless, they're a cheap and secure way to carry extra money, particularly on trips to urban areas. Both Citibank (under the Visa brand) and American Express issue traveler's checks in the United States, but Amex is better known and more widely accepted; you can also avoid hefty surcharges by cashing Amex checks at Amex offices. Whatever you do, keep track of all the serial numbers in case the checks are lost or stolen.

American Express now offers a stored-value card called a Travelers Cheque Card, which you can use wherever American Express credit cards are accepted, including ATMs. The card can carry a minimum of $300 and a maximum of $2,700, and it's a very safe way to carry your funds. Although you can get replacement funds in 24 hours if your card is lost or stolen, it doesn't really strike us as a very good deal. In addition to a high initial cost ($14.95 to set up the card, plus $5 each time you "reload"), you still have to pay a 2% fee for each purchase in a foreign currency (similar to that of any credit

d). Further, each time you use the card
an ATM you pay a transaction fee of
50 on top of the 2% transaction fee for
conversion—add it all up and it can
considerably more than you would pay
en simply using your own ATM card.
gular traveler's checks are just as secure
d cost less.

erican Express ☎ 888/412-9945 in the
., 801/945-9450 collect outside of the U.S.
dd value or speak to customer service
www.americanexpress.com.

ATIONAL PARKS

arge part of St. John is a national park,
d several of the island's most popular
ches are on national park land. You can
y a one-year America the Beautiful Na-
al Parks & Federal Recreational Lands
s for $80; this pass grants you free ac-
s to most parks that charge a fee for one
r. A Senior Pass, which replaces the
mer Golden Age Passport, costs just
) and, once purchased, grants the holder
e access to most parks; this pass must
purchased at a national park. The fee
use the beach at Trunk Bay is $4 per
son per day.

ional Park Foundation ☎ 202/238-4200
388/467-2757 (for National Parks Pass info)
www.nationalparks.org. **National Park
vice** ☎ 202/208-6843 ⊕ www.nps.gov.
ional Parks Conservation Association
202/223-6722 or 800/628-7275 ⊕ www.
a.org.

RESTROOMS

strooms across the USBVI are usually
an, neat, and free. You won't often find
endants, even at swanky resorts. Most
stations do have restrooms, but they're
ally used by staff. They'll do in a pinch,
t using the restroom in a restaurant,
raction, or shopping area is probably
etter bet.

d a Loo **The Bathroom Diaries** ⊕ www.
bathroomdiaries.com is flush with unsani-
d info on restrooms the world over—each
e located, reviewed, and rated.

WORST-CASE SCENARIO

All your money and credit cards have just been
stolen. In these days of real-time transactions, this isn't a predicament that should de-
stroy your vacation. First, report the theft of
the credit cards. Then get any traveler's
checks you were carrying replaced. This can
usually be done almost immediately, provided
that you kept a record of the serial numbers
separate from the checks themselves. If you
bank at a large international bank like
Citibank or HSBC, go to the closest branch;
if you know your account number, chances
are you can get a new ATM card and with-
draw money right away. **Western Union**
(☎ 800/325-6000 ⊕ www.westernunion.
com) sends money almost anywhere. Have
someone back home order a transfer online,
over the phone, or at one of the company's
offices, which is the cheapest option.

▌ SAFETY

In the USVI, ask hotel staff members about
the wisdom of venturing off the beaten
path. Although it may seem like a nice
night for a stroll back to your hotel from
that downtown restaurant, it's better to
take a taxi than face an incident. Although
local police go to great lengths to stop it,
crime does happen. The BVI has seen less
crime than its neighbors to the west, but
again, better safe than sorry.

Follow the same precautions that you would
anywhere. Look around before using the
ATM. Keep tabs on your pocketbook; put
it on your lap—not the back of your chair—
in restaurants. Stow valuable jewelry or
other items in the hotel safe when you leave
your room; hotel and villa burglaries do
occur infrequently. Deserted beaches on
St. John and the BVI are usually safe, but
think twice about stopping at that luscious
strand of lonely sand on St. Croix and St.
Thomas. Hotel or public beaches are your
best bets. Never leave your belongings unat-
tended at the beach or on the seats of your
rental car. Be sure to lock the doors on
your rental villa or hotel room. Break-ins

can happen across the USBVI, so it's better to be safe than sorry.

■ TIP→ Distribute your cash, credit cards, I.D.s, and other valuables between a deep front pocket, an inside jacket or vest pocket, and a hidden money pouch. Don't reach for the money pouch once you're in public.

▌TAXES

There's no sales tax in the USVI, but there's an 8% hotel-room tax; most hotels also add a 10% service charge to the bill. The St. John Accommodations Council members ask that hotel and villa guests voluntarily pay a $1 per day surcharge to help fund school and community projects and other good works. Many hotels add additional energy surcharges and the like, so please ask about any additional charges; these are not government-imposed taxes.

In the BVI, the departure tax is $5 per person by boat and $20 per person by plane. There's a separate booth at the airport and ferry terminals to collect this tax, which must be paid in cash in U.S. currency. Most hotels in the BVI add a service charge ranging from 5% to 18% to the bill. A few restaurants and some shops tack on an additional 10% charge if you use a credit card. There's no sales tax in the BVI. However, there's a 7% government tax on hotel rooms.

▌TIME

The USBVI are in the Atlantic Standard Time zone, which is one hour later than Eastern Standard or four hours earlier than GMT. During Daylight Savings Time, between April and October, Atlantic Standard is the same time as Eastern Daylight Time.

▌TIPPING

Many hotels in the USVI add a 10% to 15% service charge to cover the services of your maid and other staff. However, some hotels use part of that money to fund their operations, passing on only a portion of it to the staff. Check with your maid or bellhop to determine the hotel's policy. If you dis-

cover you need to tip, give bellhops and porters $1 per bag and maids $1 or $2 per day. Special errands or requests of hotel staff always require an additional tip. At restaurants bartenders and waiters expect a 10%–15% tip, but always check your tab to see whether service is included. Taxi drivers in the USVI get a 15% tip.

In the BVI, tip porters and bellhops $1 per bag. Sometimes a service charge of 10% is included on restaurant bills; it's customary to leave another 5% if you liked the service. If no charge is added, 15% is the norm. Cabbies normally aren't tipped because most own their cabs; add 10% to 15% if they exceed their duties.

TIPPING GUIDELINES FOR [DESTINATION]	
Bartender	$1 to $5 per round of drinks, depending on the number of drinks
Bellhop	$1 to $5 per bag, depending on the level of the hotel
Hotel Concierge	$5 or more, if he or she performs a service for you
Hotel Doorman	$1–$2 if he helps you get a cab
Hotel Maid	1$–$3 a day (either daily or at the end of your stay, in cash)
Hotel Room-Service Waiter	$1 to $2 per delivery, even if a service charge has been added
Porter at Airport or Train Station	$1 per bag
Skycap at Airport	$1 to $3 per bag checked
Taxi Driver	15%–20%, but round up the fare to the next dollar amount
Tour Guide	10% of the cost of the tour
Valet Parking Attendant	$1–$2, but only when you get your car
Waiter	15%–20%, with 20% being the norm at high-end restaurants; nothing additional if a service charge is added to the bill

EFFECTIVE COMPLAINING

Things don't always go right when you're traveling, and when you encounter a problem or service that isn't up to snuff, you should complain. But there are good and bad ways to do so.

TAKE A DEEP BREATH. This is always a good strategy, especially when you are aggravated about something. Just inhale, and exhale, and remember that you're on vacation. We know it's hard for Type A people to leave it all behind, but for your own peace of mind, it's worth a try.

COMPLAIN IN PERSON WHEN IT'S SERIOUS. In a hotel, serious problems are usually better dealt with in person, at the front desk; if it's something quick, you can phone.

COMPLAIN EARLY RATHER THAN LATE. Whenever you don't get what you paid for (the type of hotel room you booked or the airline seat you pre-reserved) or when it's something timely (the people next door are making too much noise), try to resolve the problem sooner rather than later. It's always going to be harder to deal with a problem or get something taken off your bill after the fact.

BE WILLING TO ESCALATE, BUT DON'T BE HASTY. Try to deal with the person at the front desk of your hotel or with your waiter in a restaurant before asking to speak to a supervisor or manager. Not only is this polite, but when the person directly serving you can fix the problem, you'll more likely get what you want quicker.

SAY WHAT YOU WANT, AND BE REASONABLE. When things fall apart, be clear about what kind of compensation you expect. Don't leave it to the hotel or restaurant or airline to suggest what they're willing to do for you. That said, the compensation you request must be in line with the problem. You're unlikely to get a free meal because your steak was undercooked or a free hotel stay if your bathroom was dirty.

CHOOSE YOUR BATTLES. You're more likely to get what you want if you limit your complaints to one or two specific things that really matter rather than a litany of wrongs.

DON'T BE OBNOXIOUS. There's nothing that will stop your progress dead in its tracks as readily as an insistent "Don't you know who I am?" or "So what are you going to do about it?" Raising your voice will rarely get a better result.

NICE COUNTS. This doesn't mean you shouldn't be clear that you are displeased. Passive isn't good, either. When it comes right down to it, though, you'll attract more flies with sugar than with vinegar.

DO IT IN WRITING. If you discover a billing error or some other problem after the fact, write a concise letter to the appropriate customer-service representative. Keep it to one page, and as with any complaint, state clearly and reasonably what you want them to do about the problem. Don't give a detailed trip report or list a litany of problems.

INDEX

PHOTO CREDITS

Chapter 1: United States Virgin Islands: 121, *U.S. Virgin Islands Department of Tourism.* 18 (top), *U.S. Virgin Islands Department of Tourism.* 18 (bottom), *Philip Coblentz/Medioimages.*

Chapter 2: British Virgin Islands: 121, *Philip Coblentz/Medioimages.* 122 (top), *Philip Coblentz/Digital Vision.* 122 (bottom), *Philip Coblentz/Digital Vision.* 125 (left), *Philip Coblentz/Digital Vision.* 125 (right), *Philip Coblentz/Digital Vision.*

NOTES

NOTES

ABOUT OUR WRITERS 12/07

St. Thomas–based writer and dietitian Carol M. Bareuther who lives in St. Thomas, works part-time for the government of the U.S. Virgin Islands. In her other life as a writer, she writes for local, regional, and international publications on the topics of food, travel, and watersports. She's the author of two books, *Sports Fishing in the Virgin Islands* and *Virgin Islands Cooking*. She is the mother of Nikki and Rian, as well as the longtime partner of photographer Dean Barnes. She covered St. Thomas, Anegada, and Jost Van Dyke for this edition, and she contributed the essays on island cuisine and chartering a yacht.

Long-time St. John resident Lynda Lohr lives above Coral Bay with her significant other and two chubby cats. She moved to St. John in 1984 for a bit of adventure; she's still there and still enjoying the adventure. The editor of *Island News*, a newsletter for people with a serious interest in the Virgin Islands, she also writes for numerous national, regional, and local publications as well as travel Web sites. On her rare days off, she swims at Great Maho Bay and hikes the island's numerous trails. For this edition, she covered St. John, St. Croix, Tortola, Virgin Gorda, and many of the smaller islands. She was also responsible for Essentials and the essay on diving.